THE CAMBRIDGE ILLUSTRATED HISTORY OF THE

Islamic World

THE CAMBRIDGE ILLUSTRATED HISTORY OF THE

Islamic World

edited by

FRANCIS ROBINSON

CAMBRIDGE
UNIVERSITY PRESS

DEDICATION

To my Muslim friends

PUBLISHED BY THE PRESS SYNDICATE OF THE UNIVERSITY OF CAMBRIDGE
The Pitt Building, Trumpington Street, Cambridge, United Kingdom

CAMBRIDGE UNIVERSITY PRESS
The Edinburgh Building, Cambridge CB2 2RU, UK
40 West 20th Street, New York, NY 10011-4211, USA
477 Williamstown Road, Port Melbourne, VIC 3207, Australia
Ruiz de Alarcón 13, 28014 Madrid, Spain
Dock House, The Waterfront, Cape Town 8001, South Africa

© Cambridge University Press 1996

First published 1996
Reprinted in 1998, 2002

This book was produced by
LAURENCE KING PUBLISHING LTD
71 Great Russell Street
London WC1B 3BP

Project editor: Katharine Ridler
Picture research: Michèle Faram
Layout: Andrew Shoolbred
Cartography by Hardlines, Charlbury, Oxford

Printed in China

A catalogue record for this book is available from the British Library

Library of Congress cataloguing in publication data

Robinson, Francis.
The Cambridge Illustrated History of the Islamic World/edited by
Francis Robinson
p. cm.
Includes bibliographical references and index
ISBN 0-521-43510-2
1. Islamic countries—History
DS35.63.R63 1996
909'.097671—dc20
95-37562
CIP

ISBN 0 521 43510 2 hardback
ISBN 0 521 66993 6 paperback

Contents

Contributors

Dr Sarah Ansari is a lecturer in history at Royal Holloway, University of London and author of *Sufi Saints and State Power: Pirs of Sind, 1843-1947* (1992).

Professsor K. N. Chaudhuri is the Vasco da Gama Professor of European Expansion at the European University Institute, Florence, and the author of several books on Asian Economic history, including *Trade and Civilization in the Indian Ocean: An Economic History from the Rise of Islam to 1750* (1985) and *Asia before Europe: The Economy and Civilization of the Indian Ocean from the Rise of Islam to 1750* (1990).

Dr Patricia Crone teaches Islamic history at the University of Cambridge where she is a Fellow of Gonville and Caius. Among her books are *Meccan Trade and the Rise of Islam* (1987) and *Roman, Provincial and Islamic Law* (1987).

Professor Stephen F. Dale is Professor of Islamic and South Asian History at Ohio State University. Among his books are *Islamic Society on the South Asian Frontier: The Mappilas of Malabar 1498-1922* (1980) and *Indian Merchants and Eurasian Trade 1600-1750* (1994).

Dr Robert Irwin was lecturer in medieval history at the University of St Andrews and is author of *The Middle East in the Middle Ages* (1986) and *The Arabian Nights: A Companion* (1994).

Dr Basim Musallam teaches Islamic history at the University of Cambridge where he is a Fellow of King's College. He is the author of *Sex and Society in Islam* (1983).

Professor Francis Robinson is Professor of the History of South Asia at Royal Holloway, University of London. Among his books are *Separatism among Indian Muslims: The Politics of the United Provinces' Muslims 1860-1923* (1974) and *Atlas of the Islamic World since 1500* (1982).

Dr Stephen Vernoit was formerly Research Fellow in Islamic Art and Architecture at St Antony's College, Oxford. He is currently cataloguing Islamic items in the collection of Nasser D. Khalili.

Foreword

Islam is a global religion. More than a billion Muslims inhabit the Middle East, where Islam originated, and much of sub-Saharan Africa, Central Asia, South and Southeast Asia. The world's largest Muslim populations are in Indonesia, Bangladesh, Pakistan, and India; the newest are in western Europe and the United States.

To many westerners Islam represents the East – the outside civilization to their own. For the West Islam is always problematic. It is often looked upon with curiosity, concern, contempt, or fear. Islam is a competitor. And it has been a focus of conflict and war from the Arab conquests of the seventh century, through the Crusades and the Ottoman Turkish invasions of Europe, down to Islamic terrorism today.

Yet Islam is also a source of enlightenment for the West. Toledo in the Middle Ages, part of Muslim Spain, was the centre for the transmission to the rest of Europe of Greek and Hellenistic philosophy and science with Arabic and Hebrew commentary. Scientific advances in mathematics, astronomy, and medicine came to the West under the aegis of Islam. The Muslim world had long been the hub of international trade from the Far East to Europe. Agricultural innovation such as irrigation technology, and a long list of precious crops including sugar, cotton, and oranges originated in the East. Refinements and luxuries such as spices, dyes, silk and brocades and other fine cloth came too from the Muslim world.

While westerners may still think of Islam as 'outside', the boundaries between East and West are fast disappearing. Muslim and non-Muslim peoples interpenetrate. Not only do electronic communications and travel shrink the globe, but the same life styles and values as the West have been adopted by many in the Muslim world. Science and technology and pop culture – Coca Cola, movies and rock music – are now widely shared. Islamic spirituality, sufism, has had a deep impact upon western spirituality and to this very day attracts adepts from other religions. There are close business and political alliances among Muslims and westerners. Large numbers of Muslims live in western Europe and the United States and are becoming part of the same heterogeneous cultures.

The relationships of Muslims and non-Muslims are changing rapidly. This makes is all the more important to be informed about the history, the cultural heritage, and the values and achievements of Islamic civilizations. In a brief compass this learned and calm book gives a history of the Islamic world

The development in northern Iran of a technique for over-glaze painting in enamels allowed the use of a wider range of colours and the depiction of quite detailed literary themes on ceramic dishes. The earliest surviving illustrations to Firdawsi's *Shahnama* (Book of Kings) appear not in books but on plates and bowls, as here, where the legendary Persian prince Bahram Gur, urged on by the lute-playing slave-girl Azada, aims to hit the onager in such a way that one arrow will pierce its ear and a hind leg.

on a global scale. It contains an essay on the economy which discusses agriculture and cities – the production of fine craft goods, markets, seaports, and trade. An essay on the social order reviews the place of women in society and the institution of the *hisba* which maintained moral and economic controls. A third on learning and knowledge underscores the importance of right knowledge for salvation and how this motivated Islamic accomplishments in law, theology, mysticism, philosophy, and science. The final chapter on artistic expression in poetry, music, and the visual arts, rounds out this welcome contribution to our understanding of the Islamic world.

Ira M. Lapidus
PROFESSOR OF HISTORY
UNIVERSITY OF CALIFORNIA, BERKELEY

Preface

This book has been written with the aim of making the world of Islam readily accessible to the student and the general reader. The first four chapters provide a narrative overview of Islamic history from the emergence of the Prophet Muhammad in seventh-century Arabia, through the high points of Islamic civilization in the Arab caliphate and the Ottoman, Safawid, and Mughal empires, to the enormous challenges and transformations attendant on the expansion of the West in the nineteenth and twentieth centuries. Chapters 5 to 8 examine major themes: the economic foundations of the Islamic world, the ordering of society, knowledge and its transmission, and artistic expressions. The introduction explores problems of understanding between the Islamic world and the West. The conclusion assesses current issues regarding this world – its religious revival, its apparent hostility to the West, and the position of women. All sections are supported by bibliographies designed to carry the reader further into the subject.

Ease of communication has been the guiding theme of editorial policy. Thus, in representing the words of various Islamic languages in the roman script we have adopted the simplest possible solution even though this leads to omissions and distortions which may distress some scholars. The system of *The Encyclopaedia of Islam* (2nd edn) has been employed, with the modifications that all diacritical marks have been omitted, *ain* and *hamza* have been ignored, j has been used for *dj* and q for *k*, and whenever a name has acquired an acknowledged form in English this has been retained. Arabic terms, of course, cannot be avoided, but when they are used they are explained. The Christian calendar has been used for all dates. Those who wish to convert these to the Muslim calendar may do so with the aid of G. S. P. Freeman-Grenville, *The Muslim and Christian Calendar,* London, 1977.

One of the difficulties of books of this kind is that it is impossible properly to acknowledge scholars whose work has been particularly influential both in helping to form visions of Islamic history and in providing specific ideas and pieces of information. The following works demand special mention: M. G. S. Hodgson, *The Venture of Islam,* 3 vols., Chicago, 1974, and I. M. Lapidus, *A History of Islamic Societies*, Cambridge, 1988. The section on the rulers of the Islamic world owes much to E. Bosworth, *The Islamic Dynasties*, Edinburgh, 1967.

I am grateful for advice or assistance from the following friends and fellow scholars: Vanessa Martin, Ahmed Saruhan, Felicia Hecker, Derek Blundell, Hamid Jaleipour, Graham Gardiner, Claudia Liebeskind, Venetia Porter, Sarah Ansari, and Barbara Metcalf. I am grateful, too, for the expert assistance of the editorial team at Calmann and King, in particular Michèle Faram, and Katharine Ridler.

Francis Robinson

Introduction

Since the seventh century a growing proportion of human beings have been followers of Islam. Over this period the message which Muslims believe God sent to
all people through the Prophet Muhammad has both given meaning to Muslim
lives and helped to shape the world in which they live. Now, one fifth of the
world's people identify themselves as Muslims and their increase is amongst the
fastest of humankind. They live in the main in a great swathe of territory stretching from the Atlantic shore of north and west Africa, through west, central, and
south Asia to island southeast Asia. Theirs is the dominant culture in over fifty
nation states, while they also form significant minority cultures most notably in
India but also in western Europe, north America, east Asia, and southern Africa.
This is a global presence which cannot be ignored.

The world's billion Muslims share a past of glorious achievement. For much of
the period from the eighth to the eighteenth century the leading civilization on
the planet in terms of spread and creativity was that of Islam. It was formed in the
seventh century when Arab tribesmen burst out of the Arabian peninsula and
conquered the two rival empires to the north, those of Byzantium and Sasanian
Iran. Afterwards, a great new cultural and economic nexus developed which was
able to draw on the knowledge and the commodities of lands from China and
India in the east to Spain and Africa in the west, as well as those of the west Asian
lands on which it was based. This new civilization commanded a substantial slice
of the globe's area of cities and settled agriculture. In this region there was a shared
language of religion and the law. Men could travel and do business within a shared
framework of assumptions. In its high cultures they could express themselves in
symbols to which all could respond. The first notable centres were found in the
Arab worlds of Damascus, Baghdad, and Cordoba from the eighth to the tenth
centuries; the second were found in the Turko-Iranian worlds of Istanbul, Isfahan,
Bukhara, Samarqand, and Delhi from the fifteenth to the seventeenth centuries.
There were great achievements in scholarship and in science, in poetry and in
prose, and in the arts of the book, of building, and of spiritual insight, which are
precious legacies to all humankind. For about half of what is termed the Christian era Muslims marched at the forefront of human progress.

From the nineteenth century this Islamic world system was overwhelmed by
forces from the West, driven by capitalism, powered by industrial revolution, and
civilized, after a fashion, by the Enlightenment. The symbolic moment when the
leader's standard overtly passed to the West was Napoleon's invasion of Egypt in
1798. From this moment western armies and western capital overran the lands of
the Muslims. By the 1920s only Afghanistan, Iran, Turkey, central Arabia, and the
Yemen were free from western control. The caliphate, the symbolic leadership of

A Muslim and a Christian play the ud or lute together, from a thirteenth-century *Book of Chants* in the Escorial Monastery of Madrid. Medieval Europe was deeply influenced by Arab-Islamic culture, transmitted particularly through Spain. In music some of the many works in Arabic on musical theory were translated into Latin and Hebrew, but the main influence came from the actual arts of singing and playing spread by minstrels. Amongst the living traditions thus influenced is that of the Morris or 'Moorish' dancers of England. Recent investigations in musical history have found pervasive Arab influences over the development of flamenco music, affecting everything from the style of performance to the rhythm and scales of the songs themselves.

the Muslim community which reached back to the Prophet, had been abolished. For a moment it had been feared that the holy places of Islam, Mecca and Medina, would fall into infidel hands. Muslims, who for centuries had walked hand in hand with power, had good reason to feel that history had deserted them.

The twentieth century has witnessed, from the emergence of modern Turkey in the early 1920s to that of the Muslim republics of the former Soviet Union in the 1990s, a steady decolonization of the Muslim world. But for many this has seemed a pyrrhic victory. More often than not they have found western rule replaced by that of Muslims with western values, while western capital and western culture has come to be even more corrosive of their customs and their standards than before. This challenge has elicited from Muslims throughout the world an assertion of an Islamic, and for some a totalitarian Islamic, future for their people. Such views have not been shared by all Muslims but have come to be shared by enough to represent a significant threat to the secular leaders of their societies, and on occasion, as in the revolution in Iran, to drive their upholders to power. These Muslims, who are popularly known as 'fundamentalist' in the West but are more appropriately known as 'Islamists', are seen to challenge some of the most cherished principles of the contemporary West, whether it be the position of women, human rights, or the role of revealed religion in modern life. Such is the fervour of the challenge and such is the violence with which some Islamists are prepared to press it forward, that there has been talk in the aftermath of the collapse of the Soviet Union of the red menace being replaced by a green one.

History can offer few answers to present problems, but it can place them in perspective and enrich understanding. Islamic history demands attention because of the numbers of humankind who claim that past for their own, because of the achievement of that past in the saga of human history, and because of the challenge which the inheritors of that past place before the present.

WESTERN ATTITUDES TO ISLAM

Anyone setting out to explore Islamic history should first arm themselves with some knowledge of the hostility towards Islam which has infused western culture over many centuries. Some Christians have felt bound to oppose a faith which denied the Christian doctrine of the Trinity, which denied Christ's crucifixion, and which raised the authority of its Quran over that of the Bible. Some Christian rulers, equally, have felt bound to oppose the armies of a faith which for nearly one thousand years from the Arab thrust to Poitiers in 732 to the Ottoman advance on Vienna in 1683 has threatened to penetrate to the heart of Christendom. Indeed, the Crusades from the eleventh to the thirteenth centuries, when Christian rulers took the fight against Islam into the eastern Mediterranean lands, were one of the great forces of European history.

It is hardly surprising, therefore, that from the early Middle Ages to the Enlightenment European attitudes to Islam were instinct with hostility. Early European attitudes, which out of ignorance were fashioned from hearsay and fantasy, dismissed Islam as a Christian heresy and its Prophet as a sorcerer, whose success owed much to the divine imprimatur he gave to sexual licence. With the Crusades there came the first translations of the Quran into Latin and a more knowledgeable approach. This was accompanied by a redoubled attack on the status of Muhammad as a prophet and assaults directed at those aspects of his message which seemed to condone the use of violence, to endorse sexual freedom in this world, and to promise sexual ecstasy in the next. These basic lines of attack were continued through the Renaissance and Reformation so that on the eve of the Enlightenment the widely accepted picture of Muhammad was of an impostor who had founded a heresy and given it the name of religion.

The eighteenth and nineteenth centuries saw a continuation of the old attacks against Islam. They were carried by missionaries who, taking advantage of the growing European ascendancy, now fanned out across Muslim lands; much of the medieval polemic, for instance, was repeated in a *Life of Muhammad* published in 1851 by the Bombay Tract and Book Society. But their message was broadcast, too, by westerners with purely secular concerns. Such was the impact of the writers Flaubert and de Nerval, or the painters Ingres and Gérôme, who associated sex, sensuality, and the Muslim world. Colonial administrators, their minds exercised by the tendency of Muslims to wage holy wars against their presence, found the term 'fanatic' the natural adjective for them.

Mercifully, however, the range of western attitudes to Islam was beginning to broaden. Enlightenment scholars seeking a critique of Christianity found rational qualities in Islam. It was seen, moreover, as a civilizing force which had transmitted ancient learning to the West, while its Prophet came to be viewed as a profound thinker and the founder of rational religion. This new spirit was well represented by Napoleon who, whatever his political motives, had no difficulty on landing in Egypt in declaring: 'I respect God, his Prophet, and the Quran.' For many in Europe, however, Islam was more than just a weapon in the war against Christianity, it was also an exotic playground full of novel possibilities. A good number of these were supplied by Galland's translation of the *Arabian Nights* in 1704 with its rich store of caliphs, genies, and fabulous happenings. Creative minds roamed excitedly through this new world -Montesquieu in *Persian Letters*, Mozart in *The Abduction from the Seraglio*, and Goethe in *West-Easterly Diwan*. Others preferred to travel and discover for themselves how Muslim societies might expand the potential of their lives. Not the least amongst these were women, Mary Wortley Montagu, Hester Stanhope, and a host of others, who found that Muslim women's lives were in many ways preferable to the circumscribed lives of women in the West.

Modern scholarship represents a further broadening of the range of attitudes. Arguably the modern study of Islam reaches back to the foundation of the first chairs of Arabic at the Collège de France in 1539, at the university of Leiden in 1613 and at the university of Cambridge in 1634. Later came more accurate translations of the Quran such as that of Sale into English in 1734 and the writing of the Muslim past such as Simon Ockley's *History of the Saracens* (1708–18) not as polemic but as history. Towards the end of the eighteenth century large numbers of texts, both literary and religious, began to be translated into European languages, and in the nineteenth century the range of study widened as scholars of religion, biblical criticism, and comparative philology brought Islam and the languages of the Islamic world within their purview. At the beginning of the twentieth century there emerged the Islamic specialist, like the Hungarian Ignaz Goldziher, the Dutch scholar-administrator Snouck Hurgronje, the British-American D. B. MacDonald, and the Russian V. V. Barthold, who were concerned to expose their subject to the highest standards of scholarship and interpretation. This tradition has reached its highest peaks so far in the achievement of three men – the Frenchman Louis Massignon, who greatly enlarged understandings of the spiritual dimensions of Islam, the Englishman Hamilton Gibb, who strove to provide a framework in which the historical development of Islam could be understood, and the American Marshall Hodgson, who aimed to place Islamic history in the broader context of world history. All three, too, were believers, Massignon a

Western attitudes to Muhammad

The changing image of the Prophet Muhammad is a touchstone of changing western attitudes to Islam. For a thousand years he was the false prophet, the impostor. Hence the terrible fate which Dante contrived for him in the *Inferno*. Although some Muslims, the doctors and philosophers Ibn Sina and Ibn Rushd, and the hero of medieval chivalry, Saladin, were numbered amongst the virtuous heathen and let off with slight punishment, Muhammad was consigned to the ninth of the ten gloomy ditches surrounding Satan's stronghold, where, branded a spreader of scandal and discord, he was doomed to being split in twain continuously. From the eighteenth century a more complex picture began to emerge. The historian Edward Gibbon in his *Decline and Fall of the Roman Empire* was able to admire the original genius of the Muhammad of Mecca, the moral leader, while questioning the purity of the motives of the Muhammad of Medina, the calculating politician. Some fifty years later, the historian Thomas Carlyle was able to make Muhammad his prophetic hero in his lectures *On Heroes, Hero-Worship and the Heroic in History*. 'He is by no means the truest of the Prophets', Carlyle declared, 'but I do esteem him a true one...a great soul: one of those who cannot but be in earnest.' At a less elevated but nevertheless telling level half a century later, the Victorian entrepreneur Thomas Holloway had little difficulty in having the Prophet's image affixed to the Chapel of his university college for women alongside other great teachers of humankind. In the twentieth century attitudes range from the secular that would dismiss Muhammad along with Jesus as the misguided catalyst of religious enthusiasm through to some recent Christian Roman Catholic scholars of Islam who have gone so far as to regard him as a religious genius and have wondered if he might not have been a true prophet.

Muhammad in calligraphy from Turkey. The depiction of religious figures has been discouraged in Muslim culture.

Roman Catholic, Gibb an Anglican Protestant, and Hodgson a Quaker, who brought the insights of their personal commitment to their studies.

Those involved in this tradition of scholarship considered themselves committed to the objective study of the Islamic world. In recent years, however, and in particular since the publication of Edward Said's *Orientalism* in 1978, these scholars have been accused of distorting truth, that is, of practising 'orientalism'. The charges are that they have explained Islam in terms of some unchanging essence rather than subject to processes of differentiation and change similar to those undergone by the West, that they have created a body of received truths about Islam which have authority in western academic life but little relation to Muslim realities, that they have in fact created a structure of knowledge to explain superiority of the West over the Islamic world and to justify its continuing domination. There is a grain of truth in these charges, and more than a grain when we come to the popular discourse of politicians and the press. But these charges are less fairly applied to the twentieth-century masters of Islamic studies. And they are less fairly applied to most practitioners of the subject in recent decades, who bring the

Opposite From the eighteenth century the Muslim world has been a particular arena in which westerners, in large part men, have played out their sexual fantasies. Here artists found rich inspiration. Striking was the orientalist school of painters for whom the harem, the odalisque, or the women's bathhouse were frequent subjects. Such paintings often convey a mood of sensuality, indeed sexual promise, as is the case with 'The Almeh', an Arab woman painted by the French artist Jean-Léon Gérôme (1824–1904).

insights of all disciplines from anthropology to psychology to their research, who more often than not work side by side with Muslims in their studies, and who reveal the many different ways there have been and are of being Muslim.

Contemporary attitudes to Islam contain much of the old Christian polemic in modern form, which despite the efforts of modern scholars of the Muslim world, is firmly underpinned by the continuing vigour of the old 'orientalist' understandings in popular discourse. Thus, the old objection to Islam which focused on sex and sensuality has become a new objection to the position of women. The worry about violence has become a disapproval of the approach to human rights in Muslim states. The fear of Muslim power has emerged again as the rise of the Islamists has led to talk of a green menace. Islamists, indeed, in their desire to subordinate all of human life to their understanding of revelation, provoke the strongest responses from the secular West. They commit a form of heresy in western eyes by wishing to deny the achievements of the Enlightenment and on occasion, as in the case of Salman Rushdie's *Satanic Verses*, by trying to impose their standards on the West. Ironically, Rushdie's unflattering picture of the Prophet, which has its antecedents in the Christian polemic of the Middle Ages, is one which most contemporary Christian clergy would deplore. In a secular and materialistic world, the Church, particularly the Roman Catholic branch, finds it has more in common with those who believe than with those who do not. 'Upon the Muslims too', declared the Second Vatican Council in the early 1960s, 'the Church looks with esteem. They adore one God, living and enduring, merciful and all-powerful, maker of heaven and earth and Speaker to men.' Since this Council the Vatican has found increasing reason to make common cause with forces in the Muslim world.

MUSLIM ATTITUDES TO THE WEST

Those setting out to explore Islamic history should also benefit from knowledge of the range of Muslim attitudes to the West, and how they have changed through time. In many ways they represent the reverse of the coin of western attitudes. In particular, moreover, in the passing on of received 'truths' without reference to reality, they contain elements of a Muslim 'occidentalism' to match western orientalism.

For a thousand years the Muslims were little interested in Europe. They neither wished to learn its languages nor to travel its lands. They had only the haziest idea of its geography and its peoples. They were sure that Europe contained a lesser civilization that had nothing to offer them. As far as Muslims noticed Europeans at all their attitudes contained the following strands: the Europeans, as Christians, were people of the book (*ahl-i kitab*), people to whom God had revealed knowledge, but also people who had misunderstood his message; they were *kafirs*, from the Arabic meaning to disbelieve or deny, therefore infidels, and they would be referred to as such both in speech and in official documents, often accompanied by a curse; they were dirty: 'they do not cleanse or bathe themselves more than twice a year, and then in cold water', commented one Muslim of the medieval Franks, 'and then they do not wash their garments from the time they put them on until they fall to pieces'; and they permitted their women amazing liberties: 'the women do not cover themselves decently', declared the companion of the Ottoman prince Jem on his visit to Nice in 1482, 'but on the contrary they are proud to kiss and embrace. If they grow tired of their games and need to rest, they sit on the knees of strange men.' From the sixteenth century some interest in the West developed, especially at the level of, say, the Ottoman, Safawid, or Mughal courts. The technology of warfare was of particular interest but so too were European arts, architecture, and even religion. This said, at the level of mosque and bazar, Muslims remained indifferent.

From the nineteenth century Muslims were increasingly forced to take notice of the West. Some of the old attitudes continued and were joined by new ones. The presence of Christian missionaries who were supported by European power in Muslim lands meant that it was no longer enough to dismiss Christians as infidels; in northern India Muslims went on the attack debating their faith with missionaries and developing the modern Muslim critique of Christianity based on the implausibility of the doctrine of the Trinity and the corruption of the scriptures. At the same time, ruling elites found themselves forced to admire the military strength and material achievements of the West. 'So it went on until all had passed', declared the secretary to the Moroccan envoy to France in 1846 after watching a review of French troops, 'leaving our hearts consumed with fire for what we had seen of their overwhelming power and mastery ... In comparison with the weakness of Islam ... how confident they are, how impressive their state of readiness, how competent they are in matters of state, how firm their laws, how capable in war.' It was but a short move from admiration to resentment at the bullying way in which this strength was used. Each advance of western power into the Islamic world from the Napoleonic invasion of Egypt in 1798 to the Allied occupation of Istanbul after the First World War etched bitterness yet more deeply into Muslim psyches.

In the twentieth century the complexity of attitudes increased. Christianity moved to being more an ally than a threat; the infidel is less the Christian than those who do not believe at all. Inter-faith discussion is now common, and it is possible, for instance, for Christian and Iranian Shia theologians to come together, as they did in Birmingham (England) in 1992, and to discover substantial common ground. Admiration of the West has become large-scale; secular Muslim leaders have copied its ways in order to make state and society strong enough to stand on their own feet. At its extreme this could mean a forced adoption of western ways. Thus Ataturk, the founder of modern Turkey, told his National Assembly in 1927:

Muslim images of western women

Nothing about the West has struck Muslims more forcibly than the greater liberties of all kinds which women enjoyed. Their comments reveal how differently their own societies were usually ordered and also, in the nineteenth and twentieth centuries, their concern for their own future development. The Crusades in the eastern Mediterranean offered opportunities for detached observation. Usamah, a Syrian, was astonished by the licentious freedom of the Frankish women. Their men, moreover, were 'void of all zeal and jealousy' in relation to their women. Evliya Chelebi, the seventeenth-century Turkish traveller, was amazed at the public deference shown to women. He tells how even the Habsburg emperor would make way for a member of the opposite sex. 'This is the most extraordinary spectacle. In this country, and elsewhere in the lands of the infidels, women have the chief say'. Nowhere, by common consensus, were women so dominant as in France. 'Men among them are the slaves of women', declared Shaykh Rifaa al-Tahtawi, an Egyptian who stayed in Paris from 1826 to 1831, 'and subject to their commands whether they be beautiful or not'. The Indian educational reformer Sayyid Ahmad Khan had another point to make – the high levels of education amongst European women. In Paris in 1869 he noted how a shop assistant talked four languages. In London he was amazed to discover that his landlady's sister was keen to read books of religious polemic and was able to discuss them with excellent sense. He was even more astonished to discover the female servants of the house reading newspapers and journals. The dominant response, however, at least amongst Muslim men, has always been one of shock at the freedom enjoyed by European women. If this was a source of pleasurable surprise for early commentators, it came to be a matter of deep concern as in the twentieth century European values began to make serious inroads into Muslim societies. Such freedoms led to moral degeneration. 'To develop a magnetic attraction for a man has become a mania with the women there', declared the Indian Islamist Mawdudi, who was concerned that strict rules of modesty should be enforced: 'men, on the other hand, are growing more and more voracious in their sexual appetite ... This disease is eating fast into the very vitals of the western nations. No nation in the past has survived it. It destroys all the mental and physical capabilities of man that God has endowed him with for his well-being and prosperity.'

The freedom of western women shocks and threatens but is also a subject of prurient interest for Muslims. Over the past two centuries in the West the increasing presence of women outside the home, the display of the feminine form, often scantily clad, in public, and the many opportunities openly enjoyed by women have more and more defined the difference between western and Muslim civilizations. For many Muslims, in particular Islamists, as western values have invaded public space, the seclusion of women has become the focal point of identity of an Islamically ordered society. This cartoon is from *L'Oud* ('The Lute', 1983), a strip by Farid Boudjellah for his compatriots, the Beurs, or second-generation north Africans living in France. It depicts Kader, an immigrant labourer from Algeria. The centrality of women to the differences between the two cultures to which he belongs is clear.

Gentlemen, it was necessary to abolish the fez, which sat on the heads of our nation as an emblem of ignorance, negligence, fanaticism, and hatred of progress and civilization, to accept in its place the hat, the headgear used by the whole civilized world, and in this way to demonstrate that the Turkish nation, in its mentality, as in other respects, in no way diverges from civilized social life.

As might be expected, some Muslims have doubted whether western forms of progress were appropriate for Muslims. 'The westerners', declared the Indian poet Iqbal, who was a direct contemporary of Ataturk, 'have lost the vision of heaven, they go hunting for the pure spirit in the belly.' Both communist and capitalist roads were false ones: 'The soul of both is impatient and intolerant, both of them know not God, and deceive mankind. One lives by production, the other by taxation and man is a glass caught between these two stones.'

In the hands of the Islamist movement of the second half of the twentieth century this attitude has become an aggressive rejection of western models of progress. 'Come, friends,' exhorted Ali Shariati, ideologue of the Iranian revolution, 'let us abandon Europe; let us cease this nauseating, apish imitation of Europe. Let us leave behind this Europe that always speaks of humanity, but destroys human beings wherever it finds them.' Side by side with this rejection, there has been continuing anguish at what is seen to be western bullying of Muslim peoples. Ayatollah Khomeini's howl of rage, when in 1964 the Iranian parliament granted US citizens extra-territorial rights in exchange for a $200 million loan, spoke for all Muslims who had felt powerless in the face of a bullying West from the bombardment of Alexandria in 1882 to the Gulf War in 1991: 'they have reduced the Iranian people to a level lower than that of an American dog'.

INTERACTION AND INTERDEPENDENCE

One of the misfortunes of the long history of stereotyping and conflict between Islam and the West is that it has fostered ignorance. Muslims and westerners know too little of how much they have in common and how much they owe to each other.

There are shared religious roots. Muslims, like Jews and Christians, believe in one God, in prophecy, and revelation. Twenty-one of the twenty-eight prophets mentioned in the Quran appear in the Christian Bible. Muslims are as familiar with the stories of Jacob, Joseph, and Job as any Christian. The Quran specifically recognizes the scriptures of Abraham, the Torah of Moses, the Psalms of David,

Two strands in Muslim responses to the West have been rejection of western materialism and of western attitudes to women. This repulsive image by Hussein Khosrojerdi, born in 1957 and a graduate of the College of Fine Arts, Teheran University, is infused with the spirit of rejection which animated the Iranian revolution. The westerner is portrayed as blind and deaf to the world and motivated by money and by sex. The painting is entitled 'Corruptor of the Earth'. Ironically, it was western thought that influenced groups involved in bringing about the revolution as well as those who consolidated it.

This painting from a dispersed manuscript made for the Mughal emperor Akbar underlines the point about prophets shared by Muslims, Christians, and Jews. The Persian couplet above the tent declares: 'With the compassion of Jacob, and the countenance of Joseph, with the piety of John [the Baptist], and the sovereignty of Solomon'. Under the tent Solomon (Sulayman) sits enthroned and listening to the hoopoe at his left hand, who is telling him of the imminent arrival of the Queen of Sheba. For Muslims, Solomon was the model of the perfect king, with authority over humans and animals, and natural and supernatural forces.

and the Gospel of Jesus as books revealed by God. The same angel, Gabriel, who came to Mary to announce her mission came to Muhammad to tell him to recite the Quran. Muslims, Christians, and Jews all look back to Abraham as the first prophet to receive revelation. Muslims trace their lineage back to him, through Ishmael the child of his servant wife Hagar, while Christians and Jews do so through the son of his legal wife Sarah. Muslims revere Jesus as a Prophet and they honour Mary as his virgin mother; they accept moral responsibility for their actions and anticipate a day of judgment with its attendant outcomes of heaven and hell. Major differences are that Muslims do not accept the divinity of Jesus and regard the Quran as perfecting a tradition of prophecy which Jews and Christians had allowed to become distorted through human intervention.

There are also shared intellectual roots. It is too little known that the great heritage of Hellenistic learning has been as much cherished in the Islamic world as in the West. The works of Aristotle, Plato, and their subsequent elaborators – Stoics, Pythagoreans, Neo-Platonists – were eagerly devoured by Muslims and had a major impact on theological, mystical, and political thought. The influence of Plato is evident in Islamic political thought down to the twentieth century, while to this very day Aristotle is referred to in some traditional Muslim schools as the 'first teacher'. The Greek achievement in mathematics, astronomy, and optics was greatly extended by Muslims; the names Euclid, Archimedes, or Ptolemy speak as resonantly to them of scientific achievement as they do for any westerner. In the same way Muslims developed the medical system of Galen which is practised even now in South Asia and referred to as 'Unani Tibb' or Greek Medicine.

Because the Muslims absorbed and cherished this great heritage from classical civilization, they were able to transmit its benefits along with much that they themselves had created to the West. Indeed, medieval Europe was profoundly influenced by the Arab-Islamic world, although to precisely what extent is a matter of debate. The channels of influence were in small part the Byzantine empire, in greater part Islamic Sicily, and in large part Islamic Spain. The trade networks of the Mediterranean and the international connections that developed out of Europe's crusading enterprise also played a role. The major period of influence was from the eleventh to the thirteenth century. This was the time when notable centres for the translation of Arabic texts were set up in Sicily, Barcelona, Toledo, and Seville. By this means the Hellenistic achievement and its various Muslim elaborations in mathematics, astronomy, optics, astrology, alchemy, natural history, geography, medicine, philosophy, theology, and mysticism entered the western world. Two Muslim names stand before all others for their influence on medieval Christian thought: Avicenna (Ibn Sina), whose Neo-Platonism was devoured by Christian mystics, while technical equipment was borrowed by scholars ranging from Aquinas to Duns Scotus; and Averroes (Ibn Rushd), whose commentary on Aristotle was a source of controversy and scholarship down to the end of the sixteenth century.

The material culture of the Islamic world was also influential. The impact of Muslim achievements in textiles, carpets, metalwork, glass-making, miniature painting, and bookbinding can be seen across the medieval and early modern European world. Silk and paper came to the West by Muslim hands. So, too, did the cultivation of sugar, cotton, and citrus fruit. Moreover, a host of Arabic words associated with trade have entered European languages, from magazine or the French *magazin* (Arabic *makhazin*, a storehouse) to traffic (Arabic *tafriq*, distribution).

Amongst the greatest areas of influence is Spain whose development in everything from place names to Catholic mysticism was shaped by 700 years of Muslim presence. But it should also be noted that recent scholarship has come to find the roots of medieval scholasticism and the development of universities in Muslim influence. It has even gone so far as to find the origins of Renaissance humanism in that of classical Islam. 'I have read, reverend fathers,' Pico della Mirandola begins his oration *The Dignity of Man* in the late fifteenth century, 'that when Abdala the Saracen was asked what he regarded as most to be wondered at on the world stage … he answered that there was nothing to be seen more wonderful than man.'

Over the past two centuries, on the other hand, the Islamic world has come to be penetrated and shaped by the West, and much more so than ever the West was affected by influences from its neighbour. Western power has, more often than not, dictated the boundaries of Muslim countries and fashioned the modern states under which their people live. Western power, too, has integrated Muslim economies into the new western-dominated world economy. In the process it has created whole new worlds of production and exchange which totally overshadow those of handicraft production, the bazar, the communal solidarities they have bred, and the Islamic institutions which have rested upon them for more than a millennium. Muslims have come to exist in new urban landscapes fashioned after those of the West with broad streets, glass-fronted shops, the roar of motor transport and a suburban hinterland of flats, villas, and slums. Their lives have come to be furnished by a material culture taken from the West – biros and bicycles, tables and chairs, while for men the western uniform of shirt and trousers has been widely adopted. Their minds and understandings have come to be filled with knowledge derived from the West. The new school systems of the modern nation states were concerned to transmit knowledge which it was hoped carried with it the secrets of western strength. At elite levels Muslims often came to be educated not in their own languages but in English, French, or Russian. Many, and not just at the level of the elite, came to be divorced from their heritage of learning and to seek to understand it primarily through western sources. Even those who have led cultural resistance to the West have drawn on its wisdom to make their case.

Muslims in the West: allotment-holders show off the fruits of their labours in Sheffield, Great Britain. In the 1950s and 1960s large numbers of Muslims migrated to Britain where they are now an established presence, contributing to many aspects of British life. Similar developments have taken place in France, Germany, the USA and, other western societies, where Muslims now number over 20 million.

King Fahd of Saudi Arabia and General Norman Schwarzkopf, Commander of US forces in the Gulf, review ground troops from sixteen countries before the outbreak of the Gulf War in 1991. The invasion and occupation of Kuwait by Iraqi forces in 1990, and the threat this presented both to western oil supplies and Gulf regimes, dramatically underlined the interdependence of the West and this part of the Muslim world.

Muhammad Iqbal's thought owed much to that of Nietzsche, Bergson, and Renan, that of Ali Shariati to Sartre, Fanon, and Massignon. One of the reasons why the Iranian theologians who went to Birmingham in 1992 found substantial common ground with their Christian collocutors was that they were steeped in western intellectual traditions. Not only did they know the classical Hellenic philosophers but also the work of Descartes, Kant, Hegel, and Heidegger as well as that of Christian theologians such as Barth, Tillich, and Bultmann.

The Islamic and the western worlds are not only profoundly interrelated but also increasingly interdependent. More than twenty million Muslims live in the West and are not unnaturally concerned that their societies should respect their culture and values. On the other hand the West has substantial economic and strategic interests in the Islamic world, as demonstrated by its warlike response to Saddam Husayn's invasion of Kuwait. Nor should this interdependence be restricted to the West. China has a Muslim community as populous as that in the West and no less keen for its views to be respected. Japan by the early 1990s had come to regard the Middle East as important enough to have about 100 trained Arabists in its foreign service. In this increasingly interdependent world, moreover, the rapid globalization of the media and communications is forging yet further connections. We can all, as never before, peer into each other's worlds. Such a capacity makes it crucial that we have the understanding to see through the veils of prejudice and cultural difference to grasp the common thread of humanity we all share.

PART 1

CHAPTER 1

Patricia Crone

The Rise of Islam in the World

THE PRE-ISLAMIC MIDDLE EAST

Of the Middle East in about AD 600 one thing can be said for certain: its chances of being conquered by Arab tribesmen in the name of a new religion were so remote that nobody had even speculated that it might happen. Islam came upon the world as a totally unexpected development, and the factors behind its emergence are still little known and poorly understood.

The Middle East into which Islam was born was divided between two superpowers, the Sasanian (Iranian) and the Byzantine (Graeco-Roman) empires, which held sway from Central Asia to southern Spain. The Iranians and the Greeks had been rivals in the Middle East for some nine hundred years by then and there were no signs that they were going to stop. On the contrary, their rivalry had acquired new intensity. But the superpowers could not destroy each other, nor, though they were frequently at war, did they usually try.

The Byzantine empire was solidly Christian. The dominant religion on the Sasanian side was Zoroastrianism, to which the majority of Iranians adhered; some Iranians followed other religions, such as Christianity, Manichaeism, and (in eastern Iran) Buddhism; and non-Iranians were hardly ever Zoroastrians. In Iraq, Judaism and Christianity predominated. Christianity was the fastest growing religion in western Asia at the time, and the Christians of the Sasanian empire not unreasonably hoped that the Sasanian emperor would one day go the way of Constantine, to whose conversion in the fourth century AD Christianity owed its official status in the Graeco-Roman world. Christianity was also spreading outside the borders of the two empires and was making headway in Arabia. That the entire Middle East would eventually be Christian was a sensible assumption.

The Arabs

All sensible assumptions were confounded by the Arabs, inhabitants of a large but marginal area of the Middle East comprising the Arabian peninsula and its northern extension, the Syrian desert ('Arabia' in what follows). The area was marginal because of its aridity. Agriculture was possible in south Arabia, Oman, and scattered oases, of which the most important were in central and eastern Arabia; but the rest was suitable only for nomadic pastoralism: camels could exploit what vegetation there was in the inner desert; sheep and goats could be reared on its fringes. Because the area was thinly inhabited by a mostly poor and partly mobile population, it did not lend itself to complex social and political organization.

There were some exceptions. Ancient south Arabia developed several king-doms, probably from about 500 BC. But they had disappeared by the sixth century AD, when south Arabia fell under the sway of foreigners, first Ethiopians and next Iranians. From time to time, minor kingdoms also appeared in northern Arabia. The Nabataeans of Petra (in modern Jordan, fourth century BC–AD 106) rose through trade, as did the caravan city of Palmyra (in modern Syria), which was suppressed by the Romans after the revolt of Queen Zenobia in AD 273. The Ghas-sanid and Lakhmid kings who dominated the Syrian desert in the sixth century AD were maintained by the Byzantines and Sasanians for their military services. There were also Arabs who lived as subjects of the Byzantine and Sasanian empires: one of them had risen through the army to become Roman emperor as Philip the Arab in AD 244–49. But to most Arabs, statelessness was the normal condition.

All Arabs, whether settled or nomadic, were organized in tribes, units con-ceived as descent groups. It was from these that they derived security, rather than from a state. A man's life was protected by his kinsmen, who were obliged to assist him in trouble and to avenge or seek compensation for him if he was killed or wounded, so that others would think twice about harming him; he was obliged to do the same for them. A woman's life was also protected by her kinsmen, but she had no reciprocal obligation and was thus a dependant. Most tribes also had non-tribal protégés, such as slaves, freedmen, craftsmen, and itinerant traders, who often came from outside Arabia and who were regarded as non-Arabs whatever their ethnicity might be because they depended on others for their protection.

Funerary statue of a south Arabian male, first century BC.

Tribesmen took immense pride in their ability to defend themselves and their dependants, and they regularly boasted of their strength in poetry, giving pleasure to themselves and warning potential predators at the same time. The ability to get the better of others (not of one's own tribe) by taking their camels, abducting their women, killing their men, or slitting the noses of their defenceless slaves was also highly prized. To be dominated was ignominious: 'The worst evil that can befall a people, and after which no good can come, is that their necks are bent', as one poet put it. 'The Ukl are slaves of the Taym, and the Taym are slaves themselves; if somebody says, "leave that watering trough", they leave it', another taunted. People who obeyed instead of standing up for themselves were dismissed as 'slaves' whether they were unfree persons, weak members of tribal society, or civil-ian subjects of states.

Arabian camel-rearers are first attested in the Bible c.1,000 BC; they appear under the name of Arabs in Assyrian records from the eighth century BC onwards, and there are regular references to them under this and other names thereafter. They are depicted in much the same vein throughout. They were predatory: 'And so it was, when Israel had sown, that the Midianites came up…and destroyed the increase of the earth…they came with their cattle and their tents, and they came as grasshoppers for multitude; for both they and their camels were without num-bers', as the Bible says with reference to c.1,000 BC. 'The Saracens…whom we

From time to time minor kingdoms appeared in northern Arabia. That of the Nabataeans of Petra in modern Jordan, lasting from the fourth century BC to AD 106 was based on trade. Its wealth is clear from the spectacular rock-hewn temples and tombs which remain; this one is known as the Treasury.

never found desirable either as friends or as enemies…in a brief space of time laid waste whatever they could find, like rapacious kites which, whenever they catch sight of any prey from on high, seize it with a swift swoop, and…make off', a Roman commander said some 1,350 years later. They had no rulers: 'the distant Arabs dwelling in the desert…know neither overseers nor officials', Sargon II (722–705 BC) pointed out; 'all alike are warriors of equal rank, half nude…ranging widely with the help of swift horses and slender camels', the Roman commander noted again. The Arabs depicted themselves similarly in the tribal poetry

collected after the Muslim conquests: 'we returned home with
their women captive behind us on our camel saddles, and with
the booty of camels', one poet boasts; 'we slew in requital for our
slain an equal number of them, and carried an unaccountable
number of fettered prisoners', another echoes, both referring to
raids against other tribes. 'The Himasi does not defend his honour, but is like the native of the Fertile Crescent who patiently
endures when one enslaves him', another said, referring to raids
against imperial subjects. The Arabs were most unlikely carriers
of a new world religion.

In fact, their militancy and mobility notwithstanding, they
were also unlikely world conquerors because they were few and
apparently unable to maintain large-scale political organization.
They were not nearly so alarming to the Byzantines and Iranians as the Huns,
Turks, Avars, and other tribesmen from Central Asia, who had a well-known history of political organization and conquest. The Arabs were only raiders: by the
seventh century they had been in Arabia for some 1,600 years without staging a
major conquest, so it was a reasonable assumption that they never would.

Nonetheless, in the 630s they suddenly began a coordinated invasion of the
Byzantine and Sasanian empires, severely mangling the former and wholly
destroying the latter, claiming that God had revealed the truth to them. Their new
faith not only survived but also spread and rapidly engendered new institutions,
modes of thought, and lifestyles, in short a new civilization. By the time the dust
had settled, about AD 800, the Middle East had been transformed beyond
recognition.

THE RISE OF ISLAM

The Prophet

The catalyst of all these developments was a prophet. His story is traditionally told
as follows. Muhammad was born in c.570 in Mecca, a trading city in western Arabia inhabited by the tribe of Quraysh, which is also said to have been a place of
pilgrimage (its sanctuary was known as the Kaaba). Orphaned by the age of six,
Muhammad was brought up by his grandfather and uncle, took up trade, and
married Khadija, a widow for whom he had worked as an agent and who bore him
several children. About the age of forty he had an experience that changed his life.
In a mountain cave to which he had gone for devotional purposes he was sur-
prised (one version says) by an apparition saying, 'Muhammad, you are God's
messenger.' He panicked and was considering throwing himself from the mountain when the speaker identified himself: 'Muhammad, I am Gabriel and you
are the messenger of God. Recite!' 'What shall I recite?' he replied in despair,
whereupon Gabriel squeezed him until he almost choked and ordered him to
recite the beginning of what became chapter (sura) 96 of the Quran. At first he

The Arabs settled at Nessana
in the Negev were wholly
Byzantinized, although their
names give their ethnicity
away. They were Christians
and all their inscriptions and
documents are in Greek. This
one from a sixth-century
Christian Ibn Saud petitions
for the protection of two
saints. These Arabs also
aspired to Latin culture and
adopted names such as
'Flavius al-Ubayy'; they even
tried to read Virgil in the original, as a Latin–Greek glossary
of the Aeneid excavated at
Nessana shows. We might
speculate, had Arabs of this
type led the Islamic conquests,
whether late antique civilization would have continued
much as before.

Khaybar, an oasis some 95 miles to the north of Medina. Whereas Mecca is famous for its barrenness, pre-Islamic Medina (Yathrib) probably looked somewhat like this. Khaybar, which was inhabited by Jews before the rise of Islam, fell to Muhammad in 628.

thought he had gone mad but he soon accepted that his vision was of divine origin. From then onwards Gabriel periodically brought him passages of the Quran until he died.

Muhammad began to preach, first to friends and relations and then more publicly, gaining some converts but antagonizing most of the pagan Meccans with his monotheist message. The pagans made things so difficult for his followers that he had to send some to Ethiopia and look for a place in Arabia where they could establish their own community. Eventually he encountered some Arab tribesmen from Yathrib, an agricultural settlement some 200 miles north of Mecca with a mixed Jewish and Arab population, long torn by feuds. Familiar with monotheism from their Jewish neighbours, these tribesmen found Muhammad's message intelligible and invited him to Yathrib in the hope that he might restore order to the oasis. After protracted negotiations, he and his followers left Mecca in 622, subsequently adopted as the starting point of the Muslim calendar. Yathrib came to be better known as Medina, the 'City' of the Prophet.

The emigration (*hijra*) was a turning point because it gave the Muslims their own communal organization. In Mecca they had lived by the same rules and as members of the same tribes as the pagans, but now 'they are a community to the exclusion of other people', Muhammad declared in a document he drew up shortly after his emigration. In that document, commonly known as the 'Constitution of Medina', he regulated relations between the component parts of the new community (*umma*) and its relations with outsiders, laying down that 'whatever you may disagree about shall be referred to God and Muhammad'. In other words, he assumed the role of ultimate decision-maker. Born in a stateless environment, Islam could not simply organize the believers in community for worship: it had to protect them as well. The umma had to be both a congregation and a state; and an embryonic state is what Muhammad created in Medina.

The following years were dominated by violent actions against internal and external enemies as the community established itself. The internal enemies were mostly Jewish. Initially, Muhammad's relations with the Jews of Medina were close: the Muslims prayed in the direction of Jerusalem, the central shrine of Judaism, and the Jews formed an umma 'together with' or 'alongside' that of the believers in the 'Constitution of Medina', which stipulated that they were to fight alongside the believers too. But in the second year after the hijra, we are told, Muhammad broke with the Jews by changing the prayer direction (*qibla*) to Mecca, thus endowing Islam with its own central shrine. Since Mecca was controlled by pagans, Muhammad had to conquer it, and his attempts to do so were accompanied by expulsions of the Jews. In 624 he won his first battle against the Meccans at Badr, whereupon he expelled one Jewish tribe; in 625 the Meccans

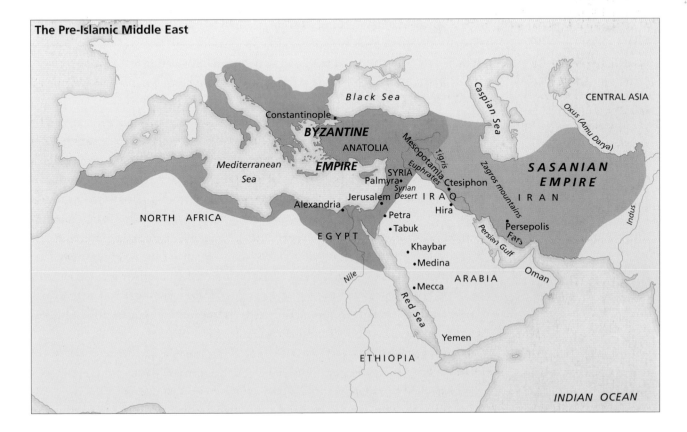

The Pre-Islamic Middle East

defeated Muhammad at Uhud, whereupon he expelled another Jewish tribe; and
when the Meccans attacked Medina in 627, he destroyed the last Jewish tribe, the
men being massacred and the women and children enslaved. The Muslims were
now ready for Mecca. In 628 the Meccans, though apparently doing well against
Muhammad, agreed to a truce, and in 630 they voluntarily surrendered. Muhammad now purified the pagan Kaaba and inaugurated it as a monotheist sanctuary
or, as the Muslims saw it, restored it to that status: they believed it to have been
founded by Abraham and his son Ishmael, whom they regarded as the first
monotheist and the ancestor of the Arabs respectively. Medina remained the
political capital.

Military activities were no confined to the Meccans: numerous minor expeditions were despatched and some notable conquests made before the surrender of
Mecca; others followed thereafter. By the time Muhammad died in Medina in 632
most of the Arab tribes had negotiated membership of his umma. He had also sent
an expedition to Byzantine Syria in 629 and gone on one in 630, though he
stopped on reaching Tabuk; and he was planning a further expedition when he
died. This is how the traditional story goes.

The Conquests

The story continues that Muhammad's death left the community leaderless. He
had no surviving sons and had not designated a successor or even indicated what
type of leadership should replace him: kings, priests, judges, conciliar government? The Muslims chose monarchy, though not kingship, by accepting Abu
Bakr, a member of the Quraysh who had emigrated with Muhammad to Medina,
as leader of the community (*imam*) with the title *khalifa* (caliph), meaning 'successor' (of the Messenger of God) or 'deputy' (of God).

Abu Bakr (r.632–34) inaugurated his reign by sending the expedition into
Byzantine Syria which the Prophet had planned. This was courageous, for
Muhammad's polity was beginning to disintegrate; many tribes considered their
membership of the umma to have expired when he died, and others rejected it by
raising prophets of their own, of whom the most important was Musaylima, active
among the Hanifa in the oases south of what is now Riyadh. But Abu Bakr successfully suppressed these revolts, extending and consolidating Medinese control
of Arabia. A tribal chief on the desert fringes of Iraq heard what was going on and
joined the Medinese venture: in 633 the Muslim commander Khalid ibn al-Walid
was sent to Iraq, where with the tribal chief he engaged in raids and induced the
city of Hira to surrender. Few in number and precariously organized, the Muslims
had now initiated hostilities on the periphery of both superpowers.

Perhaps they would have been crushed if the superpowers had not recently
been at war with each other and if they had known their opponents. When
Muhammad sent his first expedition to Syria in 629, the Sasanians had only just
agreed to withdraw their troops from Syria, enabling the Byzantines to resume

control after fifteen years. Even so, Muhammad's expedition was defeated; the Sasanians also defeated the Arabs in Iraq in 634. But Arab raiders were too familiar a nuisance to put the Byzantines and Sasanians on red alert, and the purposive return of the Arabs took them by surprise. In 634 Khalid ibn al-Walid led his army across the Syrian desert to join the Arabs on the Byzantine side, a celebrated example of the devastating use to which Arab mobility could be put when co-ordinated. Thereafter Syria was systematically wrested from the Byzantines, with decisive battles at Ajnadayn in 634 and Yarmuk in 637.

Meanwhile the leadership in Medina gathered a new army for despatch against Iraq in 637. It routed the Sasanians at Qadisiyya, thereby evicting them from Iraq. Since the Sasanian capital, Ctesiphon, was located in Iraq, the Iranians now lost the central direction the Arabs had so unexpectedly acquired. The emperor Yazdegerd did succeed in assembling another army to fight the Muslims at Nihawand in the Zagros mountains in 642; but he was defeated. After that the Muslims met only uncoordinated resistance insufficient to halt their advance in Iran.

They pursued their successes in Syria by occupying the Jazira (the northern parts of modern Syria and Iraq) in c.639–41, and by pushing into Egypt, which

The Iranian plateau was a habitat little suited to the Arabs, who did not settle there in great numbers, which was one reason why Iran was not Arabized. This picture shows the mountains of Fars (or Pars), the south-western corner of Iran from which the Achaemenian and Sasanian dynasties hailed. The Greeks called the Achaemenians 'Persians' because they came from Pars, and the country ruled by the latter has been known as Persia ever since. Its official name nowadays, however, is Iran, an old term meaning Aryans. Modern Iranians only use the word Persian (Farsi) of their language.

they had conquered by 642. They were expanding into north Africa to the west and Khurasan to the east when civil war broke out in 656, interrupting their military ventures. They had toppled the superpowers in a mere twenty years.

Explanation

What sense can we make of all this? Muhammad is clearly an individual who changed the course of history, but how was it possible for him to do so? Unfortunately, we do not know how much of the Islamic tradition about him is true. The only major literary Islamic source before about 800 is the Quran, which modern Islamicists generally regard as a collection of Muhammad's own utterances. But the Quran tells us more about Moses, Abraham, and other prophets than it does about Muhammad. Its allusions to contemporary events are unintelligible without the later tradition, which invariably purports to know what they mean but which only dates from about 800. The standard biography of the Prophet is the edition by Ibn Hisham (d.833) of a work by Ibn Ishaq (d.767), whose grandfather was a Christian prisoner-of-war taken in Iraq after Muhammad's death. But the Christians who escaped capture started writing about Islam as early as the 630s: both they and other evidence suggest that what Ibn Ishaq shows us is Muhammad as he had come to be seen some four generations after the hijra rather than what he was in his own time.

In particular, Islam may have remained closer to Judaism for longer than the Islamic tradition concedes. The substitution of Mecca for Jerusalem ascribed to Muhammad himself may well have been effected after his death, while the neat sequence of battles with Meccans and elimination of Jews culminating in the surrender of Mecca smacks of doctrinal rewriting. If Jerusalem remained the chief sanctuary in Muhammad's time, it would have been Jerusalem rather than Mecca that Muhammad was determined to conquer (though he may well have found it important to conquer Mecca too). From a classical perspective, the conquest of Mecca was the culmination of his career while the great conquests thereafter were more or less accidental; but if he actually preached conquest of Palestine, the early Muslim determination to take over Syria (in the wide sense including Palestine) makes better sense.

However this may be, Muhammad preached monotheism of the uncompromising Jewish (as opposed to trinitarian) variety and presented it as the ancestral faith of his people. On this point there is general agreement. His monotheism transcended tribal divisions and called upon the Arabs to unite in a single community, worshipping the same God, following the same law, and fighting the same holy war (*jihad*). Being an ancient people, the Arabs possessed a cultural homogeneity that was unusual in tribal societies. Muhammad's monotheism gave religious articulation to their implicit unity while also providing them with political organization and a common goal. The outcome of his preaching was a nation.

What had happened to make the Arabs receptive to his message? Perhaps they had always had the potential for fusion in the name of monotheism and merely needed Muhammad as the catalyst. More plausibly, their receptivity to Muhammad's message was the outcome of growing pressure from the superpowers. Since both Byzantine and Sasanian trade with India necessitated sailing along the coasts of Arabia, both superpowers had an interest in controlling its flanks. The Byzantines mostly manipulated the tribes indirectly via their Ethiopian and Ghassanid clients, but the Sasanians exercised direct control of eastern and eventually also southern and central Arabia. Pressures from both superpowers generated the likelihood of a political response. That a preacher should cause the peninsula positively to explode was not however to be foreseen.

THE CONQUEST SOCIETY

To the Muslims, the conquests were an amazing and exhilarating experience. 'O men, do you not see how Persia has been ruined and its inhabitants humiliated? They have become slaves who pasture your sheep, as if their kingdom was a dream', a poet disbelievingly exclaimed. 'We went out with him...barefooted, naked, with no equipment, force, arms or provisions, against the nations with the mightiest kingship, the most obvious power, the largest numbers, the densest populations, and the greatest ability to subject other nations, Persia and Byzantium...God gave us victory over them, allowing us to take their countries and to settle in their lands, their homes, and their property, we having no strength or force other than the truth', a later author triumphantly explained. To their victims, the experience was obviously less exhilarating. 'The Arabs became rich, numerous, and spread over the land which they had taken from the Byzantines and which was delivered to pillage...The Christians were in despair; some of them said, "why does God allow this to happen?"' The Christian answer was that God was punishing the Christians for their sins. But as the Muslims saw it, God was helping the Muslims because Islam was true. This was so obvious an inference that even the Christians had trouble resisting it.

The first civil war (656–61)

But the massive windfalls generated problems. How, for a start, were they to be distributed? The central government needed firm control of the newly won resources if the Muslim state was to survive. The second caliph, Umar (r.634–44), succeeded in enforcing a decision that all lands taken by force were to pass into state ownership instead of being distributed among their conquerors. The conquerors were told to stay together in armed camps (eventually garrison cities), where they received their income from the conquered lands in the form of stipends paid by the government in return for military service. Agricultural activity was forbidden. This was a far-sighted decision: without it, the Arabs might have dispersed as landlords and peasants among the conquered peoples, who

To the Arabs, crowns were symbolic of non-Islamic kingship and thus to be rejected. A story has it that Reccesswinth (r.653–72), a son of the conqueror of Spain, married the widow of the last Visigothic king and that she volunteered to make him a crown, insisting that 'kings have no kingship unless they are crowned'. After objecting that 'it is not part of our religion', he gave in; but when he was spotted wearing a crown, he was accused of having turned Christian and was killed. The story nicely illustrates how tempting it was to adopt local customs go native and how well the Muslims managed to resist that even in so isolated a province as Spain.

In 680 Husayn, the grandson of the Prophet, set out from Mecca to challenge Umayyad rule. He had with him the women and children of his household, a small band of supporters, less than 100 in all. At Karbala in Iraq he was surrounded by the forces of Yazid – Husayn was killed by an Umayyad soldier, Shemr. Commemorating his martyrdom on the 10th Mohurram (Ashura) each year is the central rite of Shia Islam. Karbala is celebrated here in an early twentieth-century coffee-house painting by Sayyid Husayn of Tabriz. Imam Husayn is the central figure on horseback.

would rapidly have absorbed them. But it made the tribesmen dependants of the state and they soon complained bitterly about its handling of the purse strings. Unfair distribution and malappropriation of the *fay* (revenues from the conquered lands) were standard accusations against the government for the next century.

Disputes over these resources were exacerbated by the fact that the conversion of powerful chiefs and wealthy Meccans undermined the status of the mostly humble men who had risen to leadership by joining Muhammad in the early days. The tribal followings of the chiefs also intensified the competition for resources in the garrison cities. Caught between an unresponsive government and eager new-comers, veterans who had settled in Iraq and Egypt went to Medina to complain to the third caliph, Uthman (r.644–56), and, finding him unresponsive, murdered him, unleashing the first civil war.

The death of Uthman showed that Medina could not remain the capital of the Muslim lands. It was in Egypt, Syria, and Iraq that Arab manpower and fiscal revenues were now concentrated, and the three contending parties in the civil war all represented centres outside Arabia. Ali, the cousin and son-in-law of the Prophet, was based in Kufa, one of the two garrison cities of Iraq; Talha and al-Zubayr, two

early converts supported by the Prophet's youngest widow Aisha, were based in Basra, the second garrison city of Iraq; and Muawiya, a late convert of the same Umayyad family from Mecca as Uthman, was governor of Syria. (Egypt did not produce a candidate.) Talha and al-Zubayr were quickly eliminated by Ali, who then fought Muawiya at Siffin in 657. The Syrians claimed to have won this battle, but according to the Iraqis they were losing when they halted it by calling for arbitration. However this may be, the dispute dragged on until Ali was murdered in 661 by Kharijites ('those who go out [to fight holy war]'), erstwhile followers of his who are said to have left him when he accepted the call to arbitration. Muawiya was recognized as caliph by the entire community in the same year. It was thus to Syria (Damascus) that the capital was moved.

Neither the Byzantines nor the Iranians had made serious attempts at reconquest while the Muslims were at war with each other, nor did they during the second and third civil wars. From this point of view the Muslims got through their potentially fatal conflicts scot-free. But the disputes, especially the first, left a deep impression on the Muslims themselves: attitudes to the first civil war enter into the self-definition of all the major Muslim sects.

The early Umayyads (661–83)

Muawiya (r.661–80) had to devise a new political organization for the conquerors. The conquered peoples had already been allowed to live as semi-autonomous *dhimmis* (non-Muslims under Muslim protection) in return for paying taxes. Ruling them proved surprisingly easy. But ruling the tribesmen was a different matter.

The solution was to keep them out of politics by governing them indirectly, while continuing of necessity to use them as soldiers. Muawiya divided the empire into a few huge provinces to which he appointed his kinsmen as governors. Being very few and closely tied to the caliphal family, these governors were above tribal rivalries. For the assessment and collection of taxes they relied on indigenous scribes, who continued to run all the central and provincial bureaucracies, thus keeping the tribesmen out of the fiscal administration. For law and order among the tribesmen themselves they relied on the latters' chiefs, who commanded them in war and were responsible for them in peacetime: if they

For a while, the Arabs continued to strike coins of the Byzantine and Sasanian types. Thus the coin on the left depicts Khusraw II (590–628) on the obverse and a Zoroastrian fire-temple with attendants on the reverse, and one would have assumed it to be a Sasanian coin if it had not been dated, in Pahlawi, to 'year one of Yazid' (presumably Yazid I, 680–83). But the caliph Abd al-Malik (685–705) experimented with ways of redesigning the coinage, and it was he who came up with the classical solution, illustrated on the right. This coin has no images, only writing; the writing is in Arabic, not in Pahlawi or Greek; and its message is aggressively Islamic: it proclaims that there is no God but God and that Muhammad is His messenger 'who He sent with guidance and the religion of truth to make it supreme over all others whether the polytheists like it or not' (Quran, 9:33). Within fifty years of the conquests the Muslims had thus reshaped the medium of exchange. They changed the Middle East as much as it did them.

Opposite The Dome of the Rock, Jerusalem, completed in 692, is the first major monument of Islamic history. Built by the caliph Abd al-Malik, it stands on the site of the Jewish temple in Jerusalem and thus amounts to a proclamation that Judaism was now superseded by Islam. It is also polemical against Christianity, with which it takes issue in its inscriptions. It consists of two octagonal ambulatories around a rock (seen here), which is classically identified as the spot from which Muhammad ascended to heaven on his nightly journey, but which was probably associated with Abraham in Abd al-Malik's time. Some sources claim that Abd al-Malik intended the Dome of the Rock to replace the Kaaba as the central shrine to which all Muslims should go on pilgrimage, but most modern scholars find this hard to believe.

misbehaved, the chief was penalized. The chiefs were richly rewarded for this role as middlemen between the tribesmen and the government. But only one chiefly house was given direct political power: Muawiya had allied himself with the Kalb, the leading tribe of the Qudaa, the major confederacy in Syria, by marrying the chief's daughter and allowing the family a substantial share in the government of Syria. In this tribe and, through it, in the Qudaa at large, his power was anchored. His system of indirect rule worked so well throughout the Muslim lands that, once the civil war was over, he never had to use the Qudaa outside Syria.

Towards the end of his life, Muawiya designated his son Yazid (r.680–83) as his successor. This was an intensely unpopular act. The caliphate was supposed to be elective, whether informally as for the first two caliphs, or formally by an electoral conclave (*shura*) as for the third caliph Uthman; nobody should monopolize it. Election had worked well enough in Medina, but now that the Arabs had an empire it was too disruptive. Hereditary succession, with its advantage of transferring power automatically on the caliph's death, was bound to be adopted.

This highlights the poignancy of the post-conquest development. The conquests were miraculous events which the tribesmen might well have expected to solve every problem they could possibly have: instead, they inexorably destroyed every feature of the society they valued by bringing wealth, social and political stratification, and a state which had to assume an imperial form if it was to survive. The tribesmen had unwittingly signed away their freedom when they allowed the state to take over the conquered lands in the days of Umar. Now they knowingly had to accept a hereditary caliphate. Within a hundred years they had come to be as thoroughly excluded from participation in political decision making as the subjects of the Byzantine and Sasanid empires whom they so utterly despised. They protested vociferously. The Umayyads 'made God's servants slaves, God's property something to be taken by turns among the rich, and God's religion a cause of corruption', they claimed, accusing Muawiya and his successors of turning the caliphate into mere kingship like that of the Iranians and Byzantines. They also rebelled. That it should be the family of a late and reluctant convert to Islam who controlled all the power and wealth with which God had rewarded the Arabs for following Muhammad was particularly bitter. Many thought that all could still be well if the Umayyads were replaced by others such as Ali's descendants. But the changes over which the Umayyads presided arose from the conquests, not from their personalities.

The Umayyads were an extremely successful dynasty. They preserved the political unity of the Muslims for a hundred years, assisted the birth of Islamic civilization, and greatly expanded the borders of Islam: when the civil war was over, Muawiya resumed warfare in north Africa; by 711 the Arabs had conquered Spain; they continued into France until finally halted at Poitiers in 732. The Umayyads also made conquests in India and more particularly in Central Asia where, shortly after the fall of the dynasty, the Muslims encountered and defeated the Chinese at

Talas in 751. But none of this made up for the Umayyads' increasingly autocratic rule. They have gone down in history as impious, secular-minded, and thoroughly dislikeable.

The second civil war (683–92)

Yazid I died prematurely in 683, with precisely the effect his father had hoped to avert by designating him his successor: civil war broke out again.

The main challenge to Umayyad rule came from the son of a contender in the first civil war, Ibn al-Zubayr, who wished to rule the Muslim world from Mecca. This was not practicable and, had he won, he would undoubtedly have been a figurehead while the real ruler would have been his lieutenant in Iraq.

Ibn al-Zubayr never gained control of Syria and Egypt, which fell to Marwan I (r.684–85), an Umayyad elected by the Qudaa. But he did establish control of Iraq, where Basra soon fell to him, though Basran Kharijites rampaged in Arabia and western Iran under 'caliphs' of their own until the civil war was over. The Kufans, who had failed to support an attempted revolt by Ali's son al-Husayn in 680 – with the result that al-Husayn and his family were massacred at Karbala – now followed a rebel called al-Mukhtar, who claimed to be the emissary of the messiah (*mahdi*). He broke convention by supplementing his Arab forces with adherents recruited from the numerous non-Arab slaves and freedmen in Kufa. But he was defeated by Ibn al-Zubayr's brother in 687, and Iraq remained under Zubayrid rule until 691. In that year Abd al-Malik (r.685–705), Marwan I's son and successor, reconquered Iraq and in 692 defeated and killed Ibn al-Zubayr himself, which necessitated bombarding the Meccan sanctuary. This act further tarnished the Umayyad image: sanctity and power, born together in Islam, were now hopelessly at loggerheads.

THE LATER UMAYYADS (684–750)

The later Umayyad period was rich in social and cultural developments, when a new post-tribal order and a distinctively Islamic culture began to emerge.

Conversion

After the second civil war, free non-Arabs began to convert on a significant scale. Non-Arabs must already have begun to outnumber Arabs in the Muslim community by then, but so far they had entered mainly via enslavement. The numerous prisoners-of-war taken by the Arabs during their expansion were sold as slaves, mostly domestic, and thus dispersed in Muslim households where they learnt Arabic and adopted Islam, and where many were eventually freed. Enslavement probably continued to be the main mechanism of recruitment until the end of the period but the conquered peoples also began to convert voluntarily.

From the time of Abd al-Malik onwards we hear of villagers migrating to the garrison cities, where they would convert in the hope of joining the ranks of the privileged conquerors. Since the defeated non-Arabs paid the taxes on which the conquerors subsisted, their Islamization undermined both the fiscal and the ethnic basis of Arab society. So far from encouraging, let alone forcing, them to convert, the authorities usually sent them back to their villages, refusing to recognize their conversion. There was no fiscal discrimination against recognized converts (*mawali*), but the Umayyad policy of admission was arbitrary and engendered much bitterness, not only among the non-Arabs but also within Muslim society among the religious leaders who were springing up against the Umayyads.

Since Muslims were acquiring land as fast as the non-Muslims were leaving it, the tax burden would have to be redistributed to fall on the land regardless of the faith of its owners. This had been largely accomplished by the end of the Umayyad period. By then the ex-tribesmen were assuring themselves that it was *not* humiliating to pay tax on land – only the poll tax paid by the non-Muslims for their protected status was degrading – but the notion that 'he who acknowledges a tax acknowledges humiliation' was not easily eradicated. The transformation of the tribesmen into taxpayers marked the final end of their glorious days as free agents when the world was for their taking. But it enabled Islam to spread freely in the countryside.

Muslim society

In the later Umayyad period, Muslim society ceased to be in the nature of an occupying army. Originally, all the tribesmen in the garrison cities were soldiers and all the conquered people were subjects, but over the years the former became unwilling to leave the comforts of their homes for campaigns against rebels and distant infidels, and from the time of Abd al-Malik onwards new professional armies were recruited from Arabs and non-Arabs alike. The main army was recruited in Syria, whose soldiers were despatched to troublespots and supplied garrisons to every province. There were also local frontier troops in north Africa, Jazira – Armenia – Azarbayjan, and Khurasan who defended their provinces in collaboration with the Syrians. In Egypt and Iraq, local troops retained only a minor role.

Everywhere, the professionalization of the army was accompanied by the emergence of a civilian Muslim society, also ethnically mixed. Some of the Arabs who abandoned their military occupation became peasants: 'you will become tillers of soil', 'you will follow the tails of cows and dislike holy war', the Prophet is said to have predicted, though the growing tradition soon credited him with having extolled the virtues of agriculture as well. But most of them stayed in the garrison towns, where they took to trade and craftwork alongside their former captives and where a new type of religious leader, the scholar, now emerged.

The scholars (*ulama*) were private individuals who presented themselves as guardians of Islamic values, always located in the past. Questions such as 'should Muslims pay land tax?', 'may women participate in warfare?', 'is birth control allowed?' (all discussed in the huge literature subsumed under the name of

As rulers of west Asia, the Arab conquerors could pick and choose between the artistic styles on offer. Palaces built by Umayyad princes in the Syrian desert combine Byzantine and Iranian art. This statue from Khirbat al-Mafjar presents the caliph (probably al-Walid II, 743–44) as a Sasanian monarch. The mosaics of the Great Mosque in Damascus (p.169) illustrate the absorption of Byzantine forms. The Arab ability to bring together separate cultural elements is significant in the formation of Islamic civilization.

Islamic law) would be answered with an examination of what the Prophet, the first caliphs, and other venerable persons were supposed to have said about them, for their opinions were authoritative. The literary genre in which statements from past figures, especially the Prophet, are recorded is known as *hadith*, a term also used of each item and usually translated as 'tradition'. Hadith is the characteristic means of expression of the ulama as distinct from other intellectuals, such as practitioners of *kalam* (roughly, systematic theology) who also appeared around this time or the philosophers who appeared in the ninth century. Traditionism lies at the heart of Islamic scholarship, above all Islamic law.

It has the by-effect of making early Islamic history difficult to unravel for, given that the only authoritative views were those of past figures, past figures were routinely used as mouthpieces for the convictions of later scholars. The Prophet and first caliphs being particularly authoritative, they are on record as having said something about practically everything, including the problem that not everything ascribed to them could in fact go back to them. The innocent reader may infer that the entirety of Islamic civilization was worked out in Medina in the thirty years between the hijra and the first civil war. This is obviously most unlikely but how to order and date the countless traditions attributed to early authorities is a controversial question.

Sect formation

The later Umayyad period was characterized by fierce debates on many issues, of which the status of past and present caliphs, especially those of the first civil war, was the most prominent. The Shiites, or members of the party (*shia*) of Ali, held that the Prophet designated Ali his successor, meaning that the first three caliphs were usurpers and that Ali's descendants were the only rightful claimants to the caliphate. The Kharijites endorsed the legitimacy of the first two caliphs but held Uthman, Ali, and all later caliphs to be in error. Still others endorsed Abu Bakr, Umar, and Uthman, holding the last to have been wrongfully murdered: these were the Uthmanis. Later, the Sunnis added Ali to the Uthmani list of rightly guided caliphs, refusing to take sides in the first civil war and endorsing all subsequent caliphs in the qualified sense that the community needed its rulers even if they were not necessarily rightly guided and hence not really caliphs at all.

It seems a mysterious issue over which to form sects but the caliphate or, as it is called in religious discussions, the imamate, was crucial to salvation. In the first place, the saving community was assumed not to exist without a legitimate leader. To choose one's imam was thus to choose the group with which one believed salvation to lie. Secondly, imams were seen as guides. 'Those whom God has guided, follow their example', the Quran says (6:90): whom had He guided, then? To answer this question was again to choose one's community. The debate was about the past because the Arabs had always defined groups by their ancestors and unselfconsciously cast the first caliphs as ancestors too, identifying their own sec-

A tradition *(hadith)*

Abd al-Razzaq from Mamar from Ayyub from Nafi from Ibn Umar, who said:

> The Prophet (may God bless him and bring him peace) prohibited travelling into enemy territory with a Quran, lest it fall into enemy hands.

A tradition consists of two parts, a chain of authorities (*isnad*) designed to guarantee the authority of its contents and the contents (*matn*) themselves. Traditions are usually short, if not always as short as this one. Their message is only binding if they are deemed authentic and have not been modified or abrogated by the Quran or other traditions; it is for the scholars (*ulama*), more precisely jurists (*fuqaha*), to decide what sort of law one can base on them. The message of this one is generally accepted, though a modern historian would not deem it authentic, for the Prophet here envisages the Quran as a tangible book, though it was only after his death that his revelations were collected between two covers. If one were to use it for historical reconstruction, one would have to decide when it came into circulation, which is less easy to say; like so many traditions, it existed by c.800.

tarian affiliation by picking out their imams where the genealogy of the umma branched out. But the debate bore on present rulers too. If the Umayyads held the leadership of the community, yet were not legitimate caliphs, where was guidance to be found? The Shiites affirmed that it was concentrated in the communal leader: only a change of personnel was needed. (It was to emphasize the centrality of the imamate to salvation that they limited the candidates to a narrow band of people related to the Prophet.) The Kharijites disagreed and the groups that were to coalesce as Sunnis also came round to the view that the caliph was only the political guardian of the community, not its spiritual leader: right guidance

Stucco heads from the Umayyad desert palace of Khirbat al-Mafjar. Classical Islamic law is hostile to the representation of animal and human beings, and this hostility must have long roots, for representations of this kind are studiously avoided in the Dome of the Rock and the Great Mosque of Damascus; the reformed coinage we have seen was also aniconic. But apparently it was only in religious contexts that images were reprehensible, for the secular art of the Umayyad period has no inhibitions about them. In fact, although the classical taboo affects secular art too, representations of animals and humans were never to disappear from Islamic art.

The Hashimites

The Hashimites were the 'family of the Prophet'. Though Muhammad did not have any sons, his lineage was continued by his cousins Abd Allah ibn Abbas and Ali ibn Abi Talib. Ali married his daughter Fatima and they had two sons, Hasan and Husayn, whose descendants are numerous today.

The Hashimites were an early focus of sect formation but only in the early Abbasid period did the classical Shiite sects begin to crystallize, partly in response to the Abbasid takeover of the caliphate. The classical Shiites concern themselves only with the Alid branch of the Hashimites. All credit the Alids with a special right to political power and a special ability to guide the community in spiritual matters: the true imam must be a descendant of Ali and Fatima in their view. But for the rest they differ.

The Imami or Twelver Shiites (found in Iran and elsewhere today) acknowledge twelve imams, whose names are numbered on the right, but hold the twelfth to have been in hiding since 873: he will return at the end of time as the messiah (mahdi). The imam is the source of all guidance, but while he is in hiding the community is guided, like the Sunnis, by scholars.

The so-called extremists (mostly extinct but represented by Alawites and Druzes in Syria, Ahl-i Haqq in Iran, and others) invested their imams with greater centrality to salvation, attaching less importance to the law. Most of them regarded their imams as divine. But the Zaydis divested their imams of such centrality, seeing them rather as superior chiefs and scholars. The Zaydis, named after Zayd ibn Ali, who staged an unsuccessful revolt in Kufa in 740, do not have a fixed line of imams: any descendant of Ali and Fatima, Hasanid or Husaynid, can claim the imamate as long as he is learned and rebels to claim his right. They survive only in the Yemen.

The Ismailis originated as extremists, though they never deified their imams. They emerged in the late ninth century, claiming that Muhammad ibn Ismail was the last imam and messiah who would soon return to abolish the literal meaning of Islamic law. Initially they were held together by belief in his imminent return but they split when the founder of the Fatimid dynasty claimed to be the person expected (c.900), and there were many other splits thereafter. The Ismailis survived in Syria, Yemen, and above all India, whence many went to East Africa; they are now dispersed all over the world. One branch is led by the Agha Khan.

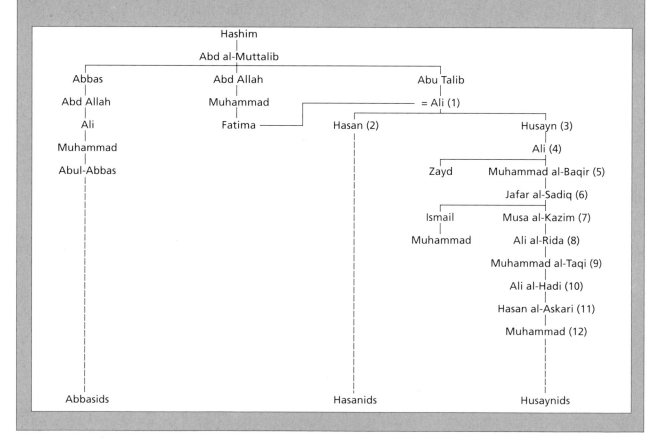

was dispersed among the Muslims at large and to be found above all among the scholars (eventually known as imams too). Differently put, guidance was a past phenomenon, not an ongoing one as the Shiites asserted: it was concentrated in the Prophet and other early figures, not in any one person in the here and now. Every Muslim was free to study the guidance enshrined in the past, and only by studying could some Muslims become more authoritative than others.

The fall of the Umayyads (744–50)

In 744 a group of Syrian soldiers killed the caliph al-Walid II and enthroned their own candidate, Yazid III, thereby unleashing the third civil war. Refusing to acknowledge the new regime, Marwan, the Umayyad governor of Jazira – Armenia – Azarbayjan, marched on Syria with his own troops, defeated his rivals, and had himself proclaimed caliph. He now had to conquer Iraq and to subdue the Kharijites, who were rebelling everywhere and whose Arabian adherents were about to spill into the Fertile Crescent when he crushed them in 748. A Shiite uprising in Khurasan was also launched in 747, led by one Abu Muslim. This revolt had long been planned and unlike the Kharijites, it could not be stopped: in 750 the Khurasanis inflicted a decisive defeat on Marwan II in Iraq. They proceeded to enthrone a Hashimite, a member of the Prophet's family; but contrary to what many had expected, they did not choose a member of its Alid branch, but

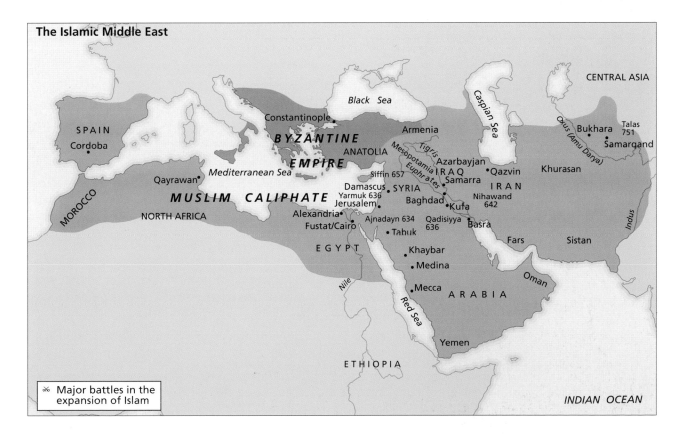

The Islamic Middle East

⚔ Major battles in the expansion of Islam

This woman from the late Umayyad palace of Khirbat al-Mafjar was probably a slave girl. The Muslim world continued to be well provided with them in Abbasid times, when they assumed the role played by hetairas in classical Greece and geishas in Japan. Many were accomplished singers and some were highly educated. When young men of the ninth or tenth centuries fell passionately in love, the object of their desire was usually a slave girl.

rather one from its Abbasid branch, which is said to have been behind the revolt in Khurasan.

THE ABBASID EMPIRE

The Abbasid dilemma

The Abbasids spent their first years pacifying the empire and liquidating Abu Muslim and other architects of the revolution. Once in control, they had to confront the problem to which they owed their own rise: there was no longer a conquest elite to hold the empire together. Again, a new political organization had to be devised, and this time it had to be openly imperial. Now that the ethnic, social, and cultural diversity of the pre-conquest Middle East was represented within Muslim society, the unity of the empire had to rest on a homogeneous elite set apart from the heterogeneous masses by culture, obviously Islamic: so Islam now had to validate the very type of imperial organization that the first Muslims had set out to destroy.

The military and political elite of the Abbasids was furnished by the Khurasani revolutionaries, who now replaced the Syrians as the imperial troops. Most were stationed in Iraq, which the Abbasids made their centre, while the rest went to garrisons all over the empire, where they filled the main governorships. The administrative elite consisted of the bureaucrats in Iraq, many of whom were Iranians and all of whom, whatever their ethnic origin, were schooled in Sasanian statecraft. But where were the Abbasids to find their religious leaders?

The religious scholars who had emerged in the Umayyad period were not entirely averse to collaboration. Most of them appreciated rulers who kept the umma united and orderly, and all were moving towards prohibiting revolt. But the religious heritage they guarded could not be made to validate the Abbasid enterprise. For the scholars had now elaborated a vision of Islam in which ideal government was exemplified by the Prophet and first caliphs in tribal Medina. The ideal ruler was a Muslim like any other, not an autocrat; he ruled in the name of truth, meaning effortlessly, not by coercion; all his adult male subjects participated in military ventures and political decision making, government being by consultation; and the only gradations were those of piety and merit, since there was no fixed social hierarchy or hereditary aristocracy. This vision lends itself beautifully to validating modern egalitarianism and mass participation in politics, but it was diametrically opposed to the imperial organization which the Abbasids sponsored and which was the only method whereby huge polities could be kept together in the pre-industrial past.

The scholars, then, could not offer full Islamic legitimation to the Abbasids. In effect, they regarded their rulers as menials doing a necessary but dirty job which involved transgression of Islamic norms, and whom one should therefore avoid for fear of moral contamination: 'the best ruler is he who keeps company with scholars, but the worst scholar is he who seeks the company of kings', as a well-known scholar is quoted. The Abbasids could increase their moral standing by building mosques, providing facilities for the pilgrims, conducting holy war, and (the rigorists notwithstanding) patronizing scholars. But they could not be seen as *representing* the Muslim community, as the first caliphs had done. Though the scholars preferred the Abbasids to the Umayyads, they implicitly condemned them too as mere kings by agreeing that the caliphate had ceased to exist: 'the caliphate will last for thirty years after my death', many quoted the Prophet as saying. The Abbasids could either accept that they were menials or try to replace the scholars with religious leaders ready to reshape their heritage. Since the scholars had come to predominate to the point where alternative visions of Islam were beginning to look impious and heretical, it was the former solution that prevailed in the long run.

The Shuubiyya

The Abbasid transfer of the capital to Iraq, where the second Abbasid caliph al-Mansur (r.754–75) built Baghdad, restored the Iraqi bureaucracy to its imperial status and gave new prominence to the Sasanian tradition of which it was the carrier. Ibn al-Muqaffa, a famous scribe and convert from Zoroastrianism killed in the reign of al-Mansur, translated numerous works from Pahlawi, practically all to do with kings and statecraft. There was also much interest in Indian science and Greek philosophy and science at court, as well as in kalam. The religious scholars looked askance at these developments because kalam and philosophy dispensed with the hadith that they themselves purveyed and because they were deeply suspicious of foreign knowledge. They and the educated laymen who flourished at court were competitors in setting the cultural tone and their rivalry found expression in the Shuubiyya controversy.

The Shuubiyya ('adherents of the [non-Arab] peoples') sponsored non-Arab culture in general and that of the Iranians in particular. They were perfectly good Muslims (though their enemies did not believe it), and they liked the Arabic language too, but they resented the identification of Islam as an Arab religion incompatible with any but Arabian culture. It was after all outside Arabia that civilization had flourished: 'all the kings of the earth belong to us, be they Pharaohs, Nimrodids, Amalekites, Persian, or Byzantine emperors', the Shuubis pointed out; 'all the prophets other than Hud, Salih, Ishmael, and Muhammad were non-Arabs'. The Shuubis indulged in lurid accounts of lizard-eating, raiding, and other aspects of tribal Arabia

This fresco from the late Umayyad palace Qasr al-Hayr al-Gharbi depicts an Iranian horseman hunting. Most archers in the early Muslim world were foot-soldiers, but the ability to shoot arrows from a horse in motion was highly prized, and Iranian horsemen were famed for it. The Turkish soliders imported from the time of al-Mutasim (832–42) onwards, however, were even more renowned for their combination of archery and horsemanship than the Iranians.

By Baghdadi standards early Muslim Spain (al-Andalus) was a rather dull and provincial place. Iraqi Muslims thought of it as backward and isolated and a non-conformist Spanish thinker by the name of Ibn Hazm (d.1064) was well aware that he might have done better in a metropolitan environment: 'My only misfortune is that I rose in the west; had I risen in the east, nothing would have been lost of my fame', he complained. Nonetheless, the culture of Muslim Spain was vastly more sophisticated than that of its Visigothic predecessor, and in the course of the eleventh century it lost its provincial imitativeness. This exquisite ivory casket was carved around 1100 in Cordoba, where Ibn Rushd (Averroes), the most famous philosopher of Muslim Spain, was born in 1126.

repulsive to a polished courtier, using the opportunity to settle old scores, for the Arab conquerors had treated the conquered people with appalling arrogance. But their point was that Islam should be a faith compatible with any worthwhile culture whatever its origin. The religious scholars responded with a barrage of statements attributed to the Prophet: 'God chose the Arabs...no believer hates the Arabs...love of the Arabs is part of the faith...love the Arabs because I was an Arab, because the Quran is in Arabic and because the language of Paradise is Arabic'.

Though the controversy dragged on for centuries, it soon became clear that the Shuubis had lost. Some Iranian culture was indeed adopted into mainstream Islam, but Islam did not become a religion that could be combined with any culture one liked, nor did the ulama lose their near monopoly of its definition. A story has it that when a scholar at the court of Harun al-Rashid (r.786–809) spoke of camels, an Iranian vizier objected that it was an unworthy subject of conversation; Harun then burst out: 'these camels have driven you from house and court and taken your crown; and even today when they are long dead, it is the whips made of their hides which you Iranians have to feel.' This graphically illustrates the problem for the Shuubis. It was thanks to the conquests that Islamic civilization existed and had an indelibly Arab imprint: they could not have one without the other. Islamic culture has retained its Arab identification to this day. Most Arabs today are Arabized descendants of the inhabitants of pre-conquest Syria, Iraq, and Egypt, but any suggestion that Islamic culture is an Arabized development of what prevailed in those pre-conquest lands deeply offends them. As they see it, Islamic culture, in so far as it was not invented from scratch, must derive from Arabia.

Al-Mamun (r. 813–33)

It would have been to the caliphs' advantage if the Shuubis had won, but they were too anxious to win the approval of the ulama to support them openly, except for al-Mamun. He was the only caliph to try ousting the ulama and he allied himself with Shuubis, practitioners of kalam, Shiites, and other enemies of the proto-Sunni scholars in the process.

Al-Mamun came to power after another civil war, the fourth. Harun al-Rashid had nominated one son, al-Amin (r.809–13), as his successor and appointed another, al-Mamun, to Khurasan with the proviso that he was to succeed al-Amin. No Abbasid prince had served as governor of Khurasan before and the friction between the two brothers rapidly developed into open war. Al-Mamun won, but since his brother represented the political establishment that his predecessors had carefully built up, his victory discredited the very organization he needed to rule, so he began a desperate search for alternatives. He stayed in Khurasan and allied himself with the local rulers and aristocrats: these were to be the new elite. In 816 he signalled his inauguration of a new order by designating the eighth imam of the Imami Shiites, Ali al-Rida, his heir and changing the black colour of the Abbasid dynasty to green. The Iraqis responded by rebelling, denouncing al-Rida's designation as a Zoroastrian plot, and raising another Abbasid to the throne. Other provinces were also chaotic and in 818 al-Mamun gave in, eliminated his Alid heir, and returned to Iraq.

He continued to favour Shiism, however, and eventually tried to claim the religious authority vested in the Shiite imam for himself. Shortly before his death in 833 he inaugurated an inquisition (*mihna*): all ulama within his reach were to sign their acceptance of a doctrine concerning the Quran to which practitioners of kalam subscribed but which the scholars loathed. By accepting it they would concede that the caliph and his court theologians knew better than they what Islam was. The inquisition continued into the reign of al-Mutawakkil (r.847–61) but it could never have succeeded. The caliph's problem was that the scholars had no organization by which he could subdue them as a collectivity. They owed their religious leadership to the informal consent of their followers; it came from below and could not be wrested from them by any means at the caliph's disposal.

Kawkaban in the Yemeni highlands. West Asia is dotted with inward-looking mountain communities, which have adopted deviant versions of Islam to insulate themselves from their neighbours in the lowlands. Thus the Yemeni highlanders have been Shiites of the Zaydi variety and (to a far less extent) Ismaili variety since the ninth century, while the highlanders of Oman have been Kharijites of the Ibadi variety since the eighth century; in both areas the lowlanders are Sunnis. In Syria the highlanders are Ismailis, Alawites, and Druzes in so far as they are not Christians.

Umayyad Cordoba

In the tenth century Cordoba, the capital of Umayyad Spain, whatever the opinion of the Muslims of Baghdad, was a leading city in wealth and in the arts of civilization not only in the Islamic world but also in the Christian lands of the west. Situated on the north bank of the Guadalquivir (Arabic *al-Wadi al-Kabir*) in Andalusia (Arabic *al-Andalus*), and served by a rich hinterland, it had been seized by the Muslims from the Visigoths in 711. The established Christian and Jewish populations were tolerated so long as they did not resist their Muslim rulers.

In 756 Abd al-Rahman ibn Muawiya, an Umayyad prince who escaped the Abbasid massacre of his family, took control of al-Andalus and made Cordoba his capital. Towards the end of the century Abd al-Rahman began to construct the Great Mosque, which was large enough to unite all Cordoba's citizens in prayer and which he called the Kaaba of the west. Other public works were also initiated - mosques, palaces, gardens, bridges, baths, and fountains. Syrian fruits were raised in his garden, including a palm tree to which he composed an ode:

> In Rusafa I came upon a palm;
> here in these western lands a sight so rare,
> I said: You stand alone, like me so far from home,
> you miss the children and our loved ones there;
> you have not grown tall in native soil.
> Like you I too must breathe the alien air.

Cordoba reached its zenith under Abd al-Rahman III (r.912-61). During his reign Spanish Islam reached its widest extent: every May campaigns were launched towards the Christian frontier. His fleet was arguably the largest of the time, his wealth barely matched in the Islamic world, and in 929 he proclaimed himself caliph. The splendour continued under Abd al-Rahman's effective successors, al-Hakam II and the usurper al-Mansur, until Cordoba was sacked by the Berbers in 1013.

Cordoba was often extolled by Arab historians. It was huge and boasted civic amenities such as running water and clean, paved, and well-lit streets. It was an intellectual centre, boasting seventy libraries. That of al-Hakam II, a noted historian who gathered learned men from the eastern Islamic lands, ran to some 400,000 volumes and was one of the greatest libraries of the Islamic world. Indeed, Cordoba was renowned for its books and its citizens for their love of the arts of the book. Women were famous as copyists, many specializing in copying the Quran in the book market. They also found roles as teachers, librarians, doctors, and lawyers. Cordoban scholarship covered the full range of sciences from the orthodox Islamic to those cultivated by the Greeks. Arts and crafts flourished too: the manufacture of crystal was one local discovery while jewellery and ivory carvings were widely exported. Non-Muslims participated in this efflorescence, Christians mainly in government and in the arts, and Jews primarily in scholarship, Jewish culture achieving a notable revival under caliphal rule. Two reminders of Cordoba's Umayyad glory remain: the ruins of Madinat al-Zahra, the palace complex built outside the city by Abd al-Rahman III which is named after his favourite wife, and the Great Mosque, the architectural masterpiece hailed in medieval Europe as one of the four wonders of the Muslim world.

The ruins of Madinat al-Zahra, Abd al-Rahman III's new capital some 2 miles northwest of Cordoba. Excavations began in 1910 and continue to the present. It was the caliph's palace, seat of government, and home to 20,000 staff, according to the chroniclers. Detailed reports exist of many receptions of foreign embassies here in the tenth century, among them one sent by the Holy Roman Emperor, Otto the Great, and two from Byzantine emperors bringing generous gifts, including a copy in Greek of Dioscorides' *Treatise on Botany*.

The great mosque at Cordoba, with dimensions of 195 by 140 yards, is the most powerful representation of the glories of Umayyad Spain. Opposite is the dome above what was al-Hakam II's prayer room, now known as the Capilla de Villaviciosa. The mosaics here and for the mihrab were made under the tutelage of a Byzantine craftsman sent by the Emperor Nicepheros II Phocas, along with over 3,500 pounds of gold mosaic cubes, at the request of al-Hakam. The caliph was determined to outdo the mosaics in the Great Mosque at Damascus.

Looking from al-Hakam II's prayer room to the mihrab, the culmination of the great mosque. The approach to the mihrab is through an extraordinary series of multi-lobed, interwoven arches, which represent a new aesthetic as compared with the parts of the mosque built by Abd al-Rahman I. The decoration of the mihrab is rich and intense; its calligraphic border mentions al-Hakam II and contains verses from the Quran.

Slave soldiers

Al-Mamun's successor, al-Mutasim (r.833–42), had begun experimenting with the solution. He recruited his crack troops from the Turks of Central Asia, famed for their mounted archery. Enslaved old enough to have acquired their native skills, they were taken to Iraq, accommodated in his new capital, Samarra, and converted to Islam. Then they were manumitted (though later they were kept as slaves) and employed as soldiers, generals, and governors. In time they ousted the freeborn Muslims of the Middle East from central government.

They were a far cry from domestic (let alone barrack) slaves: wealthy and powerful, they did not have to be coerced. But being foreigners rather than Middle Eastern Muslims, they were unencumbered by local interests and public ideals. As slaves, not free mercenaries, they were private dependants of the ruler (or his generals): he owned them and their property or had a special claim on them as their former owner. They served him as their private master, loyal to him rather than to the community he could not represent.

When Turks were not available, slave soldiers (*mamluks*) were recruited from others, such as Slavs and Africans. Later, from the fourteenth century, the Ottomans even recruited slave soldiers from their own Balkan peasantry, though this was against Islamic law, and gave them the top posts in the bureaucracy too. The institution survived into the twentieth century.

The disintegration of the Abbasid empire

The new armies, though extremely capable in al-Mutasim's hands, did not save the Abbasid empire from fragmentation. In fact, the Abbasids had never ruled the entire Muslim world, for Spain seceded under an Umayyad prince during their takeover. Most of what is now Morocco seceded soon after under the Alid dynasty of Idrisids (c.789–926). In 800 Harun al-Rashid granted autonomy to the governor of the rest of north Africa in return for annual tribute, thereby creating the Aghlabid dynasty (800–909). And shortly after returning to Iraq, al-Mamun consented to a new hereditary dynasty, the Tahirids (821–73) in Khurasan. The last two dynasties did at least co-operate with Baghdad, but thereafter the caliphate disintegrated.

In 861 the Turkish soldiers in Samarra murdered al-Mutawakkil, initiating a period of anarchy that lasted, a brief recovery apart, until 945. Ibn Tulun, a second-generation Turkish soldier, made himself independent in the wealthy province of Egypt in 868. About the same time Yaqub the Coppersmith, a plebeian leader of urban gangs in Sistan (southeast Iran), conquered Sistan, toppled the Tahirids in Khurasan, and began conquering Iraq when he was defeated in 876; he died in 879 and his brother was soon ousted by the Samanids, who ruled Khurasan and Transoxania until 1005 with caliphal consent. From 869 to 883 there was a huge slave revolt in southern Iraq, where African slaves had long been employed in restoring salinized land to cultivation by removing its marketable saltpetre. Their revolt was difficult to suppress because it was centred on the marshes where the fabled Turkish cavalry was no use at all. It was suppressed by al-Muwaffaq, a brother of the caliph's who had defeated Yaqub the Coppersmith and risen to the status of regent.

The recovery he initiated was sustained by his successors, who regained Egypt in 905. But in 908 the Baghdadi bureaucrats elevated a minor to the throne, al-Muqtadir, whose only skill as an adult was as a spendthrift: the decline became irreversible. Egypt was soon lost again, first to soldiers of slave origin and next to the Fatimids (969–1171), who led the radical Shiite movement known as Ismail-ism and had conquered north Africa in 909. Semi-autonomous rulers and war-lords also sprang up all over the Fertile Crescent. Iraq was conquered in 945 by Iranian mercenaries from the Caspian coast, the Buyids, who ruled Iraq and west-ern Iran for the next hundred years, reducing the caliph to a puppet. In 1055 Baghdad was occupied by the Seljuqs, leaders of Turkish invaders from Central Asia, and from then until 1918 the central Islamic lands (in varying degrees of fragmentation) were ruled by Turks.

THE TENTH AND ELEVENTH CENTURIES

The resurgence of Iran
In the two centuries before the Turkish invasion many Muslims feared that the era of Islam was coming to an end. The Byzantines reconquered parts of northern Syria in 969, giving the Muslims their first experience of losing land to infidels and instilling fears of losing even more. The Iranians too appeared to be return-ing, for from the Tahirids onwards they once more governed Iran. Contempo-raries lamented 'the enfeeblement and disappearance of Islam…the triumph of the Byzantines over the Muslims, the disruption of the pilgrimage, the absence of holy war, the unsafety and disruption of the roads, and the establishment of inde-pendent power by every leader'. Prognostications such as that 'a man will come forward and restore the domination of Zoroastrianism…and put an end to the power of the Arabs' were rife. But though the Byzantines were followed by the Crusaders, the eastern Mediterranean remained Muslim and Iran resurfaced within rather than outside Islam.

Zoroastrianism was not doing well as a minority religion and its chances of recovery were remote. There was a certain amount of anti-Islamic animus in the Caspian region from which the Buyids and other adventurers hailed: one Asfar (d.c.931) destroyed mosques, prohibited prayer, and threw a muezzin from a minaret in Qazvin. Another Caspian, Mardavij (d.935), reportedly adopted Ismailism. But such radicalism soon disappeared and, although the Buyids were also Shiites, Iranians did not systematically adopt non-establishment forms of Islam.

The Sunnis thought otherwise. Having discerned a Zoroastrian plot behind al-Mamun's designation of an Alid successor in the ninth century, they discerned

The main courtyard of the al-Azhar mosque, Cairo. The Fatimids were leaders of the Ismaili Shiite movement devoted to the conquest and regeneration of the entire Muslim world. They conquered north Africa in 909 and Egypt in 969, where they stayed until they were suppressed by Saladin in 1171. Their most enduring legacy there is the Cairene mosque and university of al-Azhar, which they founded in 970–72 for the greater glory of Ismailism and which were reopened in 1286 for the greater glory of Sunnism. Al-Azhar became one of the most renowned centres of Sunni learning, as indeed it still is.

another behind the rise of Ismailism in the tenth. They saw Ismailism as a *mélange* of pre-Islamic beliefs concocted by the conquered peoples, particularly the Iranians, to subvert Islam from within. Ismailism is in fact an Islamic restatement of religious notions well attested in the pre-conquest Middle East; but then Islam itself could be similarly characterized. The Ismaili vision was, however, so unlike the Sunni concept of Islam that the scholars could not consider it Islamic at all. In particular, the Ismailis expected a messiah to bring a new Islam devoid of law and ritual, the latter's spiritual meaning having been made plain to all. To mark the imminence of this new Islam, in 930 militant Arabian Ismailis slaughtered pilgrims and abducted the sacred Black Stone from the Kaaba in Mecca. With astrologers predicting the restoration of Iranian kingship and religion and Ismailis predicting the end of 'external' Islam, it was obvious to hostile (and scared) observers that Ismailism was really Iranian restoration in disguise. In fact it was not. Ismailism did have adherents in Iran, but then it had adherents in an extraordinarily wide range of milieus: for instance, the troops that conquered north

Africa and Egypt for the Fatimids were Berber tribesmen. Some continuities notwithstanding, it was not in religion that Iran made its comeback.

Nor did it recover its imperial identity. Asfar and Mardavij are both credited with plans to restore the Iranian empire, and the Buyids who occupied Baghdad in 945 actually revived the old imperial title 'King of Kings', which was blasphemous to most Muslim ears. But they did not abolish the caliphate or attempt to restore the Sasanian empire in a geographical or institutional sense. And neither the caliphate nor any state within it was perceived as an Islamized version of the Iranian empire until modern times.

Where pre-Islamic Iran did make a comeback was in language and culture. In Syria, Egypt, and Iraq converts to Islam adopted Arabic and came to be regarded as Arabs, but in Iran even the Arabs spoke Persian, which by the tenth century had come to be written in Arabic script and used as a high cultural medium on a par with Arabic. In 1010 the Iranians acquired their national epic when Firdawsi completed his monumental *Shahnama* (Book of Kings), which records the mythical and semi-historical past of Iran and ensured that with or without political organization the Iranians remained a people of their own. The linguistic and cultural resurgence of Iran, which began under the Samanids, took place under the aegis of Sunnism, and the Turks, who were also Sunnis, were to carry Iranian culture all the way to Anatolia.

Cultural efflorescence

The tenth and eleventh centuries, though politically chaotic, were a period of extraordinary cultural brilliance. All the famous names of Islamic philosophy and science belong to these centuries: for example, the philosopher and doctor Ibn Sina (Avicenna, 980–1037), the mathematician and physicist Ibn al-Haytham (Alhazen, d.1039), and one of the greatest religious thinkers, al-Ghazzali (d.1111). It is usually this era's dazzling culture that westernized Muslims have in mind when they praise the sophistication of Islamic civilization compared with that of medieval Europe. There was an unusual openness to alternative modes of life: the polymath al-Biruni (d. 1046) explored the nature of Indian paganism, poets explored the life of the underworld, and Ismaili thinkers explored that of animals (in a famous fable in which the animals stand not for humans but rather for themselves against humans). It was also in this period that Islamic mysticism (sufism) began to acquire prominence. On all this the reader will find more in the next chapter.

CHAPTER 2

Robert Irwin

The Emergence of the Islamic World System 1000–1500

In the early eleventh century, al-Mawardi, a judge in the Iraqi town of Basra, published a work of political theory entitled *Ahkam al-Sultaniyya (Ordinances of Government)*. (In medieval Islam books were published by being read out in mosques.) The *Ahkam* described how the Muslim community was governed by an imam, or caliph, elected by the community, who delegated his powers to officers chosen by him. The caliph and his subordinates had to protect Sunni orthodoxy, enforce Islamic justice, and prosecute *jihad* (holy war). Al-Mawardi's treatise bore little relation to contemporary realities: the claim of the Abbasid caliph in Baghdad to head the community was contested by a Shia Fatimid caliph in Cairo and quietly ignored by a Sunni Umayyad caliph in Cordoba.

Pious theorizing notwithstanding, the Abbasid caliphate had become hereditary and caliphs had long since ceased to command in person the armies that confronted the Byzantines. The ethos of jihad was kept alive only by Arab and then Turkish tribesmen and volunteers in the marchlands.

Even in those territories formally loyal to the Abbasid caliphate there was no unity or consensus. The caliphs were effectively the puppets of the Buyid warlords from the Caspian shore who, though Shia in their religious convictions, dared not impose those convictions on the people of Baghdad. The Buyids pretended to administer the lands of the caliph on his behalf, but in the early eleventh century their control over Khurasan was contested by the Ghaznawids, a dynasty of *mamluk* (slave soldier) origin (977–1186), whose capital, Ghazna, was in eastern

It was customary for princes to show favour to their subjects by bestowing robes of honour on them. Such costly garments were also commonly used as diplomatic gifts. Here Mahmud of Ghazna (998–1030) is shown putting on a robe of honour he has received from the Abbasid caliph. Mahmud was a Sunni Muslim prince who was careful to include the caliph's name on his coinage and thus present himself as the caliph's subject. Rashid al-Din, a vizier in the service of the Mongol Ilkhanate in Iran in whose *World History* this illustration appears, wrote in the early fourteenth century. The illustrations to this particular manuscript, produced in 1306–07 in Tabriz, show the influence of Chinese brushwork technique.

Afghanistan. Elsewhere on the fringes of Iran and Iraq the Buyids were similarly forced to surrender power to local regimes.

'Prophecy and the caliphate belong to the Arabs, but kingship belongs to the Persians' was a popular saying of the time. Firdawsi's *Shahnama*, dedicated and presented to Mahmud of Ghazna (r.998–1030), drew on pre-Islamic Sasanian political traditions and was a more realistic vision than the *Ahkam al-Sultaniyya*. Firdawsi presents kings as fallible but monarchy as a necessary evil, for it provides some protection against external aggressors. The writings of Firdawsi and other Persians offered models of rule and legitimation that influenced the ideology and rituals of medieval Islamic monarchs. Firdawsi's verses also provide evidence of racial tensions in the heartlands of Islam: Persian heroes battle first against Zahhak, a thousand-year-old demonic Arab cannibal, and later against the Turanians, the ancestors of the Turks in Firdawsi's history. Curiously, despite Firdawsi's hostile portrait of the Turanians, his epic proved almost as popular with Turks as with Persians.

THE FATIMIDS

The fourteenth-century North African philosopher-historian Ibn Khaldun wrote 'Know that it has been commonly held by all the people of Islam…that at the end of the world there certainly will be manifested a man from the family of the

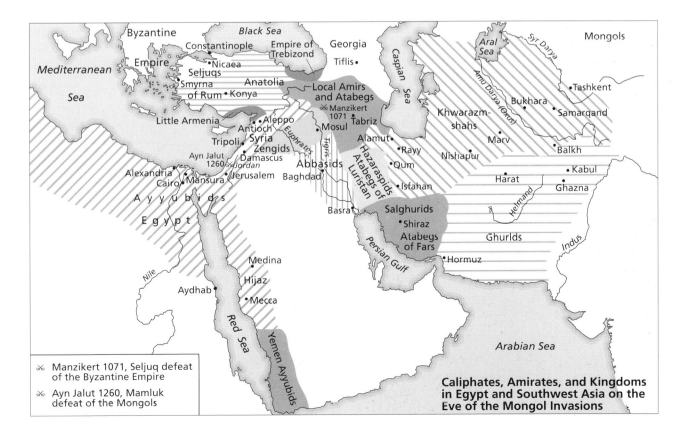

Manzikert 1071, Seljuq defeat of the Byzantine Empire

Ayn Jalut 1260, Mamluk defeat of the Mongols

Caliphates, Amirates, and Kingdoms in Egypt and Southwest Asia on the Eve of the Mongol Invasions

Prophet who will support the faith and make justice manifest. The Muslims will follow him and he will acquire dominion over the Islamic realms. He will be called the *Mahdi*.' In North Africa, the early Fatimid caliphs in the tenth century were regarded by their followers as divinely guided figures destined to impose Islamic justice upon the world. By the eleventh century, however, such eschatological pretensions were played down and the Fatimid caliphate had become a territorial regime not very different from its neighbours. Nasir-i Khusraw, a mid-eleventh-century Persian student of Shiism in Egypt, vividly evoked the gaudy ostentation of the Fatimid court. 'A balustrade of golden lattice-work surrounded the throne whose beauty defies description. Behind the throne were steps of silver. I saw a tree that looked like an orange tree, whose branches, leaves, and fruit were made of sugar. A thousand statuettes and figurines also made of sugar were placed there too.' Commercial and agricultural prosperity and the large regiments of diverse troops contributed more to the caliphate's survival than did ideology.

In Egypt the capricious and eccentric Fatimid caliph al-Hakim (r.996–1021) showered fortunes on some of his subjects and death upon others. He persecuted Jews and Christians and legislated against dogs, chess, and shops opening after sunset. He stopped shoemakers from making women's shoes and sought to ban women from going to the public baths. Those found in the baths were bricked up alive there. Yet such was the institutional strength of the Fatimids that they continued to flourish and their territory to expand. Egypt, Cyrenaica, the Hijaz, and Syria as far north as Damascus were administered by governors appointed by the Fatimid caliph. Those of Tripolitania and Tunisia professed themselves servants of the caliph, as did the Arab rulers of Sicily. The Fatimids sought to take advantage of the disintegration of the Buyids in Iraq. In 1010 the governor of Kufa rebelled against Baghdad in support of the Fatimid caliphate. Other regional princelings and military adventurers were to do likewise. In 1058 al-Basasiri, a Turkish general, even forced Baghdad and the Abbasid caliph to acknowledge the supremacy of the Fatimid caliph al-Mustansir (r.1036–94). This marked political high water for Shiism in the Middle Ages.

The Fatimids conducted a war of swords and words with the Abbasid caliphate. Indeed, they were more interested in sending *dais* (missionaries) to preach and subvert the Abbasid subjects than they were in converting their own. Thus 'Sevener' Shiism remained the faith of only a section of the elite in Egypt and the Shia were outnumbered by the Sunni Muslims, Coptic Christians, and Jews. Despite the Fatimids' despatch of spies and missionaries to eastern Islam, their efforts bore little fruit. The late eleventh century witnessed a resurgence of Sunni Islam, as Oghuz Turks, converted to Sunni Islam in the previous century, entered the Near East from Transoxania. The triumph of the Fatimids in Iraq was misleading. Al-Basasiri was forced to leave Baghdad and ethnically divided regiments fought over Egypt. North Africa came under Fatimid vassals, Sicily under the Normans, and much of coastal Syria under the Byzantines and then the Crusaders.

Ibn Khaldun

Not only was Abd al-Rahman ibn Muhammad ibn Khaldun (1332–1406) one of the most important historians ever to have written in Arabic, he has proved to be one of the world's greatest and most influential philosophers of history. Besides writing a multi-volume history of the world, the *Kitab al-Ibar*, he also composed a lengthy theoretical introduction to the *Ibar*, entitled the *Muqaddima*. In the *Muqaddima* he propounded his theories about the cyclical rise and fall of dynasties and civilizations. According to Ibn Khaldun a civilization has a predestined life-cycle. As the civilization decays, the bonds of *asabiyya*, social solidarity, weaken, and that civilization falls prey to more vigorous nomads from the frontiers. The nomads whose bonds of solidarity are strong, having triumphed, establish a new regime, but that regime will in turn fall victim to the laws governing historical decay.

Ibn Khaldun began to write his great work in a remote part of western Algeria during a three-year retirement from politics which began in 1375. He found it easy to illustrate his theories about nomads and the formation of new regimes by drawing on material not only from the early Islamic conquests but also from events in recent north African history: the successive waves of Berber Almoravids, Almohads, and Merinids that swept across the region played a major part in shaping his argument.

But his view of history was also much influenced by the ravages of the Black Death which in the 1340s had carried off his mother and father as well as many of his teachers and friends. The experience rendered his approach fundamentally pessimistic: 'In the middle of the eighth [fourteenth] century', he wrote, 'civilization both in the East and West was visited by a destructive plague which devastated nations and caused populations to vanish. It swallowed up many of the good things of civilization and wiped them out. It overtook dynasties at the time of their senility, when they had reached the limit of their duration. It lessened their power and curtailed their influence.'

Although Ibn Khaldun began writing the *Muqaddima* in the Maghrib, he completed it in Cairo from 1382 onwards. Like many others from north Africa and elsewhere, he was attracted by the patronage offered to religious scholars by the Mamluk sultans. Despite the jealous hostility of local Egyptian scholars, Ibn Khaldun lectured at the Madrasa-Mausoleum of Amir Sarghitmishiyya, pictured here, and at other religious foundations in Cairo. He marvelled at the numerous crafts, services, and entertainments to be found in such great cities, but tended to see such profusion as a sign of cultural over-ripeness.

SPAIN AND THE MAGHRIB

Morocco had never been part of the Fatimid empire. In the early eleventh century the region was divided among three Berber tribal confederacies, the Zanata, the Masmuda, and the Sanhaja. Each was widely dispersed, but the Sanhaja dominated the Sahara desert between the Atlas mountains and the Senegal and Niger rivers. Although nominally Muslims, many Sanhaja worshipped 'the gleaming mountain' and they superstitiously sought to propitiate the jinn who lurked in trees and rocks. Ibn Yasin (d.1059), a Sanhaja who in Cordoba had studied Maliki Islamic Law (after Malik ibn Anas, d.795), was invited by a Sanhaja chief to teach his tribesmen the error of their ways. In their Maliki literalistic and rigorous adherence to the Quran and *Sunna* (the practice of the Prophet), Ibn Yasin and his followers preached against the encroachment of administrative justice over the religious law, against taxes not sanctioned by the Quran, and against employing Jews and Christians in senior administrative posts. Ibn Yasin and his Almoravid followers enforced their orthodoxy by the sword. 'Almoravid' derives from the Arabic *al-murabitun*, volunteers for holy war who were lodged in *ribats* (fortified monasteries). The Almoravids were as disciplined in prayer as in fighting. Looking back on their successes, Ibn Kaldun commented that in 'the Maghrib there existed many tribes equalling or surpassing them in numbers and in group feeling (*asabiyya*). However, their religious organization doubled the strength of their group feeling through their consciousness of having the right religious insight and their willingness to die ... and nothing could withstand them.'

It was natural then that Muslim princes in Spain turned to the Almoravids for help in stemming the Christian *reconquista*. In the early eleventh century the Umayyad caliphate in Cordoba began to suffer seriously from the same sort of factional strife as was to afflict the Fatimid caliphate. In 1013 rebel Berber regiments sacked Cordoba. The Andalusian poet Ibn Shuhayd lamented the city's ruined splendour:

> A dying hag, but her image in my heart is one
> Of a beautiful damsel.
> She's played the adulteress to her men,
> Yet such a lovely adulteress !

A pretence of sustaining the caliphate under puppet caliphs was maintained for a while during this civil strife, but after the death of Hisham III in 1031 even that was abandoned. Actual rule was by the *taifa* (faction or 'party' kings), regional dynasties in Seville, Granada, Saragossa, and elsewhere, who warred continuously with one another. They took regnal names from the Abbasid caliphs, of which a poet complained that 'among the things which distress me in the land of Andalus are names like *Mutadid* and *Mutamid*: names of royalty out of place, like a cat which speaks in a puffed-up way like a lion.' These princelings individually commanded too few resources to defend their subjects against increasing Christian aggression, which took advantage of Muslim strife. Some of the taifa kings feared more from the assistance of the Almoravids than from the enmity of the Christians, but al-Mutamid, the ruler of Seville, declared that he would rather be a camelherd in North Africa than a swineherd under Christian rule. He wrote to the Almoravid general Yusuf ibn Tashfin: '[Alfonso VI of Leon] has come to us demanding pulpits, minarets, mihrabs, and mosques, so that crosses may be erected in them and monks may run them' and he begged for Almoravid assistance. In 1086, after Alfonso had captured Toledo, an Almoravid army led by Ibn Tashfin responded belatedly to appeals for help and crossed into Spain, defeating the Christians at the battle of Zallaqa. However, despite that victory and their jihad propaganda, the Almoravids proved more successful in adding the taifa principalities to their empire than in resisting the Christian advance. In time the Almoravids' fervour faded and compromises were made in the interests of the dynastic rule over large parts of Spain and north Africa.

In the twelfth century the Almoravids were replaced by another dynasty who similarly derived their power from a movement of spiritual renewal originating among the Berbers of North Africa. The Almohads, whose name derives from *al-Muwahiddun*, 'The affirmers of God's unity', recruited their followers mainly from the Masmuda Berbers. Ibn Tumart, the founder, was an ascetic enthusiast for the mystical doctrines of al-Ghazzali (1056–1111). All sorts of stories circulated about Ibn Tumart's preaching. He was credited with magical powers, with predicting the future from markings in the sand, and with conversing with the dead, but hostile polemicists accused him of hiding accomplices under the earth in the cemeteries. In 1125 he proclaimed himself the mahdi, 'And faith in the mahdi is a religious obligation, and he who doubts it is an unbeliever…No error is conceivable in him. He is not to be contended with or opposed, or resisted, or contradicted or fought, and he is…truthful in his words. He will sunder the oppressors and impostors, and he will conquer the world, both East and West, and fill it with justice as it had been filled with injustice, and his rule will last until the end of the world.' Under Ibn Tumart's lieutenant, Abd al-Mumin, the Almohads attacked Almoravid possessions in North Africa and by 1151 they triumphed in Morocco. In 1157 they crossed over into Spain and occupied Almeria and Granada. In 1195 they defeated the Christians at Allarcos but they too proved no more successful than the Almoravids in stemming Christian gains in the peninsula. After being defeated at the Battle of Las Navas de Tolosa in 1212, the Almohads withdrew from Spain, their possessions gradually taken over by the Marinids, a dynasty of Zanata Berbers.

THE COMING OF THE TURKS

In the east the revival of Sunni fortunes owed much to the massive influx of Oghuz Turks and the triumph of the Seljuqs, the paramount Oghuz clan in Transoxania, over first the Ghaznawids and then the Buyids. At its peak the Ghaznawid empire had included most of what is now Iran, Khurasan, Afghanistan, and

This Muslim battle standard, formerly believed to have been captured by the Christians from the Almohads at the Battle of Las Navas de Tolosa (1212), in fact appears to have been captured in campaigning against Spanish Muslims a little later. The inscriptions invoke blessings on the Prophet and cite the Quran. Andalusia was famous for the high quality of its woven silks.

the northwest area of India and Pakistan. Between 1016 and 1037 the Ghaznawids also held Transoxania, but their control of that region was never secure and relied heavily on hired Oghuz cavalry auxiliaries. The lands across the Oxus had been a major recruiting ground for Turkish mercenaries and mamluks since at least the ninth century, when the Persian essayist al-Jahiz wrote that the Turks were 'uninterested in craftsmanship or commerce, medicine, geometry, fruit-farming, building, digging canals, or collecting taxes, they care only about raiding, hunting, horsemanship, skirmishing with rival chieftains, taking booty, and invading other countries'.

It was not until the eleventh century that the Turks took the commanding positions in government and warfare in the Muslim heartlands - positions they did not abandon, broadly speaking, until the Ottoman empire was dismembered at the end of the First World War. In 1025 the Seljuqs were invited by the Ghaznawid ruler Mahmud to serve under him as mercenaries in Khurasan but in 1036 they rebelled and in 1038 took possession of Nishapur, the chief city of Khurasan.

In their war against the Ghaznawids, as well as in their later campaigning against the Fatimids, Byzantines, and others, the Turks preferred persisent skirmishing to pitched battles. At an assembly during their war against Masud of Ghazna they reportedly concluded that 'we are steppe-dwellers and are well able to endure extremes of heat and cold, whereas he and his army cannot, and after suffering this distress for a while, will have to turn back.' By the mid-eleventh century the Seljuq clan, who shared leadership of the Turkish tribesmen amongst themselves, had conquered the Ghaznawid lands in Transoxania, Khurasan, and Iran. In 1050 Tughril Beg received the title of Sultan from the Abbasid caliph in Baghdad; he was the first Muslim ruler regularly to use this title. Then in 1055 he drove the Shia Buyids from Baghdad, after which the caliphs found they had more flexibility. Not only were their new protectors Sunni Muslims but they rarely visited Baghdad, preferring instead to govern first from Nishapur, later from Isfahan, and often in practice from an army camp on the move. In the long run the influx of uncultivated Turkish nomads into the Middle East was beneficial. Turkish cavalry patrols provided security for merchants and the tribal economy produced meat, hides, and textiles which were traded with the cities. According to an edict of a Seljuq sultan, Sanjar (1118–57), 'Benefit is derived from their [the nomads'] wares and goods, these are a reason for the increase in prosperity, contentment, and profits of settled peoples.'

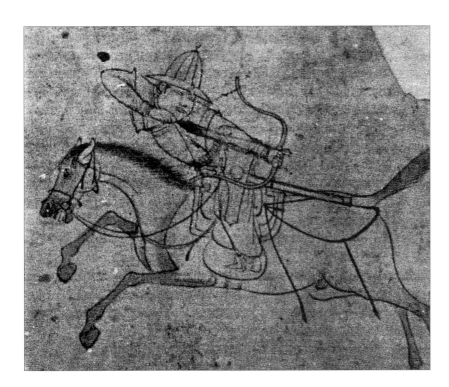

The Turkish horse-archer was a specialist in feigned retreats and in Parthian shots, fired backwards from the saddle. The archer here is shown using the composite recurved bow, made from layers of horn, sinew, and wood. This sort of bow, much favoured by the Turks, had an even greater range than the famous medieval English longbow.

The Seljuqs had converted to Islam towards the end of the tenth century, probably through the agency of sufi missionaries wandering on the Turkish steppes. Such mendicant sufis were predominantly Sunnis and the reinforcement of Sunni Islam was a clear consequence of the Seljuq triumph and the accompanying migration westwards through the Islamic lands of other Oghuz Turks.

Important to the Seljuqs' self-image was their belief that they were destined to rule the world as a master race. The eponymous and perhaps legendary founder of the Seljuq line had a prophetic dream of urinating fire over the world. In a preface to a Turkish dictionary, the eleventh-century lexicographer Mahmud of Kashgar wrote 'I have seen that God has caused the sun of empire to rise in the house of the Turks.'

Although this 'master race' was Turkish, their bureaucrats and courtiers spoke Persian. Outstanding among the Persian ministers was Nizam al-Mulk (1018–92), vizier to the sultans Alp Arslan (r.1063–72) and Malik Shah (r.1072–92). In the late 1080s Nizam al-Mulk wrote the *Siyasat-nama (Book of Government)*, which describes the administration of the Seljuq sultanate and the pompous court rituals of former Persian dynasties, gives advice on training pages and palace servants, recommends employing mamluks of various races to counterbalance the Turkish warriors, and advocates farming out tax collection to servants of the state. A striking feature is Nizam al-Mulk's treatment of the Abbasid caliphate as an institution of no political importance. Additionally, his blueprint for the well-governed society does not allot any role to the ulama as the guardians of orthodoxy and privileged interpreters of Islamic law.

Tughril Beg at prayer. With his brother Chagri Beg, Tughril Beg was one of the chief architects of the triumph of the Seljuqs in West Asia and transformed them into sponsors and defenders of Sunni Islam.

THE ULAMA

In general, the sultans offered the ulama patronage rather than power. They in turn offered the sultans legitimacy. In 1067 Nizam al-Mulk founded the first *madrasa* in Baghdad. Madrasas, colleges teaching the study and propagation of the Sunni version of Islamic law, seem to have first appeared in Ghaznawid Khurasan. But in Seljuq times the institution spread through Iran and further west. Islam is often said to have no clergy, which is true if one means an order of men, distinguished by ordination, who mediate between people and God. But if one uses 'clergy' in a looser sense, then medieval Islam possessed one. Large numbers of people were attached to mosques and earned some of their living by conducting services. Imams led prayers, *khatibs* preached sermons, *muqris* read the Quran, *muezzins* summoned the faithful to prayer, *muftis* issued legal amendments, and so on. The increase in madrasas from the eleventh century onwards greatly enlarged Islam's clergy, as professors, *répétiteurs*, and librarians joined 'the Men of the Turban'. Under the Seljuqs and their successor states the prestige of the ulama, experts on the Quran and Islamic law, visibly grew. However, since most madrasas were founded by sultans, emirs, and other politicians, the ulama who accepted employment there could be seen by rigorous religious lawyers as having compromised themselves.

Under the tolerant Shia Buyids, individualistic scholars had studied the philosophy and literature of Greek and Roman antiquity and pursued lines of speculation condemned as unislamic by more narrow-minded co-religionists. The Seljuq triumph effectively curtailed this humanist renaissance. By and large, the madrasas, with their religiously based and formally quite narrow syllabuses, became the intellectual centres. Besides providing Sunni ulama with professorial niches, the instruction was also useful in combating Shia propaganda. Several chapters of Nizam al-Mulk's *Siyasat-nama* outline the political threat posed by Shia sectarians. The theologian-philosopher al-Ghazzali (who influenced the Berber mahdi Ibn Tumart), appointed professor in 1091 at the head of the Nizamiyya in Baghdad, wrote several polemical treatises against Ismaili Shiism. But he also wrote the enormously popular *Ihya ulum al-din (Revival of the Religious Sciences)*, in which he rehearsed traditional arguments favouring the compatibility of sufi mysticism with Sunni orthodoxy. In following centuries, al-Ghazzali's doctrines and those of earlier sufis (such as al-Junayd and al-Hallaj) achieved a more widespread popularity, thanks largely to the foundation of sufi hospices and the formation of the great sufi orders.

THE SUFIS

The endowment of *khanqas* and *zawiyyas*, originally temporary resting places for wandering sufis, increased opportunities for the laity to offer patronage to and control those who had chosen the religious life. Ibn Jubayr, an Arab pilgrim from Spain who visited Syria in the late twelfth century, wrote of Damascus: 'Ribats for

Sufis which here go under the name of khanqas, are numerous…The members of this type of Sufi organization are really the kings in these parts, since God has provided for them over and above the material things of live, freeing their minds from concern with the need to earn their living so that they can devote themselves to his service.'

The early khanqas were not organized on denominational bases and individual foundations were not reserved for specific brotherhoods, but they became so when the *tariqas* (literally 'ways') formed. These were hierarchically organized sufi brotherhoods with, usually, cherished chains of transmission from master to disciple and fixed initiation rituals. The chain of transmission was customarily traced back to Ali, the Prophet's cousin, and to the Prophet himself. The tariqas seem to have begun sometime in the thirteenth century but often their alleged founders seem not to have had any role in their formation. For example, the Qadiri brotherhood took its name from Abd al-Qadir al-Gilani, a twelfth-century ascetic and preacher, but there is no clear evidence of the brotherhood until the fourteenth century. Similarly, although Ahmad al-Rifai lived in the twelfth century, the Rifai brotherhood of 'Howling Dervishes', renowned for their loud devotions, only came into existence much later.

The Suhrawardi brotherhood founded by Abu Hafs Umar al-Suhrawardi (1145–1234) in Baghdad in the 1230s was probably the first sufi tariqa. Later in the century disciples of Abul-Hasan al-Shadhili (d.1258) established the Shadhili brotherhood in Alexandria, whose lodges subsequently spread across North Africa. In India the widespread Kubrawi brotherhood traced their ancestry back to Najm al-Din Kubra (1145–1220). The Indian Chishtis similarly traced their spiritual lineage to Muin al-Din Muhammad al-Chishti (d.1236).

The social and cultural importance of the sufi brotherhoods cannot be overestimated. Sufis went as missionaries to the lands of the infidel. From the thirteenth century sufis played the leading role in advancing the Islamic frontier in Bengal, fashioning in the process one of the largest ethnic groups in Muslim lands today. The loosely affiliated brotherhood of wandering dervishes known as the Yasaviyya (after Ahmad ibn Ibrahim al-Yasavi, d.1166) were vital in converting pagan Turks and Mongols in Central Asia to Islam. Not only were some of the finest poets in the Ottoman empire affiliated to the Mawlawis, or Whirling Dervishes, but Mawlawi shaykhs (sufi leaders) served as spiritual and political advisers to some of the Ottoman sultans. The Naqshbandi brotherhood, widely spread in Central Asia, also on occasion exercised political influence: for example, the Naqshbandi Khwaja Ahrar was a leading politician in Samarqand and Bukhara in the late fifteenth century. Bektashi dervishes, despite some heterodoxy, attracted the patronage of Ottoman sultans; Bektashi *babas* (sufi leaders) became in effect the military chaplains of the Janissary regiments. The most striking involvement of sufis in politics came with the Safawids in Azarbayjan. The fourteenth-century Safawid shaykhs were Sunni sufis and guardians of a shrine in Ardabil. During the fifteenth century they became first leaders of a jihad against Christians in the Caucasus and then the militant and mahdist leaders of a Shiite movement. (The Safawids' passage from Sunnism to Shiism is one indication that the distinction between the two was by no means so clear-cut in the Middle Ages as it is today.)

Rigorous ulama, particularly those attached to the strict Hanbali school of religious law such as Ibn Taymiyya and Ibn Qayyim al-Jawziyya, campaigned against the exalted claims made for certain sufi masters and opposed pilgrimages to saints' tombs to seek their intercession with God, dancing, singing, and reciting erotic poetry during mystical assemblies. Ibn Taymiyya particularly attacked the 'miracles' of the Rifai sufi, accusing them of coating their feet with a protective ointment made from frog's fat and orange peel before staging their holy firewalking. Even so, Ibn Taymiyya and Ibn Qayyim al-Jawziyya were not opposed to all forms of sufism, both belonging to the Qadiri brotherhood. While some sufi brotherhoods had a regional or ethnic appeal, others spread throughout the lands of Islam: Qadiri lodges, for example, were found from Morocco to Indonesia. The overwhelming majority were Sunni Muslim and though there were Shiite features in, for instance, Bektashi ritual and practices, the general effect of the increased popularity of sufism assisted the Sunni revival.

BYZANTIUM AND THE FIRST CRUSADE

During the eleventh and twelfth centuries Sunni Islam gained territory at the expense of the Fatimids in Syria and the Byzantines in Armenia and Anatolia. In both areas advances were made by Turkish adventurers and war bands who were rarely controlled by the Seljuq sultan. The Seljuq conquest of the Iranian heartlands had opened the way for fresh migrations of Oghuz Turks. These pastoralist tribes did not disperse evenly throughout Islam: most pressed westwards towards the good pastures of Azarbayjan and Anatolia. There they found themselves on the edge of a war zone and in *ghazi* territory. A ghazi was a Muslim volunteer in military raids (*ghazawat*) against pagans or Christians who expected to gain either booty or a martyr's death. The Turkish tribes who joined the ghazis on the edge of the Byzantine empire took to describing themselves as ghazis too, though their advance was more like migration than raids in a holy war.

Raiding by ghazis and tribesmen provoked the Byzantine emperor Romanus Diogenes (r.1068–71) to muster a huge army and advance eastwards from Constantinople to attack the Seljuqs. An able soldier, Romanus had been made emperor precisely to solve the problem of the frontier by military means. But his campaign was misconceived, for the sultan, Alp Arslan, who had been planning an offensive against the Fatimids in Syria, had not encouraged the Turkish attacks on the Byzantine lands. Nevertheless, in 1071 the Byzantine army advanced to encounter the Seljuqs at Manzikert, near Lake Van. Romanus Diogenes reportedly declared that 'if this barbarian really desires peace, let him come over to my camp and solemnly surrender his palace at Rayy as a pledge of security'.

The encounter at Manzikert was not of Alp Arslan's seeking and before the battle he is said to have donned his burial shroud. The Byzantine defeat and an ensuing civil war in the empire removed any remaining obstacles to the migration of more Turkish tribes and war bands into Anatolia. Although Alp Arslan made minor gains on the frontier in the wake of Manzikert, he showed no interest in conquering Anatolia. Instead, two Turkish dynasties settled in the former Byzantine lands. A rival branch of the Seljuqs established a sultanate at Konya, while the Danishmendids, a ghazi lineage, controlled central and eastern Anatolia for over a century. The Turkification of Anatolia and the corresponding decline of Hellenism was one of the most important demographic and cultural changes to take place in the Middle Ages.

The Turkish advance towards the Bosphorus led to the First Crusade. The Byzantine emperor Alexius Comnenus (1081–1118), another military emperor, wrote to Pope Urban II, seeking western assistance – perhaps a relatively small and easily controllable force of mercenaries – in repelling Turkish encroachments. However, the leaders of the First Crusade which arrived in Constantinople did not want instructions or advice from the emperor. Moreover, they had grander ambitions than helping the Byzantines in Anatolia. After winning easy victories against both the Seljuqs and the Danishmendids, the crusaders pressed on into Syria with Jerusalem as their goal. When they arrived in northern Syria they were confronted by a patchwork of states controlled by rival princes and governors. Primogeniture was alien to Turkish tribal traditions and after the death of the Seljuq sultan Malik Shah in 1092 the sultanate had been rocked by dissension among Seljuq kinsmen. In Syria the city governors proved unable to co-ordinate resistance to the crusaders. After taking Antioch in 1097 the crusaders entered Palestine and captured Jerusalem from the Fatimids in 1099.

The thirteenth-century Mosuli historian Ibn al-Athir put the First Crusade in a broader context:

> The first appearance of the Empire of the Franks, the rise of their power, their invasion of the lands of Islam and occupation of them occurred in the year 478 [1085–6], when they took the city of Toledo and others in the land of Andalus …Then in the year 484 [1091–92] they attacked the island of Sicily and conquered it…Then they forced their way even to the shore of Africa, where they seized a few places, which were however recovered from them. Then they conquered other places, as you will now see. When the year 490 [1096–7] came, they invaded the land of Syria.

Even when a string of crusader principalities was established on the Syro-Palestinian coast, the capture of Jerusalem was not at first perceived as very significant. In vain the Baghdadi *qadi* (judge) al-Harawi stormed into the caliph's court and berated him: 'How dare you slumber in the shade of complacent safety, leading lives as frivolous as garden flowers, while your brothers in Syria have no dwelling

In the twelfth century this castle of Shayzar in Syria was the seat of the Arab clan of the Banu Munqidh. The most distinguished representative of the clan, Usama ibn Munqidh, wrote an exciting memoir of his encounters (not always hostile) with the Crusaders as well as his successes as a huntsman and a poet. The castle was on the front line in the Muslim struggle against the Crusader states.

place save the saddles of camels and the bellies of vultures?' Neither the Abbasid caliphs nor the Seljuq sultans took much interest in prosecuting jihad against the crusaders. It was left to the Muslim neighbours of the crusader states to devise a response. Effective preaching and prosecution of a jihad only got under way in the 1140s under the Zengid rulers of Mosul and Aleppo.

Zengi, installed as *atabeg* (governor) of Mosul by Sultan Mahmud in 1127, was a ferociously energetic Turkish officer. A hard drinker, he was otherwise extremely austere and maintained fierce discipline among his troops: when they passed through agricultural lands, 'the soldiers of the atabeg seemed to march between two ropes'. Although the majority in the Zengid armies fighting the crusader states were freeborn and mamluk Turks, the Zengids also recruited significant numbers of Kurdish warriors. From the 1150s onwards, as the Fatimid caliphate became weaker, Zengi's son and heir, Nur al-Din, ruler of Damascus and Aleppo, engaged in a race with the crusader Kingdom of Jerusalem to take over Egypt. The senior officers Nur al-Din sent to Egypt were mostly Kurds and it was a Kurd from the Ayyubid clan, Saladin (1137–93), who suppressed the Fatamid caliphate in 1171.

Saladin and his kinsmen claimed to govern Egypt on behalf of Nur al-Din but that was a pretence: when Nur al-Din died in 1174 Saladin moved out of Egypt and occupied Damascus and other Syrian towns. To many Syrians, Saladin was a usurper. However, he and his successors attempted to justify their rule in Syria and Egypt by prosecuting the jihad against the crusader states. Saladin was perhaps the most charismatic of the medieval sultans, admired by his Frankish enemies as well as by Muslims. Even Ibn Jubayr, a loyal subject of the Almohads, was constrained to write of Saladin's 'memorable deeds in affairs of the world and of religion, and of his zeal in waging holy war against the enemies of God. Because north of this land [Damascus] there is none belonging to Islam…God in his mercy gave to the Muslims here this Sultan, who never retires to a place of rest, nor long abides at ease, nor ceases to make the saddle his council-chamber.'

In 1187 Saladin defeated the Kingdom of Jerusalem at the Battle of Hattin and went on to retake Jerusalem from the Christians. This triumph notwithstanding, memories of the expensive and bloody efforts Saladin and his allies were forced to make in countering the Third Crusade (1189–92) may have blunted jihad fervour in the early thirteenth century. Not until 1291 were the last crusader ports captured by al-Ashraf Khalil (r.1290–93), the mamluk sultan of Egypt and Syria.

THE SELJUQ SUCCESSOR STATES

The Seljuq sultans of Iran and Iraq played only a minor role in this Syrian counter-crusade. The east took more of their attention. From the mid-twelfth century, Khurasan drifted out of Seljuq control as the government proved unable to stem more immigration by unruly Oghuz tribesmen. These Oghuz Turks were largely responsible for the destruction of the Seljuq Turkish regime in the Islamic heartlands. Yet more Turks found military employment with the Zengids and other petty regimes established by governors and soldiers who had formerly served the Seljuq sultans.

The empire of the Khwarazm-shahs in the east was the grandest Seljuq successor state. In 1148 the Khwarazmian Turkish general Atsiz gained independence from the Seljuqs in Transoxania, and from 1193 the Khwarazmians set about conquering Khurasan, with their army of horse-archers recruited from a different Turkish tribal group, the Kipchaks. The Khwarazm-shah Ala al-Din Muhammad (r.1200–20) ruled an empire extending from the edge of Iraq to Turkistan, and over Ghazna and part of India as well. Like the Lesser Seljuqs of Konya, the Zengids, the Ayyubids, and later the Mamluks, the Khwarazm-shahs borrowed their entitulature and protocol from the Greater Seljuqs of Iran. However, despite their pomp and vast territories, their regime proved curiously insubstantial: like the Mongol regimes which replaced it in Iran and Transoxania, the Khwarazmian empire was predatory, attracting little loyalty from its subjects. In particular, Khwarazm-shah's conflicts with the Abbasid Caliph in Baghdad and his rough handling of ulama and sufis helped to alienate the Persians who provided the bulk of the civil administration and population of the cities. Moreover, the ruler's household administration was poorly adapted to govern such a vast empire and it rapidly fell apart when the Mongols attacked.

THE MONGOLS

Before their tribes were unified in the region between Lake Baikal and the Altai Mountains, the Mongols had led a nomadic pastoralist life that was virtually identical to that originally pursued by the Oghuz and Kipchak Turks. Like them, most Mongols were shamanist, although some had converted to Buddhism or Nestorian Christianity. The founder of the Mongol empire, Temujin, was probably born in 1167. According to legend, the new-born Temujin held an ominous clot of blood in his clenched fist. Throughout his career Temujin made great play of being a 'man of destiny'. Ruthless and treacherous in diplomacy and war, Temujin began as the leader of a very small war band. Success bred success and by 1206 he had forced all the Mongol tribes of the steppe to unite under him. In that year a grand council was held at which Temujin took the title Chingiz Khan. In 1218 a Khwarazmian massacre of merchants under Mongol protection gave the Mongols a pretext for war. The Khwarazmian armies, dispersed in garrison cities, put up little effective resistance. The Khwarazm-shah (more distinguished for his knowledge of Muslim law than for military abilities) took refuge on a Caspian island where he died.

Transoxania and Khurasan were repeatedly attacked and their cities sacked. The Mongols' military successes in western Asia and elsewhere were due to the mobility and superior equipment of their mounted warriors and to their careful

Towns and cities in the Muslim world were often separated by long journeys through harsh and dangerous countryside. So rulers and local notables built caravansarais where travellers, typically traders, scholars, or pilgrims, might rest safe for the night with their animals. This magnificent entrance to the Sultan Han (Turkish for caravansarai), built by Ala al-Din Kayqubad outside Konya in the thirteenth century, indicates the importance attached to such buildings. The honeycombed vaulting of the entrance is typical of Seljuq architecture and is reminiscent of the tents of their Central Asian ancestors.

planning, as well as their attention to logistics. Promotion was by merit and, in Jebe and Subudei, Chingiz Khan had the services of two of the most remarkable generals the world has ever seen. Their campaigns are still carefully studied in the twentieth century. The Mongols also used large-scale atrocities to terrorize and intimidate their opponents. Of Persian cities it was reported that Chingiz Khan had decreed: 'All cities must be razed, so that the world may once again become a great steppe, in which Mongol mothers will suckle free and happy children.'

According to Ibn al-Athir, the Mongols 'in just one year seized the most populous, the most beautiful, and the best cultivated part of the earth whose characters excelled in civilization and urbanity. In the countries which have not yet been overrun by them, everyone spends the night afraid they may appear there too.' The sack of Nishapur in 1221 was particularly bloody. The Mongols, having made separate pyramids of the heads of men, women, and children, went on to hunt down the dogs and cats. Their profanation of mosques and Qurans was almost

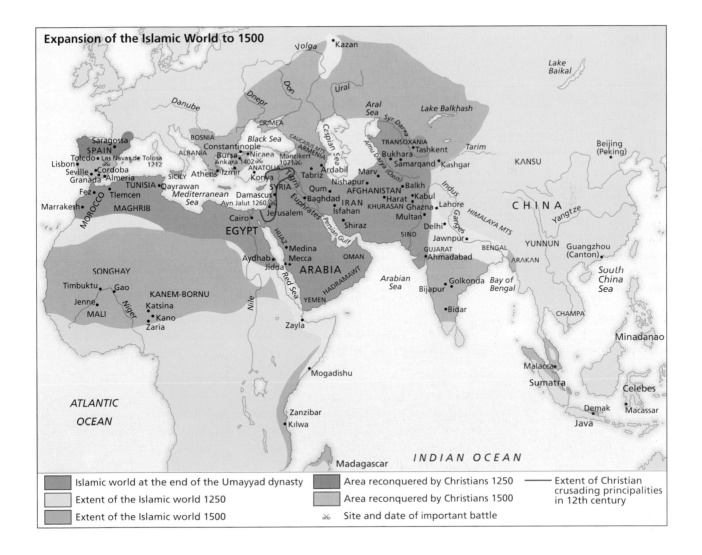

ritualistic. According to al-Juwayni, a Persian historian in Mongol service, in Khurasan and Iraq 'every town and every village has been several times subjected to pillage and massacre and has suffered this confusion for years, so that even though there be generation and increase until the Resurrection the population will not attain to a tenth part of what it was before.' Other horrified observers stressed the loss of learning as much as the slaughter. Places like Samarqand and Nishapur had been great centres of Muslim orthodoxy and scholarship, but everywhere the Mongols organized bonfires of books.

The Mongols' impact on the Near East was without doubt disastrous in its short-term effects on Muslim culture and economy. In Iran ceramic production ceased almost entirely for some forty years after 1219. The Syrian town of Raqqa on the Euphrates, a major pottery centre, was sacked by the Mongols in 1258 and thereafter abandoned. Mosul, an important centre for metalwork, ceased to be so after the 1260s.

Muslim historians claimed that Chingiz Khan communicated with devils in trances. (Similar reports circulated about the Turco-Mongol conqueror Timur in the fourteenth century.) The Muslim princes opposing the Mongols were by contrast judged as ditherers and faineants. After Chingiz's death in 1227 Mongol armies occasionally raided northern Iran and in 1243 Baiju, a Mongol general, defeated the army of the Seljuq sultanate of Konya at the Battle of Kose Dagh. Thereafter the sultanate became a Mongol tributary. However, the full conquest of Iran and Iraq began in the 1250s.

In 1253 the Great Khan Mongke sent an army of invasion under his brother Hulagu. Hulagu's first mission was to capture the castles of the Ismaili Assassins in northern Iran and particularly their headquarters at Alamut. (Probably the Assassins, or Hashishiyyun, were so named by their enemies, who claimed that they were like the deluded riff-raff who took hashish.) Alamut fell in 1256. The last Grand Master was kicked to death by Mongol troops and the castle's large and magnificent library was destroyed. The sect's territorial power shrank and the subversive appeal of their doctrines sharply declined. In 1271 the Mamluk sultan Baybars captured their last remaining centres in northern Syria.

Having destroyed the core of Ismaili Shiism in the Middle East, Hulagu advanced against Baghdad, the capital of Sunnism. Baghdad was sacked and its last caliph executed in 1258. It is unclear whether Hulagu had been given a mandate to establish a principality for himself, but his claims to some of the territories were contested by his kinsmen, so Hulagu had to fight a long war in the Caucasus against the Mongol khans of the Golden Horde established in south Russia. Although Hulagu had brought Chinese and Uighur bureaucrats with him, inevitably he and his successors also came to rely heavily on Persian men of the pen. As a Chinese minister of the Mongols observed, 'The Empire was conquered on horseback, but it is impossible to run it from horseback.' For some decades after the conquest, Persian bureaucrats and scholars were cut off from their Arab co-religionists; one effect was that the Iranian nature of culture in Iran was intensified.

Hulagu died in 1265. Possibly a Buddhist, he certainly was not a Muslim and his funeral was marked by human sacrifices. Although Hulagu's son Teguder Ahmed, who was *ilkhan* (the representative of the supreme Mongol khan in China) from 1282 to 1284, converted to Islam, his action was not welcomed by most of his Mongol following. Those in Iran were only brought over to Sunni Islam by the ilkhan Ghazan (r.1295–1304). Medieval Iran was predominantly a Sunni territory - not that it is always easy to distinguish between Sunnis and Shiites in this period. Elsewhere in the Mongol territories, Berke, the khan of the Golden Horde in south Russia, became a Muslim in the 1260s, but conversions only increased there when enforced by the khan Uzbak in the early fourteenth century. Again, though some leading Chagatay Mongols in Transoxania converted in the 1260s, Islam seems to have become widespread among this warrior elite only in the fourteenth century. Yasavi dervishes were important in converting the Mongols and their Turkish auxiliaries to Islam.

The Mongol leaders repeatedly trumpeted their God-given mandate to conquer and rule the world. 'One sun in the sky, one lord on earth.' As a letter of 1269 from the ilkhan Abaqa to Baybars put it:

> When the king Abaqa set out from the East, he conquered all the world. Whoever opposed him was killed. If you go up to the sky or down into the ground, you will not be saved from us. The best policy is that you make peace with us. You are a mamluk who was bought in Siwas [in eastern Turkey]. How do you rebel against the kings of the earth?

THE MAMLUKS

Nevertheless, the Mamluks repeatedly defeated the Mongols, preventing them from conquering Syria and Egypt. After their first victory over the Mongols at the Battle of Ayn Jalut in northern Palestine in 1260, the Mamluks generally succeeded in holding a frontier along the Euphrates against them for over fifty years. For much of this period the Mamluks also fought a successful war against the crusaders. Indeed, it was the French crusade against Egypt in 1249 that induced Mamluk officers to murder one of the last and least impressive Ayyubid sultans, Turanshah, and to take over in Egypt and from 1260 onwards in Syria. The Mamluk sultans used the ideology of the jihad to justify their usurpations of power, just as Saladin had earlier when taking Damascus. It is striking, among Muslims fighting

In spite of laws against excessive expenditure on clothing, Mamluks, as this picture of a prince and his courtiers suggests, wore elaborate and ostentatious dress. The production of luxury textiles (*tiraz*) in Egypt was the ruler's monopoly.

each other, how many regimes in this period – the Almoravids, Almohads, Ghurids, and the Anatolian beys – stressed their role as leaders of a jihad.

The Mamluks were remarkably similar to the Mongols in military skills, tactics, and equipment. The Syrian historian Abu Shama said the Mongols were defeated by 'pests of their own kind'. Imported first by the Ayyubids and then from 1250 until 1517 by Mamluk sultans, the young Turkish slaves were not only trained in military skills, but were also thoroughly instructed in Islamic doctrine and taught to read and write Arabic. Thus mamluks were trained for government as well as warfare and most of the Islamized mamluks showed the zeal of converts. Mamluk sultans and emirs followed Seljuq and Ayyubid tradition in founding and funding madrasas and khanqas. They also exercised patronage over the civilian elite in another way: the royal chancery and the *diwans* (tax offices) were vastly expanded, and the great emirs recruited Arab secretaries and financial officers for themselves.

ISLAM IN SOUTH AND EAST ASIA

In 1261 Baybars installed as caliph in Cairo a relative of the last Abbasid caliph of Baghdad. Thereafter the sultans trumpeted their piety in protecting the Abbasid caliphate and the holy cities of Mecca and Medina. In reality Cairo's jurisdiction was only sporadically recognized outside the sultanate and the thirteenth-century Persian historian al-Juzjani considered the Delhi sultanate the centre of Islam

Opposite Looking towards the Qutb Minar through the arched screen of the Quwwat al-Islam (Power of Islam) mosque in Delhi. This enormous minaret was erected in 1199 by Qutb al-Din Aybak, of the dynasty of Slave Sultans, as a tower of victory to symbolize the supremacy of Islam in India.

Below The importance of the Islamic world's relations with China are illustrated in this Persian miniature of the Turcoman school c.1470–80, which shows a Chinese bride on her way to marry a barbarian, probably Turkish, bridegroom. Chinese blue-and-white ware (as shown in the bride's dowry) was particularly esteemed and copied in the Islamic world.

China's advanced civilization was influential in the Muslim world. Muslim contacts with China were much more important than those with the Christian world. Up to the Mongol conquest Muslims, Arabs, and Persians, as well as converts, tended to be confined to the ports. Afterwards they spread throughout China. This is the Niu Jie (Ox Street) Mosque in Beijing which was founded in 1362. Note the combination of Arabic calligraphy and Chinese decorative idiom.

after the Mongol conquest of Baghdad. Like the Ayyubids in Syria, the Ghurids in northern India had stressed their prosecution of jihad, though in their case it was a war against the Muslim heretics in Sind. Just as the untimely death of al-Salih Ayyub in Egypt allowed mamluks to take power there, so in India the assassination of Mahmud of Ghur in 1206 allowed a mamluk officer, Qutb al-Din, to become sultan. Between 1206 and 1555 several Turkish and Afghan dynasties ruled in Delhi and though only a handful of the sultans were of mamluk origin, they all made extensive use of slave soldiers. Muslim-held territory greatly expanded under the Delhi sultans to include most of the subcontinent by 1335. For a long time, however, the mamluks remained an alien minority, governing in consultation with sufi advisers. Sufis, especially Chishtis and Suhrawardis, not only exercised power at court, they were also the main agents in converting to Islam a significant part of the subcontinent's population.

Even before the impetus given to Islam in India by the Turkish conquests and sufi preaching, sizeable communities of Arab and Persian merchants had established themselves in the coastal towns. In practice, the Arabian Sea between India and East Africa was a Muslim lake, until the Portuguese rounded the Cape in 1498. Islam spread eastwards from Indian ports along commercial routes: Muslim merchants from Gujarat traded in the Malay peninsula and Sumatra. In the early fifteenth century the ruler of Malacca converted to Islam, followed gradually by the Sumatrans. The Indian and Malacca Straits ports were staging posts on the trade routes to the spice islands and to China.

The importance of China, with its advanced civilization and huge cities, to the Muslim world cannot be overemphasized. Commercial and intellectual contacts with China dwarfed those with Christendom. Silks and ceramics were China's main exports to the Muslim world. As early as the ninth century there were alleged to be over 100,000 Arab merchants in Canton. Until the 1250s most Muslims, Arab and Persian as well as Chinese converts, were found in the ports. Thereafter, the Mongol conquest of 1252–79 brought many Muslim officials, soldiers, and merchants into northern China too, even though the Mongol Yuan rulers themselves never became Muslims. China's cultural prestige is reflected in Arab and Persian attempts to imitate Chinese ceramics and textiles and in the adoption of such motifs as the lotus, the cloud band, and the dragon and phoenix. In jade carving, pyrotechnics, dyeing, lacquerwork, and paper making, Chinese technical pre-eminence was obvious to the Muslims. As the eleventh-century Persian scholar al-Thalibi put it, 'The Arabs used to call every delicately or curiously made vessel, whatever its real origin, "Chinese", because finely made things are a speciality of China.'

THE RISE OF TIMUR

Arab and Persian familiarity with things Chinese increased with the regime of the Mongols and later of Timur and his successors in the Middle East, and their Chinese and sinified Turkish advisers, technical specialists, and craftspeople. After the death in 1337 of the Mongol ruler of Iran, Abu Said, contending factions fought for control over the Ilkhanate and Mongol warlords used puppet khans as foils for their regional ambitions. When in the fourteenth century Mongol power revived in the Turco-Persian heartland, its centre was further east, in Transoxania. The Chaghatay Khanate (named after one of Chingiz Khan's sons) straddled Transoxania and Turkistan. The tradition-loving Chaghatay had been slower to convert to Islam than the Mongols of the Ilkhanate. Even after conversion many remained attached to the non-Islamic customs of their steppe ancestors. Pious Muslims criticized Chaghatay emirs for revering the ordinances of Chingiz Khan more than the Holy Law of Islam.

The poorly documented early life of the Chaghatay conqueror Timur (Tamerlane c.1336–1405) is curiously, even suspiciously, similar to the story of Chingiz Khan's early years. Timur boasted no exalted lineage, for he came from a relatively minor tribe. Rather, he and his panegyrists stressed how he made his way by his own abilities. He presented himself as a man of destiny, the Turkish 'Golden Man'. Only his divinely ordained fortune and his deliverance of victory and booty to his army kept it in his service. Timur believed that 'plunder in warfare is as lawful as mother's milk to Muslims fighting for their faith' and his Chaghatay following was happy with that belief. He began as an enterprising sheep-stealer. Slowly his rustlers expanded into an army and by 1370 he controlled the entire Chaghatay Khanate. He left the khan impotently in place on the throne and took effective power as his 'emir'. Although a Turk, Timur was devoted to the Mongol idea.

Timur then commanded expeditions to Turkistan, Russia, Iran, the Caucasus, and Iraq. Like the Mongols, he used mass atrocities to cow his enemies and

The Timurid achievement

Few men in history have had a hunger for vaunting personal achievement and thirst for bloodshed on the scale of Timur. He was devoted to the idea of universal Mongol supremacy; he alone, as the representative of Mongol power, was entitled to rule in the world. Side by side with this went allegiance to Islam; he had strong support amongst both ulama and sufis. By the same token, moreover, he also sustained the wealthier urban classes against local disorder. He was especially careful to protect trade and punish corrupt commercial practices. On the other hand, he was ruthless in dealing with his enemies: cities which resisted his might were subjected to a 'general killing', opponents might be thrown over cliffs or burned, young women carried off as slaves would be forced to leave their babies to die. Towers of skulls were built as ghastly reminders of defeat at his hands; 70,000 heads went to make the tower after the massacre at Isfahan in 1387. If Timur was a military genius, many of his descendants revealed genius in other ways, amongst them his son Ulugh Beg in science, the Mughal emperor Babur in writing, and Babur's grandson, Akbar, in ruling. So awe-inspiring was Timur's achievement, as well as its style, that he captured the imagination of Muslims and non-Muslims for many generations after his death. A theme of Mughal painting was the portrayal of Timur and his successors, drawing clear links between contemporary rulers and Timur's overwhelming might. Today in Central Asia his memory is being revived as Uzbeks and others ransack the past for images of power to identify with their fledgling states.

In 1941 Timur's mausoleum in Samarqand was opened by scientists of the Soviet Archaeological Commission. M. M. Gerasimov was able to reconstruct what Timur's Mongoloid face must have looked like when he was alive.

In the fifteenth century the Kunlun Mountains, a major source of jade (nephrite), lay within the Timurid empire, which shared a long frontier with Ming China. Jade was one of Muslim Central Asia's main exports to China but the Timurid elite also seem to have made a cult of it and numerous finely worked drinking vessels have survived from this period. Such cups may have been used in the drinking rituals of the Chaghatay warrior elite, for imperfectly Islamicized Chaghatay Mongols adhered to the old Mongol traditions of heavy drinking. Clavijo, a Spanish envoy to Timur, noted that 'the man who drinks very freely and can swallow the most wine is called a hero'.

Throughout his career Timur was careful to cultivate the good will of the sufi shaykhs and their followers. The shrine of the twelfth-century sufi missionary and poet Shasykh Ahmad Yasawi was the focus of a cult among the nomads of Central Asia. Yasawi was buried in his home town of Yasi. In about 1397, after making a pilgrimage to the place, Timur erected this splendid mausoleum for the shaykh. Through such acts of architectural piety, Timur hoped to be associated in popular memory with the holy man.

subjects. The massacre at Isfahan after that city's revolt in 1387 was particularly spectacular. The Chaghatay decapitated all the citizens they could find and built minarets with their skulls. Nizam al-Din al-Shami, Timur's historian and craven encomiast, commenting on the slaughter, quoted a saying popular among medieval ulama: 'One hundred years of tyranny and oppression by kings is preferable to two days of trouble and popular revolt.' In 1398 Timur and his army crossed the Hindu Kush, defeated the Delhi sultanate's army, and sacked Delhi. In 1400 he invaded Syria and captured Aleppo. The Mamluks defending Damascus fell apart without giving battle and Timur's troops sacked the city in January 1401. A tribute was imposed and when the notables were slow to hand it over Timur berated them: 'I am the scourge of God appointed to chastise you, since no one knows the remedy for your iniquity except me. You are wicked, but I am more wicked than you, so be silent!' In 1402 Timur turned on the rulers of Anatolia and the Balkans, defeating the Ottoman sultan Bayazid 'the Thunderbolt' (r.1389–1402) at the Battle of Ankara. Timur had designs on China and died while on his way to conquer it in 1405.

Although Timur's campaigns in effect reconstituted much of the thirteenth-century Mongol empire, after his death the empire was split among four sons, and most of his successors preferred to deepen their knowledge of Islam than to perpetuate the Turco-Mongol warrior culture. In 1429, for example, Timur's son Shah Rukh, the ruler of Transoxania and Khurasan, wrote to the Mamluk sultan in Egypt for a copy of Bukhari's collection of hadiths, and works by the religious scholars Ibn Hajar and al-Maqrizi. In the fifteenth century Timurid Samarqand and Bukhara rivalled Cairo as capitals of Islamic culture. Under Timurid patronage literature written in Turkish gained in status, a development paralleled in the Mamluk and Ottoman lands.

THE RISE OF THE OTTOMANS

The origins of the Ottoman beylicate are extremely obscure. The Turkish tribal group, of which the family of Osman was the paramount clan, appeared at the beginning of the fourteenth century as pastoralists and raiders around Bursa in northeast Asia Minor. Probably the Ottomans were at first the subjects or clients of Mongol overlords. However, after the Mongols had lost their grip in Anatolia in the early fourteenth century, Ottoman chroniclers retrospectively focused on the Ottomans' religiously inspired raids against Byzantine towns and villages. The Ottomans took Bursa in 1326 and Nicaea in 1331. Strife within the Byzantine empire allowed them and other Turkish tribesmen to cross the Dardenelles and in 1354 an earthquake rendered Gallipoli defenceless against Ottoman occupation. Neighbouring Muslim beylicates in Asia Minor were no less vigorously attacked. The sultans took care to legitimize these wars by seeking *fatwas* (legal opinions) in their support. Bayazid I briefly annexed most of Anatolia until defeated by Timur in 1402, who re-established Anatolia as a buffer for his empire.

The Alhambra

It took over two centuries for Muslim Spain finally to give way to Christian forces. In that period the kingdom of Granada presided over a brilliant late flowering of Islamic culture which all but rivalled that of the Umayyad golden age some three hundred years before. The most remarkable remnant of this flowering is the Alhambra.

Just as the tenth- and eleventh-century Umayyad caliphs of Cordoba had preferred to reside in the Madina al-Zahra outside Cordoba, so the fourteenth-century Nasirid rulers of Granada eventually moved their royal residence to a hill overlooking the city. Like so many Islamic palaces (among them, those of Abbasid Samarra and Mamluk Cairo), the Alhambra was not one palace but several within a large enclosure. Although at one time there were as many as seven palaces within the walls which encircled the crest of Sabika Hill, today only two palace complexes remain substantially intact – those clustered round the Court of the Myrtles and the Court of the Lions.

The Alhambra gained its name from the Arabic *al-Hamra*, 'the red'. Such was its magic that Christians imitated its style, as in the Alcazar of Seville. Moreover, its capacity to transport the viewer into a world of fantastic imagination continued to be celebrated down to the twentieth century when its name was given to cinemas in the 1920s and 1930s.

The complex of buildings around the Court of the Lions, built for Muhammad V in the 1370s, is richly decorated with geometric, vegetal, and calligraphic designs. Some of the calligraphic inscriptions are quotations from the Quran, but others are poems by the courtier Ibn Zamrak celebrating Muhammad V's munificence and his (rather minor) victory against the Christians at Algeciras in 1369.

Horoscope drawn up in Shiraz, Iran, in 1411 for one of Timur's grandsons, Iskandar Sultan, who had been born in 1384 (the date is given in Persian, Uighur, and Chinese). Timurid princes, especially Iskandar Sultan and Ulugh Beg, were great patrons of both astronomers and astrologers. The horoscope predicts success and happiness for Iskandar Sultan, despite the designs of envious relatives. In fact, the prince was blinded and put to death by Shah Rukh a few years later.

Bayazid's death in captivity was followed by civil war among his sons and only in the reign of Mehmed I (1413–21) did the empire regain its former frontiers. The Turks continued to expand in the Balkans and in 1453 Mehmed II (r.1451–81), after a hard-fought siege, took Constantinople. The capture of Constantinople, renamed Islambol ('Islam abounds') or Istanbul, was seen as the fulfilment of apocalyptic prophecies circulating since the seventh century, for the Arabs had first besieged it in 668. The location of the new Ottoman capital, between Europe and Asia, could be taken to symbolize the sultans' ambition in both those continents. Its possession encouraged Mehmed II and his successors to consider themselves not only descendants of ghazis but also in some sense the heirs of Alexander and the Caesars.

Mehmed II was also a noted legislator. The Ottomans, like some other Muslim dynasties, paid strikingly little attention to the prescriptions and restrictions of the religious law. They not only initiated legislation but much of what they ordained and practised flagrantly contradicted Islamic law as traditionally interpreted. Their Law of Fratricide sanctioned the killing by the heir to the throne of his brothers, in order to secure the succession. The *devshirme*, a levy of Christian boys who were forced to convert before service in either the Palace or Janissary regiment, breached the traditionally protected status accorded Christians. Then again, Ottoman qadis had powers to investigate and prosecute that were not traditionally sanctioned.

The Ottoman conquest of Gallipoli and Constantinople included important dockyards and, for the first time since the decline of the Fatimids, Muslim fleets dominated the eastern Mediterranean. Ottoman successes in the Balkans and the Aegean in the fifteenth century – adding Greece, Bosnia, Herzegovina, and Albania to earlier conquests of Bulgaria and Macedonia – might be seen as compensation for losing the last Muslim foothold in Spain.

Granada, ruled by the Nasirids from 1230, had survived as a tributary of the Christian kingdom of Castille. However, the unification of Castille and Aragon in 1469 and improvements in western artillery techniques made this survival precarious. The Nasirids had sought help from the Merinids, the Mamluks, and the Ottomans, but to no avail. In 1492 Boabdil, the last Nasirid ruler, surrendered the

Trade in spices and silks between the Mamluk lands and Venice and Genoa was of great importance. Here we see Venetian ambassadors being received in Damascus in the late fifteenth century. The Venetians maintained a *fondaco* or commercial colony in the administrative capital of Mamluk Syria. The governor of Damascus sits on a low platform and he alone wears a strange horned hat as a sign of his high rank. Note the brightly coloured Mamluk heraldry on the walls of the building.

city to Ferdinand and Isabella. Although toleration was at first the declared policy, many Muslims emigrated to North Africa. And so did Jews, who flourished in the Muslim lands of the Mediterranean basin.

ISLAM IN WEST AFRICA

The loss of Granada sent a thrill of horror throughout the Muslim world, but Islam continued to spread not only in the Balkans but also in Asia and sub-Saharan Africa. In East Africa, as in India, large Muslim communities were found in such ports as Aydhab, Zaylan, Mogadishu, and Kilwa. In the interior, however, despite jihads organized from Kilwa, Islam was all but unknown. Further northwest, in northern Sudan, Islamization was more or less synonymous with Arab conquest. Although in the eleventh century the Muslim regime of Takrur in West Africa, the Almoravids, and others sporadically attempted jihads against paganism, in general the triumph of Islam in such regions as Senegal and Mali was due to other factors. Berber traders seem to have been largely responsible for the spread of Islam in sub-Saharan Africa. Their caravans carried salt south across the Sahara and returned north with spices, dyes, and slaves. Timbuktu (founded c.1100), a staging post between the Maghrib and Black Africa, was also a religious and scholarly centre with its own madrasa. The sixteenth-century traveller Leo Africanus, who visited Timbuktu, noted that 'here are brought diverse manuscripts or written books out of Barbary which are sold for more money than any other merchandise'.

Muslim merchants and political advisers enjoyed prestige in the African gold kingdoms. Those literate in Arabic were much prized for their administrative skills. Some African kings declared their conversion to Islam to add legitimating ideology for their rule but they tended to be casual about Islamic prescriptions. Muslim ideology was often combined with a thoroughly pagan cult of the ruler. Among the subjects, sexual segregation was rarely observed and scanty clothing and the freedom accorded women shocked Arab travellers.

In most sub-Saharan kingdoms Islam remained the religion of an elite. When in 1324 Mansa Musa, the ruler of Mali, made a pilgrimage to Mecca, his lavish distribution of gold as he travelled made a great impression: on his return to Mali he acquired a considerable retinue of Arab and Berber advisers and servants. Most of his Sundiata subjects, however, remained pagan. Even when the monarch was an avowed Muslim, relations between him and his co-religionists could be difficult. Sunni Ali (1464/5–92), the Muslim ruler of the West African Songhay, claimed that he could turn himself into a vulture and make his armies invisible. When the Timbuktu ulama criticized the pagan elements in his rule, they were savagely persecuted.

In his history of Egypt, the Egyptian scholar Jalal al-Din al-Suyuti (1445–1505) boasted that his books had travelled to Syria, the Hijaz, the Yemen, India, the Maghrib, and Takrur. This shows both the prestige of Mamluk Egypt's scholars and the Islamic world's intellectual cohesion. However, not all was well. In his voluminous writings al-Suyuti listed the catastrophes which had afflicted the Islamic world in the fifteenth century, prominently the conquest of Granada by the Christians; secondly, the appearance among the Songhay of Sunni Ali, whose persecution of good Muslims was comparable to Timur's; thirdly, the disappearance of scholars of real distinction (al-Suyuti comfortably excepted himself). In al-Suyuti's view, the Islamic world was in crisis, sorely needing spiritual and intellectual renewal. He did not share Ibn Khaldun's interest in economic and social history, so failed to list probably the greatest catastrophe to afflict the Arab lands in the late Middle Ages, the recurrence, from the 1340s onwards, of devastating plague epidemics. He took little interest in the Mamluks and the occupation of their territory by the Ottomans in the early sixteenth century. He also failed to anticipate the revival of military Shiism by the Safawid rulers of Iran and the threat posed by Portuguese maritime ventures in the east. It would indeed seem to be true that, after al-Suyuti's death, few distinguished scholars were to be found in Cairo. However, in the sixteenth century, Islamic civilization flourished elsewhere, under the patronage of the Ottoman, Safawid, and Mughal dynasties.

CHAPTER 3

Stephen F. Dale

The Islamic World in the Age of European Expansion
1500–1800

In the sixteenth and seventeenth centuries the armies of the great Muslim empires were major forces to be reckoned with. For years the Ottoman army was arguably the most efficient fighting machine in the world. Here we see the army of Sulayman the Magnificent before Vienna in 1529.

RISE AND DECLINE

In the sixteenth, seventeenth, and eighteenth centuries the Islamic world comprised two major regions. One was the contiguous territory encompassing the Near East, India, and Central Asia where Turco-Mongol forces had established four major states by the early sixteenth century – the Ottoman, Safawid, and Mughal empires and the Uzbeks of western Turkistan, whose capitals were respectively Istanbul, Isfahan, Agra, and Bukhara. The second region included North Africa and large parts of Sudanic Africa and Southeast Asia. There it was usually Arabic-speaking merchants, ulama, or sufis who either founded dynasties or converted local elites to Islam. Despite their cultural and political differences, the two regions were linked by a common body of Islamic scholarship and the pilgrimage to Mecca, which Muslims undertook in greater numbers as security and transportation improved.

In 1500 Muslims seemed likely to carry all before them, as Ottoman armies penetrated eastern Europe, and other Muslims founded new states in Africa and Southeast Asia, where Islamization also was broadly diffused. The magnificent Ottoman, Safawid, and Mughal capitals alone seemed adequate testimony to the coercive power and wealth of these regimes and the brilliant artistic and architectural creativity of Islamic civilization. But by 1800 much of the Islamic world had entered a period of economic, political, and cultural challenge from Europe which its states were unequal to match. The Turco-Mongol states had either collapsed or were in decline. Independent Muslim states of Southeast Asia had either disappeared or become subordinated to European powers, and African Muslim states were about to suffer a similar fate. Many individuals offered solutions for their states' military and political collapse and the economic, military, and technological challenges of the West. They usually pressed for more vital and authentic Muslim societies, succeeding in some cases in reformulating and revivifying their faith, but not ulama or bureaucrats or political theorists could slow the pace of western European expansion in the Islamic world.

THE TURCO-MONGOL EMPIRES

The Ottoman, Safawid, Uzbek, and Mughal states represented an unparalleled triumph of Turkic military and political influence. Ruling families in all four states spoke related Turkic languages as their native tongues, and relied upon Turkic or Turco-Mongol tribes or military units to gain power. In cultural terms, though, the Turkic triumph was muted. The baroque court dialect, Ottoman Turkish, evolved into the imperial administrative, historical, and literary language of the Ottoman elite, as did Chaghatay Turkish, or old Uzbek, in Uzbek Turkistan. Yet Arabic continued to be not only the language of religion and theology of the entire region, but was also the spoken, literary, historical, and commercial language of the Ottoman empire's Arabic provinces. Persian, too, the first language of the majority of educated Muslims in Iran and Mughal India, as well as the principal administrative and literary language of the Safawid and Mughal states, was the most prestigious lingua franca in Istanbul, Anatolia, Iran, Turkistan, and northern India. Early in this period it was still the language that Ottoman Turks, Iranians, Uzbeks, and Indian Muslims had to know well enough to be able to compose poetry if they wished to become cultivated members of the ruling elite. Thus when the Ottoman bureaucrat and intellectual Mustafa Ali summarized his literary output in 1596–97, he specified that he 'had composed four eloquent *diwans* [volumes of poetry] in Persian and Turkish.'

The common Turkic identity of these states bequeathed to most of the Ottoman, Uzbek, and Mughal elite the Hanafi code of Islamic law. The Safawids, in contrast, led a militantly evangelical Shia sufi order, and imposed the Shia faith over most of the Iranian plateau, which intensified conflicts with the Ottomans and the Uzbeks. Safawid rulers threatened the Ottoman Anatolian frontiers, for most of their Turkic tribal supporters had originally been settled in this region. They continued to recruit followers there, and a significant number of its inhabitants who held Shia or proto-Shia beliefs were naturally regarded as a potential fifth column by Ottoman authorities. Aggressive Shia Islam also imparted a religious quality to the persistent warfare between the Safawids and Uzbeks in the Khurasan area of northeastern Iran. This conflict was a reprise of the historic antagonism between Iran and Turan, one of the leitmotifs in the mythology of Iranian kingship. The Sunni-Shia boundary allowed Turkic tribes in Uzbek territories to justify their enslavement of thousands of Iranian Muslims whom they captured in Khurasan. However, religious differences had little effect on generally amicable Safawid-Mughal relations, whose military confrontations were largely aimed at controlling the strategic and wealthy agricultural and commercial centre of Qandahar in south-central Afghanistan. Not only were Mughal emperors indebted to the Safawids for restoring Mughal power in the mid-sixteenth century,

By the end of the sixteenth
century, the Ottoman,
Safawid, and Mughal empires
had constructed a huge, relatively stable, low-duty commercial zone. This bridge over
the river Drina at Visegrad on
the Bosnian–Serbian border
was built by a Bosnian peasant's son, Muhammad
Sokollu, who became grand
vizier in 1565 and governed
the Ottoman empire till his
death in 1579. Its history
over more than 300 years is
celebrated in arguably the
greatest novel in Serbo-Croat,
The Bridge on the Drina,
which won its author, Ivo
Andric, the Nobel Prize for
literature in 1961.

but early Mughal rulers did not associate religious identity with dynastic loyalty –
understandable considering they employed both Iranian Shia Muslims and Hindus, and ruled a predominantly non-Muslim population.

Whatever their political or religious differences, the rulers of all four states promoted commerce. They stimulated trade directly by providing an infrastructure of
bazars, caravansarais, roads, and bridges, and indirectly by enforcing security
throughout these vast regions. As the French Huguenot jeweller Jean Chardin
accurately observed after travelling in Ottoman territories, in Iran, and in Mughal
India in the late seventeenth century, 'In the *East* Traders are Sacred Persons. . .
'Tis on their account especially that the Roads are so safe all over *Asia* and especially in *Persia*.' These conditions also encouraged pilgrims, poets, and historians,
ulama and sufis to move between states with relative ease. Merchants commonly
paid low customs duties of no more than three per cent on goods they imported
and exported. By the end of the sixteenth century the Ottoman, Safawid, and
Mughal empires, and to a lesser degree Uzbek Turkistan, had thus become an
enormous, contiguous, relatively stable, low-duty commercial zone. Commerce
was also catalysed by the influx of New World silver that Europeans brought to
pay for Asian products, particularly Turkish and Iranian silk and Indian cloth,
indigo, and spices.

A large percentage of the silver that entered Ottoman provinces and Iran eventually went to Mughal India, the largest economy among the four Turco-Mongol
states. Its enormously wealthy fertile crescent, the Indo-Gangetic delta stretching
from the Arabian Sea north to the Punjab and down to the Bay of Bengal, helped
to support a predominantly rural population estimated at between 60 and 100
million people in 1600. It produced many cash crops and cotton textiles that were
exported throughout the region and to Europe. These sales yielded an enormous

cash surplus for the Mughals and also other South Asian states. In contrast, the economies of the Ottoman, Safawid, and Uzbek states were more fragile enterprises. They had much smaller agrarian resources, suggested by their smaller populations. At the end of the sixteenth century their combined populations were probably little more than half that of the Mughal empire, with approximately 22 million in Ottoman territories, and possibly 6 to 8 million in Safawid Iran, and no more than 5 million people in Uzbek Turan.

The Safawids largely relied on their renowned silk industry to generate foreign exchange, although the nomads of the Iranian plateau also raised a surplus of horses. Even more horses were sold to China, Russia, and India by the proportionately greater nomadic population of the Uzbek khanates, and these hardy animals were the pre-eminent Uzbek export. Ottoman sultans commanded substantially larger resources than Safawid or Uzbek rulers. They derived income from agriculture in the Near Eastern fertile crescent, such manufactures as the cloth produced by the well-known Bursa silk industry, and wealth from international trade. Commerce was also stimulated by building elaborate commercial complexes; best-known was the Bedestan of Istanbul with its covered bazar. However, by the mid-sixteenth century even these resources were proving inadequate to pay for the escalating expenses of constructing Istanbul, continued military campaigns, and Indian imports.

The Ottoman Empire

The oldest and ultimately the most enduring of the four Turco-Mongol dynasties, the Ottomans had evolved from their origins as leader of one of many Turkic, ghazi principalities that emerged in the chaotic post-Mongol period on Byzantium's eastern Anatolian frontiers. After taking Constantinople in 1453 the Ottoman emperors Mehmet the Conqueror (r.1444–46/1451–81), Bayazid II (r.1481–1512), Selim (r.1512–20), and Sulayman the Magnificent (r.1520–66) conquered the fertile crescent, Egypt, and the Hijaz, thus gaining control of Mecca and Medina, Yemen, and north Africa up to Morocco. Under Sulayman they removed the Christians from the Aegean and in the mid-sixteenth century twice tried to take Malta, the key to the western Mediterranean. Their power was not severely lessened by their defeat at the hands of the Venetians at Lepanto in 1571. In the Balkans their progress was even more striking. In 1521 they captured Belgrade, in 1529 they besieged the Hapsburg capital Vienna, and by the 1540s controlled a great swathe stretching in a crescent from Trieste in the west, passing within sight of the walls of Vienna, to the Crimea in the east. At Sulayman's death they had created the largest and arguably the most militarily powerful empire in the world at that period.

To reflect these remarkable conquests Ottoman sultans articulated an imperial ideology that authorized and exalted them. Selim claimed both religious and steppe legitimacy when he described himself in Perso-Islamic terms as the

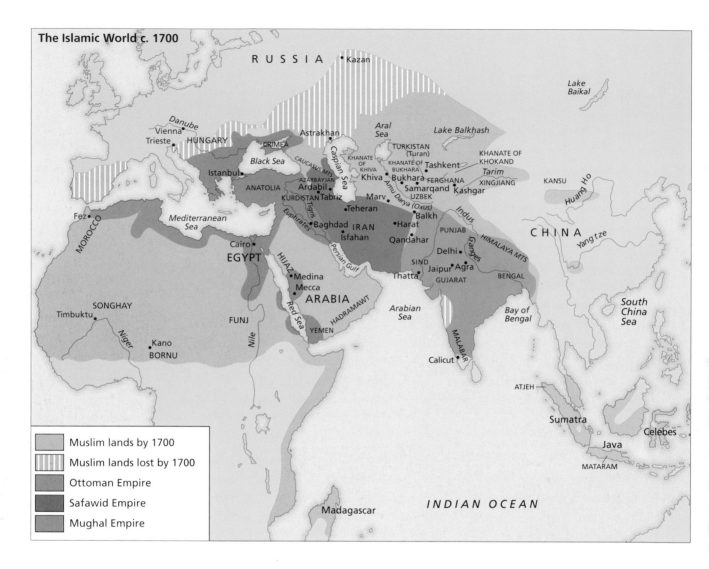

The Islamic World c. 1700

Legend:
- Muslim lands by 1700
- Muslim lands lost by 1700
- Ottoman Empire
- Safawid Empire
- Mughal Empire

'shadow of god' and the *sahib-qiran*, lord of the planetary conjunctions. The latter was a Timurid title that the Timurid-Mughal emperor Shah Jahan (r.1628–57) appropriated with considerably more justification. Chroniclers and theologians also invested the sahib-qiran with a messianic element, but by the 1550s, when Sulayman was approaching sixty, that had yielded to a more traditional definition of the ruler in Iranian terms as *padshah* (king). This evolution paralleled and may have directly resulted from changes in the Ottoman state, for the mid-sixteenth century was also when Sulayman presided over the elaboration of a dynastic code, the *Qanun*, and began to be identified as the defender of Hanafi Sunni orthodoxy. Sultans increasingly emphasized this role when Ottoman rule declined, attempting to subordinate their Turkic identity to a broader Islamic legitimacy.

The change in Ottoman titles at the end of Sulayman's reign can be taken as a metaphor for the end of the most creative, dynamic, imperialist period in Ottoman history. The empire had expanded at a remarkable rate following the setback of Timur's defeat and capture of the emperor Bayazid at the Battle of Ankara in 1402. Active sultans had presided over successful campaigns, staffed both by the old Anatolian Turkic aristocracy and the Janissary corps. Sulayman the Magnificent embodied the apogee and turning point of Ottoman history. While consolidating the empire's gains he laid the foundations of a more conservative bureaucratic state. He also began the practice of withdrawing from active participation in government, which by 1595 was almost an ensured tradition. Henceforth Ottoman male heirs were brought up largely confined to the elaborate palace harem in near complete isolation from military and political affairs. Safawid monarchs adopted this custom in the seventeenth century, but Mughal rulers never emulated it.

The result was that even intelligent and dynamic individuals were very inexperienced when they succeeded, their selection now based on longevity rather than the rigorous Darwinian process determined by success in war. The declining vigour of Ottoman dynastic leadership was exacerbated by the simultaneous triumph and factionalization of the devshirme, the levy of an elite cadre of slaves

The Sulaymaniye Mosque complex, built between 1550 and 1557, proclaims the power and confidence of the Ottoman empire under Sulayman the Magnificent. Commanding the old city of Istanbul and the Golden Horn, it is a masterwork of the great Ottoman architect, Sinan, surpassed only by the Selimiye Mosque at Edirne. It incorporates schools for Quran recitation and learning traditions, four madrasas, a medical college and hospital, and the tombs of Sulayman and his much-loved Russian wife, Haseki Hurrem.

Sulayman the Magnificent, who ruled from 1520 to 1566, presided over the zenith of Ottoman fortunes, when the empire was in its most creative and expansionist phase. He personally led the Ottoman armies in many victorious campaigns. He also laid the foundations of a bureaucratic state in which the ruler increasingly withdrew from active participation in government. Known as *Qanuni*, the Lawgiver, he established a dynastic code to cover those areas of life about which the sharia offered little guidance. The engraving of 1559 by Melchior Lorichs gives a strong sense of the power associated with this Ottoman sultan.

from the non-Muslim population. This bureaucratic equivalent of the Janissaries gained the upper hand over the Turkish aristocracy in the late sixteenth century. Yet their triumph did not reinvigorate the role of the sultans: instead they dissipated royal authority in factional manoeuvring. Individual officials, such as the Grand Vizier Mehmed Koprulu (in office 1656–61), sometimes restored centralized control but, overall, dynastic authority and energy deteriorated and administrative efficiency declined.

The loss of dynamism and direction at the Ottoman state's centre dating from Sulayman's reign raises the question of how the empire then survived until the First World War, outlasting the Safawid and Mughal empires by more than 150 years. Its endurance is often attributed to its strong bureaucracy and military, whose inertial force was significant. But in the sixteenth and seventeenth centuries the Ottoman regime benefited from the insignificance of the principal states on its periphery – Iran, Russia, Hungary, and the Holy Roman Empire. The Safawids posed a serious threat only under Shah Abbas the Great (r.1587–1629), when they reconquered the western Iranian plateau and temporarily occupied Baghdad and substantial areas of Mesopotamia. Muscovite Russia was exceptionally weak. Hungary and the southern Slav territories represented fragile feudal entities. With the consolidation of the early modern European monarchies in Russia, Austria-Hungary, Spain, and France in the late seventeenth and early eighteenth centuries, the Ottomans began to face more formidable opponents. From that time they were nearly always on the defensive, gradually ceding earlier conquests to Hapsburg and Russian monarchs. By the end of the eighteenth century the fundamental shift in the balance of power between the Ottomans and European powers was unmistakable, marked by the Russo-Ottoman Treaty of Kuchuk Kainarjı in 1774: under this the Ottomans ceded territory to a European power for the first time and implicitly agreed that Russia could intervene on behalf of Christian minorities in Ottoman provinces.

In the midst of Ottoman political and military deterioration the state still benefited from the pervasive, effective *ilmiye* institution, the large cadre of those learned in Islam. Unlike the Safawid state, where the ulama evolved into an independent body, and the Mughal empire, where the religious classes retained great autonomy, Ottoman rulers shaped the ulama into a state bureaucracy. They developed a hierarchical system of religious institutions that trained religious scholars and other potential members of the ruling class. Culminating in the eight madrasas established by Mehmet the Conqueror, this system trained religious functionaries, teachers, *qadis* (religious judges), and the scribal elite. Qadis became the most important civil officials of the empire, as they enforced both religious law and the Qanun, the imperial code. Their innumerable administrative duties included supervising local markets and assessing and collecting taxes. Qadis effectively ran the local administration in predominantly Muslim provinces, and when central control weakened they assumed more power, some becoming de facto local governors.

This system also trained and employed many great Ottoman writers and thinkers. One such individual was the encyclopaedist Taskoprulu Zade Ahmet Husamuddin Effendi (d.1553), who compiled biographies of ulama, scientists, mathematicians, and sufis and compendiums of religious and secular science. However, the pervasive influence of the ilmiye discouraged scientific, philosophical, and even theological experimentation, a trend already marked in the late sixteenth century. In 1580, for example, the supreme Ottoman religious official, the Shaykh al-Islam, objected to the construction of a new observatory in Istanbul intended to correct the tables from the Samarqand observatory of the fifteenth-century Timurid ruler Ulugh Beg. The Janissaries were ordered to raze the half-finished building. Its destruction was symptomatic of the lack of mathematical, scientific, and technical innovation in all four early modern Islamic empires. Ironically, one of the Mughal's Hindu Rajput courtiers constructed observatories in Jaipur and Delhi that were inspired by Ulugh Beg's astronomers.

Ottomans not only created a state-controlled religious system but also closely supervised and sometimes persecuted the most popular form of Islam, sufism. They suppressed the more unkempt personification of devotional, mystical Islam, the Qalandaris, who had been influential in early Ottoman Anatolia – not surprising after a Qalandari tried to assassinate Bayazid II in 1496. Sultans instead sanctioned more 'orthodox' or at least such acceptable orders as the Bektashis. In the sixteenth century this order became closely associated with the Janissaries, acting, indeed, as their chaplains. Like the Chishtis patronized by Mughal rulers, Bektashis willingly absorbed non-Muslim practices. Apparently as a result, they successfully converted nomads in eastern Anatolia and Christian agriculturalists in southern Europe. A mid-sixteenth century description of a Bektashi dervish provides a vivid contrast with 'orthodox' ulama:

> Beardless and heart-wounded, with a
> halberd in his hand and a sheepskin
> apron round his waist; decked with
> bells and plumes: his pocketbook of
> love and palheng-stone at his waist,
> his 'waterpot' awry on his head, his
> chest gashed and shirtless; mad, wild,
> naked and hairless; barefoot and bareheaded;
> his doe-eyes tinged with collyrium.

The Ottoman bureaucracy had gained the upper hand over the Turkish aristocracy by the late sixteenth century, and is often seen to have enabled the empire to survive down to the end of the First World War. This is a *firman* (decree) of Sultan Murad III (r.1574–95), whose name and titles appear in the *tughra* at the top of the document; each sultan had his own elegantly calligraphed tughra. The text is in the busy *diwani* script much used by the Ottoman bureaucracy.

Piri Reis: Ottoman admiral and cartographer

Cartography was one of the sciences that flourished in the Ottoman empire in the formative sixteenth century, when Ottoman conquests stimulated exploration and map-making. One of the foremost practitioners was Piri Reis, nephew of the mariner Kemal Reis. Piri Reis (b.c.1470) began serving with his uncle in the Ottoman Mediterranean fleet in the 1490s, later as a commander in Ottoman - Venetian wars between 1499 and 1502. In 1516–17 he served in the fleet that captured Alexandria, and drew a map of the Nile Delta while in Cairo. In 1547 he was appointed as Hind Beylerbeyligi, the commandant of the fleet responsible for challenging Portuguese fleets in the Red Sea, the Persian Gulf, and the Indian Ocean. After losing battles in the Persian Gulf and favour at court, he was recalled to Egypt and executed in 1554.

Three of Piri Reis's works have survived: fragments of two maps and his major navigation text, *Kitab-i bahriye*. His earliest cartography, a large world map, he presented to Sultan Selim on the latter's conquest of Egypt in 1517. In drawing it he used Arab, Portuguese, and Spanish charts and maps, including a copy of one drawn by Columbus. The complete map, which has not survived, evidently included outlines of India, China, and Columbus' discoveries in the Americas. He wrote in the *Kitab-i bahriye*: 'Having made use of new maps of the Chinese and Indian seas which no one in the Ottoman lands had hitherto seen or known, I presented them to the late Sultan Selim Han (may he

rest in peace and reside in Paradise) while he was in Egypt.' A second map, which he completed in 1528–29, showed the north Atlantic Ocean and the shore of North America. However, the *Kitab-i bahriye*, 'The Book of Seafaring', represents Piri Reis's most formidable achievement. It is a comprehensive collection of navigational charts and sailing instructions for the Mediterranean and the Persian Gulf, with descriptions of the Portuguese discoveries and technical information for navigators on compasses, wind directions, and his own charts. After the first draft of 1521, written partly in verse, Piri Reis revised and presented it to Sulayman the Magnificent.

Ottoman conquests, and especially the expansion of Ottoman naval power in the late fifteenth and early sixteenth centuries, stimulated cartography. This map from the *Kitab-i bahriye* of Piri Reis shows Venice and the lagoon.

Piri Reis's maps and his *Kitab-i bahriye* exemplify sophisticated cartographic and navigational techniques, but they are also testaments to the rapid diffusion of knowledge around the Mediterranean between two religious communities that are often perceived inaccurately as hermetically separated armed camps. Reis's knowledge and use of copies of Portuguese maps and those of Columbus show the speed of this dissemination, and demonstrate that the Islamic-Christian frontiers could be permeable when it came to exchanging certain types of knowledge. However, the permeability depended upon the biases of each civilization. In the Ottoman case this allowed the diffusion of cartography and medicine, but not printing and astronomy, a reflection of the profound conservatism of the early modern Islamic world.

A more restrained and intellectual counterpoint to the Bektashis were the Mawlawi sufis, whose stately devotional dance caused them to be known as the 'whirling dervishes'. Founded by the Persian-speaking poet Jalal al-Din Rumi in the thirteenth century, this order attracted well-educated urban devotees, many of whom were government officials. The Mawlawis helped to sustain the knowledge of Persian literature in Ottoman provinces, because they wanted to comprehend Rumi's devotional poetry.

The Safawids

Ottoman suspicion of populist or heterodox sufism was partly related to the rise of their eastern rivals, the Safawid dynasty of Iran. The Safawids first gained prominence as leaders of a sufi order in the small Azarbayjani town of Ardabil during Mongol rule in Iran in the thirteenth and fourteenth centuries. Initially led by shaykhs with an eclectic, quasi-messianic religious message, including even Jewish and Christian references, the Safawids increasingly inclined to Shia beliefs during the fifteenth century. Later in the century they sought support for their religious claims among the rough Turkic tribes of Azarbayjan and eastern Anatolia, creating a threat to the Ottomans' eastern Anatolian frontiers. Then too the Safawids became militarized in defending their interests against the predominantly nomadic Sunni regimes, the Aq and Qara Qoyunlu, the 'white' and 'black' sheep dynasties dominating western Iran from the 1450s. By 1500 the Safawids had evolved into a cohesive and formidable military force. In 1501 Shah Ismail I (r.1501–14) founded the Safawid dynasty with the capture of Tabriz, which became the first capital of the new state.

The emergence of the Safawid state in the early sixteenth century - and its precipitate dissolution two centuries later – resembled the model Ibn Khaldun had proposed in the fifteenth century for interpreting the cyclical histories of north African states. Khaldun hypothesized that north African dynasties typically relied upon nomadic social cohesion and military prowess. He believed that tribes became especially formidable when unified by a charismatic religious leader, which Muhammad had accomplished in the Hijaz in the seventh century. According to the theory, these dynasties always declined within three to four generations, since the very characteristics that brought them to power deteriorated when they established bureaucratic regimes in urban areas. In that environment both their ferocity and social cohesion declined until they were overthrown by yet another tribal confederation.

Safawid shaykhs were the kind of charismatic leaders who Khaldun thought could unite otherwise disparate tribes. They appealed to their followers with a dual sufi and Shia ideology, functioning simultaneously as sufi shaykhs, often in authoritarian control over their disciples' spiritual life, and as descendants of the seventh imam, nearly sacral figures who could present themselves from a Shia point of view as the only legitimate leaders of the Islamic community. Shah Ismail

The shrine of Safi al-Din (1252/3–1334), the founder of the Safawid sufi order, at Ardabil, eastern Azarbayjan. It was erected by Shah Tahmasp I (r.1524–76).

In 1612 Abbas I, the greatest of the Safawid shahs, endowed the family shrine at Ardabil with about 1,215 pieces of Chinese porcelain and 6 of jade. All the Ardabil pieces were engraved with the personal seal of Shah Abbas recording the endowment. This seal from one of the jade pieces says: 'Abbas, slave of the King of Holiness [i.e. Ali], made endowment of the shrine of Shah Safi.'

I effectively invoked this ideology to unite an otherwise unlikely coalition of Azarbayjani and eastern Anatolian Turkic tribes. As he wrote in one of his early Turkic poems:

> From Pre-Eternity the Shah is our sultan our *pir* [spiritual leader] and *murshid* [teacher], our soul...We are the slaves of the Imams, in all sincerity. Our token is to be martyrs and ghazis.

These tribes came to be known as the Qizilbash or 'redheads', after their distinctive headgear. Ismail used this coalition, most of whose tribesmen evidently thought him semi-divine, to conquer the northern Iranian plateau within the first decade of his rule. In 1510 he capped these successful campaigns by defeating and killing Shaybani Khan Uzbek at Merv in western Turkistan.

In these years Shah Ismail began transforming the religious landscape of Iran by imposing Twelver Shiism on the populace. He did so by persecuting and executing recalcitrant Sunnis, using state patronage to develop Shia shrines, institutions, and religious art and by importing Shia scholars from Syria and Iraq. (Few well-educated Shia ulama had lived in predominantly Sunni Iran.) Ironically, one of the principal targets of Safawid persecution were sufi orders, because they represented potential ideological alternatives to a sufi dynasty claiming religious infallibility. In consequence significant numbers of sufis and quasi-sufi poets emigrated from Iran, usually to Mughal India, driven out by persecution or withdrawal of patronage. As the Safawid poet Kawsari wrote of Safawid Iran, 'In this dominion there is no purchaser of speech . . . Now go I ought towards Hindustan.' This literary stream assumed such proportions that a modern Iranian writer has referred to it as *The Caravan of India*. The emigration helped to produce a distinc-

tive Indo-Persian literary school known as *sabq-i Hindi*, literally 'Indian style'.

Safawid influence over their Qizilbash followers was badly damaged when Shah Ismail was defeated in 1514 by the Ottomans. They had sent an army to their eastern frontier to cauterize the social and political wound caused by Safawid recruitment of more and more tribes in eastern Anatolia. Not only was the tribes' assumption of the shah's sacral invincibility destroyed, but Ismail himself thereafter largely withdrew from directing the Safawid state. During the sixteenth century his successors often had to struggle to retain control in the face of Qizilbash independence. Before Shah Abbas came to the throne in 1587 tribes controlled most provincial regions and sometimes usurped the power of the Safawid family itself.

The Safawids had often sought to strengthen their authority, but only in Shah Abbas' reign (1587–1629) did they systematically follow the policy that had brought the devshirme class to power in the Ottoman empire. Abbas reduced the military and political power of Qizilbash tribesmen as he replaced them with slave troops and bureaucrats, many of whom were Georgian slaves. Possibly as a corollary, he also accelerated the family's change of status from that of sacred sufi and Shia leaders of a tribal coalition to traditional Iranian autocrats of a bureaucratic state. In Ibn Khaldun's schema, these policies initiated the process that severed the Safawid's ties with their tribal supporters and predisposed the dynasty to eventual collapse.

As part of his attempt to revive Safawid fortunes Shah Abbas instituted an Iranian mercantilist policy to stimulate the development of his relatively impover-

This engraving by Cornelius le Bruyn in 1704 depicts the Maydan-i Naqsh-i Jahan (Exemplar of the World), one of the key features of Isfahan, which Shah Abbas made the capital and economic centre of his state. To the right of the great open space is the Lutfullah Mosque, one of the masterpieces of Safawid architecture, to the left is the Ali Qapu, both entrance to the royal palace and pavilion from which ceremonies on the maydan could be watched. In the distance is the entrance to the bazar which covered over 11 square miles. By night the maydan was the resort of entertainers, storytellers, prostitutes, and holy men. By day, as we see here, it was a place of trade.

صُورَةُ المُؤَلِّف "قدِّسَ"

A feature of the later Safawid period was the assertion of the authority of the ulama against that of the shahs. Mulla Muhammad Baqir al-Majlisi (1627–98) was the most powerful religious figure of this era. The author of over sixty books, he was appointed Shaykh al-Islam of Isfahan in 1687 and Mullabashi (head mulla) in 1694. When the new shah, Sultan Husayn, asked Majlisi what reward he wanted after he had presided at his coronation in 1694, the mulla asked for royal decrees forbidding the drinking of wine and the flying of pigeons, and the expulsion of all sufis from Isfahan.

ished state. He restricted currency exports and supported local industry. In particular, he developed the nascent Iranian silk industry into a highly profitable state enterprise, and forcibly co-opted influential Armenian merchants to be his agents in marketing this most valuable Iranian export. Abbas so successfully transformed the military structure and economic health of the state that he was able to regain territories lost to Ottomans during the sixteenth century, and expanded or consolidated Safawid control at all points of the compass. His energy and vision is commemorated by the reconstruction of Isfahan in the early seventeenth century as his new capital and the economic centre of his state. Like Ottoman Istanbul, it contained an exquisite ensemble of religious and royal buildings and elaborate bazars and caravansarais. These included a separate suburb for the protected Armenian merchant community, who linked Iran with both Asian and European markets.

But it was during the reign of Shah Abbas that two trends emerged which contributed to the collapse of the Safawid regime in 1722. One that he initiated was the Ottoman policy of ending succession battles by confining potential heirs to the haram, with the same effect in Safawid Iran as in the Ottoman empire. It fatally compromised the military and political acumen and experience of potential new rulers, just as it increased the influence of the harem. Simultaneously, Shah Abbas lost control over the Iranian Shia ulama, whom his predecessors had introduced by inviting Shia scholars from Iraq and Syria. The ulama began openly to assert the logical implication of the early Shia doctrines that only the descendants of Ali, the imams, could understand the meaning of the Quran, and therefore only they could legitimately lead the Islamic community, represented by the ulama themselves. By 1722 they had effectively usurped the religious authority of the dynasty and claimed that they collectively embodied the *naib imam*, the imams' earthly representative (a claim that some Iranian Shia ulama openly made for Ayatollah Khomeini in the 1980s).

In retrospect, the Iranian Shia ulama may have provided some stability in the seventeenth century. At least their increasing assertiveness paralleled the period of stasis and then decline of the regime after Shah Abbas' death. By the late seventeenth century even casual European observers were aware that the regime was exceptionally fragile. Abbas' army had been allowed to wither away, and his austere practicality was replaced by self-indulgent, haram-educated princes who drained Iran's modest revenues by ostentatious consumption. When in 1722 Afghans rose against the Safawids' Georgian governor of Qandahar they dis-

covered no force capable of resisting their motley tribal army, and they took Isfahan after a desultory battle. However, these men were incapable of running a
major bureaucratic state. After a few years they left a power vacuum in Iran that
was largely filled by the old Qizilbash aristocracy in the eighteenth century. First
the draconian Nadir Shah of the Afshar tribe seized the remnants of the Safawid
regime. He conducted ruthless campaigns, administering the *coup de grâce* to the
decadent Mughul empire when he invaded India and sacked Delhi in 1739. Then
at the end of the eighteenth century another Qizilbash tribe, the Qajars, gained
control of most of the Iranian plateau and established the last of the many Turkic
tribal dynasties that ruled Iran in the Islamic period. They shifted the capital to
the unimportant city of Teheran, because it was located near their winter pas-
turage on the southern slopes of the Elburz mountains.

The Uzbeks

The Shia ulama's challenge to Safawid legitimacy had no parallels in Uzbek Turan
or Mughal India. The Uzbek khans and Mughal emperors possessed impeccable
Chingizid and Timurid lineages, genealogies that Ottoman chroniclers admired.
Shaybani Khan Uzbek (r.1500–10), the founder of the Uzbek confederation, was
a genuine Chingizid, even if most of his followers were Turks. From the first,
Uzbek khans ruled as leaders of a coalition of clans. One Shaybanid descendant,
Abd Allah Khan II (r.1583–98), attempted to transform the confederation into an

From the sixteenth to the nineteenth centuries the city states of the Uzbek khans came to be marked by a strict Sunni orthodoxy. The madrasa was the typical building of the age and Khiva, Khokand, Samarqand, and most notably Bukhara were centres of scholarship. The great Registan Square in Samarqand, with the Ulugh Beg madrasa to the left, the Shir Dar madrasa to the right, and the Tila Kara madrasa straight ahead, symbolizes the spirit of the age. 'I know of nothing in the East', declared Curzon, the British statesman and traveller, 'approaching it in massive simplicity and grandeur.'

Iranian-style imperial regime but he was ultimately unsuccessful. None of his successors, the Janids, in the seventeenth and early eighteenth century seriously attempted to emulate him. While politically divided and militarily relatively weak, Uzbek khans struggled with the Safawids to control the wealthy and strategic Khurasan province. They also clashed with Mughal rulers when the latter tried to reconquer their ancestral homelands north of the Hindu Kush moutains. These khans exercised a decentralized dominance for more than three centuries in western Turkistan, principally the cities and hinterlands of Bukhara, Tashkent, Samarqand, and Khiva, the rich alluvial lands along the Amu Darya and Zarafshan rivers, and the fertile Ferghana valley.

The 'supreme' Uzbek khans in Bukhura ruled the most substantial of these 'city-states'. The others included independent dynasties of Khiva, founded in 1512, and Khokand, in the Ferghana valley, established in 1700. Bukhara also became the theological centre of the region; its madrasas were famous for producing conservative Hanafi Sunni ulama. Protected by their remoteness from power in Iran, South Asia, and China, these city-states survived until they were overrun by Russian armies in the second half of the nineteenth century. Russian forces had annexed the Kazan and Astrakhan khanates on the middle and lower Volga in the mid-sixteenth century and conquered the Crimean khanate in 1783. In Chinese Turkistan, on the eastern boundary of Uzbek Ferghana, descendants of Chingiz Khan's grandson Chaghatay continued to rule until the mid-sixteenth century, when their rule disintegrated, threatened by Mongols in the northeast and displaced by lineages of ambitious Naqshbandi sufis in the south.

The political prominence of Naqshbandi sufis in sixteenth-century Central Asia highlights the pivotal role of sufis as missionaries to Turco-Mongol inhabitants of the region. Three orders, the Naqshbandi, Qubrawi, and Qadiri, were especially influential in drawing pagan or half-Islamized tribes into Islamic urban culture. The sufis' close association with tribesmen also helps to explain the sufi shaykhs' political involvement, some even becoming rulers themselves. Typical of such association was the alliance of the Naqshbandi shaykh Khwaja Ubayd Allah Ahrar (d.1490), and his lineal and spiritual descendants, with the Timurids, the Uzbeks' predecessors as rulers of western Turkistan. This alliance was particularly strong in northern India under the Timurids of South Asia, the Mughals, when Naqshbandi sufism became something of an aristocratic cult.

Naqshbandis were politically involved in widely separate areas of the Islamic world in the eighteenth and nineteenth centuries where Muslim political power had lessened or had never effectively existed, as when they led resistance to Russians in the Caucasus. Other shaykhs revived earlier Naqshbandi influence in Kashgar. Further east, in China's Kansu province Muslims inspired by Naqshbandis spread reformist teachings, eventually sparking a rebellion against Manchu rule in the late eighteenth century. Naqshbandi shaykhs also spread into Ottoman territories, with less dramatic effect than on the margins of the Islamic world. Yet they laid the basis for a Naqshbandi presence that subtly but pervasively persists in the modern Turkish state and among present-day Kurds in both Turkish and Iraqi Kurdistan.

The Timurid Mughals

The principal victims of Uzbek conquests in western Turkistan were Timur's fractious descendants the Timurids. Shaybani Khan had virtually eradicated Timurid power there by 1510, but in South Asia the Timurids enjoyed a spectacular renaissance. In ethnic and linguistic terms, the Timurid Mughal dynasty, which Zahir al-Din Muhammad Babur founded in 1526, was predominantly Turkic. In other respects it differed markedly from its contemporaries. Unlike the Ottomans, Safawids, and Uzbeks, all of whom relied on particular tribes to bring them to power, Mughal armies were composed of fragments of tribal groups. They lacked a coherent ethnic or social identity partly because Timur had weakened or destroyed tribal cohesion during his struggle for supremacy in western Turkistan in the fourteenth century. Perhaps because their supporters did not possess the same tribal coherence and independence as the Iranian Qizilbash or the Ottoman Sipahis (cavalrymen), Mughal rulers never felt the need to establish a slave soldiery or slave bureaucracy to balance or weaken tribal power. The Timurid Mughals also abstained from transforming the haram into a political institution housing potential heirs. Mughal princes reached the throne through open competition among experienced administrators, governors, and military leaders. When Ottoman and Safawid rulers remained largely confined to the court, the late-seventeenth-century Mughal ruler Awrangzeb was a dynamic and indefatigable general – although those qualities may have shortened rather than lengthened the life of the dynasty.

Neither Babur nor his son and successor Humayun established Mughal control over the historic centre of the Indian empires in the Ganges-Jumna basin. Babur garrisoned but had not pacified most of the strategic, wealthy Gangetic valley before he died in 1530, and Humayun was defeated by Afghan forces in 1540, forcing him into exile in Iran. He did not regain the throne until a year before his death in 1556. His exile, though, had long-term effects on Mughal India, for large numbers of Iranians accompanied him upon his return, a pattern of emigration that persisted throughout the dynasty. It was Babur's grandson Akbar (r.1556–1605) who transformed the nascent Mughal state into the Mughal empire. Akbar succeeded through tireless military campaigns in northern and northwestern India for thirty years of his reign, by co-opting still autonomous indigenous lineages into the Mughal regime and

Akbar transformed the nascent Timurid state into the Mughal empire. Aware that he could rule only in collaboration with Hindus, he curbed the influence of the ulama, enforced religious toleration, and enjoyed religious discussions with those of all faiths. Not surprisingly some were not displeased to see him die. One, for instance, typified his reign as the time when 'the sun of guidance was hidden behind the veil of error.' This sympathetic study of Akbar in old age reveals the strands of humanism which flourished at the Mughal court.

Babur: a renaissance prince of Central Asia

Zahir al-Din Muhammad Babur (1483–1530) founded the Timurid Mughal empire of India in 1526, but his fame rests more on his writings than his military exploits. His memoir, known as the *Baburnama*, and his poetry offer unique insights into the personality and life of an early modern Muslim prince – ranging widely over Islamic culture and society in Central Asia, Afghanistan, and India. There are portraits of disparate individuals whose idiosyncrasies can scarcely be imagined from traditional Muslim historical writing, which tends to present Muslims as stereotypes. If, like all autobiographers, Babur presents himself in a favourable light, he still reveals his society as Benvenuto Cellini does Renaissance Italy. He demonstrates that the cultured violence of Italy was typical of his Central Asian world, and he himself was every bit as much a *l'uomo universale*, a 'Renaissance man', as the Medicis or Castiglione's idealized courtier. In his memoirs he one moment describes military campaigns or the decapitation of enemies and then turns to an informed discussion of Turkic or Persian prosody. He writes throughout in a plain, unadorned style marked by frank, matter-of-fact observations on men and nature.

Consider his description of a comrade in arms:

Zulnun Arghun distinguished himself among all other young warriors in the presence of Sultan Abusaid Mirza by the use of a scimitar, and afterwards, on every occasion on which he went into action, he acquitted himself with distinction. His courage is unimpeached, but certainly he was rather deficient in understanding. He was a pious and orthodox believer, never neglected saying the appointed prayers, and frequently repeated the supererogatory ones. He was madly fond of chess; if a person played at it with one hand, he played at it with two hands. He played without art, just as his fancy suggested. He was the slave of avarice and meanness.

Or equally here is his description of how he submitted an early poem, written at age nineteen, to be evaluated by his uncle, the Mongol khan of Tashkent:

I had written a quatrain in an ordinary measure but was in some doubt about it because at that time I had not studied poetic idiom so much as I have now done. The Khan was good-natured and also he wrote verses, though ones somewhat deficient in the requisites for odes. I presented my quatrain and I laid my doubts before him but got no reply so clear as to remove them. His study of the poetic idiom appeared to have been somewhat scant.

Merely the idea of a young Timurid Muslim analysing the verse of a good-natured Mongol khan transforms our images of the Islamic world, which are too often shaped by orientalist assumptions. Babur's autobiographical presentation and his literary taste for the particular and idiosyncratic reveal the dynamism and creativity of Islamic culture.

Babur spent thirty years trying to win an empire that would match those of his ancestors, Chingiz Khan and Timur. Since Babur's *Memoirs* were translated into English in the early nineteenth century they have won many western admirers. 'What a happiness to have known Babur!' exclaimed the novelist E. M. Forster, 'he had all that one seeks in a friend. His energy and ambition were touched with sensitiveness; he could act, observe, and remember; though not critical of his senses, he was aware of their workings, thus fulfilling the whole nature of man.'

by elaborating a carefully surveyed land revenue system initiated by his Afghan predecessors. This provided the economic basis for both royal revenue and the military fiefs that were the principal sources of Mughal power.

In histories that focus on Akbar's ostentatious religious tolerance and pragmatic politics it is often forgotten that he stabilized the Mughal state only after decades of fighting. His most important conquests were those of the Rajput states in the Rajasthan desert west of Agra, for these Hindu warrior clans commanded the best armies in northern India. Mughal generals erected towers of skulls – Timurid terror tactics – from thousands of slain Rajput troops who resisted Akbar's early campaigns. Their draconian practice persuaded other Rajput dynasties to submit, several offering their daughters to the Mughal haram. What distinguished Akbar's conquest was that he married Rajput princesses without forcing them to convert to Islam. He thus conciliated Rajput chiefs who were then usually given special Mughal military fiefs within their own territories. His policy successfully transformed the Rajput chiefs into Mughal loyalists, and from the late sixteenth century Rajput contingents represented some of the most formidable and reliable elements in the imperial forces.

Akbar's Rajput relations astutely recognized political reality in an empire in which 80 to 90 per cent of the population was non-Muslim – predominantly Hindu but also Jain, animist, Christian, Jewish, and Zoroastrian. The Mughals were a Turco-Mongol garrison state that controlled the urban centres and

The Taj Mahal (1632–54) is a tribute to love. The Mughal emperor Shah Jahan built it as a mausoleum for his dearly beloved wife Mumtaz Mahal, who died trying to bear their fifteenth child in 1631. The Taj is also a tribute to the capacity of the Mughals to attract skilled craftspeople from all over the eastern Islamic world; the draughtsmen and calligraphers came from Shiraz, the clerk of works from Qandahar, the finial makers from Samarqand, the dome builder from Ottoman Turkey, the stone-cutters from Bukhara. These people worked with Muslim masons from Multan, Hindu inlayers also from Multan, and a Hindu garden expert from Kashmir.

Nothing symbolizes the different tone of Awrangzeb's reign, compared with his predecessors, more than his humble grave, open to the skies, at Khuldabad, near Aurangabad in the Deccan. The earlier Mughals rest in great tomb complexes that proclaim power and connoisseurship, Awrangzeb in the bare earth preferred by the strictest Muslims. The earlier Mughals were all great patrons of the arts, Awrangzeb patronized ulama and waged war. In his will he decreed that 305 rupees from the sale of Qurans he had copied himself should be distributed to holy men on the day of his death.

agricultural heartlands of the Indo-Gangetic fertile crescent. Mughal emperors exercised a fragile paramountcy over a bewildering variety of Hindu and Muslim rulers who, like the Rajputs, Afghans, and Marathas of west-central India, had deep roots in the countryside. The Mughals' Timurid identity did not legitimize their rule in the eyes of most South Asian inhabitants, and even their Islamic faith was not sufficient to co-opt Afghan clans for more than temporary service.

Akbar responded to these realities by restraining the ulama's influence and enforcing religious tolerance throughout the empire. His public policies also seem to have been driven by a profound non-sectarian spirituality. Akbar's eclectic piety often found expression in his association with sufis or later in the remarkably open religious discussions over which he presided in his new palace at Fatehpur Sikri, itself located to commemorate his reverence for the Chishti sufi order. His son, the emperor Jahangir, proudly said of his father that 'He associated with the good of every race and creed and persuasion…The professors of various faiths had room in the broad expanse of his incomparable sway. This was different from the practices in other realms, for in Persia there is room for Shias only, and in Turkey, [non-Mughal] India and Turan there is room for Sunnis only.' Akbar's lack of education during a tumultuous childhood that left him at best semi-literate may have encouraged his latitudinarian religious inclinations.

Apart from its sufi links, Fatehpur Sikri, just west of Agra, represented only one of several architectural complexes that Mughal rulers and nobles erected from Thatta in the Sind to Bengal in the east. Their number and sized reflected the remarkable wealth the Mughals extracted from South Asian subjects. The bulk of Mughal income derived from India's enormous agrarian economy. Specific buildings were usually supported by *awqaf* (charitable endowments), from the revenue of neighbouring villages. This was true of the Taj Mahal and most other tombs and mosques, and of similar structures in the other early modern Islamic empires. However, Mughal rulers also benefited from the enormous currency influx from all Eurasia to pay for India's exports of cash crops and, most of all, its dazzling variety of cotton textiles. The state directly siphoned off only a small percentage of the income from foreign trade, 2 to 4 per cent as customs and mint duties, but it indirectly gained because the currency stream produced high levels of monetization. The wealth, especially from agrarian taxation, financed the imperial army, largely cavalry and artillery. Mughal officers were appointed as *jagirdars*, literally place or land holders, whose agricultural income would support contingents of cavalry, as was true of *iqtadars*, holders of *iqtas* (land grants), who supplied soldiers to the Safawid shahs, and the holders of *timars*, who furnished cavalry to the Ottoman sultans.

Despite the wealth and manifest splendour of the Mughal empire, symbolized by the Taj Mahal, it disintegrated in the quarter century after Awrangzeb's death in 1707. The collapse was unrelated to European pressure, and was far more complex than the sudden disappearance of the Safawid state in 1722. Much of the responsibility has to be assigned to Awrangzeb himself, who reigned as long as his great-grandfather Akbar. Some attribute the collapse to the emperor's austere personality and ascetic Islam. His increasing preoccupation with ruling as an orthodox Sunni may have offended some Rajput chieftains, but the state's financial and administrative deterioration was immediately due to Awrangzeb's relentless, unsuccessful, and ruinously expensive twenty-year wars against the Marathas in the jungle and mountains of Maharashtra. In personal command of Mughal armies, he was nearly always absent from his capital and unable closely to supervise administrative affairs.

Awrangzeb's longevity also contributed to the eventual collapse of the Mughal imperial system, for when his successor, Bahadur Shah, ascended the throne he was already an old man, and ruled for only five years before his death in 1712, without asserting control over the state. The empire was once again plunged into debilitating strife just when the Marathas and the new sectarian power in the Punjab, the Sikhs, threatened the empire's heart. So when Nadir Shah Afshar, the Safawids' successor, entered India in 1739, he was met only by a provincial Mughal army. After he sacked Delhi and seized the Mughal treasury, Mughal rulers could not finance a new army and, while a Mughal state persisted in the Delhi-Agra region, the empire was effectively dead. However, neither indigenous powers nor Mughal governors could fill the power vacuum: the British East India Company then stepped in. The Company took control of Bengal by 1764 and over the next century absorbed both Mughal and non-Mughal South Asian territories.

ISLAM IN AFRICA AND SOUTHEAST ASIA

Morocco

Contemporaneous with the Turco-Mongol empires were the Arabic-speaking or Arab-influenced dynasties and populations of Africa and Southeast Asia. In terms of the early confrontation between Europe and the Islamic world, the most important states were Morocco and the Malay and Sumatran sultanates of Malacca and Atjeh. Morocco had been included in earlier north African kingdoms, but in the fifteenth century it had fallen into prolonged economic and political crises, and was threatened by Portuguese expansion. From the late fifteenth century the Saadian dynasty, direct descendants of the Prophet Muhammad through his elder grandson Hasan, resuscitated the state. They invoked their sacred lineage and initially utilized the support of sufis in successful campaigns against the Portuguese.

Between 1500 and 1800 the Moroccan state was fully established by two dynasties, the Saadians who ruled from Marrakesh till the mid-seventeenth century, and the Alawites who ruled from Meknes afterwards. Royal power was expressed in the construction of vast palaces such as the el-Badi at Marrakesh, whose walls we see here, and that of Mawlay Ismail (r.1672–1727) at Meknes.

In 1550 the Saadian ruler al-Shaykh entered Fez and took the title caliph and al-Mahdi. His victories and religious claims evidently led the Ottomans to assassinate him in 1557, for if left unchallenged he might have expanded eastwards into Ottoman territories. Saadian rulers had relied upon Berber tribes for their principal forces but by 1600 they had created a modern army. It included formidable artillery and European components, which in 1591 were used to conquer the Sudanic state of Songhay, centred south of the Sahara on the middle Niger river.

Sub-Saharan Africa

Songhay was typical of a group of small Sudanic or sub-Saharan states of this period that became at least nominally Islamic when indigenous elites responded to Muslim merchants and ulama by converting to Islam. They imported Arabic-speaking Muslim educational and religious specialists to legitimize and help to administer their regimes. The central Sudanic states of Bornu and Kano are other examples in this period. The Funj kingdom, in the territory of modern Sudan, was a similar east African example. Direct commercial contact with thoroughly Islamized societies in Nubia, upper Egypt, and Arabia attracted numerous ulama and sufis from these regions. Timbuktu exemplifies this trans-Saharan connection. An oasis market town, it had been a dispersal point for Islamic studies

Timbuktu drawn by René Caillie in 1828, when its days of glory were past. In the sixteenth century it had been the largest of the west African cities, capital of the Songhay empire and boasting a trade that was probably equal to that of contemporary London. It was also a great centre of scholarship. Most of its importance derived from its position on the huge bend of the Niger where it flows furthest into the Sahara desert. Here the primarily agricultural world of the Sudanic people of the savannah met the pastoral world of the nomads of the desert. To the south lay the rich hinterland of the middle Niger floodplain and the routes to some of the wealthiest regions of west Africa to the north was the harsh and arid land across which caravans would travel to Egypt and the Maghrib.

under Mali in the fourteenth century. It retained its cultural significance into the eighteenth century, despite fluctuating political fortunes.

Islam continued to spread south of the Sudan in the person of merchants, ulama, and sufis. In the sixteenth century the most dramatic manifestation of the increasing Islamic presence in west Africa was a remarkable wave of jihads. These campaigns gradually coalesced into a broad movement to establish Muslim-dominated states. Many of these reform movements, as they are often described, were in origin political and social protests expressed in Islamic idioms. Africans absorbed the ideology of the jihad and of a pure Islamic state when they studied in Mecca and Medina during their hajj. The jihad in Senegambia that led to the foundation of a Muslim-dominated state in Dundu in the 1690s was an ambiguous example. However, for Uthman dan Fodio (1754–1817), who began militant missions in Hausaland in the 1770s, there was an unmistakable connection between these jihads and the teaching in Arabian schools of hadith studies. Dan Fodio was a student of Jabril ibn Umar, who after studying in Mecca and Medina had returned to Africa to preach a rigorous personal Islam and the establishment of a theocratic state. In most respects Dan Fodio's jihad was a central-Sudanic variant of the much better known contemporary Wahhabi movement in Arabia.

Muhammad ibn Abd al-Wahhab (1703–87) preached a puritanical doctrine rejecting Arabian folk Islam as well as sufi beliefs and practices. When the minor chief Ibn Saud joined Abd al-Wahhab, the movement assumed the classic appearance of an Ibn Khaldun-like tribal confederation energized by prophetic mission. In 1773 the Saudi-Wahhabi alliance made Riyadh its capital. In 1803 the alliance seized Mecca and in 1805 Medina. To the horror of the Muslim world, destruction of tombs and shrines followed, including that of the Prophet Muhammad. This aggressive regime, however, did not last long: in 1818 it was destroyed by the Ottoman governor of Egypt, Muhammad Ali. The Wahhabi movement stimulated reformist movements or gave its name to similar fundamentalist and puritanical expressions in other regions of the Islamic world. Such phenomena were common in South or Southeast Asia where Muslims were responding to commercial and political dislocation brought by European and indigenous rivals.

Southeast Asia

Southeast Asia was the second region of the Islamic world to experience aggressive European expansion. The Portuguese and the Spanish arrived there in the sixteenth century, with an ideology like the medieval Christian crusaders'. The Portuguese assaulted Muslim communities in south Arabia and the western Indian coast, where Vasco da Gama arrived in 1498 at Calicut in Malabar, and in Southeast Asia, especially in the strategic areas around the Straits of Malacca. By 1565 the Spanish had also reached the Philippines from their South American bases. Both Iberian powers quickly realized that the spice trade they sought to monopolize was largely controlled by Muslim traders, whose centuries-long presence in the region had generated substantial Muslim populations and states. When Spanish forces arrived at the site of the present city of Manila they discovered an embryonic Muslim principality expanding rapidly in the archipelago. The Philippines would probably have become predominantly Muslim and formed into one or more sultanates had not the Spanish intervened.

Between 1500 and 1800 Islam made great strides forward in Southeast Asia, partly through traders and trading connections with the west coast of India, the Persian Gulf, and the south coast of Arabia. Atjeh in northern Sumatra was a notable Muslim stronghold which had strong scholarly and diplomatic links with other parts of the Muslim world. In this Dutch engraving of 1596 we see an envoy from Mecca (the fully clothed personage) and the governor of Bantam in west Java.

Hadrami sayyids: the diaspora of sacred merchants

In the sixteenth century increasing numbers of Arabs from the southern Arabian region known as the Hadramawt spread out as merchants along Indian Ocean trade routes. They settled temporarily or permanently in coastal market towns in east Africa and South and Southeast Asia. Many of these merchants were also sayyids, that is, they claimed descent from Ali, the Prophet's son-in-law, through Ahmad bin Isa al-Muhajir, who is said to have emigrated to the Hadramawt from Basra in the tenth century. As sayyids they exercised spiritual influence over Arab tribes in their homeland; certain sayyid families were hereditary religious arbiters for specific tribes, and came to wield similar influence in Muslim societies around the Indian Ocean. Such families as the Aydarus of Tibi, the Alawi of Tarim, or Ba Faqih of Duan and Shihr often became leaders of the local ulama in port towns of the Indian Ocean. In Calicut, the spice-trading centre of the Malabar coast, nearly all leading ulama claim sayyid status and are known as Tangals; in

Atjeh, the predominantly Muslim region of northern Sumatra, they are known as Teungku. Both are honorific terms denoting high religious status or achievement.

Most sayyids were nothing more than merchants, but even those without a religious vocation usually enjoyed special reverence among African and Asian Muslims. Hadrami sayyids exemplify the association between commerce and the spread of Islam that is so obvious in the African town of Timbuktu. They tended to enunciate a conservative Quran- and hadith-based faith linked to teachings in Arabia. Their diaspora is well documented in genealogies, like that possessed by the Alawis of Calicut, which show that one Alawi had settled in Calicut while others had gone to Atjeh or another port. These carefully preserved family trees document the existence of a remarkable ethnic and kin-based network that could and did serve both commercial and religious purposes in the early modern Muslim world.

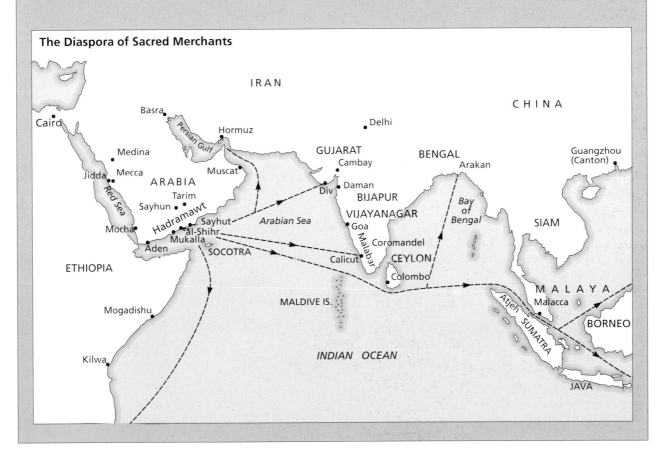

The Diaspora of Sacred Merchants

Three centuries of warfare and colonization forcibly confined Muslim influence to the southwest province of Mindanao. Nonetheless, Muslims fought a sporadic but continuous defensive jihad against the Spanish throughout the period and even into the early twentieth century. These jihads parallelled a similar Atjehnese struggle against first the Portuguese and then the Dutch, culminating in a Dutch campaign of conquest which stretched over three decades from the early 1880s. In both the Philippines and Atjeh the contests bequeathed a tradition of religious militancy that still distinguishes the Islamic culture of these regions. The Atjehnese were eventually incorporated in the officially Muslim state of Indonesia. Muslims in Mindanao, though, are persisting in sporadic fighting for their own state in the southern Philippines at the end of the twentieth century.

Conversion

The history of Islamic settlement and the growth of indigenous Muslim societies in Southeast Asia parallels that of Islam in Africa. The progress of Islam in sub-Saharan Africa may even offer insights or models for interpreting the scarce data for Southeast Asia. Two fundamentals of both regions are unmistakable: Islam spread initially along the trade routes and with Muslim merchants, and the majority of these merchants were Arabs or Arabic-speaking. In Southeast Asia such merchants came from south Arabia or the Persian Gulf or from Arabized trading communities in Gujarat or Malabar. Their origin is generally indicated by the prevalence of the Shafii legal code in Muslim Southeast Asia and the coasts of India. This was the dominant school in Cairo, the east African coast, the Arabian peninsula, and the Persian Gulf. Some of the Muslims who brought Islam to Southeast Asia may have been Gujarati or Malayali Indians, but their 'Islamic' language was usually Arabic rather than the Persian or Turkish that was spoken in the Mughal heartlands.

The process of conversion in Southeast Asia was gradual but less well documented than in Sudanic Africa. While sufis are often held to have been the primary agents of conversion, in reality Islamization, which probably began as early as the seventh century, was undoubtedly more complex. It is highly likely, first of all, that ulama, merchants, and sufis were not generally distinct individuals. In the case of merchants from the Hadramawt in southern Arabia who were sayyids (descendants of Muhammad's cousin and son-in-law Ali), one individual could have blended all three in his own person. The example of the Hadrami sayyids is especially important, because in the early modern era they were dispersed across the Indian Ocean region from east Africa to the Philippines.

Merchants of Hadrami sayyid families frequently became important ulama in east Africa, coastal India, and Southeast Asia, merely on the strength of their sacred descent. Local Muslims believed that this conferred spiritual power on them as on the Moroccan Saadian dynasty. The Hadramis' mercantile occupations did not dilute their spiritual standing and may even have enhanced it. The Alawi lineage also developed a sufi order, though of limited influence and organization. Hadrami sayyids formed an important network that was closely linked with the Hadramant itself, a centre of austere, puritanical Islam, and with the Hijaz. After 1500 many became political and even military leaders of the community, in south-west India and in Southeast Asia. Their descendants led Atjehnese forces in the later phase of the Atjehnese – Dutch war in the early twentieth century.

After Muslims had established substantial trading settlements, Southeast Asians may have converted to Islam for a variety of reasons. Most obvious were the attractions of a wealthy, relatively egalitarian society for lower social castes or classes, particularly those in the port cities. Islam may also have appealed politi-cally to local monarchs who perhaps saw in it the same ideological utility that Hinduism had for their predecessors in the early Christian era, a faith they could use to justify claims of independence or legitimize expansion. Rulers might also have found that an Islamic identity offered a clearly articulated ideology with which to defend themselves against increasingly aggressive European mercantile and colonial powers. This ideology would have made them allies of other Muslim states around the Indian Ocean and even possibly of the great Ottoman empire. Atjehnese sultans offered fealty to Ottoman rulers during their confrontations with the Portuguese for this reason.

Despite early Portuguese victories in Malacca in 1511 and nearby Pasai in 1522, several Muslim states successfully resisted Portuguese attacks in the six-teenth century. At the same time Muslim communities were growing rapidly in the old Hindu areas of central Java. The Atjehnese were the foremost opponents of the Portuguese and other European powers in the sixteenth and early seven-teenth centuries. Atjeh became the centre of resistance for all non-European traders, and assumed the main burden of defending Islam in the region. Its sultans vigorously patronized Islamic worship and education. They also maintained close contact with the Hijaz and other Muslim states and communities of the Indian Ocean, including those on the Malabar coast assaulted by Portuguese and later Dutch and British forces. Unlike the Javan kingdom of Mataram, whose Muslim rulers had ambiguous, often hostile, relationships with ulama and sufis, Atjehnese sultans worked with the religious classes. Both states, though, ceased to be inde-pendent by the late eighteenth century. The Dutch occupied the Atjehnese coast by the 1660s, and later in that century the sultans of Mataram began compromis-ing their independence by relying upon the Dutch to support their rule. By the nineteenth century few independent Muslim powers remained. Yet despite this decline Islam had irreversibly penetrated Southeast Asia, taking root in Sumatra, Java, Malaya as far north as Thailand, Borneo, and the southern Philippines.

CHINA

China was the other region where Islam penetrated largely via merchants and sufis. They arrived along the Silk Road trading routes in northwest China and the

Mosque in Kashgar in the
Tarim Basin, now China's
province of Xinjiang, which
was the capital of the
Chaghatay Khanate in the sixteenth and seventeenth centuries. During this period the
khans found themselves
increasingly opposed by sufi
brotherhoods under leaders
known as khojas. The last
Chaghatay Khan was over-
thrown in Kashgar by a khoja
in 1678, by which time the
oasis cities of the region,
which also included Yarkand,
Khotan, and Aqsu, were competing under their khojas as
rival city states. In 1758–59
the Manchus brought the area
within the Chinese empire.

ports of the southeast Chinese coast. Now China's Muslim population includes
two distinct groups, the mainly Turkic tribes of Xinjiang province and the Hui,
descendants of converts to Islam or marriages between Muslims and Chinese.
During the early modern period, which in China included the latter half of the
Ming and the first century of the Manchu dynasty, Xinjiang was brought under
Chinese administrative control. However, it is culturally and geographically part
of Central Asia rather than China proper. Nonetheless, some of the Hui were
found in west China where they had been converted or influenced by Muslim
merchants. During the Ming dynasty (1368–1644) and under the Manchus
(1644–1911) Chinese Islam was allowed to prosper, first encouraged by the Ming
rulers' policy of toleration. Many mosques were built at this time and the first
works of Chinese Muslim literature were written in the later Ming. Under the
Manchus a genuine Chinese-Muslim literary tradition was created. The most
notable figure in this development was Liu Chih, a native of Nanking, who
between the 1650s and 1720s wrote works on Islamic philosophy and law and a
life of the prophet Muhammad. Unlike Southeast Asia, though, Islam never
threatened the integrity or supremacy of Chinese culture. In China proper it
remained largely a cultural artefact of the apogee of Muslim commercial influence
in the years before Europeans established supremacy in the Indian Ocean and in
Central Asia.

REACTION AND REFORM

The growing political peril of Muslim states at the end of the eighteenth century
was signalled by Napoleon's invasion of Egypt in 1798. By this time Muslim schol-

ars were preoccupied with what they perceived as the ethical and spiritual crises in Islamic societies. Sometimes, as in Uthman dan Fodio's jihad or the puritanical Padri movement in Minangkabau in Indonesia which began in 1803, this concern was directed against dynamic indigenous cultures and entrenched local elites. In many cases, as in these two, the need for reform was directly linked to the teachings of theologians in Mecca and Medina. People like Shaykh Abu Tahir Muhammad al-Kurdi and Taj al-Din al-Hanafi, who taught in the Hijaz in the first half of the eighteenth century, criticized sufi doctrines and associated saint-worship in favour of shaping society more fully by the Quran and hadith. One man who personified many of the intellectual trends was Shah Wali Allah of Delhi. His early career also exemplifies the degree to which pilgrimage to and education in the Hijaz linked ulama from Africa to South and Southeast Asia.

Born in 1703, Shah Wali Allah was the son of an important Mughal legal scholar and a member of the Mujaddidi Naqshbandis, who followed the early seventeenth-century Indian shaykh Ahmad Sirhindi. After a classic Perso-Islamic education in India, he studied hadith in Medina with al-Kurdi and in Mecca with al-Hanafi and he was a contemporary of Abd al-Wahhab. He absorbed the Medinan focus on the example of the Prophet and the subordination of sufism to a hadith-based ethics and legal system. However, Wali Allah was probably unusual in emphasizing the importance of *ijtihad* (personal reasoning) in interpreting the law in response to evolving conditions of society. He was typical of most Muslim thinkers of this period, though, in believing that traditional rulers could restore the political vitality of decaying Muslim states. In his case he invited Afghans to invade northern India to ward off non-Muslim rule in the Mughal heartland, although as an urbane intellectual he would probably have detested Afghan rule.

Many ulama made remarkable efforts to revitalize their communities in the troubled world of the eighteenth century. Shah Wali Allah's intellectual energy contrasts markedly with the inertia of great Muslim states and the relative technological and scientific decline of the Islamic world. Some of the ulama's efforts bore fruit, contributing to the institutionalization of religious reform. In northern India Wali Allah's ideas helped to shape Muslim responses to colonial rule. Wali Allah's career also showed that ulama in distant regions of the Islamic world were linked by an Arabic textual tradition that transcended political boundaries. The shared world of scholarship illustrates how Muslims in the eighteenth century might have common religious concerns even if they were otherwise marked by cultural, linguistic, and political differences.

CHAPTER 4

Sarah Ansari

The Islamic World in the Era of Western Domination: 1800 to the Present

By 1800 Muslim rulers faced mounting internal problems made all the more diffi-cult to handle by the accelerating challenge from the West. Developments in Europe in the previous two centuries first brought the Christian world to rival the Muslim world, and then propelled it further ahead, effectively ending any hope of parity between Muslims and non-Muslims. Politically, the Muslim world was vul-nerable and this weakness was reinforced as more and more Muslims became incorporated into the empires acquired by European powers during the nine-teenth and early twentieth centuries. Like most other non-European people, Mus-lims faced the problems of how to survive western imperialism and make the transition to modern independence in a world still dominated by the West.

Apart from the threat to their political autonomy, Muslims everywhere since 1800 have come face to face with the implications of the main spin-off of western imperialism -modernization. The impact of the expanding, modernizing state was profound, whether the state was a European colonial one or a Muslim one responding to the more technologically advanced West. It introduced new demands and opportunities for many Muslims who were caught up in its drive to implement new systems of government and production. Advances in technology and communications enabled Muslims to be more aware of developments else-where in their world at precisely the time when interaction with the strengthened West and the changes which flowed from this encounter meant that they had new experiences in common with each other. Increased physical mobility, illustrated by the steadily mounting numbers of pilgrims who made their hajj to Mecca, com-bined with the increased circulation of ideas, new printing techniques, and improved literacy rates, meant that Muslims were able to keep in touch with each other in new and easier ways than in the past.

THE MUSLIM WORLD ON THE EVE OF EUROPEAN EXPANSION

The expansion of the West eventually turned the Muslim world upside down. But even before the European thrust had begun in earnest, there were signs that Mus-lims were rising to the challenge it posed to their identity. While some Muslims accepted their political misfortunes quietly as 'the judgment of God', others set about finding ways of 'remedying the evils which beset them'. As a result, in direct contrast to Islam's political vulnerability, the eighteenth and nineteenth centuries were a period of increasing religious vitality, highlighted by a surge of religious reform and revival. Religious leaders, ulama and sufis alike, seized the initiative with the emergence of movements emphasizing the reform of outward religious practice as well as inner renewal. They sought to establish new ways of looking at the world which involved first and foremost the purification of Islam. In some the Wahhabi message was most vocal, in others reformed sufi orders led the way; more often than not, a mixture of influences was at work.

Islamic revival was often influenced by intellectual movements in Arabia which were carried along the networks of connections of learned men. With the steadily increasing flow of Muslim travellers in and out of Islam's Holy Places, it is not surprising that reform movements elsewhere echoed developments in the Arabian peninsula with their own combination of ideas. In particular, ulama connected with the hadiths school at Medina influenced visiting scholars and pilgrims who returned home carrying the ideas of the reformers with them. These same Muslims were also influenced to a great extent by the mid-eighteenth-

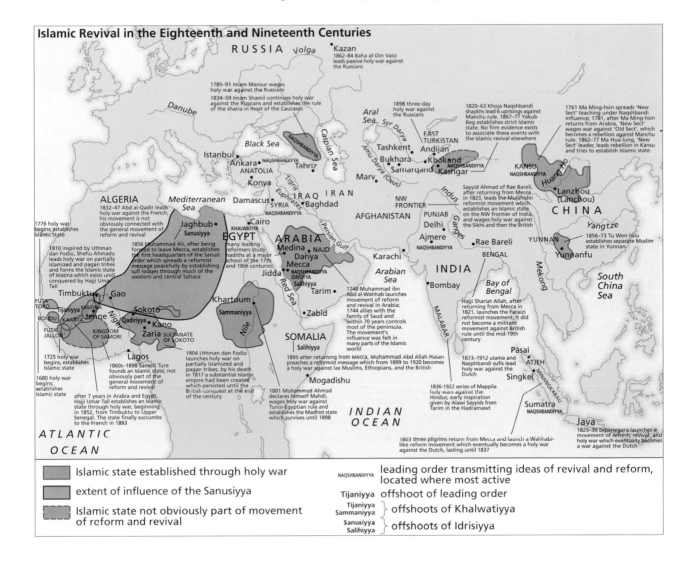

Islamic Revival in the Eighteenth and Nineteenth Centuries

century campaign for purification and renewal in Najd in eastern Arabia, led by Muhammad ibn Abd al-Wahhab (1703–87). In what became Indonesia, the island of Sumatra experienced a reform movement launched in 1803 by three pilgrims who had witnessed the Wahhabi occupation of Mecca. Known as the Padri movement, it led to a much greater Islamization of local Minangkabau society but got entangled, like many others, with expanding western, in this case Dutch, power and fought a 'holy war' which lasted well into the 1830s.

At a time when the world which they had known seemed to be disintegrating, one of the reformers' main lessons was the importance of action. Muslims could no longer wait for change to happen. Instead, it was their duty to bring it about, and to fight for their beliefs if necessary. This period therefore witnessed a number of jihads in pursuit of the reformers' vision of the future. So in places where European imperialist expansion had begun, many of these movements got caught up in individual struggles for survival. An important Idrisiyya offshoot, the Salihiyya, led by Muhammad Abd Allah Hasan (1864–1920) whom the British labelled and libelled the 'mad mullah', preached its particularly puritanical reformist message in the Somali region where by 1900 it was waging holy war against both foreigners – Ethiopian and British – and those whom it regarded as 'lax' local Muslims. Other sufi orders elsewhere in Africa similarly provided a structure of resistance to foreign control.

But despite the number of physical confrontations, jihad was not simply a question of fighting infidels in the flesh: just as important was the inner fight to produce the kind of Islam which could resist the mounting encroachments of the West. Blaming the contemporary difficulties of Islam in large part on compromises which Muslim rulers had earlier made in order to accommodate local religious practices, Islamic reformers stressed a purer vision of Islamic life and society. They sought a return to the so-called first principles – the Quran and the hadiths – for guidance and placed great importance on the Prophet Muhammad as the best model for correct behaviour. The Faraizi movement of eastern Bengal, for example, launched in the 1820s after its leader Hajji Shariat Allah (1781–1840) had been on pilgrimage, had a typical reforming programme which emphasized the example of the Prophet and condemned those Muslim practices which were in conflict with the sharia. In general, this renewal attacked all aspects of popular religion which challenged the unity of God. In particular, it involved an assault on supposedly dubious practices associated with sufi traditions, such as worship at saints' tombs, and, on a more philosophical level, a rejection of Ibn al-Arabi's unity of being which had been so useful in the process of absorbing new semi-Islamized recruits to the faith. But this attack on sufism did not prevent certain sufis from becoming involved in reform: the Naqshbandiyya in Asia and the Khalwatiyya and Idrisiyya in Africa cleansed their practices and beliefs of much that was objectionable to the reformers as part of the wider attempt to erect the kind of moral defences that could repel the Christian, western advance.

THE EUROPEAN TAKE-OVER

The urgent message of Islamic reform was intensified after 1798 when the forces of Napoleonic France occupied Egypt. After that Muslim independence steadily crumbled as region after region fell under European control. From west Africa to the eastern fringes of Southeast Asia, from the steppes of Central Asia to the tip of the Indian peninsula, European powers proceeded to capture territory ruled by Muslims. By the time of the First World War, most of the Muslim world had come under varying types and degrees of European colonial control.

Great rivalry within Europe fuelled and drove forward the imperial machine. The early French attempt to occupy Egypt was largely aimed at curtailing British supremacy in the east and gaining the upper hand in the imperial contest. France was assisted by the fact that Ottoman authority had reached a low ebb as Egypt's Mamluk rulers tried to secede from their nominal Turkish masters. Like the other European powers who followed them into Muslim lands, the French recognized

The French suppress the Muslim revolt in Cairo in 1798. On 21–22 October, four and a half months after the French landed in Egypt, the citizens of Cairo, irritated by French fiscal policies and by their interference with Islamic customs, rebelled. The uprising failed because the leaders were unable to win the support of all Cairo. 'After the first watch of the night', wrote the eyewitness al-Jabarti, 'the French entered the city like a torrent rushing through the alleys and streets.'

the need to pay special attention to the religious sensibilities of their inhabitants. Hence the French swiftly issued proclamations: 'shaykhs, qadis, imams, and officers of the town, tell your nation that the French are friends of true Muslims' – a clear indication that Napoleon wanted to stabilize his occupation by attracting the cooperation of native leaders including the ulama. It was the tyranny of the Mamluks not the Islamic faith which was the target of French actions.

This particular round of European involvement was short-lived: the occupation was over by 1801 when the French army surrendered to a British expeditionary force. But the continuing decline of the Ottoman empire, which was designated Europe's 'sick man' by the middle of the nineteenth century, meant that the Eastern Question – how to resolve the potential power vacuum in the Middle East – continued to dominate European perceptions of the region. Egypt, whose significance increased once it became home to the Suez Canal in 1869, had practically detached itself from Istanbul during the reign of its ruler Muhammad Ali (r.1805–48). But the intervention of the British in 1882 prevented it from securing complete independence and in theory restored Ottoman authority. In reality Egypt fell under British control and, although it did not become an official protectorate until 1914, it displayed most of the features associated with such an arrangement. By the First World War, the whole of north Africa was under some form of European control, France having conquered Algeria between 1830 and 1890, transformed Tunisia into a protectorate in 1881, and occupied Morocco in 1912. In 1912 Italy began its conquest of Libya. By the second decade of the twentieth century, the Ottoman empire was reduced to Arab Asia, Anatolia, and some Aegean islands, its European remnants lost in the Balkan wars of 1912–13.

For much of the nineteenth century the Dutch found the sultanate of Atjeh in northern Sumatra, which by the 1820s produced over half the world's pepper, a major threat to its imperialist ambitions on the island. From 1873 to 1912 the Dutch waged almost continuous war against the Atjehnese which became a jihad for the latter. The struggle only began to turn in favour of the Dutch when they adopted the advice of their orientalist, Snouck Hurgronje, that the ulama were not to be appeased and could only be crushed. Here Panglima Polem Muhammad Daud (1857–1940), the main Atjehnese military leader of the latter stages of the war, surrenders in 1903 to the governor of Atjeh, van Heutsz. Daud was to become a leading official under Dutch rule.

The year 1800 similarly proved a turning point in the relationship between more far-flung parts of the Muslim world and European powers. In island Southeast Asia, where Islam had come to influence most of its people and where Muslim states in earlier centuries had already had to struggle against first the Portuguese and then the Dutch, the nineteenth century confirmed political power in European hands. The Dutch East India Company had been active in Java for approaching 200 years and for more than 100 years it had been involved in the interior of the island. Now the Dutch government assumed direct control and began to extend its authority the length and breadth of the Indonesian archipelago. With the end of violent resistance in Atjeh in 1912, this process was complete. In the Philippines under Spanish rule, Islam remained largely confined to the southern island of Mindanao, and little changed when power passed to the United States following its victory in the Spanish-American war of 1898. Meanwhile, Britain with the Treaty of Pangkor in 1874 accelerated its involvement in the states of the Malay peninsula, which had started with Stamford Raffles's landing in Singapore in 1819 and produced a protectorate in 1914.

Britain's interest in Malaya was influenced, as was much of its imperial policy, by its stake in India, which grew steadily during the nineteenth century. By 1800, the Mughal empire had effectively disintegrated as factionalism at court had increased and control over the provinces had slipped out of its hands. Britain took advantage of Mughal decline to convert its commercial and strategic interests in the shape of the East India Company into something which approached political control, first in Bengal and gradually over the other Mughal provinces. To the revenue management of Bengal, granted by the powerless Mughal emperor to the British in 1765, were added other prizes, won by the 'slow attrition' of the Company's fiscal and military demands. In 1818 Britain was recognized as paramount and by the middle of the nineteenth century it ruled most of India. The uprising of 1857 sounded the final death knell for indigenous rule in India. The mutinous soldiers and other disaffected groups gained support from the last Mughal emperor, which afterwards provided Britain with final justification to end all remaining vestiges of Mughal power and exile him to Burma. The East India Company was abolished and from 1858 the British crown assumed direct administration of its Indian empire.

As in the Middle East, the consolidation of British power in India was influenced by the imperialist competition of European powers – in this case British fears about a threat to its position from either France or Russia, or both. Russia was carrying out its own imperial expansion eastwards into the Muslim-dominated lands of the Caucasus and Central Asia following the conquest of the Giray Khanate of Crimea, Kazakhstan, and Daghistan in the eighteenth century. In the Caucasus it conquered northern Azarbayjan at the beginning of the nineteenth century and by 1864 had occupied the whole region. After the end of the Crimean war of 1854–56, the tsarist drive into Central Asia intensified. In 1868 the emir of

Imam Shamil (c.1796–1871). Two notable movements of religious reform in the Caucasus merged into resistance against Russian expansion; both received support in particular from the people of Daghistan. The first was led by Imam Mansur (d.1794) who waged jihad against the Russians from 1785 to 1791. The second was led by Imam Shamil, a Naqshbandi shaykh, who between 1834 and 1859 imposed the sharia on the Caucasus and resisted Russian might. He was defeated only when the Russians cut down the forests on which his forces depended for cover.

Bukhara was intimidated into signing a treaty which preserved his domestic power but made his lands a Russian protectorate. There was a similar fate for other Muslim areas such as Khiva in 1873. Both Khiva and Bukhara remained protectorates until absorbed into the Soviet system in 1920. Other Muslim lands were taken away from Afghanistan, Iran, and Turkey at the turn of the twentieth century. Thus, the main centres of Islamic civilization for twelve centuries in Central Asia fell to Russian colonialism at the same time as their counterparts elsewhere in the world fell victim to the colonial thrust of other European powers.

European states began to compete more seriously for direct stakes in Africa in the late nineteenth century. While European intrusion into parts of Muslim Africa dated back to the fifteenth century, the scramble for power there intensified after the Berlin West Africa Conference of 1884, which effectively divided the African continent among the Great Powers. By 1900, Britain and France had become the major foreign 'shareholders': France occupied three times as much territory as the British in west Africa but Britain governed a population twice as large as that of the French colonies. In east Africa, Britain and Germany divided the spoils with some left-overs going Italy's way. This loss of political independence coincided with the continued expansion of Islam throughout the belt of Africa lying between the Sahara and the equator. Here European rule stimulated the conversion of Africans to Islam as much as to Christianity. In west Africa Muslims 'reached' the coast while in east Africa they pressed further and further inland. Either way, the overall number of Muslims grew dramatically as European empires grew and the twentieth century gathered pace.

By the beginning of the twentieth century, world power had passed firmly into European hands. All the same, the direct defeat of the Ottoman empire in 1918

General Franchet d'Esperey, Supreme Commander in the Orient, lands in Istanbul beneath the walls of the former palace of the sultans, Topkapi, on 22 November 1918. He is greeted by General Wilson of Great Britain behind whom stands Mustafa Kemal Ataturk who was to lead the struggle to found the modern Turkish state. The defeat of the Ottoman empire meant the end of the last powerful Muslim state; it also meant that the Europeans were free to impose their will on the heartlands of the Muslim world.

still came as a great shock to Muslim pride. Indeed, the nadir of Muslim fortunes was the political settlement which constructed a new map of the Middle East after the First World War. Instead of remaining neutral, as the Allies had hoped, Turkey had joined the Central Powers in October 1914. During the course of the war, Britain, France, Italy, and Russia made secret agreements on dividing what remained of the Ottoman empire in the event of an Allied victory. The arrangements were complicated by the fact that Britain in particular seemed to be making conflicting promises. As well as the Sykes-Picot agreement with France, Britain appeared to promise an independent Arab state and the establishment of a national home for the Jews in return for support against the Turks.

The 'humiliating' defeat inflicted on Turkey caused Muslims elsewhere to be fearful about the kind of postwar treatment that the Ottoman sultan, still caliph or spiritual head of much of the Muslim world, would receive. In the event, the political settlements produced by the Paris Peace Conference, the 1920 Treaty of Sèvres, and the 1923 Treaty of Lausanne failed either to placate Muslim fears or to satisfy local, Arab, aspirations. Ottoman power shrank to within the borders of Turkey while most of the Middle East was parcelled into political units or mandates assigned to Britain and France by the newly created League of Nations. The last of the great Muslim empires had been laid rather unceremoniously to rest.

THE NATURE OF THE EUROPEAN CHALLENGE

In political terms, the European challenge of the nineteenth and early twentieth centuries was insurmountable. But the nature of this challenge went far deeper than the simple loss or shrinking of Muslim political power. As many Muslims noticed, both in places which remained independent and in those which experienced the 'trauma of defeat' and 'rule by infidel powers', the Muslim world as a whole had fallen behind Europe materially, technologically, and in terms of intellectual and political development. Islam directly challenged by western philosophical and scientific theories made Muslims think about how far their faith could reconcile itself with what appeared to be the new twin 'religions' of reason and materialism. Likewise, unquestioned certainties of Muslim society were threatened by the strength of European hegemony. Europe without the benefit of Allah's guidance, it seemed, had risen to unassailable heights armed with the modern state as the prime weapon of its success. Muslims could see the state at work – directly if they had been colonized by it, indirectly if they dealt diplomatically and traded with it – and they recognized its awesome efficiency. The modern state had very little time for God: the people legitimized its existence and it created for them a political framework which no longer owed anything to divine revelation. Indeed, popular sovereignty posed a direct threat to Islam by challenging the sovereignty of God. Since the modern state was also the nation-state, secular nationalism rather than religious community could now act as the argument for binding a people together.

Political cartoons

As in the West, the cartoon has been a powerful vehicle for political and social comment. The form developed with the press, which began in Muslim lands in the early nineteenth century and by the early twentieth century could boast 150 titles in Egypt, 160 in Central Asia, 370 in Iran, while in India over 700 had been founded in Urdu alone and even in China by the 1930s there were about 100. They were inspired in part by Western models. *Awadh Punch*, for instance, which was the leading satirical journal of Muslim India from the 1870s to the 1930s, derived its inspiration from *Punch*, the humorous magazine of Victorian Britain. But they were inspired in part, too, by indigenous models. *Karagoz*, a satirical journal of Istanbul in the Young Turk period, drew its inspiration from the Turkish village tradition of shadow puppets. Cartoons have had a vigorous existence into the late twentieth century as a source of comment – affectionate, witty or savage – on all aspects of life. In the Arab world, for instance, they exist as a significant part of mass culture,

Here *Mulla Nasreddin* (1909) attacks the willingness of the Emir of Bukhara and his chief justice to assist the Russian capitalist in fleecing his state of Bukhara. *Mulla Nasreddin* was a lively and noncomformist weekly published by a group of Azeri intellectuals from Tiflis; the title was taken from the prominent figure of Turkish folklore noted for his humour and wisdom. The journal attacked all forms of conservatism, all forms of humbug, and those who were prepared to compromise with the Russians. On the other hand, it was a vigorous supporter of the reformer Ismail Bey Gasprinski.

Intellectuals increasingly contrasted the attributes of western dominance with the elements of decline and apathy which they had identified in their own cultures. They began to work out new ideas about the relationship between themselves and their religion and between their religion and the modern world, particularly ideas from the West. This led to a development in reform by which Muslims sought to use the West's own strengths, its rationalism and efficiency, to build up their intellectual stamina and equip them to reassert their independence. Everywhere these intellectuals, called reformists or in their more radical form modernists, sought to maintain their cultural identity and integrity in the face of western colonial rule.

This quest was given unity by one of the movement's founding fathers, Jamal al-Din al-Afghani (1839–97), an activist who travelled widely in the Middle East. Afghani regarded the West 'not only as the enemy and conqueror of Islam but also a model to follow in order to acquire a new strength, which would lead to liberation and the rebirth of a strong community'. Like other modernist thinkers, he would invoke a verse from the Quran to stress that Muslims were responsible for their own futures: 'in truth God does not change a people's condition, if that people does not change its own condition'. Muslims had to free themselves from the influence of conservative ulama who, by forbidding the pursuit of modern science and technology, had revealed themselves as the real 'enemies of Islam'.

often providing the vehicles through which the intellectual class endeavours to counter state-sponsored propaganda. The rise of Islamism with its intolerance of pictorial propaganda raises a question mark over the future of the tradition. That it survived the Islamic revolution in Iran, it should be noted, was a consequence of the adoption of iconographic propaganda by Twelver Shiism; it is no guide to the future of the tradition in the Sunni world.

Zakiyya al-Dhakiyya (Zakiyya the Clever) is the fount of wisdom in the most successful comic strip magazine in the Arab world, *Majid*. This weekly designed for children, published from Abu Dhabi since 1979, is read in every Arab state except Syria. Zakiyya is a source of comment on politics, science, general knowledge, even religion. It is revolutionary in an Arab Muslim context that a source of authority should be both female and juvenile.

This cartoon from *Al-Sharq al-Awsat* (1982), the Arabic language newspaper published from London, underlines the Muslim view of the bias of the western media towards Israel.

Al-Azhar in Cairo became the intellectual centre of the modernist movement. Its rector, Muhammad Abduh (1849–1905), had been a pupil of Afghani whose ideas he developed on a purely religious level. Widely regarded as the other founder of Islamic modernism, Abduh wished to promote a progressive interpretation of the sharia, stressing individual interpretation based on reason. He strongly advocated ijtihad (personal reasoning), or in other words the free exploration of what was best here and now within the framework of the moral norms of Islam. This approach enabled Muslims, if they wished, to accept modern scientific and technological advances as part of God's revelation and to reconcile Islam and modern European thought.

Abduh and his circle in Cairo generated ideas which spread far beyond the Arab Muslim world. Indonesians who studied at al-Azhar, for instance, were greatly influenced and Indonesians at home absorbed the new teachings from imported books disseminated via a fast-expanding Muslim press. They formed the Muhammadiyya (The Way of Muhammad) in 1912 to propagate their reforming message by establishing schools and clinics. The broad appeal of these reforming ideas was also reflected in the Sarekat Islam (Islamic League), similarly founded in 1912 and Indonesia's first attempt at a mass modern political organization. In the Malay archipelago reformist ideas were popularized by newspapers such as *al-Imam* whose birth in 1906 was 'a bombshell on the quiet Malayan scene of Islam'.

Shaykh Muhammad Abduh, the leading Egyptian reformer, the influence of whose ideas was felt in much of the Muslim world, with friends in Beirut in 1885. He is in the centre of the front row. The purpose of his life was, he declared, 'to liberate thought from the shackles of imitation (*taqlid*)...to return, in the acquisition of religious knowledge, to its first sources, and to weigh them in the scale of human reason, which God has created in order to prevent excess or adulteration in religion...and to prove that, seen in this light, religion must be accounted a friend to science, pushing man to investigate the secrets of existence, summoning him to respect established truths and to depend on them in his moral life and conduct.'

In their writings Malay reformists emphasized the importance of education and modernity for Malay Muslims and the need to get rid of un-Islamic practices in their lives.

The most radical theologian of the period was not an Arab or an Indonesian but an Indian Muslim who arrived at his intellectual position independently of developments at al-Azhar. Sayyid Ahmad Khan (1817–98), whose family had served the Mughals and who was himself a loyal servant of British rule, believed that Islam was entirely compatible with modern science. Appealing strongly to Muslims from northern India where the decline of Muslim political power had been most profound, Sayyid Ahmad, who was knighted by the British for his political and educational services, established the Muhammedan Anglo-Oriental College at Aligarh in 1877 for Muslims to study western learning without severing their religious roots. The finished products of this centre of modernist thought were able to compete successfully with non-Muslims for jobs in the new system created by the British. Their subsequent political activities covered the entire span of options open to Muslims, but they became particularly associated with Muslim separatist politics. Many were strong supporters of the All-India Muslim League, established in 1906 to safeguard Muslim rights in a majority Hindu society, even when this involved supporting the British administration in its role as the supposedly neutral arbitrator of Indian political life. The Pakistan movement which gained ground in the run-up to independence encompassed different kinds of Muslims but its intellectual development was deeply affected by the poet Muhammad Iqbal (1878–1938), who made an ambitious attempt to rethink Muslim principles in the light of contemporary experience. Ideally, Iqbal argued, all Muslims belonged to the one 'fatherland' that was Islam. In reality the lure of the individual nation required Muslims to create a compromise between Islam and the modern nation. So to Indian Muslims he presented a separate state as a realistic goal for them to pursue:

Now that brotherhood has been so cut to shreds

That in the stead of community

The country has been given pride of place

In men's allegiance and constructive work.

Acknowledgment that the Muslim world needed reform that would embrace what the West offered was not restricted to religious thinkers or spiritual poets. The declining Ottoman empire was quick to appreciate that 'reform' along modernist lines offered a practical means of keeping the West at bay. Mahmud II (r.1808–39) and Abd al-Majid I (r.1839–61) instituted wide-ranging measures to overhaul and modernize state institutions. They particularly wished to strengthen the central

The Dolmabahce Palace.
The process of reform in the
Ottoman empire in the nineteenth century is symbolized
by the move of the sultans
from the old palace of
Topkapi overlooking the
Golden Horn to a new
European-style palace, in
outward form at least, stretching for 310 yards along the
Bosphorus. The Dolmabahce
Palace was designed by
Nikogos Balyan, from the
distinguished family of
Armenian architects who did
much work for the sultans in
the second half of the nineteenth century. Its interior
was the work of a French
decorator, Sechan, who
designed the Paris Opera.
Abd al-Majid I took up residence in 1856.

authority's control over the provinces and to extract taxes more efficiently and
regularly. Knowing that reform was long overdue in the armed forces, in 1826
they disbanded, against their wishes, the arch-representative of the traditional
military order, the Janissary corps. In its place they created a modern Prussian-
trained army. With opposition held in check, the full flourishing of the *tanzimat* –
the collective name for the various measures of reform introduced between 1840
and 1870 – could now take place. The new legal code based on the French model
clearly indicated the extent to which the Ottomans sought to become secular: the
state no longer turned to the authority of the sharia for guidance.

In Egypt where the de facto independent governor Muhammad Ali created his
own strong central government, the 'New Order' provided the framework for the
country's drive for modernization over the following 100 years. Crushing the
power of the ulama and the Mamluks, the traditional military elite, and making
profitable use of the resources this released, Muhammad Ali proceeded down
much the same path as his nominal Ottoman overlords. Cairo, which combined a
western-style city growing separately from the eastern, Islamic, one, now presented a powerful image of the way that new, usually French, ideas were entering
the country and developing alongside older convictions. Since the ulama had formerly controlled the state's legal and educational apparatuses, they formed a substantial section of the opposition to the overhaul of the administration. The
debate about Egypt's future was reflected in the press which, as in Turkey, multiplied but was able to express more freely than under the Ottomans the range of
problems facing Muslims coming to grips with the process of modernization.

To a large extent, Ottoman and Egyptian reforms provided models for other
Muslim rulers to follow. In neighbouring Qajar Iran, the drive for modernization

started during the reign of Nasir al-Din (r.1848–96). He and successive rulers sought to build up the central government's power against the ulama, the tribes, and the merchants through military and bureaucratic reforms. For some, such as the ulama, the reforms went far too far. For others, such as Iran's western-educated radicals, they fell short of what was required. When in the first decade of the twentieth century the Shah seemed to be sacrificing Iranian interests to the exploitation of the British and the Russians, these different opposition groups coalesced to impose a democratic constitution on the monarchy. This constitution, however, failed to live up to the expectations of the ulama, so they withdrew their support.

Iran's Central Asian neighbours also experienced the impact of modernist reform. To contemporary Europeans, Bukhara exemplified 'Muslim stagnation': in 1911 one traveller wrote of his delight at having seen 'all the features of the country at a time when it and its population [were] still the same as in Tamerlane's day'. In fact, significant change had been taking place, especially under Emir Nasr Allah (r.1827–60) when work began to reinforce the central authority of the state. After 1868, the West in the guise of tsarism offered ideas of constant progress towards power and prosperity. At the same time, the Orthodox Church was in the midst of expanding Christianity among the Muslim and 'pagan' peoples of the Russian empire. It was the Tatars who responded most vigorously to these challenges and who were largely responsible for introducing reformist ideas to Muslim Turkistan. The leading Tatar intellectual Shihab al-Din Marjani (1818–89), in the spirit of Muhammad Abduh, denied that the door of ijtihad had been closed, declared the compatibility of the Quran and modern science, and called for, among other things, the study of both science and the Russian language in madrasas. The Crimean Tatar journalist, pedagogue, and western-educated Ismail Bey Gasprinski (1851–1914) then used his newspaper *Tarjuman* (The Interpreter) to propagate the reform of religious education. In 1884 he established his first *jadid* (new method) school, and by 1910 jadid schools operated in all the Islamic territories of the Russian empire.

In time the movement produced Muslims who joined protests against the Tsarist monarchy. The Bolsheviks under Lenin realized that an active anti-Islamic programme would alienate so-called Muslim Communists who were combining Marx with the Quran to win over substantial support. Hence they initially followed a policy of caution and patience in dealing with Islam. Among the ulama, the New Mosque group advocated reform and urged cooperation with the Bolshevik regime. In their writings, they pointed to common characteristics in Islam and Communism, and they reinterpreted many of Islam's traditional beliefs in a socialist light. But by the mid-1920s, the Soviet government had changed its outlook. To implement its control more thoroughly, it clamped down on Muslim institutions. Muslim Communists such as Mir Sultan Galiev (1880–1928?), whose national Muslim version of Communism led to calls for resistance to Russian

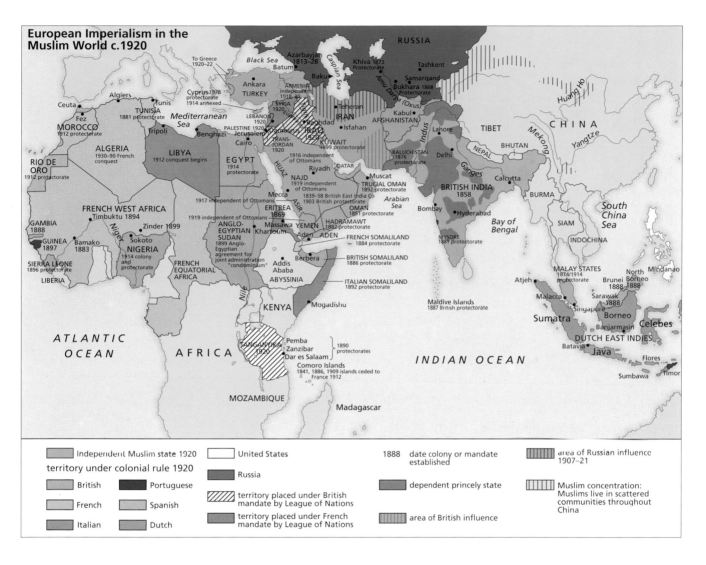

interference, were vilified as dangerous promoters of local nationalism. The jadids became main targets of the state's long and bloody anti-Islam campaign, and what remained of Islam in the Soviet Union went underground.

THE EMERGENCE OF MUSLIM NATION-STATES

The combined impact of western political control and intellectual ideas created the scenario for the emergence of Muslim nation-states in the twentieth century. In constructing empires for themselves, western powers very often provided a framework for nationalist activity. Interaction with the West established a new set of ground rules and political vocabulary for Muslims seeking to free themselves from subservience. To be heard in a world in which nation-states were supreme, Muslims now had to communicate in similar ways. The problem which emerged in many of these new Muslim states, however, was how to balance competing sets of national identities. By and large, their rulers rejected religion in favour of

Much of the sharp western orientation which Ataturk wished to give the Turkish people is evident in this picture of the founder of modern Turkey arriving in Istanbul from Ankara to take up his summer residence at the Dolmabahce Palace. He and his entourage have adopted a strict western formality, the uniforms of the military are modelled on western lines, while the women go unveiled.

secular alternatives: ethnicity, language, or simply the apparatus of the state itself became the binding forces which defined and kept these new nations together.

The Ottoman state had begun to create a secular framework during the nineteenth century. It had also confronted the problem of what identity to adopt once the Young Turks had rejected the Islamic option in 1908: the supra-communal Ottoman one or a new Turkish identity? With the loss of the remnants of its empire after 1918, the dilemma was resolved in favour of the Turkish nation-state. Under Mustafa Kemal (1881–1938), later known as Ataturk (the father of the Turks), the new Turkish government pushed through a sweeping programme of reforms which aimed at turning the country into a modern secular nation-state on western lines. Over fifteen years, 1923–38, an array of secularist laws transformed public life. Turkey became a republic in 1923; in 1924 the caliphate was abolished. The government introduced a written constitution on European models, and new legal codes replaced the Islamic legal system; Islam was no longer the religion of the state. Westernization also meant suppressing religious orders, abolishing the fez, introducing family surnames, and substituting the Roman script for the Arabic. Although in time popular pressure forced the government to retreat from strict secularism, allowing Islam gradually to re-enter the public arena, Turkey managed to retain this secular identity forged largely in opposition to its Muslim past.

During the nineteenth century there had been increasing antagonism from Arab subjects towards Ottoman Turkish rule. This growing political consciousness was linked to a literary revival in Syria in the 1850s and 1860s where newly established societies studied Arab history, literature, and culture. While most of the early pioneers of secular Arab nationalism were Christians, the bitter experience of Ottoman rule ensured that for many Muslim Arabs the way to political emancipation lay in nationalist activity, even if it involved rejecting the right of a spiritual leader – the Ottoman caliph – to rule over territory which was at the heart of his religious domain. The despotism of Abd al-Hamid II increased nationalist awareness and, despite the Young Turk Revolution of 1908, Arab opposition became more vocal and organized in the years preceding the First World War.

The Arab revolt of 1916–17, which played a part in the Ottoman downfall, created expectations of an independent Arab state centred on Damascus which were not fulfilled at the end of the war. Despite the assertion of Arab leaders such as the Hashimite King Faysal, temporarily of Syria and then of Iraq, that 'we are Arabs before being Muslims and Muhammad was an Arab before being a prophet', the political scene established by the First World War settlements dictated the shape of the independent Middle East to come. Egypt was technically independent in 1922 but the Anglo-Egyptian Agreement of 1936 underlined Egypt's semi-colonial status. Real independence was not achieved until Colonel Jamal Abd al-Nasir (Nasser) seized power in 1952. The Free Officers' revolution led to the British exit from the Suez Canal zone in 1954. Two years later Egypt withstood the western assault which followed its decision to turn to the Soviet bloc for arms denied by the USA and to nationalize the Suez Canal Company. Egyptian self-confidence rubbed off on its Arab neighbours. In 1956, King Husayn of Jordan dismissed Glubb Pasha, the British officer commanding his army, and in 1958 an army-led coup toppled Iraq's Hashimite rulers, dramatically ending British involvement that had endured despite Britain's formal withdrawal in 1932. Meanwhile France in 1946 had granted independence to Syria and the Lebanon.

Nasser acknowledges the acclaim of his people as he drives through Port Said in June 1956. The son of a postal clerk, he rose through the army. In 1949 he helped to found the Free Officer's Movement which led the Egyptian revolution of 1952 and brought an end to British imperialism in Egypt. In 1956 he nationalized the Suez Canal Company, crowning a series of anti-imperialist actions which were to make him an Arab leader as well as an Egyptian one.

The issue of transition to independence was complicated in Palestine by Jewish immigration. Britain increasingly saw its role as arbitrator between the Arab and Jewish communities. As Zionist settlers rose to around one third of the population, Arab protest succeeded in persuading the British in 1939 to put a ceiling on Jewish immigration. The horror of the Holocaust intensified moral pressure on Britain to reverse this decision, and mounting political tension eventually caused Britain in 1948 to hand over the problem of partitioning Palestine between Arab and Jew to the United Nations. The 1948–49 war with the Arab states secured the political future of the independent state of Israel. It also generated hundreds of thousands of mostly Muslim Palestinian refugees whose stateless condition, just as much as the existence of a Jewish state in their midst, served to concentrate the opposition of Arab states towards their new Israeli neighbour.

Arab nationalism reached a peak in the 1950s and 1960s, when it became the creed of the radical Arab parties which achieved power during this period. All the same, it still could not resolve the central problem of how to reconcile Arab unity with Islam or competing national identities. From 1958 to 1961 Egypt and Syria formed the United Arab Republic (UAR), later joined by the Yemen. The initiative was widely believed to be the first step towards a broader Arab unity but an unequal balance of power and competing national interests led to its collapse. The UAR was ended by a Syrian army coup, fuelled by resentment of Egyptian dominance. The Hashimite monarchies of Jordan and Iraq, alarmed by the UAR, had formed their own union – the Arab Federation – but the downfall of the Iraqi monarchy ended this attempt at union, for the new republic of Iraq immediately declared its close alignment with Egypt. Although in both Syria and Iraq military regimes with socialist tendencies made way for radical Arab nationalist Baath (Resurrection) parties, later schemes of unity with Egypt also foundered. 'Nasserism' and the promotion of Arab socialism aroused the hostility of pro-western and conservative, Arab states. With the failure of Egypt's Palestine policy – including defeat in the 1967 Six-Day war with Israel, the loss of Sinai, and the closure of the Suez Canal – 'the hero of Arab nationalism in 1956 had become its victim in 1967'.

Nationalist sentiment continued to be fired by reactions to Israel but the disaster from the Arab perspective of the 1967 war highlighted divisions within the Muslim Arab world. Political developments revealed how fragmented it had become and how removed in practice the rhetoric of Arab nationalism was from the reality of Arab disunity. Competing national interests virtually reduced Arab nationalism to a call for Arab solidarity in the foreign policies of the individual states. The Arab nationalism of the Baath parties represented the subordination of the Islamic umma to the Arab nation. For Michel Aflaq (1910–89), co-founder and ideologist of the Baath Party, who was from a Greek Orthodox family, the nation predated Islam. In his view, the Arab identity was the common denominator which could overcome sectarian and ethnic divisions. In practice, the separate

Baathist regimes in Syria and Iraq placed national priorities above any pan-Arabic sentiment and came to be dominated by powerful Alawi military interests.

Further west along the north African coastline, the call for Arab unity was much fainter. Here the Second World War nationalist feeling grew in Tunisia and Morocco where France, handicapped by economic difficulties and its Indo-Chinese commitments, was unable to restore its former colonial position. By 1954 both countries were in open revolt and the French made concessions. The Sultan of Morocco, exiled in 1953 and leader of the Istiqlal (Independence) Party, returned and Morocco achieved full independence in 1956. In the same year Tunisia became an independent republic with Habib Bourguiba, its first president, continuing the secular programme of the nationalist Neo Destour (New Constitution) Party, founded in 1934. Algerian Muslims found their position less easy to change. Despite some reforms giving them representation in the French parliament and a greater say locally, the influence of the French *colons* (settlers) persisted, helping to generate support among Muslims for a complete break with France. The strength of the *colons* and their allies proved to be the sticking point: it was only after de Gaulle came to power that the delicate process of preparing French opinion for Algerian independence was begun. The French authorities had to crush a potential military revolt and when agreement was finally reached in 1962 the cost of independence was high with hundreds of thousands of Muslims killed and displaced. The Algeria constructed by President Ben Bella was a socialist one, which paid no more than lip-service to Islam. Later under Boumedienne, Algeria experienced rapid industrialization very much on a western model of development.

The Algerian war of independence from 1954 to 1962 was the most bitter and bloody of all those involved in the decolonization of the Muslim world. It is not surprising that it gave birth to Frantz Fanon's *The Wretched of the Earth*, an analysis of the role of violence in effecting historical change, which became a most influential handbook for those seeking revolutionary changes in the 1960s and 1970s. The situation was exacerbated in early 1957 when important oilfields were discovered in southern Algeria: there was an increased incentive to hold on to the land. Here in July 1957 French paratroopers frisk citizens after a raid on Algiers.

In July 1951 Dr Musaddeq, the Iranian prime minister, appeals for a vote of confidence in the Iranian Parliament in a debate on the nationalization of the Anglo-Iranian oil company. To raise the resources to fund Iran's modernization, in early 1951 the shah tried to force a quick and profitable renegotiation of the Anglo-Iranian oil concession through Parliament. The issue became one of Iranian independence and the power of the shah. Parliament responded by nationalizing the oil industry on 20 March 1951. Musaddeq, who had a reputation for integrity, became prime minister in May with a brief to put Parliament's nationalization policy into operation.

In the Arabian peninsula, the Saud family had managed by the First World War to drive Ottoman forces out of northern and eastern Arabia. Steadily, Abd al-Aziz ibn Saud's army of Wahhabi Ikhwan (Brothers) accumulated territory. In January 1926 Ibn Saud (1880–1953) was proclaimed King of the Hijaz and by the end of the 1920s the shape of the new state had virtually been settled. Saudi Arabia, created from the kingdoms of the Hijaz and Najd in 1932, in contrast to the majority of its Middle Eastern Muslim counterparts, made the sharia the basis of its legal system but it also embarked on selective modernization within this framework of divine law. Indeed, the religious idealism of the Ikhwan, and their opposition to western symbols of modernity such as the motor car and the telephone, had become too much of a liability for the new state, which defeated their attempted rebellion in 1929. Although the King set up a *Majlis al-Shura* (consultative council), its powers were never really exercised and were eventually emasculated.

The coastal areas of the Arabian peninsula had become British protectorates by the turn of the twentieth century. As they moved towards full independence, British support helped to establish and preserve conservative regimes who, like their Saudi neighbours, sought to create modern states politically acceptable to the West. In 1961 Kuwait became independent and the British withdrawal from the rest of the Gulf was completed by 1971 with the formation of the United Arab Emirates and the separate states of Oman, Qatar, and Bahrain. Only in Aden, which the British had left in 1968, were the local rulers deposed by nationalists who established the pro-Soviet People's Republic of Yemen (or South Yemen).

In Iran, the emerging modern nation-state followed a strictly secular path which played down the country's Muslim identity in favour of its pre-Islamic past. Ataturk's contemporary, Riza Shah (1878–1942) was a colonel in the Cossack brigade who seized power in 1921 and in 1925 made himself shah, founding the Pahlawi dynasty which revelled in the glories of Iran's Persian inheritance. In essence a military dictatorship, his rule brooked no opposition as he set out with the help of bulging oil revenues to centralize properly the state's authority and create a modern infrastructure for a secular Iran. But, despite the sweep of these reforms, most of the population did not feel that they benefited. On his abdication in 1941, forced by the British and the Russians because of his pro-Nazi sympathies, Riza Shah bequeathed to his young son a state that was top-heavy and overcentralized. The war had also strengthened nationalist resentment at western control of Iran's oil resources. In 1951, the prime minister, Dr Musaddeq, nationalized the oil industry to strengthen Iran's unity and independence. But the effect of an international boy-cott of Iranian oil dissolved Musaddeq's broad coalition of support and soon he was overthrown with foreign assistance. The shah returned from abroad and aligned Iran to the West even more firmly than before. The onward march of the modern secular state appeared relentless, spilling over into neighbouring Afghanistan, which became during the 1960s a constitutional monarchy. King Zahir Shah, following the example of the earlier Afghan ruler Aman Allah Khan (r.1919–29), now introduced development programmes incorporating administrative, educational, and social changes, but the impact of the reforms remained limited while offending conservative and religious opinion.

Pakistan stood out from the bulk of Muslim nation-states which emerged after 1920 by virtue of its deliberate creation as a home for the Muslims of the Indian subcontinent. As Indian independence approached, increasing numbers of Muslims feared the consequences of becoming a permanent minority in a Hindu-dominated Indian republic and gave their support to the Muslim League's campaign to secure some kind of separate Muslim state. The political circumstances of the Second World War enhanced the League's position, winning it vital support in provinces where Muslims formed a majority. These regions provided the territorial basis of the new 'Islamic state' in 1947 despite being divided by over 1,000 miles of Indian Republic. Religious appeals certainly helped to win Muhammad Ali Jinnah (1876–1948) enough votes to realize a separate political future for some of India's Muslims, however Pakistan's early rulers envisaged Pakistan as a modern secular state. Pakistan's first constitution, finally inaugurated in 1956, assigned religion a largely symbolic role. The modernizing policies of General Ayub Khan pushed Islam further into the background and Pakistan dropped albeit temporarily the 'Islamic' tag from its title between 1958 and 1963. Islam's failure to hold the country together was revealed most forcefully when in 1971 Pakistan's eastern wing broke away in a war of secession to become Bangladesh. A shared religion, it seemed, could not overcome differences of ethnicity, language, and culture or make up for the imbalance of political and economic power between East and West Pakistan.

Ethnic differences proved to be the main obstacle to Islam's chances of determining the character of Malaysia at independence. The fact that religious divisions followed ethnic lines very closely meant that, throughout the twentieth century, the strength of specifically 'Malay' ethnic demands continually checked the influence of Islamic reformism. As Malay Muslims found their majority at risk from a growing non-Muslim, primarily Chinese population, ethnicity rather than

Muhammad Ali Jinnah, who had almost single-handedly created Pakistan, stands with Lord Mountbatten, the Governor-General of India, outside the Constituent Assembly building, Karachi, on the first day of the state's existence, 15 August 1947. To Jinnah's right stands his sister, Fatimah, on Mountbatten's left is his wife, Lady Edwina. In the speech which Jinnah had just made to the Assembly he had emphasized that in the state of Pakistan religion was to be a private matter. Within a year popular protest had forced Pakistan's leaders to change tack. The precise role which Islam should play in public life has since been a major feature of political discourse.

Sukarno, leader of the Indonesian nationalist movement from the 1920s and president of the country from 1950 to 1966, addresses the Indonesian Party's convention in Jakarta under a massive picture of himself. Indonesia has by far the largest population of Muslims in the world. Although Muslim organizations have been involved in acts of violence – for instance, the slaughter of tens of thousands of communists after the coup of 1965 or terrorist activities in the late 1970s – Islam in Indonesia is renowned for its moderation and tolerant attitudes.

religion emerged as the primary source of political identity for most inhabitants of the peninsula. The leadership of the independence movement was assumed by the United Malay National Organization (UMNO), whose prime concern was to safeguard Malay communal interests vis-à-vis non-Malays. UMNO's commitment to Islam remained limited and it opposed the establishment of an Islamic state, choosing rather the aim of bringing communities together.

Leading political parties in neighbouring Indonesia were also consciously secular. Not facing the same ethnic divisions, they still had to contend with a variety of competing styles of Islamic adherence among the majority Muslim population. Secular groups led the fight to expel the Dutch in 1945–49 and the leadership which emerged at independence sought to distance itself from efforts to impose a legalist version of Islam on the country. The state's first president, Sukarno (1901–70), who called himself 'a convinced nationalist, a convinced Muslim, a convinced Marxist', urged, like Atatürk, that Islam should remain a private religion. Both Sukarno and his successor Suharto regarded Islam with considerable apprehension and caution, and tried to maintain Indonesia as a secular state in which the political activities of religious groups were strictly regulated. As a result the state managed to check Muslim political ambitions while rural ulama, reformers, and modernists continued to present a variety of Islamic opinion and practice to Indonesia's Muslims.

Not all Muslims had to obtain a separate independence in order to start thinking of themselves as nation-states. The consolidation of Soviet power in the 1920s ended any dreams Central Asian Muslims might have retained about achieving true self-determination. Stalin's insistence on central interests before regional ones clashed with their growing desire to be free of Soviet control. The Soviet system divided Central Asia into separate republics, based on ethnic and linguistic similarities, to forestall the growth of a pan-Muslim, pan-Turkic national movement. These Muslim societies developed on Soviet terms, which emphasized economic development, land reform, and mass educational and literacy campaigns. But the promotion of national culture was accompanied by efforts to undermine Islam behind both its public and private face. The Soviet Union's priorities were secularization, and political and economic assimilation, even when official policies on religion and culture were relaxed after Stalin's death in 1953, and the leaders of official Islam, in return for the opportunity to maintain a Muslim organization, became much more open in their backing for the Soviet regime. Sufi orders often provided a parallel Islam which distanced itself from the compromises of the ulama. During the 1970s attempts by the Soviet hierarchy to expand contacts with the wider Islamic world increased official interest in state-sponsored religious activity. But popular religious observance started to be officially accepted only after *glasnost*. The breakdown of the highly centralized Soviet system in the late 1980s pushed the Muslim republics, like their non-Muslim counterparts, into a limbo of semi-independence, in which 'national' differences still defined the physical boundaries between them but in which Islam looked set to play a much more prominent political role.

Bosnia's Muslims too developed their 'national' identity as one component of the federal state of Yugoslavia. These were Muslims of Slav, Croat, and Serb origins who converted to Islam during the 500 years of Ottoman rule in the Balkans. They had become identifiable as the landowning aristocracy of Bosnia, associated by class and religion not nationhood. After the Second World War, most Yugoslavian Muslims remained well integrated members of the wider communities to which they belonged. In 1961, a new official category of 'Muslims in an ethnic sense' was introduced by Tito's Communist government with the hope that this would halt any trend towards the formation of a distinct Muslim community. Gradually, however, some Bosnian Muslims reached a new definition of their political identity ironically encouraged by the government's recognition in 1972 that Bosnian Muslims represented a nationality with its own separate characteristics within the Yugoslavian multi-national state. It was not until much later, however, that the stronger sense of Bosnian identity -involving Catholic Croat and Orthodox Serbs as well – broke up in response to the Serb and Croat fight for spoils elsewhere. In the 1990s, as Yugoslavia tore itself apart, bloody confrontation replaced any lingering sense of collaboration between Bosnia's parts, confirming the separate 'national' identity of its Muslim community.

ISLAMISM

The extent to which the Muslim world has accommodated itself to western secular visions of progress has often been overshadowed during the late twentieth century by growing support among Muslims for so-called fundamentalist responses to the challenges arising from their encounter with the West. Militant Islam everywhere has raised its political profile. In many of the newly independent and overwhelmingly Muslim sub-Saharan states, for instance, Islam has become an important unifying force. In others such as Nigeria, a multi-religious state, it has been a source of division. Here, in the 1980s, heightened Muslim consciousness and social dislocation prompted by an oil boom encouraged a 'fundamentalist' streak of Muslim revivalism in the powerful northern provinces, which called for the introduction of the sharia.

The label 'fundamentalism', however, is not applied only to Islam, nor is it a particularly new one. It has also been attached to both radical and conservative schools of thought and often applied inaccurately to anything Muslim which

Sudanese women's forces go through their paces while the Islamic Conference organization meets in Khartoum, December 1993. In the 1980s the Sudanese government, under pressure from the moderate wing of the Muslim Brotherhood led by Dr Hasan al-Turabi, took a sharp turn in an Islamist direction. Quranic punishments were introduced and a total ban on alcohol was dramatically initiated with the pouring of thousands of bottles of beer, wine, and spirits into the Nile. Islamism has few problems with women participating in most areas of public life, provided that Islamic sensibilities are respected when they do so. The formation of women's fighting units such as these has been a feature of some aspects of Islamist assertion in the late twentieth century.

challenges what the West assumes to be progress. A better term, more accurately embodying what is distinctive about Muslim fundamentalism, would be 'Islamism'. Central to it is the notion of activism – creating a new religio-political order while preserving orthodox religious observances. It therefore appeals for reinterpretation of the sources of doctrine rather than the reassertion of traditional values. Islamism is definitely a twentieth-century phenomenon; it has not developed in a political vacuum. The pressing need to confront western ideas, and the dramatic changes which have taken place in many Muslim societies have encouraged some Muslims to demand the establishment of an Islamic system, a *nizam* as against the materially based systems of western capitalism and socialism. Islamism therefore does not represent a return to the past. Then the traditional Islamic view of government was limited to creating and maintaining the right conditions for Islam to flourish. Islamists, in contrast, usually consider, like the West, that government, with the enhanced power of the modernized state at its command, should exercise much greater responsibility for the people. This difference gives a distinctly modern look to the relationship between Islam and the state.

The Ikhwan al-Muslimin (Muslim Brotherhood), the leading Islamist force in the Middle East, was founded in Egypt in 1928 by Hasan al-Banna (1906–49) as 'a new soul in the heart of the nation'. It disagreed with traditional orthodoxy about modernization, which it neither accepted nor rejected but reinterpreted to fit an Islamic model. Leaders of 'official Islam' were 'parrots of the pulpits', out of touch with reality. Revivalist Islam was a means of overcoming social and economic injustice imposed by the 'secular' controllers of the state. Banna himself was, like many leaders of Islamist movements, not one of the ulama but a poorly paid schoolteacher in the provincial city of Ismailia; his supporters belonged to similar lower middle class backgrounds and were very often the recent urban migrants who were fuelling the rapid growth of Middle Eastern cities such as Cairo. At the end of 1948 the Egyptian government dissolved the Brotherhood for its involvement in the murder of the prime minister, Nuqrashi Pasha, and shortly afterwards Banna himself was assassinated. The dissolution led to the emigration of many Brothers, who spread their message to neighbouring Arab states. Equivalent parties grew in strength in Syria and Yemen with active support in Palestine and Transjordan. Despite activity in anti-British disturbances in the early 1950s, the Brotherhood was again suppressed in 1954 by the new Free Officers regime, disappearing from politics for at least a decade. Another purge in 1965 followed a second alleged plot to overthrow Nasser: its leader, Sayyid Qutb, was among the members executed by the authorities.

The Brotherhood gradually re-emerged in the more favourable circumstances of the 1970s when Nasser's successor Anwar Sadat (1918–81), sought to present a more Islamic image for his regime, exploiting Islamic symbols to build support against Communism and Nasser's followers. This change was closely related to Egypt's 1967 defeat by Israel which had sharpened dissatisfaction with secular nationalism and acted as a catalyst in the resurgence of Islam. Although Sadat encouraged the moderate leadership of the Brotherhood, its more extreme affiliates kept up the pressure for armed insurrection. By the early 1980s these two wings had come together to oppose the government's peace negotiations with Israel. In September 1981 Sadat rounded on the opposition, concentrating on Islamic militants and sympathetic army officers. One month later, he was

Nothing demonstrated the nature of the challenge levelled by Islamism against the secular leaders of Muslim states so graphically as the assassination of President Anwar Sadat of Egypt in 1981 as he reviewed a military parade celebrating the October War against Israel. The failure of the Camp David accords with Israel in 1978 to create a settlement acceptable to the Palestinians, and economic policies which had exposed Egypt to the full force of western capitalism, stimulated increasingly vocal opposition from Islamists. Sadat replied by arresting more than 1,500 opponents and purging the army of 200 officers friendly to the Muslim Brotherhood. The Islamists, led by Lieutenant Khaled Islambouli, the brother of one of those arrested, wreaked their vengeance at the parade stand.

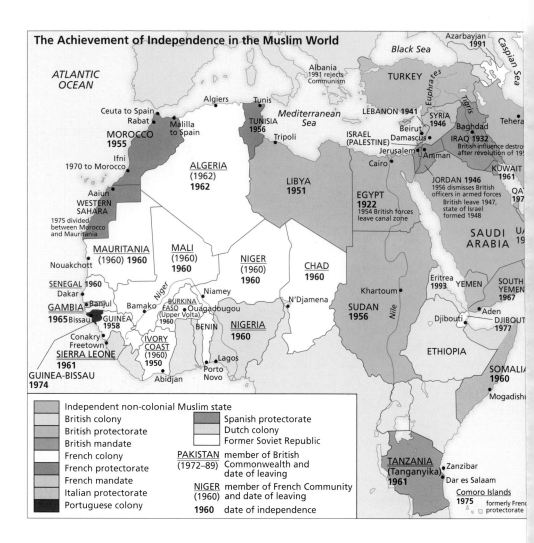

The Achievement of Independence in the Muslim World

assassinated by military supporters of a Brotherhood offshoot, the Takfir wal Hijra (Repentance and Flight from Sin). Under Hosni Mubarak, the Brotherhood has continued to press for the Islamization of Egyptian society. Elections in 1984 and 1987 demonstrated its political influence: Islam had become the chief source of opposition to the regime as militants accelerated attacks directly on the government and more indirectly against the symbols – often tourists – of the West.

In Syria, where Hafiz al-Asad's faction in the Baath Party had seized power at the end of 1970, the Muslim Brotherhood trod a similar path, joining forces in the 1980s with other Muslim parties to form an Islamic front against Asad's regime which was brutally suppressed in a military action which left much of the city of Hama destroyed. In North Yemen in 1988 a quarter of the elected seats on the state's consultative council were won by Muslim Brothers. Another major centre of Brotherhood activity was the Sudan where it campaigned after independence in 1956 for a permanent constitution based on the Quran and Sunna. This war of attrition contributed to President Numeiri's action in September 1983. Faced with

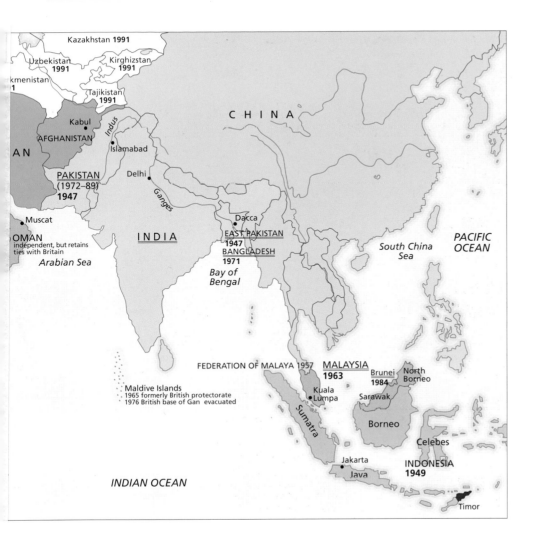

an economic crisis and serious erosion of his political base, he announced the introduction of Islamic law in its entirety. In Algeria, the late 1980s witnessed a determined challenge by Islamists who succeeded in unsettling the political equilibrium by winning in 1991, albeit temporarily, an electoral showdown with the country's secular rulers. Libya produced another variation on the theme when, following an army coup in 1969 which overthrew King Idris, the policies of Colonel Muammar Qaddafi – a modern technocrat – combined correct Islamic practice with Arab socialism to produce a 'Third Way' of 'Islamic socialism' that was highly revolutionary. Qaddafi's insistence on the Quran as the sole source of legitimacy denied the authority of the hadiths and earned the enmity of more traditional Muslim states such as Saudi Arabia.

The Indian subcontinent saw its own versions of Islamism emerge. In Pakistan, the Jamaat-e Islami (Islamic Society), founded in 1941 and led by Mawlana Abul Ala Mawdudi (1903–79), reversed its earlier opposition to the creation of a separate nation-state for India's Muslims and called for the construction of a truly

Benazir Bhutto campaigns in the Pakistani province of the Punjab. One of the paradoxes of the period of the rise of Islamism, which on the whole is opposed to women political leaders, is that it has also been the time when women have become premiers of Muslim states. Benazir Bhutto was the first to achieve this status in 1989. Since then she has been followed by Khalida Zia in Bangladesh and Tansu Ciller in Turkey.

Islamic society with Islamic government, banking, and economic institutions. Like Sayyid Qutb in Egypt, Mawdudi's totalitarian vision condemned western notions of political sovereignty as denying God's authority on earth and, like the Brotherhood, the Jamaat drew support from the fast-expanding cities whose inhabitants, often former migrants from India, were disillusioned with the new Pakistani state. The prime minister Zulfiqar Ali Bhutto (1926–79), leader of the populist Pakistan Peoples' Party, declared Pakistan an 'Islamic Socialist Republic' in 1973 as a way of keeping Islamism at arm's length but dissatisfaction with his policies encouraged a drift to religio-political alternatives. This opposition mainly gave its support to General Zia ul-Haq (1924–88) after he seized power in 1977.

Strongly influenced by the Jamaat, Zia embarked on Islamization which confirmed the sharia as the supreme law of the land. His own strongly held religious views, however, did not disguise the political motives at the root of these policies on Islam: he firmly believed that Pakistan's political system had to be Islamized in order to forge an ostensible national unity. This task was eased by events in Afghanistan where his support for *mujahidin* resistance to the Soviet-backed Kabul government after 1979 helped to bring him substantial western backing. Despite attempts at Islamization during this period, electoral success for religio-political parties such as the Jamaat remained limited. However, the strength of general religious sentiment persuaded subsequent governments, including that led by the world's first Muslim woman prime minister, Benazir Bhutto, of the pitfalls in seeking to amend the Islamic status quo.

All Muslim societies, majority or minority, came by the late 1970s to contain an Islamist wing. Everywhere there were Muslims striving to purify their communities of the taint of westernization and to restructure them along more consciously Islamic lines. Even in Saudi Arabia, renowned for the conservatism of its rulers, the Islamist opposition movement had emerged by the 1990s as the main challenge to the existing order. But it was in Iran that the secular western mould was broken most spectacularly. Its revolution of 1978–79 appeared to sum up Muslim rejection of western-style modernization. The identification between the state and Islamism in post-revolution Iran also meant that Iran came to be regarded as the prime mover in the Islamist network that forms an element of the politics of Muslims everywhere, and this in spite of Shia-Sunni sectarian differences.

The Iranian revolution was a hybrid incorporating secular left-wing opposition to the Shah's regime as well as the Shiite clerics whose religious teachings determined the nature of the new Iranian state. One persistent critic of the Shah's secularizing policies was Ayatollah Khomeini (1902–89) who had long rejected the quietist stand of many of his fellow ulama by condemning the Pahlawi regime in colourful terms: 'all the idiotic words that have proceeded from the brain of that illiterate soldier [Riza Shah] are rotten…Only the law of God…will remain and resist the ravages of time'. His call for Iranians to rise up in 1963 led to his exile in Iraq but did not stop his voice of opposition, which with the help of tape recorder and telephone was still heard back in Iran.

Dissatisfaction with the Shah's policies grew as modernization gathered speed. 'Mushrooming' cities, as economic circumstances in spite of oil revenues deteriorated, spawned increasing numbers of Iranians whose disillusionment with the regime was intense. The opposition now included Iranians with western educations, who were influenced by the writings of Dr Ali Shariati (1933–77) which used central Islamic symbols and principles to express radical themes of social justice flagrantly violated by the regime of the Shah. By 1979, the Shah had fled and Khomeini had returned triumphant. In the aftermath, the ulama gained complete control as their secular allies fell by the political wayside. Khomeini's view that the purpose of government was to apply the law of God meant that the sharia became the law of the land with the provision that 'the religious expert and no one else…should occupy himself with the affairs of government'. Public adherence to the stated norms of Muslim behaviour meant the compulsory veiling of women and other symbols of propriety. The bloody Gulf war with Iraq between 1980 and 1988 unified the country politically but made the task of governing more difficult because of its colossal human and material cost.

Khomeini's death enabled the Iranian authorities to become more flexible with the outside world but the Teheran government remained a potent inspiration for movements and Muslims with similar aims elsewhere in the world. Its decision to uphold Khomeini's fatwa condemning to death the author of *The Satanic Verses* provided leadership for those Muslims who objected in principle to Salman Rushdie's novel. More specifically, it assisted Islamist groups to achieve high public profiles, particularly in the troubled political arena of the Middle East. Militant

organizations such as Hizballah (Party of God) dominated the headlines in the Lebanon, while Iran was able to exploit hostility between secularists and Muslim activists among Palestinians. Islamic Jihad and Hamas (the Islamic Resistance Movement) were obvious targets for Iranian backing, and the extent of their support was revealed in the remarkable *intifadah* (uprising) of Palestinian youth after 1987. Here the Iranian revolution offered practical and moral support, just as it has done for Islamists in places as far apart as North America, Britain, Yugoslavia, Nigeria, India, and the Philippines.

ISLAM AS A CONTEMPORARY WORLD PRESENCE

The two centuries since 1800 have marked an important break with earlier times for the Muslim world. The vast empires so characteristic of it before this period disappeared from the map. Muslims, who formerly had ruled so many non-Muslims, more often than not instead found themselves being ruled by non-believers. With the decline of western imperialism, Muslims reacquired much of their political independence, but the result has been a patchwork of separate states, each one trying, with varying success, to balance its religious and national identities. For some, Islam and political life were inexorably intertwined. For others, their citizens, or perhaps only some of them, just happened to be Muslims and the state tried to maintain a neutrality on the question of religion. Hereditary monarchs, democracy, theocracy, dictatorship, military rule, radical revolution – the Islamic world has experienced it all since 1800.

The most striking thing about the contemporary Muslim world therefore has to be its diversity. Statistics confirm this: only about one in four of today's 1,000 million Muslims live in the Middle East. Indonesia has the world's largest Muslim population; more Muslims live in South Asia than in the whole Middle East; even the former Soviet Union had a larger number of Muslim citizens than any Middle Eastern country save Turkey. Indeed, Muslims now very often represent one element in a rich mosaic of different peoples living side by side. Thanks to decolonization and migration patterns since the Second World War, Europe now possesses a much bigger Muslim population, communities forming permanent strands in the fabric of western society. Organizations such as the Muslim Parliament in Britain and the Islamic Society of North America (ISNA) reflect the growing claims of sections of these Muslims who, as they have put down roots in their new homes, have become much more assertive over issues such as Islamic education where state and community interact.

Not surprisingly, the Middle East continues to dominate popular perceptions about Islam and Muslim society. Apart from the fact that the religion emerged and developed here, Arabic, the language of Islam and the Quran, retains its emotional hold as a sacred liturgical language, despite the widespread availability of religious guidance in the vernacular. In addition, from a western perspective, the Middle East was where Europe first encountered Islam. The Middle East's oil wealth has

Ayatollah Khomeini dominated the Iranian revolution of 1979 and the minds of many of those who experienced the first decade of the revolutionary regime up to his death in 1989, as this work by the young artist Mostafa Goodarzi clearly suggests. Shia Islam has always had a powerful iconographic tradition and this was harnessed with vigour to serve the purposes of the revolution.

Islam in the West

It is one of history's ironies that the Christian West, after spending more than a millennium trying first to hold back the expansion of Islam in Europe and then to drive the Muslims out, should in the nineteenth and twentieth centuries have assisted in establishing their presence. In Britain, France, and Germany, Muslims came after the Second World War to seek work in economies which were short of labour. In the USA and Canada they came to societies eager to attract the best of the world's talent and enterprise to their shores. Only in the Balkans, where Albania, Bulgaria, and the states of the former Yugoslavia have significant Muslim populations, is their presence the result of earlier Muslim conquest. These Muslim peoples of the Balkans are in the main the outcome of conversion to Islam. Indeed, wherever Islam has established a presence it has usually succeeded in winning adherents from the host society. Most striking in this respect has been the USA where the number of Muslims has grown by a factor of six since 1971. Many American Blacks have converted to Islam as a means of rediscovering a lost African identity, and the progress of the faith has become closely linked with their struggle for civil rights. Prominent in the process has been the Nation of Islam founded in 1930, in which Elijah Muhammad (d.1975) and Malcolm X (d.1965) were leading figures. Currently, under Louis Farrakhan the organization attacks white racism and seeks separate development for Blacks.

Where Muslims are established in the West their presence has often led in recent years to key questions being asked of the societies in which they dwell. In the former Yugoslavia, where Muslims were recognized as a separate nationality in 1972, the emergence of a Muslim political identity in the 1980s has helped to destroy the political consensus under which the province of Bosnia-Herzegovina was governed. In Britain and France, Muslim demands for respect for their identity, whether it be to extend the blasphemy laws to non-Christian religions in the former, or that Muslim girls should be permitted to wear headscarves at school in the latter, have raised issues about the values of these societies and their future direction. The importance of such issues, moreover, is not restricted to these societies. Muslims regard the respect with which their co-religionists are treated by the states of the West as an indication of the respect with which they are likely to be treated by these states in the world at large.

Significant Muslim populations in the West.
Country/Number of Muslims/% of Total Population

Europe		
Albania	2,275,000	70.0%
Belgium	250,000	2.5%
Bulgaria	1,200,000	13.0%
France	2/3,500,000	4.4/6.1%
Germany	1,700,000	2.1%
Greece	120,000	1.2%
Italy	150,000	0.3%
Netherlands	350,000	2.3%
Spain	300,000	0.8%
UK	1,500,000	2.7%
Former		
Yugoslavia	4,500,000	21.1%
Bosnia	2,000,000	
Kosovo	2,000,000	
Other areas	500,000	

Americas		
Argentina	370,000	1.1%
Brazil	500,000	0.3%
Canada	350,000	1.3%
Guyana	130,000	13.0%
Surinam	150,000	30.0%
USA	6,000,000	2.4%

A key issue in Europe has been the extent to which religious Muslims are allowed to assert their preferences as they move within the spaces controlled by the state. A manifestation of this issue has been the dispute in France over whether Muslim girls might wear headscarves in school or not. Here in 1993 a headmaster, Jean Demestoy, forbids his Muslim pupil, Fouzia Aoukili, from entering the Xavier-Bichat high school in Nantua, eastern France.

reinforced its disproportionate importance by seeming to anchor the Muslim centre of gravity ever more firmly here. But the late twentieth century reassertion of
Muslim identity and confidence in Islam has been matched by the rekindling of
the pan-Islamic spirit and the emergence of international organizations which
reflect the changed relationship between the Middle East and Muslims elsewhere
in the world.

Both the Rabetat al-alam al-Islami (World Muslim League), a religious organization set up in 1962, and the Islamic Conference, established in 1969 as a permanent political organization by King Faysal of Saudi Arabia (r.1964–75),
maintain their headquarters in the heart of the Middle East. But their member-
ships stretch right around the Muslim world: the Islamic Conference possesses
more than forty member states with leading officials who have come from countries as far apart as Malaysia and Senegal. Even OPEC has played a part in this
regenerated sense of pan-Islamic cooperation with 11 out of its 13 members in the
mid-1970s effectively Muslim states, including non-Arab Nigeria, Gabon, and
Indonesia. Similarly, the Teheran authorities have been able, with the help of Iran's
oil resources, to establish international Islamic organizations which have been in
direct competition with their Saudi-sponsored counterparts.

Yet, while it has proved relatively easy to express pan-Islamic sentiment, to
maintain a consistent common front has been much more difficult. Even in relation to Israel, political forces in the Middle East, following the lead of Egypt, have
in recent years been willing to consider a compromise solution, and a purely religious solidarity has been hard to maintain. The 1990–91 Gulf war, which pitched
Iraq against the West, further fractured the Muslim world as different states lined
up on opposing sides of the divide. The Gulf crisis revealed, as other recent periods of tension had demonstrated, the divisions which still exist within the Muslim world despite the very obvious solidarity that holds it together. This diversity
and unity was highlighted in the early 1990s amid much anguish by the plight of
Bosnian Muslims who had little choice, thanks to the civil war tearing their country apart, but to accept being evacuated half way round the world to new homes
in Muslim states such as Malaysia. Culturally, these two societies are worlds apart.
They are linked, however, by their Muslim heritage.

PART 2

CHAPTER 5

K. N. Chaudhuri

The Economy in Muslim Societies

THE TRANSOCEANIC ECONOMY

In popular imagination, Islam was a religion of the desert which arose in the oasis towns of Syria, Iraq, and Egypt in the seventh century AD. Of course, neither Mecca nor Medina, the twin cities of the Prophet Muhammad, really belonged to the desert or the bedouin nomadic way of life. The Umayyad military victories in Iraq, Syria, Egypt, and Iran within a decade of Muhammad's death in 632 produced immediate and tangible results, the most notable of which was the consolidation of the two transcontinental trade routes through the Red Sea and the Persian Gulf. The economic foundation of the Muslim world system created by the Umayyads and the Abbasids in the first century of Islam rested on three factors: settled agriculture, urbanization, and long-distance trade. Nomadism and its economy had provided the backdrop to the early Arab expansion and they were not entirely marginalized in the development of urbanized Islam. The bedouin of Arabia did not give up their nomadic way of life; the desert and the camel continued to signify certain aspects of Islam and certainly to signify the context of its movements. Anyone who contemplates the magnificent mihrab of the Great Mosque in Cordoba built in the eight century, with its pure Arab geometry, must be aware that the historical roots of the Islamic world were already strong by the Umayyad and Abbasid periods. But those political leaders and their Arab followers who did migrate to the old and new towns to adopt an urban life soon revived the economic unity of the ancient world, which had been lost with the decline of Rome and Persia.

The diffusion of Islam as a social and cultural structure, besides its religious and spiritual vitality, carried with it a distinct material life, expressed through food, clothing, architecture, objects, and artefacts. These materials were of course implicated in the economic underpinning of Islam. The identity between the two could clearly be seen through the perception and control of space. Ahmad Ibn-Majid al-Najdi, one of the most famous Arab navigators of all time, wrote in his scientific treatise in the second half of the fifteenth century that the Red Sea was the most dangerous of all the seas in the world and yet people sailed on it more than in any other ocean that covered the earth. According to Ibn Majid, people used the Red Sea because of the Ancient House of God and the pilgrimage of the Prophet, and because the inhabitants of the Hijaz and the faithful of the annual hajj caravans alike had to be supplied with food and means of subsistence. The Hijaz, the middle coastline of the Arabian peninsula in the Red Sea, was almost barren land. The southwest monsoon winds which brought rains and agricultural

Preceding page A mural from an Egyptian village. In western and southern Egypt villagers commission paintings such as these for the outer walls of their houses to celebrate their performance of the pilgrimage to Mecca.

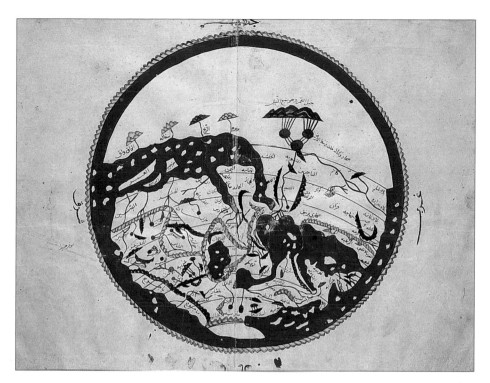

The broad reach of the Islamic world system and the trading networks which crossed it encouraged the emergence of geography as a subject of study. Amongst the first to apply scientific method to studies of the known world was the Arab al-Idrisi (1100–66), who was born at Ceuta (Morocco) and studied at Cordoba. Most of his adult years were spent in the service of the Norman King Roger II of Sicily at Palermo. This map of the world is derived from an encyclopaedic work he produced under Roger's patronage, the *Kitab al-Rujari*, the 'Book of Roger'.

prosperity to the lands of the Yemen and Oman seldom reached the Hijaz. The coming and going of the Egyptian grain fleets bearing the gifts of the Nile, together with the ships which came from other parts of the Indian Ocean, was an economic and social necessity which the 'miracle' of Islam created at the epicentre of the spiritual empire. As long as Mecca and Medina retained the allegiance of Muslims, pilgrims had to converge on the Red Sea from the four points of the compass. Ocean-going ships – capable of carrying hundreds of passengers – camel caravans, merchant houses, and trade fairs contributed to the movement and well-being of an astonishingly large number of people each year. Arabs had always excelled in controlling the landscape of the desert. For them to learn how to exercise a similar command over oceanic space was a new skill developed by political and economic expansion.

The combination of local geography, global climate (as evinced by the monsoon winds), and the social conventions of Islam undoubtedly gave the Red Sea its historical importance. Yet that was not the whole story. Ibn Majid's work demonstrated beyond question that the navigation and trade associated with the Red Sea and the Persian Gulf was part of a much larger structure which included not only the caravan journeys across the sand dunes of the Nafud and the stony wastes of the Syrian and Iraqi desert but also voyages across the Indian Ocean and the Mediterranean. Historically, the Muslim world was a civilization of both the West and the East. It absorbed as much the Mediterranean economies and societies of Byzantium and Rome as it did those of imperial Iran. Basra, one of the

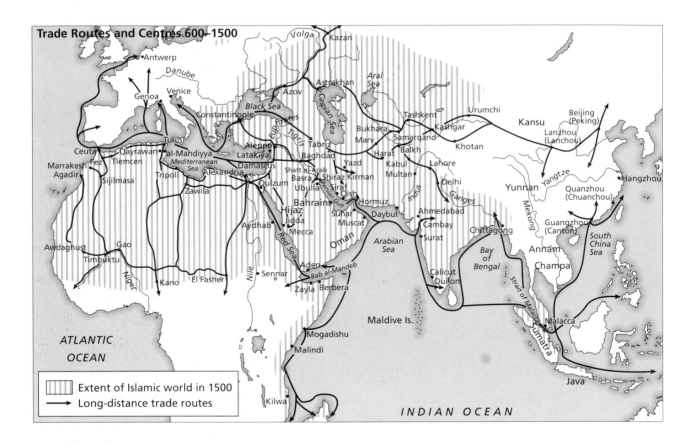

earliest Islamic cities outside the Arabian peninsula, was founded not only through nomadic expansion but also because it was a port which served both the desert grazing grounds and the rich canal-irrigated lands of Mesopotamia.

Arab control of the Persian Gulf, the Red Sea, and the eastern Mediterranean placed at the disposal of the caliphate the nautical skills of the seafaring people of Bahrain, Oman, and the Coptic shipbuilders of Egypt. A Muslim fleet soon emerged in the Mediterranean which could challenge the formidable sea power of Byzantium. By 674 the sea walls of Constantinople itself were under Arab siege, though the city successfully resisted all Muslim attacks until 1453. When Damascus became the capital of the newly founded Arab Empire in about 660, there was a distinct economic shift that operated in favour of Iraq and Syria, benefiting Basra and other towns in Iraq. When Baghdad was founded in 762 by the Abbasid caliph al-Mansur, trade in the Persian Gulf received an even greater impetus. By this time, the caliphate included the maritime province of Sind in India, most of Iran and Iraq, Syria, Egypt, and north Africa as far as the Atlantic coast of Morocco. The conquest of Andalusia and large parts of Iberia brought the Muslims into proximity with a Christian and Frankish Europe that was to produce a lasting influence on both social perceptions and the exchange of technology.

During the Umayyad caliphate, the immediate problem for the rulers of the newly conquered provinces was to establish a uniform system of land taxes, followed by reform of the chaotic currency and monetary systems. As the four-teenth century Moroccan historian Ibn Khaldun reminds us, the early Arab rulers never forgot the celebrated dictum ascribed to the Iranian model king Anushir-wan (Khusraw I, 531-79): that royal authority rested on the army, the army on money, money through taxes, taxes through cultivation, cultivation through jus-tice, officials, and the quality of political advice. The growth of economic produc-tion and consumption in the enlarged market of the Muslim world was made possible by three parallel developments. First, the Islamization of the conquered people created a partially homogenous religion, moral, and juridical system. Sec-ondly, the Arabization of the army and the administration helped to break down ethnic and national barriers by recruiting local entrants or by the incorporation of the warlike steppe people. Finally, the Semitization process was completed through the adoption of Arabic as the universal language of communication, edu-cation, literary expression, and government. The linguistic mastery over the sub-ject people, even in the case of the Iranians, who had by far the strongest cultural identity in the caliphate, was a remarkable triumph for the Muslim conquerors.

The geographical and commercial significance of Muslim unification was not lost on contemporary writers. Al-Muqaddasi, perhaps the most perceptive and thoughtful Arab geographer with extensive first-hand knowledge of the world of Islam, observed c.980 that the sun set on the extreme side of the territory into the Atlantic, the all-encircling ocean. In the east, the Arabian peninsula was sur-rounded by the Sea of China, as Arab geographers described the Indian Ocean. The Mediterranean they called the Sea of Rome. And it was China rather than India or the islands of Java and Sumatra which identified the great eastern sea in Arab minds, because Muslim shipbuilders, sailors, navigators, merchants, and geographers knew that the same sea which touched the landing jetties of Suez and Basra also stretched as far as China, providing a maritime highway to the Pacific, just as the Mediterranean was a highway to the Atlantic. Indeed, by the time Baghdad was founded, Arab merchants and sailors had already accumulated nearly half a century's experience of sailing to China and India. A sizeable colony of Arab and Iranian merchants traded with and lived in the imperial port city of Canton. Each year not only Arab merchants but also those from Frankish Europe sailed east towards India from Suez, Jidda, and Basra. This transoceanic and transcontinental trade, originating in China and terminating in western Europe, had begun in ancient times. In the fourth century BC the Greeks of Alexan-dria already knew the sailing route across the Indian Ocean. Muslim sailors were aware that the Red Sea carried dangers which could be fatal to ships. Long, uninterrupted coral reefs with branches extending far into the open sea obstructed the coastlines. To find a safe pas-

Items were traded across vast distances. One of the notable goods traded over a long period was Chinese porcelain. Muslim potters responded to the techniques and styles of the Chinese. This ninth-century bowl from Iraq belongs to a group which dis-plays Chinese influence in their low feet, flowing sides, and everted rims. It is deco-rated in blue kufic with the single Arabic word 'blessing'.

sage through these reefs and shoals, to master the local winds often blowing up into sudden squalls and gales, and to arrive at a port with ship, crew, and cargo intact needed both courage and exceptional seacraft. The Persian Gulf, less dangerous than the Red Sea, had its own hazards: lack of safe harbours, shortage of drinking water, and the vast marshland at the entrance to the rivers Tigris and Euphrates, the twin waterways to the cities of ancient Mesopotamia. The caravan trade, whether from Aden up the steep escarpments to the valleys of the Yemen or across the Syrian desert to the Mediterranean ports, needed careful planning in order to secure water and food supplies and the support of the nomadic tribes, who guarded the caravans in return for a financial indemnity. In spite of all these dangers and difficulties, maritime trade continued to flow through the area for two millennia, supplemented by the equally hazardous caravan journeys across almost waterless deserts. Why was it so? All through the ages, the great products of civilization – silk, porcelain, spices, incense, fine horses, and precious objects of all kinds – joined with the humbler necessities of daily life – food grains, fuel, timber, and cooking oils – have enabled towns and cities not just to live but to exist against the dictates of pure geography and economics.

MARITIME TRADE TO THE EIGHTEENTH CENTURY

The Roman natural historian and geographer Pliny complained that the trade of India, China, and Arabia drained at least 100 million sesterces every year from the Empire in imported luxuries. His long descriptions of the ancient trade in frankincense and myrrh grown in the mountains of southern Arabia and Ethiopia reveal how a single item of long-distance trade can play an indispensable role in the religious and social life of an entire empire. Incense remained a sought-after and rare commodity – few religious rituals could be performed in India and China without the burning of incense – which sustained the seaborne trade of both the Indian Ocean and the Mediterranean. At the foundation of Islam in the seventh century this transit trade of southern Arabia included an active and long-established flow of precious metals among the three continents of Europe, Asia, and Africa. The camel masters of the Quraysh tribe, to which the Prophet belonged, knew how to deal in gold and silver, both of which moved both eastwards and westwards. It was in the commercial buildings of the ancient cities of Arabia, Syria, and Egypt that bankers from Spain, Italy and north Africa engaged in the trans-Saharan gold trade, met to do business with bankers trading to India and China.

In the post-Islamic centuries the commercial traffic which passed through Basra, Jidda, and Suez followed the caravan routes which had probably existed from antiquity, although ancient desert emporia such as Petra and Jerash had long since fallen into ruins. Goods were unloaded from ships at Qulzum, at the upper end of the Red Sea, and were despatched on camels to Fustat (Old Cairo) and to Alexandria. In the Persian Gulf, the deep-berthed ocean-going ships discharged

The Seaport

From the early days of Islamic expansion, the seaport was vital to Muslim economies and civilization. In the Red Sea, Jidda, the maritime gateway to Mecca, rose to prominence as a result of the pilgrimage to Mecca, the *hajj*, undertaken by devout Muslims from Egypt, Africa, India, and later from the Malay archipelago. Through prosperous and difficult times, Jidda remains a focal point of both the pilgrim and the trader. Each year with the arrival of ships from Egypt, Iran, and India, local and foreign merchants engaged in commercial transactions of considerable value, selling linen from Damietta, cotton textiles woven in Gujarat, luxury Iranian carpets, and many other goods from Africa, Southeast Asia, and Europe. As the Arab military leaders moved into Iraq in the middle of the seventh century, Basra was founded to become the second great port in the Muslim world.

First, Basra was a military garrison with good access to the desert routes and grazing grounds for the bedouin camels. Soon its situation at the mouth of the rivers Euphrates and Tigris and its easy passage to the open sea attracted a large number of merchants who traded with Oman, the Yemen, and India. In the tenth century ship captains from Basra and the neighbouring port of Siraf on the Iranian coast sailed as far as the Straits of Malacca and Sunda in the Indonesian archipelago and even to the ports of southern China. On the Mediterranean, the strength of Alexandria as a port of trade revived with the expansion and economic unification of the Sea of Rome with that of India. The Muslim seaport was first and foremost a spontaneous urban creation with only minimal intervention from rulers. However, it was widely recognised that international merchants needed a special form of protection which guaranteed both their personal safety and the security of the goods. This was achieved by the minimum rate of customs duty being imposed on trade and by enacting strict laws for maritime contracts. The seaports were governed by high state officials with subordinate officers supervising the dockyards, warehouses, and the sale of commodities. There was a sophisticated infrastructure including a regulated currency, banking facilities, and standardized weights and measures.

The harbour of Muscat which, with the exception of Aden, is the finest natural harbour in Arabia. Traders sailed to and from here as they participated in the trading networks of the Indian Ocean. Conquered and burned by Albuquerque in 1507, it remained in Portuguese hands for a century and a half – their forts guarding the harbour can still be seen, that of Marani to the left and Jalali to the right. Most visitors to the port complained of the heat, including a fifteenth-century Iranian who talked of how roasted fowl fell out of the air and boiled fish could be scooped out of the sea. On the other hand, they also reflected on the humility and urbanity of its inhabitants.

their cargo either at Ubulla or Basra onto river boats. While the towns and cities of Mesopotamia absorbed a large amount of the goods from India, Java, Sumatra, and China, those for the Mediterranean markets were forwarded from the upper Euphrates by camel caravans to Aleppo and Damascus. During the trading season, Alexandria and the ports of Syria – Antioch, Latakiya, Tripoli, Byblos, Sidon, Tyre, and Acre – were crowded with ships belonging to Greek and Italian merchants as well as those of Muslim north Africa. But the Arabian peninsula together with Egypt, Syria, and Iraq was the core of a world system that was economic as well as spiritual. North and east Africa, parts of Anatolia, India, and Central Asia were historically important but belonged to the periphery, and the islands of Southeast Asia were incorporated in the Muslim world only in the fifteenth century and even then conversion remained incomplete.

While the Mediterranean trade was largely shared between the Muslims and Christians, in the Indian Ocean Arab and Persian shipmasters rapidly established themselves as commercial carriers over oceanic routes. Their maritime exploits in the South China Sea were recorded by Buzurg Ibn Shahriyar (c.900–53), whose accounts of these voyages, often told as fantastic sea stories, bring to light a remarkable feature of Arab trade from the late seventh century: Muslim ships sailing out of the strait of Hormuz and out of Bab al-Mandeb in the Red Sea went all the way to China, returning two or three years later with silk, porcelain, jade, and other rare goods whose high value in the Middle Eastern markets made such lengthy and hazardous journeys worthwhile. Some Muslim traders lessened the risks by taking on Far Eastern cargo at Southeast Asian ports. About 916, the Arab encyclopaedist al-Masudi visited many countries bordering the Indian Ocean and noted that ships from the west, from Siraf and Oman, met those from the Far East at a port called Kalah Bar in the Malayan archipelago. He also described the Muslim merchants from Oman, Siraf, Basra, and Baghdad who had married and settled in Indian ports.

A single voyage from Arabia to China not only meant extended stop-overs in safe anchorage while the monsoon winds shifted, but it also imposed considerable constraints on the mixture of cargo and the margin of profit. Most ships, in the Indian Ocean as well as the Mediterranean, needed heavy ballast goods complementing their cargo of high-value fine items in order to stabilize the vessel. As the level of consumption and the sophistication of market operations increased in the Middle East with the growth of urban centres, single round voyages to China and back through the Strait of Malacca and Sunda were gradually replaced by that of emporia trading. The wealthy merchants of Fustat, Jidda, Aden, Suhar, and Siraf no longer traded directly with Guangzhou (Canton) and Hangzhou; instead, they stopped at Quilon and Calicut on the Malabar coast, or in the ports of Johore, Sumatra, Java, and Annam. But their transoceanic trade was also affected by political and social conditions in the regions surrounding the Persian Gulf and the Red Sea.

الفـــــ ن تم ربعـد اساطيـر بلدهـا و ذخارف جلـهـا وفـا ل ازكبـوا فيها بسم الله مجرها

ومسا هات ... ة نفس نفر المعمبر ا و عباد الله للذكر مين وقا ل اما انا

The peoples of the Muslim world traded on water from the Mediterranean through to the China Sea. From the eighth to the sixteenth centuries Arabs and Persians dominated the trading routes of the Indian Ocean. Here an illustration to the twelfth-century *Maqamat* of al-Hariri shows a boat sailing from Oman to the great port of Basra. Note that the crew are apparently Indian and the passengers Arab.

The military uprising of the African slaves working in the sugar plantations of lower Iraq around the marshes of Shatt al-Arab between 868 and 883 severely disrupted the commercial traffic of Basra. By the early tenth century, Baghdad and the Abbasid empire were faced with a crisis of social identity, expressed in the growth of religious dissension and bloody internal conflicts. The conquest of Egypt in 969 by the Fatimid dynasty of north Africa and their claim to the spiritual headship of Islam further weakened the Abbasid caliphate. The Red Sea route began to attract the attention and the economic preference of the leading Indian Ocean merchants which raised Aden, Jidda, Aydhab, Qulzum, Alexandria, and Cairo to a new level of power. Their ascendancy would continue into the period of Venetian trade with Egypt and up to the arrival of the Portuguese in Calicut in 1498. How-

Knowledge of the heavens was central to the capacity of Muslim merchants to steer a course by sea. A major tool in using the heavens as a guide was the astrolabe. This plani-spherical version was made in Safawid Iran by two crafts-people from Yazd. On the front suspension bracket is this quotation from the Quran, Sura 36, verses 38–40:

And the sun – it runs to a fixed
  resting place;
that is the ordaining of the All-
  mighty, the All-knowing.
And the moon – we have determined it by stations,
till it returns like an aged palm-
  bough.
It behoves not the sun to over-
  take the moon, neither
does the night outstrip the day,
each swimming in a sky.

ever, the leading ports in the Persian Gulf continued to serve the caravan trade which covered the huge area from the coast to the oasis towns of Transoxania.

Increasing specialization in shipping and navigation only through the Red Sea and the Persian Gulf meant that the main centres of redistributive trade shifted outside these two seas. Furthermore, as ports of trade, both Basra and Jidda had several disadvantages. The known hazards of the seas and the local winds dis-couraged the ships from the other side of the Indian Ocean from stopping too long in the area. The prospect of missing the monsoon winds was one which few ship captains and their owners were prepared to contemplate. Then there was the dif-ficult channel of Shatt al-Arab. It was much more convenient for the large deep-sea vessels to discharge their cargo at Siraf and Aden. Gradually, other centres of trade emerged both in the Persian Gulf and the Arabian Sea. Siraf was followed by Qish, Hormuz, and Suhar in Oman. Bahrain handled the local trade on the Ara-bian coast of the gulf. The commercial traffic of Aden was supported by Raysut in the Hadramawt and by the two ports in the Horn of Africa, Zayla and Berbera, and those further down the coast such as Mogadishu, Kilwa, and Malindi.

From the mid-tenth to the fifteenth century, Islamic trade in the Indian Ocean and the South China Sea was restructured into three segments based on Aden and Hormuz, Cambay and Calicut, and Malacca and Guangzhou. In the first area, already by al-Muqaddasi's time in the 980s, Mecca, Jidda, Suhar, and Bahrain were large trading towns that handled a range of commodities, both local products and imported items; and in the fifteenth century the commercial life of the two great eastern cities of Cambay in India and Malacca in Southeast Asia turned on the emporia trade of Aden and Hormuz. Many other lesser towns and cities in the Red Sea and the Persian Gulf were equally flourishing and prosperous. Exported lux-ury items such as frankincense, myrrh, scent distilled from rose petals (attar), pure-bred horses, gold brocades, silk piece-goods, fine carpets, and high-quality swords and personal armaments appeared on the ships' bills of lading along with heavy bulk goods – dates, fresh and dried fruits, leather, coffee, rock salt from Hormuz, and dried fish. Importing regions in the Mediter-ranean, India, east Africa, Southeast Asia, and China paid for these famous products with their own exports: gold and silver, fine woollen textiles, and metalware from Europe; gold, ivory, timber, and foodstuffs from east Africa; cotton textiles, precious stones, wheat, rice, and sugar from India; spices, black pepper, sandal-wood, tortoise-shells, and gold from Malacca, Java, Sumatra, and the Spice Islands; porcelain, silk piece-goods, tea, and cam-phor from China. The composition and volume of Middle East-ern exports clearly depended on the economic specialization both in and outside the exporting regions. Egyptian linen weavers and Indian cotton weavers supplied large quantities of fine and ordinary cloth to the Muslim markets. Each year from the 1430s to the 1730s the

An incense burner in the shape of a lion from Iran, of the tenth or eleventh century. Metal goods were among the most important possessions for Muslims of this time for use both inside and outside the home. Hence they were valuable trade items, as was incense itself.

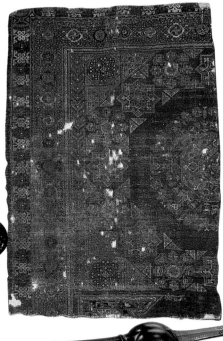

Fine carpets were among the items traded: this fragment of a Mamluk carpet dates from the late fifteenth century. The workshops of Cairo were particularly productive from the fifteenth to the seventeenth centuries, exporting carpets not only to the Muslim world but also to Europe. Carpets from the Mamluk era are notable for their geometric designs.

A damascened sword from eighteenth-century India. Damascening was a form of steel ornamentation developed in Damascus

silk producers of Ahmedabad in India were commissioned to manufacture a brocade covering for the Kaaba in the sacred mosque of Mecca; nearly all centres of silk weaving in the Middle East competed for the same honour.

The extent and influence of maritime trade in the urban life of the Muslim world is revealed in the business papers of a group of Mediterranean merchants who migrated from Tunisia first to Cairo and then to all the main port towns of the western Indian Ocean. These papers, known as the Cairo Geniza records, and other sources often mention a commercial association or organization called the *karim*. What exactly a karim was cannot be ascertained, though it may have been a trading convoy of some kind. Merchants continually faced the many organized communities of pirates in the Indian Ocean and financial demands from political authorities and ruling elites who saw their commercial wealth as a legitimate object of appropriation. If the karim was an annual convoy trading with India, those who joined it might have found better political and naval protection than on their own. By the mid-fourteenth century, the Karimi merchants of Egypt had become a powerful group, with most of the Indian Ocean spice trade in their hands. The favourable policy of the Ayyubids in Egypt and the Yemen kept the Indian Ocean trade flowing firmly towards the Red Sea and Fustat. A senior civil servant in the late thirteenth century cites a policy document of about 1280: 'A decree has been issued, may God exalt the Sultan's exalted command...He offers a genuine welcome to those who come to his realm, as to the garden of Eden...

A mosque at Quanzhou on China's east coast. Built in 1310, it is possibly the oldest existing mosque in China. The style of the arches is reminiscent of Indian Islamic architecture. By the time this mosque was built Muslims had been trading from Arabia and India through the Southeast Asian seas to China for over five centuries.

from Iraq, from Persia, from Asia Minor, from the Hijaz, from India, and from China. Whoever wishes to set forth – the distinguished merchants, the men of great affairs and the small traders – from the countries enumerated…let him come to a country whose inhabitants have no need either of supplies or reserves of food…Whoever brings merchandise with him, such as spices and other articles imported by the Karimi merchants, will suffer no unjust impost nor be subjected to any burdensome demand.'

By 1429, when Barsbay, the Mamluk sultan of Egypt, monopolized the entire pepper trade of his kingdom, it was known in every trading city of Asia and Europe – in Calicut, Cambay, Malacca and Canton, in Venice, Genoa, Seville, Frankfurt, and Antwerp – that the rulers in India and Egypt made a fortune from eastern spice. Indeed, in 1433 a large Chinese fleet from Canton arrived in the Yemen and for the first time requested permission to trade in Jidda for the hajj fair. But it was the last Chinese fleet to sail from China, for the Ming dynasty then discouraged overseas trade in pursuit of making China economically self-sufficient.

THE PORTUGUESE, THE ENGLISH, AND THE DUTCH

Among those who had noticed the profits of the spice trade in the Mediterranean and the Indian Ocean were the royal court, counsellors, and admirals of a small European nation on the edge of the Atlantic. The Portuguese economic onslaught against Muslims and their trade began with the conquest in 1415 of the Moroccan caravan town of Ceuta. During the rest of the century, Portuguese explorers pushed further and further down the west coast of Africa until Bartholomew Diaz rounded the Cape of Good Hope in 1487–88 and Vasco da Gama in 1498 dropped anchor in the harbour of Calicut. The Portuguese ships carried a new style of armament, heavy cannon mounted in ports cut on either side of the hull which could be fired simultaneously: the effect of the gunpowder revolution applied to the mastery of large oceanic space was shattering on the Muslim merchants of the Red Sea and the Persian Gulf. Contemporary chroniclers from the Hadramawt record their shock at the seas exploits of the 'Franks': 'His first appearance in the land of India was at Calicut, Malabar, and Goa at the beginning of the 900s [Hijra]. So too his first appearance off the Arabian coast at Husn al-Ghurab near al-Shihr in this year [900 AH/1502–03 AD].'

The Portuguese soon realized that the structure of transoceanic commerce precluded any hope of monopolizing the spice trade unless they could exercise naval and political control over the leading emporia and ports. It was particularly essential to seal off the Strait of Hormuz and Bab al-Mandeb in order to prevent Muslim shipping from gaining access to India. The Portuguese declared a perpetual war against the merchants of Arabia and by 1507 were freely cruising in the Gulf of Aden and Oman and in 1515 had overcome Hormuz. Their maritime state in India, based on the newly founded capital Goa, enforced its monopolistic policy by controlling Hormuz and by an annual naval blockade of Bab al-Mandeb.

During the sixteenth century, the situation began to change. Portuguese officials and private residents in India found a profitable income from the maritime trade of Asia; they were not inclined to follow too strictly the policy laid down in Lisbon if it interfered with their own trade. Secondly, the Ottoman conquest of Egypt in 1517 and of Baghdad in 1534 under Sulayman the Magnificent brought the formidable military and naval power of the Turks closer to the Red Sea and the Persian Gulf. The celebrated expedition of the Turkish admiral Piri Reis in 1522 was the first of many attempts to gain control of the western arm of the Indian Ocean. Thirdly, the Indian and Malay merchants also began to arm their ships with heavy artillery and effective fighting capacity. Both Cambay and the Sumatran port city Atjeh reopened their spice trade to the Red Sea, though not without many battles with the Portuguese. By the end of the century, not only were pepper and spices once again flowing through the Middle East to reappear in Alexandria and Beirut but the Portuguese empire in the Indian Ocean was about to be challenged by the rising sea power of England and Holland.

The English and Dutch East India Companies were founded in 1600 and 1602 against a background of wars against Spain and its associated kingdom Portugal. The active war which both the Companies pursued with the Portuguese Estado da India had the effect of liberating Asian and particularly Muslim navigation through Bab al-Mandeb and the Strait of Hormuz, while at the same time diverting, far more effectively than the Portuguese had ever done, the transoceanic trade of Eurasia via the Cape route. In 1622 a joint English and Persian force captured Hormuz and destroyed the century-long Portuguese control of the Gulf. As the Portuguese fleets were relentlessly defeated by the Dutch throughout the Indian Ocean, the ruler of Oman besieged Muscat in 1649–50 and forced the Portuguese garrison to surrender. The wheel had made a full circle: it was now the turn of the Portuguese church in Muscat to be converted into a mosque.

Alfonso d'Albuquerque (d.1515). In this year [900AH/1502-03AD]', records a contemporary chronicler from the south Arabian shore, 'the vessels of the Frank appeared at sea en route for India, Hormuz, and those parts. They took about seven vessels, killing those on board and making some prisoners. This was their first action. May God curse them.' Albuquerque, Portugal's leading naval strategist and Viceroy of India, was a strong supporter of this campaign of violence. He burned Muscat after the town had surrendered, even though it had been promised that it would be spared. Its beautiful mosque, built of timber and plasterwork, was demolished.

The eclipse of the Lusitanian empire in the Indian Ocean gave renewed impetus to the emporia trade of the Middle East, which once again turned east, towards Surat in India, Bantam in Java, and even to Canton. The pilgrim traffic from Indian ports and the Muslim towns of Sumatra and Java returned to its former strength. In the west, the Egyptian grain trade with the Hijaz continued and European goods imported from Italy, Holland, England, and Germany were brought to Mocha and redistributed to the rest of the Indian Ocean by that most enterprising group of international merchants, the Armenians. Operating from New Julfa, a suburb of Isfahan, they specialized in the overland caravan trade and in the freight traffic of local ships. North European companies also began to dominate the maritime trade of Mocha and Gombroon, which had come to replace the entrepot trade of respectively Aden and Hormuz. By 1700, the transoceanic trade of the Red Sea and the Persian Gulf was finally lost by the Arabs mainly because the Cape route was used to bring large volumes of Asian goods to Europe. Middle Eastern trade nevertheless found a new source of strength in coffee, raw silk exported from the Caspian province of Iran, and in the redistribution of Spanish-American silver, which had begun to move eastwards from the middle of the sixteenth century.

The eighteenth century was a period of major economic and political change in West Asia. The overthrow of the Safawids in Iran and the resurgence of tribal,

Whereas in the arid landscape of West and Central Asia the camel was king of the road, in South Asia the pack animal was joined by wheeled transport, typically the bullock cart, as revealed in this mid-eighteenth century painting from Murshidabad in Bengal.

nomadic politics in large parts of western India, Central Asia, Iran, and the lands bordering Syria and Mesopotamia disrupted both caravan trade and general economic life. The naval dominance of the western Indian Ocean by the English and the Dutch reduced the participation and the share of the Muslim merchants even in the inter-regional trade of Asia.

OVERLAND TRADE

Nothing illustrates better the interdependence of religion, urbanization, settled agriculture, and nomadism than the symbiosis that existed between maritime and overland trade. It arose from the geography of the Muslim world, suspended between three oceans – the Indian, the Mediterranean, and the Atlantic. There were three factors underlying overland trade from the rise of Islam to the eighteenth century. Coastal towns handling seaborne trade were rarely the major centres of economic consumption and production, which were usually at some distance from the sea. Distribution of goods from the ports to consuming areas therefore had to be overland. Where water transport was available, as in India, Iraq, and Egypt, the large rivers were the primary highways, the roads secondary. But for most other regions of Islam, there was little alternative to carrying goods by land transport. Secondly, it was the widely dispersed inland producing centres that supplied both fine goods and low-value bulk items. Textiles, ceramics, and precious metals and heavy raw materials were transported over vast distances, from the Great Wall of China to Constantinople. The al-Amarya mosque and the madrasa at Radda in the Yemen, for instance, contain stone columns carved in northern Gujarat, which were exported to Aden as ballast goods and then transported over mountain passes by camels or mules. The third factor was the declining use of wheeled vehicles. By the late Roman period the wheeled vehicle had virtually disappeared from the Near and Middle East. It was replaced by pack animals, mainly camels but also mules, donkeys, and oxen. The camel is an efficient and cost-effective load-carrier. It is possible that the economics of long-distance land carriage by camel caravan, combined with the expense of maintaining roads suitable for wheeled transport, caused the demise of the chariot and the wagon which had once dominated the technology of Egypt, Mesopotamia, and Persia.

The difference between an arid landscape of barren mountains, desolate rock-strewn tracks, and pack animals, and a landscape of high vegetation and abundant water, with a multitude of wheeled vehicles, was noted by at least one traveller. In 1677 John Fryer, physician to the English Factory in Surat on the west coast of India, visited Persia. He sailed to Gombroon and then followed the old caravan route to Isfahan through the desert. Back in India, he was called out to visit a sick colleague some fifty miles from Surat. Fryer went by road, travelling on horseback but with a carriage following. The contrast between the Iranian desert landscape and the busy agricultural and industrial scene in western Gujarat impressed him. Road transport between the ports and the inland markets, towns and villages

Camel trains were a familiar sight in many parts of the Muslim world, and so they also featured in art, as in this plate from Mongol Iran. Textiles, ceramics and precious metals might be transported over vast distances. But equally grains, foodstuffs, and essential raw materials – heavy timber, cut stone, roofing tiles, iron, lead, tin, and copper, various kinds of dying substances, indigo and redwood, hides and skins – would all need to be gathered together from widely dispersed inland producing centres.

characterized both areas. But on Iranian roads, Fryer noted, there were no carts, coaches or wains. Here in India the way was clogged with caravans of oxen and camels. Bullocks teams of eight, twelve, and sixteen were yoked to heavy wagons loaded high with merchandise. In Iran, the main danger facing caravan traders came from bandits hiding in the mountain passes; in India the roads were infested with bands of soldiers from the irregular cavalry forces belonging to the local princes or even the central government.

From the seventeenth century onwards there are many European accounts of caravan routes throughout the Muslim world. Comparison of these narratives with those by earlier Muslim writers, such as Ibn Jubayr (during 1183–85) and Ibn Battuta (died 1368/69), shows that caravan trade was an indispensable adjunct of civilized and urbanized life in Islam. Public authorities and wealthy individuals both constructed roads, caravansarais, water cisterns, and covered markets and planted trees along the most frequented routes. Furthermore, the caravans – comprising thousands of pack animals, their commercial owners, and ordinary people travelling in security – needed the organized services of the people living along the route. Food for the passengers, fodder for the animals, and above all the guarantee against robbery were provided by the nomadic communities of the desert and the steppe, who in turn needed some of the goods carried by the caravans.

Four leading Muslim cities acted as the hubs to the overland trade in the Middle East, Africa, India, and Central Asia: Mecca, Damascus, Baghdad, and Cairo. These were joined, after its Turkish conquest in 1453, by Constantinople which had been the terminus of a northern route from Kiev, Samarqand, and the oasis cities of Asia such as Kashgar, Turfan, and Urumchi. Of course, besides the four metropolises, there were other famous caravan towns. In north Africa, on the periphery of the Muslim world, there were caravan towns which had attracted Arab migrants and witnessed the conversion of local Berber tribes from Umayyad and Abbasid times. On the edge of the Western Sahara, Sijilmasa was founded around 757 AD by the Kharijite dissenters who had been seeking a sanctuary in the desert. In the central Maghrib, around 776, Tahert rose to rapid fame under the Rustamids who migrated from Iran. And in the ninth and the tenth centuries, Tahert, Zawila, and Sijilmasa formed the points of a vast triangular caravan trade in the Sahara, visited by merchants from Basra, Kufa, and Khurasan. As the chronicler Ibn Saghir put it, Muslims and Jews found it profitable in Tahert and traded with it because of its opulence, the praiseworthy conduct of its religious leader towards the subjects, and the security of life and property. The roads to the Sudan and all the countries east and west of the Sahara as a result were busy with the exchange of all kinds of goods. African gold and slaves from beyond the great desert were traded in the bazars of Fez, Tlemcen, Qayrawan, and Tripoli. A series of long caravan routes connected the markets of Alexandria with towns which

traded with the Sudan. Tripoli, al-Mahdiyya, Qayrawan, Tlemcen, Ceuta, and Fez
were all part of a classic Muslim urban tradition and yet their economic life
depended in great measure on the integration of a different African experience.
Textiles, cowry shells from the Maldive Islands in the Indian Ocean, glass beads
from Cambay in India, and bronze objects were carried by the caravan traders in
return to Awdaghust in modern Ghana and the towns of the Niger. The dispersion
of such objects from India to Atlantic Africa from prehistoric times demonstrates
that overland caravan trade enjoyed a stability perhaps not shared by sea lanes.

ORGANIZING THE HAJJ

The north African caravan routes along the Mediterranean and across the Sahara
from Chad converged on the twin turntables of both Christian and Muslim trade,
Alexandria and Cairo. The latter shared with Damascus and Baghdad the distinction of organizing the three annual *hajj* caravan journeys to Mecca. It is the pious
duty of every Muslim to visit Mecca and perform the circumambulation of the
Kaaba. The movement of such a magnitude of people was highly profitable to
both the caravan traders and the nomadic tribes, but little else is known about the
hajj caravans from Damascus and Cairo in early Muslim times. It is the route from
Abbasid Baghdad that is well documented. This was the Way of Zubayda, named
after the wife of the fifth Abbasid caliph Harun al-Rashid (r.786–809). The road
runs for nearly 900 miles through the Iraqi desert and across the Nafud to Medina
and Mecca. Every 15 or so miles, or one day's march, there are artificial water cisterns, caravansarais, and eating-houses. For the intermittent rain in the desert
enables grasses to grow and to support a flourishing nomadic economy. Conserv-
ing the water also provided a constant if limited supply for the travellers passing
through the arid landscape. This was achieved by the hydraulic engineers of the
Way of Zubayda, utilizing a technology more than 1500 years old.

The Way of Zubayda was probably constructed mainly during the reign of al-
Mahdi, who preceded Harun al-Rashid. According to the historian al-Tabari, al-
Mahdi ordered substantial improvements on the stretch from al-Qadisiyya to
Zubala, providing every station with cisterns and excavating wells. Both Harun al-
Rashid and Zubayda performed the hajj on foot and must have discovered what
the conditions actually were on the Kufa-Mecca road. According to the historian
al-Yaqubi, Zubayda sponsored and promoted public works in the name of Islam
out of a desire to outdo the deeds of her famous husband both in serious and triv-
ial matters. The most eloquent tribute to Zubayda's pious work on the desert road
comes from Ibn Jubayr, who joined the Baghdad caravan in 1184. As the pilgrims
were approaching the cisterns of the important station at Thalabiya, something
terrible happened: maddened by thirst, the pilgrims fought desperately to reach
the water and in the resulting stampede seven people were crushed to death.

The number of people joining an established annual event like the hajj was
extremely large. An English merchant who accompanied the Cairo to Mecca hajj

caravan in the second half of the sixteenth century estimated the total size at about 200,000 people. Such a gathering clearly called for considerable organization, not only to provide food and water through the desert but also to keep law and order among the travellers themselves. All three hajj caravans were headed by a high ranking army officer with a substantial force of soldiers. The caravan of which the English merchant was a member also carried six pieces of artillery to be used against nomadic attacks and to celebrate the safe entry to Mecca. Once the caravan entered the true desert, the tribal leaders took over as protectors and the bedouin came to the camping stations to barter their animal products for textiles and other imports.

THE TRANSCONTINENTAL CARAVAN TRADE

Merchants and traders supplying the needs of the pilgrim caravans in the Middle East were also involved in the transcontinental trade to India, Central Asia, and China. The caravans supplied the local markets and redistributed seaborne goods from the leading seaports in India, the Persian Gulf, and the Red Sea. Similarly, the great desert cities such as Isfahan, Yazd, and Kirman in Iran and Samarqand and Bukhara in the steppes of Transoxania, had an overland trade with Indian towns. The early Muslim sources mention Daybul and Lahari in Sind and Multan in the western Punjab as the most important places visited by Muslim overland traders. These towns specialized in the export of coarse and fine cotton textiles and Multan also conducted large financial and banking transactions, acting as a market for bills of exchange and precious metals imported from Central Asia. They were joined later by the three imperial cities of Islamic India – Lahore, Delhi, and Agra.

Each year the Turkoman, Uzbek, and even Chinese traders arrived at the Indian markets with luxuries such as fine porcelain, Chinese brocade and damask, jade objects, high-quality paper, and above all purebred horses. The Turkish and nomadic styles of warfare based on large cavalry forces introduced to India during the 700 years of the Sultanate and Mughal periods needed war horses. Central Asian breeders supplied animals strong enough to carry armour-clad men, while Iranian and Arab horses were used for show-riding and prestige. The Chinese and Central Asian imports to the Middle East and India throughout the history of Islam prove that sheer distance did not prevent the good organization and profitability of such transactions. For the routes across the Gobi or the Iranian salt deserts demanded exceptional transport animals and marching discipline from the caravan-masters. The two-humped Central Asian camels used on the Gobi route and on the Himalayan passes had the endurance and ease of handling necessary for a round trip that could easily take two years. More troublesome than the problem of distance was that of protection for the overland traders.

The transcontinental caravan routes, both in Africa and Asia, crossed territories imperfectly controlled by the centralized governments or passed through tribal pasture grounds: the possibility of robbery and large organized attacks was

Opposite The pilgrimage caravans which converged each year on Mecca were both one of the great sights and one of the great experiences of the pre-modern Muslim world. The caravan might be led by a band, as in this illustration from the *Maqamat* of al-Hariri. The numbers involved were vast. 'Over the immense extent of the plain you could see the thrust of a crowd filled with pain and fright and the knocking together of litters', wrote Ibn Jubayr of the pilgrimage of 1184, 'who has not seen with his own eyes this Iraqi caravan has not experienced one of the genuine marvels of the world.'

a real danger. In remote areas, the overnight resting-houses (known variously as *khans*, *sarais*, and *wakelahs*) were built like fortresses with high walls and bastions. Their massive gates could be closed to protect the travellers and their goods from petty theft, and the fortifications were strong enough to withstand sudden attack from nomadic raiders. Regular indemnities to organized bandits provided some protection for the caravans when on the march, and the owners would also engage soldiers to defend them. In the Mughal empire, a caravan of two hundred carts generally carried two soldiers for every valuable wagon. The mobile cavalry of the central government was also frequently used to subdue the outlaws and bandits sometimes sheltered by local chiefs. In the 1670s, a French jeweller, Jean-Baptiste Tavernier, journeying from Surat to Agra saw the severed heads of captured bandits and even that of the local raja displayed on the city ramparts after a Mughal expedition had successfully carried out a raid. Such rough justice both showed that the Empire was capable of protecting its subjects and upheld the Islamic, and indeed widespread, principle of letting merchants pass unmolested along public highways.

URBAN LIFE IN THE ISLAMIC WORLD

The later Arab historians noted a continuing paradox about the bedouin dispersion and assimilation into the settled societies which took place in the aftermath of the foundation of Islam. The Umayyads and the early caliphs who led their tribal followers to Damascus and Alexandria retained their passion for a wandering, desert way of life while at the same time showing a marked preference for the comforts and values of an urban civilization. As the memory of a nomadic origin faded, the taste for urban luxuries increased on the part of the Arab newcomers, who would exceed the converted Muslims in ostentatious consumption and other displays of personal wealth. By the time that the Syrian geographer al-Muqaddasi was writing about Islamic cities (c.980), educated Muslims had almost forgotten the realities of nomadic existence and regarded the bedouin as an element in opposition to the true significance of Islamic history. The periodic incursions of the nomads and their military victories over settled people and capital cities were considered synonymous with ruination. The most extreme expression of this point of view was that of Ibn Khaldun, who proclaimed that wherever the desert Arabs settled, from the eleventh to the fourteenth centuries, flourishing Muslim cities fell into ruins.

As a religious, economic, and social system, Islamic civilization remained centred on the town which, however, could function effectively only by drawing on the surplus of rural areas. Food, industrial raw materials, and fuels were transported to towns over considerable distances. But the urban manufacture of industrial products and their distribution made the town markets a natural meeting-ground for long-distance merchants and traders, and farmers and tribesmen from the hinterlands. The nomadic contribution to the Islamic urban economy may have been small in terms of quantity but it was vital in that it was the sole source of baggage animals.

Contemporary historians pointed out that the origins of many leading Islamic towns – Kufa, Basra, and Cairo – were to be found in the temporary military garrisons. The purpose of these early settlements was to separate the Arab tribal warriors from the sedentary populations of the conquered land and to keep the military contingents in a state of alert in case of any sudden uprising. Within a few decades of the conquest of Iraq, Kufa had grown to about 100,000 inhabitants, while Basra was nearly double the size. The rapid growth of these two entirely new towns on the edge of the desert and the river systems underlines the fact that the Arabs were no strangers to urban life in spite of their avowed predilection for the open country. Both Mecca and Medina were substantial pre-Islamic urban centres, and the existence of an ancient caravan trade through the high plateau of the Yemen and the Hijaz points to a long chain of similar towns, which became important religious and economic centres in the Muslim centuries. Radda, Jibla, Sana, Thula, and Shibam straddled the road from Aden to Taif, Mecca, and Medina, and thence to the oasis towns of Wadi Sirhan in the western Nafud to join up with the great trunk route to the ports of the eastern Mediterranean.

Muslim towns varied according to their economic specialization, cultural and education roles, and administrative functions. According to al-Muqaddasi's

Shibam, an ancient walled city in the Wadi Hadramawt, Yemen. The Wadi takes the form of a canyon 1,000 feet deep in a flat gravel plain; it is, according to one visitor, 'a forgotten bit of paradise waiting for the Day of Judgment'. Shibam's tall houses were pressed close together for defence, the windowless lower stories often forming the outer wall of the city.

categories, capital cities such as Baghdad, Cairo, and Damascus were comparable to royalty; provincial cities are given the ranks of ministers; while ordinary towns and villages appear as cavalry and infantry respectively. The Arabic expression for a metropolis was given different interpretations by jurists, linguists, and common people. The legal and religious definition of an Islamic town was a place with a large number of inhabitants, with law courts, political officers, and an income sufficient to pay for all its internal expenditures. The linguistic usage defined a town as a dividing point between two regions, such as al-Basra, al-Raqqa, and Arrajan. The public, however, applied the term metropolis to any large and important town. Muqaddasi was careful enough to reserve a definition of his own: a capital city in the Muslim world included the residence of the supreme ruler, the location of the departments of state, and the investiture of the provincial governors. When his classification is compared with other descriptions of the towns and cities visited by al-Muqaddasi, it is clear that his theories were not pure invention but were derived from actual experience.

There were two distinctive features associated with urbanization in Muslim history. First, the religious and cultural expressions of Islam came to be concentrated in towns, although the peasants and the bedouin both professed the same faith as the townspeople. Secondly, the social composition became extraordinarily diverse and heterogeneous compared with towns in western Europe, India, and China. Indeed, the garrison settlements expanded into towns with separate quarters for not only different Arab tribal peoples but also Christians, Jews, Turks, Persians, and Indians. The purpose of this separation was economic, social and political. The historical experience of three leading cities – Damascus, Cairo, and Baghdad – are cases in point. Damascus, an old Aramaic town which grew into a Hellenic settlement, was a Byzantine city when conquered by the Muslims during the early phase of expansion. It was ideally placed between the desert and the fertile mountain valleys of western Syria, attracting the oasis-dwellers in the immediate hinterland, the inhabitants of the high valleys to the north and the west, and the nomadic migrants from as far away as the desert bordering the Euphrates and the central Arabian peninsula. According to later traditions, the caravan masters of pre-Islamic Mecca regularly visited Damascus, and in Byzantine times the city clearly had a wide sphere of economic influence. The first task assumed by the Islamic conquerors was to designate a place of worship for the Muslim faithful in a town dominated by Christian churches. The construction of the Great Mosque (709–15), begun under the caliph al-Walid, allegedly involved not only the entire tax revenue of the province for seven years but also grew into associated projects for aqueducts, covered markets, and new suburbs. Although the city lost its prime political role with the Abbasid revolution in 749–50 and the subsequent foundation of Baghdad as the capital of the caliphate, it continued as a cultural centre of Islamic learning and grew into a considerable industrial city producing fine brocaded silk, muslin, and the famous inlaid – damascene – swords and armour. The

Great Mosque with its Byzantine-styled mosaics and enormous colonnaded prayer hall would signal to all ambitious Muslim rulers, along with the al-Aqsa mosque in Jerusalem, that there were certain urban symbols over which it was necessary to exercise political control.

Cairo lacked such a symbolism but from the tenth century its influence in the Muslim world was greater than any other leading city. In 641 the Arab invaders under Amr had built a military camp near the site of a Coptic town. Known as Fustat, the town controlled the route to the cities of north Africa and was also the starting-point of caravans setting out along the Red Sea to the ports of Suez and Aydhab. The real expansion of Cairo came in the late tenth century when the Fatimid dynasty of Tunisia established their regime in Egypt. The construction of the new city al-Qahir next to Fustat and of the al-Azhar mosque and its associated madrasa, which became an influential centre of theological teaching, were two signs of the changing balance of power in the Middle East. The gradual diversion of transoceanic trade from the Persian Gulf to the Red Sea brought economic prosperity to both Cairo and Alexandria, reflected in the sumptuous houses built for the visiting merchants. At its commercial height in the early fourteenth century, the port area of Cairo, the Bulaq, had several hundred wakelah bazars. Cairo's population remained substantial through epidemics, fires, and military disasters, until the pandemic of the 1340s drastically reduced it.

These random calamities did not spare Baghdad, despite its epithet of 'City of Peace'. But for nearly five hundred years from its foundation by Caliph al-Mansur

The mosaics of the Great Mosque at Damascus depict buildings and an idyllic landscape; these come from the mosaic above the central portico. It is not known what the purpose of their depiction was – a representation of heaven, perhaps, or of the subjection of the world to Islam. Whatever the purpose, it offers a glimpse of an urban vista of the eighth century.

in 766 to its destruction by the Mongols in 1258, the famous round city symbolized in every sense the spiritual and material centre of Islam. The only challenge to Baghdad as the economic, cultural and political capital came from Samarra, built to the north of Baghdad in 836 by Caliph al-Mutasim, when he grew tired of the constant disturbances created in the streets of Baghdad by the Turkish mercenaries. But Samarra's capital role lasted only until 889 when the administration was transferred back to Baghdad. The power of the Abbasid caliphate was closely connected with the cultural and economic reputation of Baghdad. Its numerous mosques and religious schools were matched by busy artisan quarters where fine cotton textiles and gold brocades were manufactured. The bazars and merchant houses in both the city and the outer suburbs looked after the commercial needs of the caravans from Aleppo and Mosul in the north, from Khurasan in the east, and from Medina across the great desert.

Above The round city of Baghdad has been well described as 'a piece of ideology walled off from the world'. This plan has been constructed on the evidence of classical Arab authors. At the centre was the caliph's 'Palace of the Golden Door' with its 'Green Dome'. The caliph's sons lived in the first circular layer, the departments of government in the second. The city plan sets out the value placed on proximity to the successor of the Prophet as the leader of God's community on earth.

Wherever Islam spread, from Andalusia to India, its cities had certain features in common. Most private houses, even in Damascus, Cairo, or Baghdad, were built with sun-dried bricks, whose fragility made the cities seem constantly dilapidated to foreign travellers. Only the architecture of power – mosques, palaces, citadels, and city walls – could make a claim to permanency by using kiln-baked bricks or cut stones. However, in the Yemen and many parts of Iran the town houses of the wealthy were constructed in solid masonry. The skill of Muslim architects and builders showed itself in a style that was varied by different materials but perfectly integrated with the arid environment and the climate. The austere geometric lines of the buildings, the artistic motifs created in white plaster, and the ornate painted timber ceilings inside expressed a sensibility as unmistakably Islamic as the Quranic inscriptions at the entrance to a mosque. While public buildings were carefully planned and executed, the rest of the city was left completely unplanned. The original circular inner city of Baghdad was an exception. Most other Islamic towns were characterized by narrow, winding streets flanked by tall structures with very little space between them. The main streets, lined with shops, were often covered in order to provide shelter from the fierce sun in summer and rains in winter. The open space around the citadel palace and the Friday mosque – used for communal recreation, religious processions, and the display of horsemanship– compensated to some extent for the dense and solid urban landscape.

The social milieu too was far from featureless. The artisan workshops and craft associations located around the bazars and the Friday mosques. Most of the workforce was organized into corporations of some kind. Urban crafts and service people such as metalworkers, gold and silversmiths, shoemakers, cabinetmakers, carpenters, papermakers, bookbinders, calligraphers, printers, butchers, bakers,

Opposite The Great Mosque at Damascus, which was built by the Umayyad caliph al-Walid I between 709 and 715, is the earliest surviving monumental mosque in the Muslim world. It was designed to be the place where the whole Muslim community of the city could worship.

The bazar

No urban centre can exist without markets. The Islamic city was no exception. The Arabs and the converted Muslims had inherited from the ancient Iranians, Greeks, and the Romans an active and thriving urban tradition but endowed it with a special vigour from the seventh to the tenth centuries. The market – *suq* in Arabic and *qaysariya* in Persian – became an integral part of Muslim urban development. The most distinctive feature of Muslim markets is their separation from the residential quarters. Private housing, whether rich and spacious or large tenement blocks for poorer people, was surrounded by blank exterior walls, since personal privacy was highly valued. The suq, by contrast, with its numerous shops and stalls, needed open access to customers and suppliers. As a result, the markets were arranged in a system of connecting streets or lanes, often roofed over with clay domes to protect the shoppers from the fierce sun in summer and rains in winter. Each street specialized in a particular trade or article of goods. Thus the suqs of Basra, Damascus, Cairo, and Baghdad contained quarters for spice, food, cotton and silk textiles, leather goods, metal, jewellery, money-changing, and perfumery. Behind the shops, there was usually an enclosed courtyard with, at right angles to the suq, a building that was used as a warehouse and temporary residency by the caravan merchants and traders. The market was strictly supervised by officials who ensured that the traders used only standard measures and that the quality of goods was not fraudulently adulterated. Prices were also regulated in times of scarcity to prevent food sellers and grain merchants from making undue profits at the expense of consumers. Apart from its retail activities, the market also acted as a meeting place. Eating-houses and restaurants were always located in the suqs and were used by a large number of people who had few facilities at home for preparing cooked meals. In Cairo the number of cooks engaged in preparing public meals was estimated as 12,000. After the discovery of coffee and tobacco, the café became a common feature of the market from the sixteenth century.

The covered bazar in Istanbul in the nineteenth century. At this time it had over 4,000 shops, 2,000 workshops, 500 stalls, as well as mosques, fountains, and storehouses. The central area, the Bedesten, dates back to the Ottoman conquest of the city. Over one of the gates to this area there is a formidable bird. According to the seventeenth-century writer, Ewliya Chelebi, the meaning of the bird is: 'Gain and Trade are like a wild bird, which if it is to be domesticated by courtesy and politeness, may be done so in the Bedesten.'

The fully planned circular city of Baghdad was an exception. Most Muslim towns had carefully planned public buildings and spaces surrounded by densely packed housing, as can be seen in this view over the rooftops of Yazd in Iran. This was a world of narrow winding streets, high blank walls, and blind alleys. Often it was divided up into quarters inhabited by homogenous communities bound by common religious, ethnic, or occupational ties. Such quarters themselves might be units of administration and have gates which would be closed at night.

and tanners were all carefully differentiated by long apprenticeships and internal regulations. While the craft guilds looked after the economic interests of their members, the urban markets were not left entirely unregulated by the authorities. The city governor, a police chief, and judges represented the central administration. But there were other officials whose duty was to supervise the markets and see that there was no excessive profiteering at the expense of consumers and that the goods were not adulterated or debased. The long and sustained history of Muslim cities from their inception to the present proves that periodic social disturbances, famines, and other demographic disasters have never fundamentally affected their economic base or organization.

THE RURAL ECONOMY

The urban success of Islam was due in no small measure to the contributions made by the peasant and the nomad. The farmer often attracted the unwelcome attention of both rapacious tax officials and nomadic overlords, but towns were still dependent on the rural surplus for their supply of wheat, barley, millet, sugar cane, cooking oils, garden produce, dates, milk products, and livestock. Industrial raw materials such as cotton, wool, dying substances, hides and skins, timber, firewood, raw metals, silicon-sand for glass manufacture, and a host of other semi-finished products were brought to town by specialized producers, dealers, and nomadic tribal people. This urban–rural trade was freely transacted through market deals and voluntary contracts between farmers and traders, despite the image of a politically oppressed peasantry. It provided a sufficient income for farmers to increase their families and their capital stock. For, in common with peasant agriculture elsewhere in the Indian Ocean and the Mediterranean, labour supply in

The first centuries of the Muslim world saw developments in farming techniques and the spread of many new crops from rice and cotton through to sugar cane and citrus fruits. In this scene from the Arabic version of Pseudo-Galen's *Book of Antidotes* (1199) we see the work of digging, harvesting, threshing, and winnowing, with the pleasing addition of the arrival of the labourers' lunch, top left.

the rural Middle East was dependent on the size of farming families.

Agronomic science drew on the long experience of settled farming, which optimized the use of small or medium plots of land, a plough drawn by draught animals, and the application of irrigation combined with fertilizers. The agricultural technology of Mesopotamia, Egypt, parts of Syria, and Iran had developed over several millennia before Muhammad. Indeed, so legendary was the reputation of these productive areas in the minds of the Muslim invaders that some tribal leaders even proposed to Umar, the conquering caliph, that all the land belonging to the vanquished people should be redistributed to the Arabs. The suggestion was rejected on the grounds that such a policy would penalize as much a future Muslim state as the existing owners and cultivators. So the earlier Arab land taxation and management continued based on Sasanian, Byzantine, and Coptic systems.

Since the income of the central state and individual landowners in the Middle East was largely derived from the economic surplus of cultivated land, a finely adjusted system had evolved for estimating the annual outturn of crops and calculating the rent or tax payable by the farmers. The value of the surplus was measured in cash or a proportion of the subsistence grains was taken as rent in kind. Where an active market for agricultural produce existed either through rural specialization or demand, it was not difficult to make tax assessments in money terms. This was the case in the highly efficient agricultural economy of Mesopotamia. The land survey carried out by Umar's agents immediately after the conquest of Iraq differentiated between various kinds of land and crops. Where irrigation was available from the river Euphrates, fields closely sown with wheat incurred an assessment of 1⅓ *dirhams* for every *jarib* measure; if it was thinly sown, the assessment was only ⅔ of a *dirham*; average production of wheat paid 1 *dirham*. Valuable cash crops planted on garden plots paid a much higher rate. Date plantations were taxed at the rate of 10 *dirhams* per *jarib*, as dates were the most valuable of the commercial crops.

AGRICULTURAL DIVERSITY

Agricultural treatises from other parts of the Muslim world – Egypt, the Yemen, and Iran – reveal that cereals, sugar cane, cotton, oil seeds, vegetables, and fruits were cultivated by the peasants not merely at the subsistence level but included a surplus calculated according to price movements in a competitive market. Just as the Arab expansion and military conquests in north Africa, Spain, Sicily, Iran, and India in the classical period from the seventh to the eleventh centuries created an expanded market and brought with them the Arabic language and legal institutions, so they diffused crops and agronomic techniques. Sugar cane, bitter oranges, aubergines, melons, and some varieties of rice were brought from India and Southeast Asia first to new areas of cultivation in the Middle East and thence carried to north Africa and Spain. Indeed, the qasbah economy of Tunisia and Morocco was an extension of the Muslim system of combining date plantations with vegetable and fruit growing, to which pastoral stock-breeding added another dimension. North Africa was an important producer of wheat, barley, and olive oil in the classical period. After Arab occupation arable farming became more mixed and, depending on the relative strength of the main Arab and Berber tribal groupings, nomadism and transhumance (the seasonal movement of livestock) expanded. The date plantations in the river valleys on the edge of the Sahara came to be run and maintained by imported African semi-slaves.

Irrigation

The fundamental factors behind the crop diffusion and the agronomic innovation of the early Muslim centuries were irrigation and the technology of lifting water developed in tandem with other crop-growing techniques. Intensive agriculture in the river valleys of northern India, Mesopotamia, and Egypt incorporated several crop cycles within the year. The winter crops composed of wheat, barley, various kinds of lentils, and oil seeds were followed by the summer crops such as rice, millet, maize (introduced after the discovery of America), cotton, sugar cane, indigo, aubergines, sweet peppers, and melons. If the climate permitted, a third crop of rice or green vegetables was planted between the harvesting of the summer plants and the sowing of the winter ones. The success of both the winter and the summer crop-cycles lay in the management of the water resources. In parts of India and the Yemen where the southwest monsoon winds brought a sufficient level of rainfall between June and September, the summer plantings presented few problems. For the winter crops, on the other hand, most of the arid areas of monsoon Asia did not have sufficient rainfall to provide the irrigation needed at the critical stage of plant growth. Although wheat and barley were both dry crops and could be grown extensively with a smaller amount of labour than for rice or sugar cane, the timing of the water supply was the deciding factor in their cultivation. The solution adopted in those areas lacking winter rain was to construct wells, reservoirs, or water channels that tapped the natural aquifers in the mountains in order to provide artificial irrigation. The problem for western Asia and the Mediterranean was the opposite to that of the Indian Ocean. These regions had ample autumn or winter rains but the summers were excessively dry and hot. Successful cultivation of the summer crops in north Africa, Spain, and Sicily required the construction of irrigation works that would supply sufficient water during the summer.

Hydraulic technology

As the Arabs became familiar with the hydraulic technology utilized to harness the waters of the Euphrates, the Tigris, the Indus, and the Nile, they were able to combine it with their own techniques based on the *wadi* (river) irrigation of the desert. The introduction of artificial irrigational works to new areas of conquest in the Mediterranean led to an astonishing redevelopment of land which had declined in agricultural productivity or which had never had the facilities for double cropping. The central problems in subsistence or commercial crop production were the conservation of a seasonal water supply and its distribution. Mechanisms allowing water to be raised from one ground level to another were as necessary as the construction of channels directing the water to the fields. The use of the pulley, differential gearing, and the cantilevered beam had evolved in parallel with the different methods of intensive farming. Over the same time, civil engineering developed masonry works with graduated levels to control the speed and volume of the water flow. The complex system of social rights connected with the distribution of scarce water introduced a complexity to property ownership that was absent in sub-Saharan Africa as well as in western Europe. For cultivatable land was valued not only by its natural fertility but also by its access to available water. Customary laws specified the amount of water a plot of land sown with cereals or planted with date palms was allowed to have. Valves fitted to water pipes were opened and closed according to standard lengths of shadows cast in the date plantations by trees, or an analogue measuring rod, made from the stem of a palm leaf, inserted in a water tube controlled the flow.

The construction of brick – or stone-lined wells presented few engineering problems, apart from their depth, which could run to nearly 150 feet in areas with a low water-table. But drawing water from such deep wells was excessively laborious for humans and animals alike. In India special cattle were bred for strength to work at the well-head ramps, which sloped away to give the bullocks extra pulling-power. A large leather bucket discharged water into a stone reservoir from which masonry channels led to the fields. In the oasis gardens of central Arabia or in the deserts bordering the Euphrates, the semi-fortified villages growing dates, pomegranates, vegetables, lemons, and oranges also depended on well water for irrigation, using camels instead of oxen to draw the water. Where the lift was not too high, draught animals were yoked to the most famous hydraulic mechanism of Islam, the *noria* or water-wheel. This was composed of two articulated wheels operated by gears. The first and large wheel fitted with earthenware pots was lowered upright into the water and its pinion meshed with that of the other smaller wheel, turned by a camel, donkey or bullock. As the larger wheel revolved, the pots filled with water and discharged the supply into a tank.

The large noria could also be used by swift-flowing streams and rivers. In the Orontes valley of upper Syria, great norias with wheels measuring more than 30 feet in diameter have survived to the present day, but similar wheels were already working in Roman times, as noted by Vitruvius in the first century AD. Similar devices operated on the Euphrates, Tigris, and Nile, whose currents turned the slotted rim of the great wheels. The technology optimized the natural features of these three rivers – the seasonal fluctuations in the water level and the flow rate. The annual floodings of the Tigris and the Nile were so steep that the agronomic engineers had realized their potential nearly a thousand years before Muhammad: they built an elaborate system of subsidiary canals to distribute irrigation water to land at some distance from the rivers. The famous Naharwan canal developed during the Abbasid caliphate drew its head water from the Tigris near Samarra and

A noria (waterwheel) at Hama on the Orontes in Syria. From late Roman times such waterwheels could be found from Iran through to Spain. Mastery of hydraulic technology and water management enabled Muslims to bring areas of new land into production.

A qanat being repaired near Tabas in Iran. This is a specialized irrigation technique employed in Iran, north Africa, and Spain which uses subterranean water by means of underground channels known as qanats. A mother well is dug in the hills where there is an aquifer and the water sent along a mined tunnel to where it is needed. The path taken by the water tunnel can be charted from above by the vertical shafts sunk at intervals along its route. In this picture the mounds formed by the vertical shafts can be seen in the distance.

was linked to a network of lesser canals to bring a huge area of the alluvial plain under the plough which would otherwise have remained a wasteland. On a small island between Fustat and Cairo, the famous Nilometer recorded the spring rise in the level of the river. At the height of 16 arms, peasants could be certain that sufficient water was available for them to plough and sow the fields successfully. At 20 arms the land would remain submerged beyond the period of cultivation, and at anything less than 16 arms the volume of water would be insufficient for a normal harvest. The daily recordings at the Nilometer during the inundations were treated by the financial markets of Cairo almost as an indicator of the immediate economic prospects for Egypt, the traditional breadbasket of much of the Hijaz and the Middle East.

Although neither Mesopotamia nor the Nile valley were totally free from the risks of flooding and even water shortage, their agriculture was more fortunate than that of most of Iran, parts of Oman, Afghanistan, and north Africa on the fringe of the Sahara. Water management here consisted in the construction of conduits below ground (*qanats*) which were linked to natural reservoirs located in the mountains. From this original aquifer a series of tunnels lined with baked clay pipes was dug, interconnected by airshafts which resembled wells. Some of the Iranian and north African underground conduits ran for more than 40 miles. The main challenge facing the engineers was to determine correctly the fall and force of the water flow. They did this with the aid of a levelling tube made of glass. A number of holes were made along the shaft and it was filled with water to test the rate of flow. The irrigation system enabled many towns and villages to operate date plantations and a flourishing agriculture, complementing their role as industrial centres and commercial entrepots.

NOMADIC PASTORALISM

The productivity of these oasis settlements exposed the inhabitants to constant danger of financial exactions and demands by the warrior nomadic tribes, who lived either on the fringes of or deep within the desert itself. Two factors of the arid ecology contributed to the nomadic economy. First, the grain production and irrigated agriculture needed the traction power of domesticated animals besides their dairy products, wool, and hides. Secondly, the climate's low rainfall could not support stock-rearing as well as the cultivated fields of settled arable farming. It was possible, however, to raise animals on marginal land because winter and spring rains brought forth a luxurious growth of nutritious grass and other plants for a brief period. Nomadic pastoralism had evolved in the steppe land of Eurasia and in the deserts of the Middle East and north Africa in parallel with settled agriculture from prehistoric times. Because of the role played by the desert Arabs in the history of Islam, nomadism occupied an important if ambivalent function in society as a whole. While the economic contributions of the nomads were acknowledged to be useful and even vital for the welfare of settled people, misgivings arose from the nomads' in-built capacity for military activities. When the centralized bureaucratic empires were strong they could easily contain the warlike nomadic tribes on or within their frontiers. In times of political and military weakness, however, they were vulnerable to nomadic attacks. Villages and date plantations on the edge of the desert could not be adequately protected even in times of peace, and the inhabitants were forced to come to a settlement with the leading tribes who offered protection in return for regular payments in agricultural products.

The pastoral economy and society associated with Islam included many different forms, developed over the centuries. The prophet Muhammad's tribe, the Quraysh, had a strong base in Mecca and seems to have been engaged in organizing the caravan trade across the desert to the Mediterranean ports. But the political and military methods adopted by his immediate successors in Islamic expansion were mainly bedouin. Political and economic inter-tribal relations were principally concerned with the hierarchy of grazing rights in the desert which was demarcated by a migrating schedule, access to drinking water, and fixed agreements with the villagers in the irrigated oases. Military power and the capacity for mounted warfare determined in the final instance how the economic gains were to be shared. These regular raiding expeditions tested the tribal warriors' fighting and ambushing skills. The success of the raiding mission was measured by the number and the quality of camels taken as a prize. Pedigree camels raised by the specialized bedouin who lived wholly in the desert enjoyed individual reputations equal to those of the famous purebred Arab horses. These animals were rarely sold to dealers and for outsiders their acquisition implied either a successful raid or a gift-exchange with the original owners. However, the bulk of the camels, horses, donkeys, and sheep bred by the nomadic people, whether Arab, Turkish, or Berber, fell in the category of non-pedigree stock and was sold to farmers, professional transporters, and urban citizens for cash sums.

Each year the main tribal confederacies would move across the desert to visit Damascus, Kufa, Baghdad, and the cities of Oman to buy and replenish their stocks of textiles, food grains, coffee, sugar, tea, tools, and armaments. From the high mountains of the Atlas in Morocco to Anatolia, the Zagros, and the Pamirs in Afghanistan, a similar movement of livestock took place in a cycle of summer and winter pastures. The social composition of the nomads always remained fluid. The great bedouin tribal confederacies of the nineteenth to twentieth centuries

Shepherds from the Ait
Hadidou Berber tribe bring
their sheep to market at
Imilehi in the Upper Atlas
Mountains, Morocco.

such as the Ruwala or the Shammar were made up by several tribes of different genealogical origins. In Iran, the Bakhtiaris and the Qashqays could include Arabic, Persian, and Turkish-speaking groups. The ownership of the flock and the herd and the mobile way of life was the social cement that bound the groups together. Warfare, natural calamities, and epidemic animal diseases could spell disaster for all nomadic communities and reduce them to the status of destitute labourers working for farmers. In general, a free nomad was a much richer individual than the rural counterpart, the peasant. The cash value of the stock and the freedom from fixed taxes and rents put the nomad in an enviable position compared to the peasant.

MODERN DEVELOPMENTS AND THE IMPACT OF OIL

The arrival of Europeans in the Indian Ocean, during the sixteenth and seventeenth centuries, radically changed the structure of transoceanic trade. British naval supremacy in the Arabian Sea and the establishment of a British empire in the Indian subcontinent in the succeeding centuries likewise delivered a severe blow not only to Muslim political power, which had remained unchallenged to the east of Suez from the time of Saladin, but also to its economic independence. The construction of the Suez Canal would reopen the ancient channels of trade after 1869. But the British occupation of Aden (from 1839) and Egypt (from

1882), followed by the *de facto* control of the Arab states in the Persian Gulf, opened the door in the Muslim world for western economic domination that would follow a path of turbulence and revolutionary changes almost to the present. The discovery of petroleum in Iran, Iraq, the Gulf states, and parts of north Africa in the 1920s and 1930s introduced another dynamic factor in the regional economies, leading to far-reaching changes in the 1960s and 1970s. Today, the populations of many Muslim countries of the Middle East enjoy a standard of living and a level of prosperity that are among the highest in the world and unprecedented in their history. The transfer of resources from the consumers of oil to the producing countries such as Iran, Iraq, Saudi Arabia, Kuwait, the members of the

A diagram issued in 1913 to show the planned extent of the Baghdad railway. The British and the Germans invested substantially in railway development in the Ottoman empire. After the completion of the Vienna-Istanbul line in 1888 such investment was particularly attractive to European capital. It has been estimated that between 1899 and 1909 railway companies operating in the Ottoman empire made a 5 per cent annual return on capital.

The procession of ships at the opening of the Suez Canal in 1869. This event led to an intensification of European economic pressure on the Muslim world. It was not surprising that in 1956 the British and the Egyptians should come to blows over the control of the canal. The former saw it as the lifeline to their economic and political interests further east, the latter saw it as a symbol of colonial domination.

United Arab Emirates, Oman, and Libya provided opportunities for not only improving the living standards of the ordinary people but also restructuring the economy and society. The pressures for change generated by the oil boom after the Second World War led to very different results in different countries, but the factor common to all is an awareness that economic modernization also challenges the conventional forms of social behaviour. It is universally recognized that the role of Islam as a religion and a social system consequently needs to be reinterpreted. If the Muslim oil-rich countries face problems of adjustment brought about by increasing wealth, there are others such as Pakistan, Bangladesh, Indonesia, Egypt, Tunisia, and Morocco for whom the real question is how to combat the impoverishment of the poorer sections of their societies engendered by rapid population growth and lagging technological progress.

The failure to keep up with Europe

The period between 1500 and 1800 is seen as one of decline and stagnation, although precise statistical information is lacking to substantiate this hypothesis. The reasons are to be found in the inability of Muslim countries, along with India and China, to keep up with the rate of economic growth in western Europe, stimulated by rapid technological change and the resultant transformation of industrial production. By the 1550s, most of the Arab world was directly or indirectly

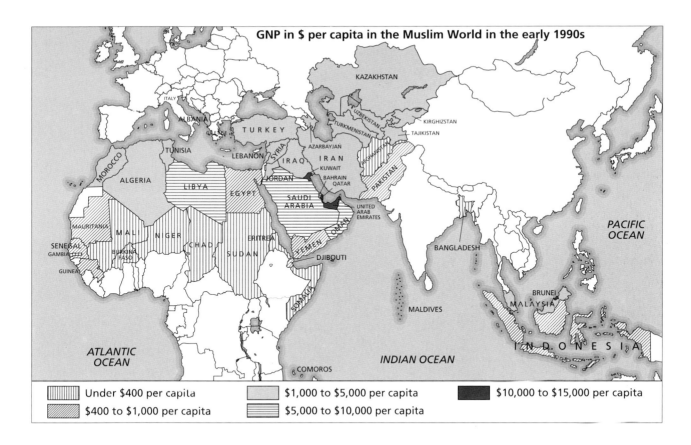

GNP in $ per capita in the Muslim World in the early 1990s

Under $400 per capita	$1,000 to $5,000 per capita	$10,000 to $15,000 per capita
$400 to $1,000 per capita	$5,000 to $10,000 per capita	

under the political control of the Ottoman empire, centred in Istanbul and Anatolia. Although the administrative structure set up by the Ottomans to rule Arab provinces continued intact until the First World War, Egypt had effectively become independent by the 1820s and lower Iraq always proved difficult to control. Iran, of course, remained outside Turkish influence, while north Africa was gradually brought inside European hegemony, both political and economic. The migration and settlement of a substantial European population, mainly French and Italian, to selected areas of north Africa, was matched by an influx to the rest of the Middle East of western capital, the introduction of modern banking and financial institutions, the construction of railway lines, and a modest industrial development. Thus the stimulus for economic growth in the period from 1800 to 1914 seems to have come mainly from outside.

Population and economies intertwined

After many centuries of demographic calamities caused by repeated plagues and destructive warfare, the population of the Middle East began to increase during the nineteenth and twentieth centuries. Nothing illustrates the favourable economic situation of the Middle East relative to the rest of the ancient world better than its density of population in classical times. It has been suggested that in the second century AD the region had something like 40 to 45 million inhabitants or about a fifth of the world total. The great pandemic of 1346–48 and the subsequent outbreaks reduced the figures by about a third, and around 1830 the total population of north Africa and the Middle East was probably no more than 35 million. By 1914 the estimated figure had risen to 68 million and for 1930 the total was 79 million, or just over four per cent of the world's population. The rate of growth was not uniform in different areas. In Egypt due to an expansion of cultivated land, the demand for labour grew. In north Africa after 1870 there was also a sustained demographic expansion along with agricultural development. As a result of the industrialization of European economies, the external demand for Middle Eastern commercial crops increased strongly throughout the nineteenth century. The rise in agricultural output during this period can be attributed to internal workings such as demography, fiscal centralization, and the modernization of currency, and to the demand for exports.

The increase in Middle Eastern population and external trade was spectacular, but it was accompanied by a decline in traditional industries, which were unable to compete with the machine-made European production. Similarly, in British India the hand-loom cotton spinning and weaving suffered a severe and protracted decline in the first half of the nineteenth century. From being one of the leading industrial countries in the world the Indian subcontinent became largely a producer and exporter of agricultural crops and industrial raw materials.

In parts of Egypt and the grain economy of Syria and Iraq, agricultural expansion occurred using the existing technologies by bringing new land under cultivation with an additional supply of labour. There was little incentive on the part of richer landowners and substantial farmers to finance expensive agronomic innovations. In other areas, however, the growth of agricultural production for a discriminating market, such as that of citrus fruits, silk, tobacco, and oil seeds, required considerable investments in improved techniques and irrigation.

Tradition and change
The basic forms of traditional economic production based on peasant farming, industrial crafts, nomadic stock-rearing, and urbanized markets continued for much of the Middle East in the later period. The changes in the external economy were not only reflected in a sustained expansion in the value and composition of the exports and imports but also in the direction of trade and its control by different social groups. Western opposition to the Ottoman naval dominance of the eastern Mediterranean had greatly reduced the volume of Muslim trade with western Europe in the sixteenth and seventeenth centuries. At the same time, however, coffee from the Yemen and silk filaments from the Caspian province of Iran added a new economic strength to the Middle East. And the diffusion of American silver through the Red Sea and the Persian Gulf would supply financial liquidity to the rest of Asia for more than three centuries. The main export markets for the Middle East appear to have been in India, Southeast Asia, and China. But the eigh-

teenth century was a period of renewed activity for European merchants trading with the Levant. The traditional imports of currants and raisins increased together with raw silk, wool, dying substances, skins, and hides. Exports of European glass, china, woollen textiles, and metal goods also greatly expanded in Egypt, Syria, and the Red Sea. By the beginning of the twentieth century, trade with the industrial countries of the West was a leading sector of the different economies of the Middle East, although for parts of Mesopotamia, Iran, and Afghanistan, the Indian subcontinent remained a substantial and important market. The new commercial expansions benefited the coastal towns at the expense of the old urban turntables on the caravan routes. Smyrna (Izmir), Beirut, Alexandria, and Basra acquired fresh economic prominence relative to Bursa, Aleppo, Baghdad, and Isfahan. European, Armenian, and Jewish merchant houses complemented the financial activities of western bankers who underwrote large-scale enterprises such as the construction of the Suez Canal and the Baghdad–Hijaz railway.

Oil

From the 1920s, the discovery and the exploitation of petroleum first in Iran and Iraq and then in north Africa and the Persian Gulf accentuated the influence and control exercised by European businesses in the Middle Eastern economies. The framework of oil exploration and extraction was provided by a small number of

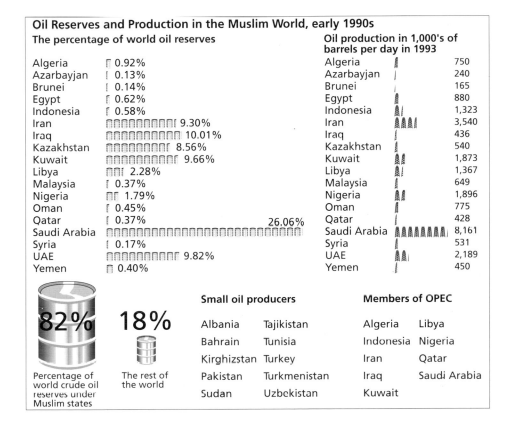

Oil Reserves and Production in the Muslim World, early 1990s

The percentage of world oil reserves

Country	%
Algeria	0.92%
Azarbayjan	0.13%
Brunei	0.14%
Egypt	0.62%
Indonesia	0.58%
Iran	9.30%
Iraq	10.01%
Kazakhstan	8.56%
Kuwait	9.66%
Libya	2.28%
Malaysia	0.37%
Nigeria	1.79%
Oman	0.45%
Qatar	0.37%
Saudi Arabia	26.06%
Syria	0.17%
UAE	9.82%
Yemen	0.40%

Oil production in 1,000's of barrels per day in 1993

Algeria	750
Azarbayjan	240
Brunei	165
Egypt	880
Indonesia	1,323
Iran	3,540
Iraq	436
Kazakhstan	540
Kuwait	1,873
Libya	1,367
Malaysia	649
Nigeria	1,896
Oman	775
Qatar	428
Saudi Arabia	8,161
Syria	531
UAE	2,189
Yemen	450

82% Percentage of world crude oil reserves under Muslim states

18% The rest of the world

Small oil producers

Albania	Tajikistan
Bahrain	Tunisia
Kirghizstan	Turkey
Pakistan	Turkmenistan
Sudan	Uzbekistan

Members of OPEC

Algeria	Libya
Indonesia	Nigeria
Iran	Qatar
Iraq	Saudi Arabia
Kuwait	

Kuwait was the first of the Gulf states to receive the benefits of oil production. What had been an economy focused on pearling and the maritime trade became one dominated by oil in which, by the late 1860s, 70 per cent of those employed worked for the state. The monumental Kuwait Towers erected on the gulf shore in the 1970s symbolizes the confidence felt by such oil-rich economies. The wealth of such states has to some extent been recycled to other Muslim economies both by the remittances of emigrant workers and by grants, investments, and loans by funds ranging from the Kuwait Fund for Arab Economic Development to the Islamic Development Bank.

British, American, and French joint-stock companies and by a system of commercial and political concessions obtained from the states which had territorial rights over the prospective oil fields. The concessions granted were generally for period of sixty to seventy years and covered huge areas in Iran, Iraq, Saudi Arabia, and the entire territories of Kuwait, Bahrain, Qatar, Muscat, and Oman. In return for the favourable commercial rights, the oil companies had to pay royalties and taxes to the host governments, employ local people on the oil fields, and supply petroleum products to the internal markets at lower than world prices. These arrangements proved highly profitable to the foreign companies because of the low cost of exploration and technical operations; they continued until the 1950s and 1960s. When the economics of Middle Eastern oil production are related to the political dependence of the Muslim countries on the West – especially Britain, France, and the United States of America – it is not difficult to see why the producers' demands for changes in the status of foreign oil companies should have spearheaded the change in the balance of power between the Middle East as a whole and the rest of the world after the Second World War. The cost advantage of the Middle East fields was matched to the technological changes in industrial fuel consumption which favoured oil at the expense of coal. As the world demand for petroleum products rose, the economic supremacy of the Arab and Iranian fields holding more than 50 per cent of the total world reserves also increased.

The first to take advantage of the changing situation was Iran. It nationalized the giant Abadan oil fields in 1951, which led to a political crisis with Britain. Within a decade, most of the foreign oil companies operating in the Middle East were forced to share a large proportion of the net oil revenues with the national governments. After the establishment of the Organization of Petroleum Exporting Countries (OPEC) in 1961 and the Arab–Israeli war of 1973, a massive transfer of purchasing power took place from the consuming countries of oil to the producers. For Arabic-speaking countries such as Saudi Arabia, the Gulf states (Kuwait, the United Arab Emirates which include Abu Dhabi and Dubai, Bahrain, and Oman), and Algeria, the transfer of real resources also brought higher standards of living for the masses in the form of better housing, educational and medical facilities, and the provision of public services. Considerable investments have been made in improving the industrial base of these countries' economies. For other countries with a large population (Iraq, Iran, Nigeria, and Indonesia), the economic benefits were not quite of the same order, but they too enjoyed considerable prosperity as a result of the oil boom. At present, the world demand for petroleum remains below the level of potential supply, and the economic future for the Muslim oil producers is not as optimistic as it was in the 1980s. But the story of oil in the Middle East points to a remarkable capacity for the region to remain in the forefront of world attention.

CHAPTER 6

Basim Musallam

The Ordering of Muslim Societies

The classical form of Muslim life developed in the cities of the Islamic world. Here Muslims lived in communities under the law. Here was achieved the balance between the imposition of public morality and the freedom for the working of individual conscience that produced a system remarkably tolerant of human weakness and difference. This is the environment in which we can learn something of the lives of women. It is also the environment in which the transformation brought about by European power was most fully felt.

THE COMMUNITY AND THE CITY

Umma, the Arabic word for 'community', made no distinction between the citizen body of each city and the worldwide Muslim community. There was such uniformity in the laws and institutions which bound each citizen to the urban community, and which were common to every Muslim city, that one can truly speak of a universal society which joined the urban centres of Islam from the Atlantic to China. This was the highway of coherence which cut through continents of political and cultural division to link the paths of divergent communities of peasants and tribes. Medieval Muslims said that the Muslim city had two focal points, the Friday mosque and the market. When Ibn Battuta, who came from Morocco, visited the Muslim quarter of a Chinese town in the fourteenth century, he found its market arranged exactly as in the towns of the central Muslim lands.

Attendance at the Friday prayers in the central mosque was the most dramatic manifestation of communal solidarity within the city. Its equivalent for the universal society of Islam was the *hajj*, the pilgrimage to Mecca. Undoubtedly, this was the single greatest incentive to travel within the Muslim world. And just as a visit to the mosque might be combined with a business deal, so the hajj became an opportunity for commercial exchange and professional advancement. The vast annual hajj caravans that set off from Damascus and Cairo, and from cities as far as Fez in Morocco, were laden with merchandise; a fairly impoverished pilgrim like Leo Africanus in the sixteenth century expected to work his passage, either by providing secretarial services or by speculation on merchandise.

The accounts of Muslim travellers give a vivid picture of the Muslim city in the Middle Ages. All of them were highly educated members of the *ulama* (Islamic scholars) and what immediately strikes the reader is the ease and confidence with which they could move within the elite, from Cordoba to Fez, from Fez to Cairo, from Cairo to Damascus, and so on, with Arabic as the common medium of religion and law, science and learning. Wherever they went they could expect respect, hospitality, and employment.

The historian Ibn Khaldun, for instance, was born in Tunis in 1332, but spent several interrupted years in Merinid employ at Fez, first as the writer of the *alama* (the ruler's official signature), later as an official member of Sultan Abu Ishaq's literary circle. In 1362 he was at the court of Granada in Spain and when twenty years (and at least as many episodes) later he turned up in the Mamluk capital of Cairo, students flocked to his courses at the *madrasa* (college) of al-Azhar and he was appointed Maliki chief *qadi* (judge) of Cairo.

Perhaps the best example is Ibn Battuta (1304–c.77) who came originally from Tangier but after thirty years of travel, which extended from China in the East to Spain and the Niger in the West, finally settled in Fez, where he wrote an account of his travels. We learn that he so ingratiated himself with the Sultan of India that he was made chief qadi of Delhi and was later sent as his ambassador to China. It would, however, be too much to say that 7,000 miles from home Ibn Battuta did not encounter a single cultural barrier, unless one understands this to mean there were no barriers to his acceptance and promotion.

To describe Islamic society as traditionally urban has become something of a cliché. The history of the Middle East is the history of its cities, where commerce and learning, industry and art, government and faith flourished. Its hinterland has rarely known a landed gentry with rural power bases. Power bases were urban. Tribal chiefs often formed armies from men of the desert or mountain, and led them to conquer the cities. But once they established their power, their interests lay in a stable and prosperous urban life.

Many of these cities – Baghdad, Cairo, Qayrawan – were actually founded by the Muslims; the others were enlarged and enriched by them. Instead of demolishing the Roman, Byzantine, and Sasanian heritage, they conceived the idea of upstaging it. Sixty years after the Prophet's death (632 AD) they signified their arrival on the world scene by building the Dome of the Rock in one of the most sacred sites in Jerusalem, a city then widely portrayed as situated in the dead centre of the world. Twenty years later came the Umayyad mosque in Damascus, today still one of the noblest buildings in the world. And fifty years on, in 762, Baghdad was under construction, the first integrally planned Muslim capital.

In north Africa the site of Qayrawan had been chosen and a start made on what developed into the most classical of Arab mosques. To the east, Fustat, the main Muslim settlement in Egypt since 640, grew into a major city and was enlarged in 969 by the Fatimid foundation of al-Qahira, Cairo. And in the west, following the conquest of Spain in the eighth century, a princely refugee from the struggles in Baghdad, Idris Ibn Abd Allah, came upon a well-watered valley that nestled in the skirts of the Atlas and abreast the road to Spain. There in 788–89 was founded the city of Fez.

Seen from the low hills above, the densely packed houses of Fez followed the valley's contours in gentle terraces, their flat roofs a jumble of dazzling cubes. The first impression of Fez was that the city was clearly not built for effect. Vistas,

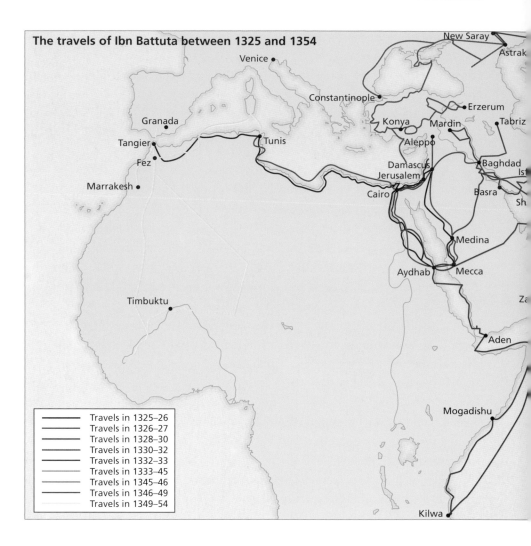

The travels of Ibn Battuta between 1325 and 1354

——	Travels in 1325–26
——	Travels in 1326–27
——	Travels in 1328–30
——	Travels in 1330–32
——	Travels in 1332–33
——	Travels in 1333–45
——	Travels in 1345–46
——	Travels in 1346–49
——	Travels in 1349–54

boulevards, waterfronts, and facades were conspicuous by their absence. Leo Africanus thought the fortified city walls and crowds of people were worthy of remark: 'A world it is to see how large, how populous, how well-fortified and walled this citie is', he wrote in his *Wasf Ifriqiya* (Description of Africa) in 1526. The man who became known in Europe as Leo from Africa was properly Hasan al-Wazzan (d.c.1550), born in Granada but brought up in Fez. The city was not a collection of magnificent buildings but a congregation of people. Whether rich or poor, their homes were not detached in gardens or semi-detached in terraces, but huddled hard together, three walls shared and the fourth blankly shutting off the street. 'Believer is to believer,' said the Prophet, 'as the mutually upholding sections of a building.'

At street level the mud walls were continuous and blank save for heavy doors. Each door opened into a twisted narrow passage at the end of which, hidden from the street, a very different and private space was revealed. For the centre of the house was a courtyard, flanked on three sides by galleries, with a fountain or a

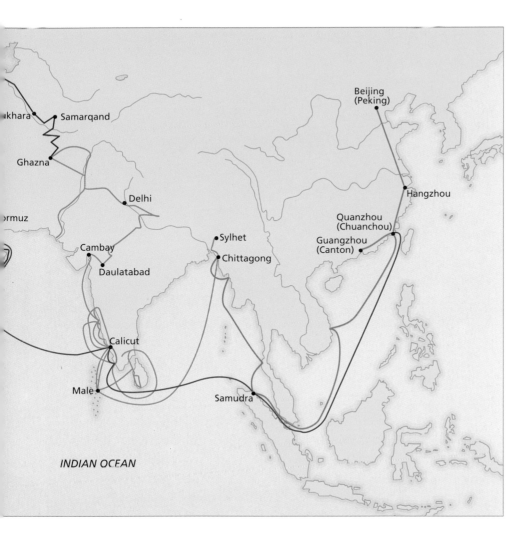

Fez in its well-watered valley
in the foothills of the Atlas
mountains.

Looking at Fez from above we can see how the city was above all things a 'congregation of people'. Respect for individual privacy was essential if living in such close proximity was to work. Disputes over issues such as access, boundary walls, water supplies and the management of animals were inevitable in such an environment. Muslims, as al-Ghazzali (*see pp. 173ff*) reveals to us, had considerable wisdom regarding the management of such communities and their problems.

pool in the middle. The courtyard was paved, the walls and the pillars supporting the galleries might have had faience tiling and carved or stucco capitals. It was a place of unexpected elegance, a sanctuary for private life.

The open patios of the houses found their public equivalent in the open space at the centre of the city. This was the mosque. Seen from the air the Qarawiyyin mosque of Fez appears as a spacious ordered clearing at the heart of the city's maze. Fez had dozens of mosques but here as in other Muslim cities, a distinction was made between the Jami mosque and the local mosques. 'City mosques are of two kinds,' wrote Ibn Khaldun, 'great spacious ones which are prepared for holiday prayers, and other minor ones which are restricted to one section of the population or one quarter of the city and which are not for generally attended prayers.' The Masjid Jami, the 'great spacious one', was the centre of worship for the whole city. It had to be large enough to enable everyone to assemble there. The call to prayer resounded five times a day; it was the pulse of the city. In the city's circulatory system the mosque was truly the heart. As a gathering point at the community's focus, it filled the same role as a Roman forum or European marketplace, but with one important difference; in the Islamic city the sanction under which the community assembled was not that of political or corporate authority but of religious hegemony.

The mosque was much more than a place of worship. The Qarawiyyin mosque remained until the twentieth century the foremost educational institution in Fez. Like al-Azhar in Cairo it was the city's college. Here the elite of students who had emerged from the local Quranic schools embarked on their higher education. Here they sat in circles round their chosen professor and entered the realms of Islamic learning. As the students absorbed their professor's commentaries on the

The house

Houses vary throughout the Islamic world according to the influence of pre-Islamic cultures, climate, geography, building materials, and construction techniques. Nevertheless, their nature is profoundly influenced by two concerns widely shared by Muslims: the right of the family to keep its affairs secure from neighbourhood and state, providing it did not flaunt wrongdoing, and the impact of Islamic law and Muslim preferences with regard to women.

Little can be guessed of the interior of the houses of Fez from their exterior. Tall blank walls face the outside world. If they are pierced by windows at ground level, they are small, grilled, and high enough to prevent passers by from peeping in. Windows higher up may be larger but must not overlook the courtyards of neighbours. Not a hint was to be given externally of the nature of the life within. Wisdom, moreover, taught men to conceal their women from the prying eyes of neighbours and their wealth from the jealous sight of the authorities. In effect, the houses looked inwards. Resources were spent in making beautiful interiors using tilework, stucco, and wood. The family lived around a courtyard, or courtyards, where trees and lush vegetation would be grown for coolness and shade, and water might flow to cisterns and fountains - Fez had a plentiful supply of water.

'Believers, do not enter the dwellings of other men', exhorts the Quran, 'until you have asked their owners' permission and wished them peace.' But even when a Muslim did enter the house, he was most unlikely to penetrate beyond the men's reception room. This might be separated from the woman's area, *harem* (related to *haram*, sacred), by screens, through which women might witness the men's gathering, or by substantial distance. If the man of the house had more than one wife, the harem would be furnished with separate but equal apartments for each wife, often the architecture itself distinctively reflecting the requirements of the faith.

The heart of the house was the courtyard. Note the tiled floor and the provision for a pool and fountain.

The courtyard of the Qarawiyyin mosque which lies at the centre of Fez. The mosque was begun under the Almoravids in 859 and extended in the tenth, twelfth, and seventeenth centuries. It was the place where the best students in the city would be taught as they prepared to enter the ranks of the ulama. Down to the twentieth century it was the leading centre of education in the city.

Quran and hadith, as they explored the Islamic sciences and Arabic arts, and above all as they debated points of Islamic law, so they approached the status of the ulama, the learned and immensely influential caucus of Muslim society.

Around the Qarawiyyin mosque were located most of the madrasas. Except for the famous and favoured Bu Inaniyya madrasa at the western end of the city, the Fez madrasas were more student hostels than teaching establishments. They had halls of prayer, some even a minaret, but they were essentially the academic equivalents of the inns for visiting merchants which were also located near the mosque. Of these latter establishments Leo Africanus reckoned there were almost 200, and to them came a continuous stream of merchants, encouraged by the city's location at the crossroads of two vital trade routes: the long east-west route from Tunis and Egypt to Spain and the Atlantic coast, and the trans-Saharan route from the kingdoms of Timbuktu and the Upper Niger to the Mediterranean. They brought to Fez the luxuries of the whole Muslim world – gems and sandalwood from India, furs from Central Asia, incense from Yemen, pearls from the Gulf, saffron, indigo, and carpets from Iran, gold from west Africa. And they took away the products of Fez, the silks, thread, and fabrics, the saddlery and the shoes.

The area beside the Qarawiyyin mosque was the *qaysariyya*, the commercial centre of the city. Here in the narrow streets and cul-de-sacs were jewellers' shops, a whole bazar for shoes and leather goods, another for spices, and another for fabrics. Here too were the *funduqs*, the warehouses for each trade where goods were sold by auction from wholesaler to retailer. Local markets in Fez dealt in food-stuffs and basic commodities but the qaisariyya was the prestigious centre of the long-distance trade.

Doubtless it was the vision of springs welling from the ground and rushing to form the Wadi Fez that dictated the site of the city. It was certainly to the convenience and abundance of the clear mountain water of the river that Fez owed its development and prosperity. Using the lie of the land and conducting supplies by an elaborate system of channels, the Fez engineers brought water to every mosque, madrasa and funduq, to the street fountains and the public baths, and to every household of consequence. There was even enough supply and sufficient fall to operate an effective system of flushing drains.

But what made water the lifeblood of the city was the opportunities it offered agriculture and industry. The proximity of good grazing and arable land was an obvious necessity for any medieval city. In Fez extensive fruit and vegetable gardens flourished within and without the city limits. Beyond, the mountain pastures supplied meat, the olive groves oil, and the coastal plain grain. The essentials for growth were there. But to create the wealth to realize it, Fez turned to industry.

In both English and French, Morocco denotes leather. Both the city and the country of which it is the ancient capital became known by their products. Ever since craftworkers from Andalusia settled on the south bank of the river, Fez has been famous for its handicrafts. During the prolonged death of Muslim rule in Spain there were further influxes of refugees from Cordoba, Seville, and Granada. An artistic and industrious people, they brought with them skills and endowed the city with its gracious mosques, stuccoes, and mosaics.

A local bazar in Fez. Such bazars concentrated on foodstuffs and basic commodities, while the qaysariyya next to the Qarawiyyin mosque was the centre for the long-distance trade. Here were the shops specializing in jewellery, leather goods, and spices; here too were the warehouses where goods were sold by wholesalers to retailers.

The tanneries in Fez where skins and hides were tanned and dyed. Oil, mineral, and vegetable tanning agents were all used and finishes achieved in a good range of colours which included red, brown, blue, olive green, yellow, and black. Morocco gave its name to a distinct form of leather as did Muslim Cordoba to 'cordovan'.

Some trades, like the working of precious metals (a speciality of the important Jewish community, also expelled from Spain in 1492), weaving, and leather finishing, required little or no water so could be conducted in the heart of the city. But others – pottery and milling, and, above all, dyeing and tanning – required vast quantities. Hence they were located downstream of the residential and commercial areas and added a considerable dimension to the city plan. 'Dyers have their abode by the river's side and have each of them a most clear fountain or cistern to wash their silk-stuffs in', noted Leo Africanus. The tanneries, where skins and hides were prepared and cured in a variety of vats, were also located downstream. Twenty different operations were involved in the processing alone – a good reason for production-line methods. But the tanneries were not factories so much as communal workshops to which the craftsman brought his own team of apprentices and journeymen, his own tools and materials, and in which he rented space and facilities. There may have been a hundred such teams in one tannery.

How, before modern times, this labour was organized has been the subject of acrimonious debate. Were the trade organizations to which, for instance, each tannery belonged, 'guilds' or not? In Fez at any rate they were important institutions.

Headed by an *amin*, they regulated the hierarchy of each trade, operated a system of initiation, and settled internal disputes. They also operated rudimentary social benefits for their members. Each 'guild' patronized certain mosques and identified with certain sufi brotherhoods. They also provided the *muhtasib* with a consensus of opinion within each trade and with specialized advice on trade practices.

The muhtasib was the official guardian of public morality and as such had many responsibilities. He saw to it that the Friday prayers and the Fast were observed and also kept an eye on decent public conduct in, for instance, the baths and inns. The humane treatment of children, slaves, and animals was his concern, as was the cleanliness of the streets and mosques. But his principal function was as a supervisor and arbitrator in the market. He controlled weights and measures – his standard cubit is still to be seen marked on a marble slab in the Fez qais-ariyya; he checked prices, exercised quality control, and punished fraud. It is significant that the post of muhtasib was considered to be a religious institution. The incumbent was practising officially that primary religious obligation of the individual believer to exhort his or her fellows to good and to denounce evil. He was a classical example of how Islam entered daily life and provided Muslim society with a sense of solidarity and conformity.

THE COMMUNITY, THE STATE, AND THE INDIVIDUAL: THE DUTY OF *HISBA*

When we speak of a certain society as Muslim, if we do not mean that Islamic law has formed to a recognizable extent its social institutions (so that marriage or inheritance arrangements, for example, show its distinctive stamp), we do not mean much. The sharia was an ideal system of social morality which constantly pressed to shape society. But it was more than the sum of legal regulations, for it embodied a certain general outlook or attitude, which combined the certainty that God-given truth ought to guide individual lives, with the understanding that right behaviour depended primarily on the individual conscience and the need to conform. It is commonplace to point out the sharia emphasis on the individual, in Albert Hourani's words: 'The emphasis was on the freedom of the individual to seek the goods of this world and the next in his own way, and to dispose freely of them.' The medieval community was very sensitive to the dangers of direct coercion, or state involvement in matters of belief. Its moral regime was at once firm on principles and distinctly inclined to forgive human weaknesses and diversity. The key note was moderation or balance, the middle way, which al-Ghazzali (1056–1111) identified completely with the *sirat al-mustaqim*, the 'straight path' of the Quran.

When al-Ghazzali wrote his *Ihya ulum al-din* ('Revival of the Religious Sciences') in the last decade of the eleventh century he had already lived in several important cities, including Baghdad, Damascus, and Jerusalem. In this remarkable book, one of the most influential in the literature of Islam, he devoted a section to condemning the offences which he said were common in the streets, mosques, markets, public baths, and private houses. It is a good place to get a sense of the dominant attitude of the ulama and thus the sharia.

Street offences included encroachment on public space by adding protruding balconies to the houses or benches to the shops; obstructing passage by piling large supplies of wood or grain in the street (only the amount needed for home consumption should be allowed); slaughtering of animals outside butchers' shops and polluting the path with blood; dumping water and making the street dangerously slippery; keeping riding animals tied longer than was necessary to mount and dismount, which obstructed the street and fouled it with dung; bringing into the narrow streets pack animals with sharp-edged loads that tore people's clothes (the wider avenues should be used instead when available); loitering by groups of adolescent boys outside the women's public baths to ogle them on their way in and out. Al-Ghazzali explained that such behaviour defeated the public good which streets were meant to serve. Pedestrians had a right to go about their business reasonably unhindered, and without their clothes being torn or soiled. Streets should be free from refuse for reasons of public health and safety, but also for aesthetic reasons. He pointedly said that 'human nature abhors filth.'

Al-Ghazzali had harsh words for pretentious or overly eager conduct of religious services, for the muezzin who exaggerated and stretched his call to prayer, or began it in the middle of someone else's. He said that excessive enthusiasm of that kind produced a cacophony of jarring noise which only confused the congregation. The custom of repeating the call to prayer at daybreak in the same mosque he called a nuisance which served no purpose, since no one within earshot could have been left sleeping after the first call. There were also many worshippers who disturbed the concentration of others in the mosque by their ritually unclean clothes, their wrong qibla orientation, or by reciting the words of the Holy Book incorrectly. This last was especially widespread and al-Ghazzali emphasized the merit of teaching correct recitation. In any case, they should be politely asked to keep their voices low.

On Fridays in particular the mosques were crowded with pedlars hawking medicines, foods, and amulets. The quack doctors and sellers of magical amulets were frauds who ought to be banned inside and outside the mosque. But there was nothing wrong with allowing merchants to sell clothing, medicines, books, and foods in the mosque so long as they did not disturb worship or turn the mosque into a daily market. Similarly, children were welcome and free to play in the mosque but not to turn it into a regular playground. The insane too were welcome, provided they did not rant obscenities or expose themselves. Equally, the inebriated were free to stay provided they did not vomit or become aggressive and unreasonable. Al-Ghazzali opposed those who wanted to beat and remove them: he favoured inviting the drunkards to stay until they were sober enough to be counselled against drink. Nevertheless, he supported punishing a drunk seen swaying in public, principally to stop the flaunting of sin. But the secret offender must not be pursued, for to spy on people in the privacy of their own homes was a more serious offence than drinking.

This discussion of offences was part of al-Ghazzali's invaluable analysis of *hisba*, the primary duty of every Muslim 'to promote what is right and to prevent what is wrong' (*Al-amr bi al-maruf wa al-nahy an al-munkar*). The office of market inspector was conceived as a specialization of this general duty, muhtasib

Travellers arriving at a small town in the thirteenth century. This scene, painted with a humane and humorous eye, enables us to approach the urban world of the time. Of course there is a mosque and a minaret, but there are also chickens on the domes of what appears to be the bazar. A woman sits outside the town gate spinning, while a guard stands at the gate with a long spear. A man and a woman appear to be arguing, various animals go about their business, and the travellers are welcomed with courtesy. The clothing of all, as well as the saddlecloths of the camels, are decorated with strips of cloth known as *tiraz*.

meaning someone who practises hisba. For al-Ghazzali the duty of hisba was 'the main pivot of the religion, and the high purpose for which God sent His Prophets.' There was much at stake in his argument that hisba was the inalienable right and obligation of the *individual* believer, male or female, free or slave, upright or even persistent sinner (*fasiq*). Only the insane, the minor, the disabled, and the unbeliever were exempt or excluded. He unequivocally rejected the opposing view that individuals had no right to hisba except with the permission of the ruler (*imam, wali*), finding no basis for it in the religious sources, which, he said, taught that every individual believer was unconditionally obliged to disapprove of the wrong, and that he or she did not need the permission of any other creature to do so.

In the first two centuries the nascent Muslim polity had undergone a crucial struggle to decide who was to be the ultimate authority in matters of law and legislation, the caliphs or the ulama. The conflict came to a head in the first half of the ninth century, and by al-Ghazzali's time it had long been decisively settled in the ulama's favour. It was the Caliph al-Mamun (r.813–33) who had defined the conflict by his determination to establish caliphal authority as supreme and exclusive in matters of religious doctrine. Al-Mamun desperately understood, probably too late, that the caliphal state would not survive without unquestioned supreme authority over all matters, religious as well as worldly. He had even claimed, consistently enough, that the caliph could decide who was and who was not qualified to transmit hadith. Towards the end of his reign he created the inquisition (the *mihna*) in order to subdue the self-appointed religious leaders who claimed that they, rather than the caliph, were the rightful arbiters of right and wrong.

These religious leaders asserted that the Quran and Sunna stood above the caliph; that allegiance to their divine commands superseded all other loyalties; that the community itself through its specialists was responsible for the interpretation of these commands; and finally that a caliph who did not follow Islam thus understood could not command the obedience of the community. It is very significant that the ulama who were the targets of the inquisition had mobilized the civil community in the capital Baghdad against the caliph under the banner of *al-amr bi al-maruf*. The basis of their claims was precisely that they represented a community of all the individual believers.

The drama of the inquisition has obscured the importance of al-Mamun's earlier, more subtle strategy to control the revolutionary potential of the hisba. It was he who invented the muhtasib as a state official, by giving the title to the ancient office of market inspector, and claiming that only his appointed muhtasibs were entitled 'to promote what is right and prevent what is wrong'. For men in authority there was an understandable need to tame the revolutionary potential of the hisba, and its consignment as a precisely defined job to a government-appointed official proved very successful; it spread to every city in the Islamic world. It has not always been easy to see beyond the muhtasib-as-market-inspector to the original conception of hisba and its profound 'constitutional' implications.

Two centuries later, the first comprehensive work of Islamic political theory, *Al-Ahkam al-Sultaniyya* (Ordinances of Government) of al-Mawardi (d.1058), confirmed the success of the muhtasib as a city official. Al-Ghazzali, however, a generation later, did not mention this official at all and, as was his wont, went straight to the heart of the original matter. He evoked the great constitutional struggle by marshalling a relentless sequence of episodes in which the early ulama performed heroic hisba, and mouthed some of the most incendiary political rhetoric ('There

This bazar scene from a late sixteenth century Ottoman manuscript shows the *muhtasibs* (market inspectors) at work. The life of the bazar proceeds: vendors shout their wares, men haggle, a woman negotiates the sale or purchase of a bracelet. The market inspectors are the men with swords.

A ruler and his followers attend a mosque service, from a sixteenth-century Iranian manuscript. The mosque was a great place of congregation for the community and Muslims were expected to behave there with all due consideration for others. Note the presence of women in a separate area. In the early Islamic centuries women took full advantage of their right to pray in the mosque. Subsequently, however, they were not able to do so in all Muslim societies.

is a valley in Hell called Habhab which God has specially prepared for every tyrannical imam'), against practically all the caliphs of Islamic history from Muawiya to al-Mamun. He summed up the case nicely: 'Given that it is right to censure the imam because of his oppression, how can it be right to ask for his permission?... If the wali approves when someone practises *al-amr bi al-maruf*, so be it; but if he is displeased, then his displeasure is an offence which must be condemned.'

In one episode a self-appointed muhtasib was dragged in front of al-Mamun who told him, 'I am informed that you consider yourself fit to "promote what is right and prevent what is wrong" without our permission...when God has assigned this right to us.' The man answered back, 'You have been given dominion in the world, but here is God's Book and the Example of his Prophet – if you obeyed them you would show gratitude to those who help you to protect their sanctity.' Another story brought a man who had just smashed a whole boatload of the caliph al-Mutadid's best wine to him: '– Who are you? – A muhtasib. – And who appointed you to the hisba? – The One who appointed you to the imama appointed me to the hisba.'

Caliphal authority, such as it was, did not long survive the death of al-Mamun's immediate successors. Meanwhile the Abbasid caliphs continued their frantic search to find a stable basis for their authority. The caliph al-Mutasim's (r.833–42) momentous decisions to move away from the people of Baghdad to his purpose-built capital of Samarra and to recruit an army of Turkish slaves from beyond the borders of the Islamic world, signalled the fateful alienation of the state from society in Islam and hugely contributed to it. Writing from the vantage point of eleventh-century Spain, Ibn Hazm (d.1063) had no doubt about the significance of Mutasim's policy:

> Al-Mutasim became caliph after his brother al-Mamun: he departed from Baghdad and made Samarra his capital; he degraded the state of the Khurasanians, the armies of his fathers; and he sought strength from the Turks whom he imported and made into an army. From that time the Islamic State perished, and the pillar of corruption began to rise.

The introduction of Turkish armies to the Middle East with Turkish generals who soon became the *de facto* rulers, was reinforced in the mid-eleventh century by the migration of huge numbers of Turkish-speaking nomads who formed, with their Turkish cousins who remained in Central Asia, a formidable military class that would control most of the governments of the Middle East until modern times.

When the Abbasid caliphs lost actual control of vast provinces of the Islamic empire, any hope that the central government could preserve the umma was also lost; and the community began to rely largely on its own resources. At the very time that the unified Muslim empire disintegrated into separate political units, the civil community itself, notwithstanding the political fragmentation and without political cover, built up classical Islamic society with all its defining institutions,

from the schools of law to the sufi orders. The several types of self-chosen frater-
nal associations that began to appear simultaneously in the eleventh century,
whether spiritual brotherhoods or paramilitary groups such as youth gangs, cannot be understood socially unless we see them also in the same light.

Henceforth the umma was founded upon loyalty to principles formulated by
religious scholars independently of the state. It expected the government to
uphold the law and the truth, but not to define their contents. Instead, the community vested this basic function of legislation in itself, leaving a distinct hollow-
ness at the heart of the Muslim states which reduced their authority for centuries
to come. Medieval Muslims believed, as we said, that the Muslim city had two
focal points, the Friday mosque and the market. It speaks volumes about the Muslims' view of their polity that the palace, or government house, was conspicuously
absent from their list of the indispensable elements of the city. The dominant
ideology now saw the government as an outside agency to be kept at arm's length
from the spheres of personal life. Insecurity led to stronger emphasis on the

One of the great celebrations
of communal feeling each year
was the feast at the end of
Ramadan, the month of fasting. Muslims would don new
clothes, the congregational
mosques would be full to
overflowing, and there would
be mingled senses of relief,
joy, and achievement, widely
shared. Here a cavalcade
comes together to celebrate.
Note the flags bearing religious inscriptions.

intimate areas of social life, which turned in towards the quarter and neighbour-hood, small group, family, and personal loyalties.

Throughout his treatment of hisba al-Ghazzali tried to do two things at the same time. The first was to uphold hisba as the right of the individual without the permission of the state, a foundation principle of the existing community. The second was to curb what the zealous could take as an open invitation to search and destroy whatever they deemed offensive, by regulating hisba so that individ-ual rights were protected and communal conflict avoided. This second concern was patently not directed against the state as such, but against any agency which could infringe on the individual's privacy and conscience. Here, al-Ghazzali was taking extraordinary care that the civil community itself and the guardians of its sharia law do not act illegally. For he did not leave his argument – that hisba was the right of the individual – to be undermined by the claim that only 'good' Mus-lims were entitled to hisba. He openly rejected moral integrity as a prerequisite. Those who required integrity had asked how someone who was morally corrupt could reform others ('how can the shadow be straight if the stick is bent?'). He rejected their argument as baseless:

> Should it be required that the muhtasib be free from sin? Such a prerequisite
> would be against the consensus of the community *ijma*, and would put an end
> to the possibility of hisba, for even the Companions of the Prophet, not to men-
> tion lesser people, were not free from sin. There is even disagreement as to
> whether the prophets themselves, peace be upon them, have been immune from
> sin. The Quran itself associates Adam, peace be upon him, and other prophets
> with sin. That is why Said Ibn Jubayr said: 'If no one but the blameless were to
> command the right and check the wrong, no one will ever command anything.'

An individual Muslim who sinned, even persistently, by drinking wine or forni-cating, was nevertheless still obliged to disapprove of the wrongdoing of others. His obligation did not end because of his own offences. Again, al-Ghazzali was unconditionally forthright: 'The armies of the Muslims have always been full of the good and the bad, of those who drank wine and those who oppressed widows, and they have not been forbidden to fight [in the cause of Islam], neither in the Prophet's own time nor after him.'

Hisba, then, was simply the inalienable right of the individual Muslim as a believer; it was also his or her foremost religious and civic duty. Al-Ghazzali warned of the consequences that neglect of this duty would bring about – the destruction of prophecy and religion, and the ruin of countries and societies. Given this apocalyptic emphasis, the extent to which he was prepared to limit the application of hisba by considerations of respect for the rights of individual Mus-lims, and the fear of communal conflict, is remarkable. In a city divided between two religious groups any attempt to enforce right belief might lead to civil war. Generally, he was troubled by the possibility that 'the gathering of supporters and the brandishing of weapons might provoke a wide communal conflict.' So he defined the target of hisba very strictly. The offence had to be deemed objectionable by all orthodox jurists without question; and there was to be no intervention in matters about which Muslims disagreed. A Shafii had no right to object to a Hanafi doing what the Hanafi school of law permitted – consuming 'non-intoxicating' wine, or marrying without the presence of a legal guardian. In effect this limited the targets to the most common offences such as the drinking of wine, fornication, eating pork, and failure to pray.

Furthermore, the offence had to be *in progress*. Intervention was not lawful after the fact, for example against someone who had already finished drinking wine; nor was it lawful before the fact. Finally and crucially, the offence had to be *overt*. The firmest feature of al-Ghazzali's treatment of hisba was his repeated emphasis that it was unlawful to search for evidence of wrongdoing. Absolutely no one had a right to spy on someone's home in order to detect forbidden music or wine; intervention was possible only if boisterous noise or an overwhelming smell of wine aroused the public outside. It was equally unlawful to question people about the behaviour of their neighbours. He quoted with approval the words of the wise Luqman (the ancient Arabian sage after whom chapter 31 of the Quran is named): 'It is better to keep quiet about what you know than to broadcast what you merely suspect.'

It was also unlawful to enter a house without the occupier's permission. Al Ghazzali gave the telling example involving the second caliph Umar, who climbed over the wall of a man's house to find him with wine and a woman in the middle of a forbidden act. As Umar began to admonish him, the man said to the Caliph: 'Granted that I have committed an offence, but you have committed three offences: God said "Do not spy", and you have spied; and He said, "Enter houses through their doors", and you came in through the roof; and He said, "Do not enter other people's houses without first asking their permission and saluting them" [Quran 24:27], and you have failed to do so.'

Hisba applied only to offences committed publicly: 'A sin committed in private damages only the sinner; only when it is done openly and left unchecked does it damage the public at large.' But even in public extraordinary care had to be taken. It was not even permitted to stop a notorious drunk on the street with something looking suspiciously like a bottle hidden under his clothes. The man's bad name did not necessarily mean that he was carrying a prohibited substance, for even sinners needed perfectly legal things, like oil or vinegar. What was required for intervention was transparent and unsolicited direct evidence. The muhtasib could not demand inspection of the hidden bottle, for that was *tajassus* (spying), inquisition which was positively forbidden.

The inquisition of al-Mamun had been an invasion of privacy and the individual conscience on a massive scale. Those caught in its net were forced to undergo an interrogation which determined not only their chances for life and

Opposite Muslim life was notable for the great respect which was shown to the dead. Cemeteries came to be features of the urban world. Here citizens might perform pilgrimage, hold festivals, gather in meetings, or enjoy picnics. In the great cemeteries a range of buildings embracing hostels, hospitals, libraries, and free kitchens might be constructed, as princes and local notables demonstrated their piety. Amongst the more striking cemeteries which have survived are the City of the Dead in Cairo and the Shah-i Zinda in Samarqand. Here we see a burial from a thirteenth-century Arab manuscript. Note the domes of the larger tombs, which were typical of these places, as was the presence of trees, and often cats.

livelihood but also their very standing as members of the umma. The inquisition failed, but its lasting effect in classical Islam was that no group of mainstream ulama would ever again think of using the state to enforce belief. It was an enduring lesson of the dangers of prying into private life. In late fifteenth-century Cairo al-Suyuti (d.1505) even condemned as spying the reprehensible 'new habit of some persons to ask their fellows: Where have you been? Where are you going?'

Al-Ghazzali's discussion of actual intervention reinforced his restrictions. Hisba was governed by respect for the rights to life, personal dignity, privacy, private property, and social peace. Intervention which violated these values was unlawful. Intervention itself was a complex procedure, in eight stages, which he demarcated with supreme care. It was to proceed from one stage to the next in reluctant escalation, only when absolutely necessary.

The eight stages of intervention fell into two distinct groups, the first four relying on moral persuasion, and the last four on coercion. To cross the line separating persuasion from coercion was fraught with difficulties, and therefore invited important qualifications. Physical coercion applied only to certain offences. Those of the tongue and heart, and every offence inside people's souls, could be dealt with only by moral exhortation. Significantly, the use of force was not permitted against one's superiors. The muhtasib might not use force against his own father, or teacher, or the ruler, for that would undermine the social order and social peace. It will be recalled that al-Ghazzali had argued forcefully that even the persistent sinner was fully entitled to practise hisba. Here he conceded that moral integrity was necessary in moral intervention, since a muhtasib's effectiveness was compromised if his bad name was known. Ironically, hisba involving force did not require this condition, and a sinner was obliged to practise it: 'Shouldn't someone who drinks wine still stop a murder?'

The muhtasib was not allowed to push or drag the offender if he could talk him into walking away voluntarily. He was not to use his own hands if the offender could be persuaded to spill the wine himself. He should avoid breaking the wine jugs. These were legal private property and the muhtasib might have to pay compensation if he were to destroy them unnecessarily. When removing silk clothing he was not allowed to tear it, only to loosen the seams!

Furthermore, hisba was binding only if a person was able to suppress the offence without suffering serious harm. No one had an obligation to intervene if he or she feared retaliation, and intervention was actually forbidden if a friend, companion, or relative might suffer reprisal. There were also circumstances when hisba was positively prohibited. The Quranic condemnation of suicide meant, for example, that there was no place at all for intervention against a villain with a glass of wine in one hand and a sword in the other (al-Ghazzali's image of the government's soldiery), for he might cut the muhtasib's head off and drink the wine. The principle of self-preservation did not prohibit all action that could lead to death. Heroic hisba was legitimate – provided it could definitely stop the offence or raise the morale of the believers, but to risk death otherwise was meaningless and prohibited. Intervention was also prohibited if the suppression of an offence led directly to something worse.

The eight stages of intervention were: (1) Recognition: the offence had to be an unambiguous public breach of Islamic law. (2) Instruction: sometimes a person does wrong simply because of ignorance. It is essential to teach without insulting him or her merely because of ignorance. (3) Counselling: a persistent offender who knows that the action is forbidden, for example a habitual drunk, should be patiently and politely counselled. (4) Rebuke: when gentle counselling fails, the muhtasib may use harsh words of disapproval, provided he avoids overstatement and obscenity.

The next stage (5) which specifically targeted the sin rather than the sinner, nevertheless marked the critical line separating persuasion from coercion: if strong rebuke fails, the muhtasib may act directly to stop the prohibited act or destroy the prohibited substance, for example by spilling the wine. (6) Intimidation: the *threat* of force must precede any actual use of force against the person of the offender, and it must not include impossible or unlawful threats, such as, 'I will plunder your house, or beat your child, or enslave your wife.' (7) Coercion: when necessary the use of force is permitted provided it is confined, in the first instance, to the use of the bare arms and, always, to the minimum necessary to stop the offence.

The highest stage of hisba (8) called for the deployment of weapons and assistants when the muhtasib was not able to carry out his duty alone. In such circumstances the offender might also muster help, and two armed groups would be likely to form and face each other, and ultimately street fighting might break out. This was the most problematic stage of hisba, and here al-Ghazzali was rather ill at ease. The possibility of armed conflict had provided one of the weightier arguments for the opinion that individual Muslims had no right to hisba without appointment. Extremely sensitive to the dangers of fighting in the streets, al-Ghazzali nevertheless maintained that the risk should not be allowed to undermine the principle that hisba was the unconditional right of the individual. His solution was to restrict intervention to precisely those few symbolic things (wine drinking, fornication, failure to pray) whose open transgression would outrage the community as a whole, making intervention essential to uphold the law within the community. Thus, al-Ghazzali accepted the risk of riot if it arose from an attempt to check an ordinary common offender; it was therefore all the more telling that he was emphatically not willing to risk the sectarian strife that might follow from hisba against different religious belief, or heresy. This was the unique and consequential circumstance where he limited the individual believer's absolute right to hisba.

Originally al-Ghazzali had presented the question in this way: if it was right to refrain from objecting to the Hanafi on account of his marriage without a legal guardian simply because he believed it to be right, should not one similarly refrain from objecting against the Mutazilite who claimed that God cannot be seen, or that only good, but not evil, issued from Him, or that the Quran was created, or the philosopher who said that only souls, not bodies, will be resurrected, or the wrong views of Christians and Jews? After all, they too believed they were right. Al-Ghazzali made a radical distinction between the two types of differences. The different opinions of Muslims about what acts were allowed or forbidden were equally legitimate because they were matters of detail; but on the basic articles of faith there could not be two contradictory points of view.

In principle, therefore, the duty of hisba against heresy was evident. Al-Ghazzali's main argument, however, was that it might not be possible or even desirable to introduce it. One must consider conditions in the city: if the population was divided between the orthodox and the heretics, so that condemnation of the heresy might provoke communal conflict, then for the sake of peace individual Muslims were forbidden to get involved. Al-Ghazzali understood the source of the difficulty well: 'The heretic believes that he is right, and believes that the man of right belief is wrong; each claims that he is right, and denies that he is a heretic.' Only the ruler could bring to the task the kind of overwhelming force that would maintain civil peace (but the duty of government to suppress heresy was to be carried out in obedience to the views of the ulama who, on behalf of the community, determined who was and who was not to be considered orthodox). The requirement that individuals needed permission in order to fight heresy was the culmination of al-Ghazzali's cumulative curbs which were designed to shield society from the heedless application of hisba. Muslims must refrain from practising hisba in mixed societies – and outside the inner Arabian peninsula all Muslim societies were mixed – in order to avoid sectarian violence and civil war.

The 'preference for social peace at almost any price' was a guiding principle of later medieval Muslim society. The pronounced tendency of the urban elites of ulama and notables to accept any government provided it was able to maintain civil peace governed their attitude to all changes of regime, if not generally to all rulers. Equally, the governments were not able to rule without expensive bargaining with these urban elites. The sultans made vast financial investments in the religious endowments which provided the ulama with much of their social power. Such institutions of urban society were basically independent of the rulers, which is why modern historians invariably use the word 'alliance' to describe the relationship between rulers and ulama.

THE LIVES OF WOMEN

The ulama were the authors of most of the written records of Muslim societies before modern times, and their biographical dictionaries offer detailed information about the origins and contributions of thousands of them. The biographical dictionary was a distinctive creation of Muslim societies; in it the ulama

فاطمه

ام المؤمنين

مسلم...

وام...

Women associated with the Prophet offer Muslim women a range of ideal types. Here his daughter Fatima, his favourite wife Aisha, and his wife from the Makhzum tribe Umm Salama are kneeling, their faces veiled and their heads surrounded by a nimbus of flames. Fatima has gained amongst the Shias a position almost equivalent to that of Mary for Christians; Aisha is one of the most respected sources of traditions relating to the Prophet and remembered for her willingness to go into battle to avenge the murdered caliph Uthman in 656; while Umma Salama is recorded as having dismissed summarily and with pride Abu Bakr and Umar, who were to become the first two caliphs, when they tried to intervene in the relations between the Prophet and his wives.

immortalized themselves. 'The conception that underlies the biographical dictionaries', as H. A. R. Gibb put it, 'is that the history of the Islamic community is essentially the contribution of the individual men and women to the building up and transmission of its specific culture; that is, it is these persons (rather than the political governors) who represent and reflect the active force in Muslim Society in their respective sphere; and that their individual contributions are worthy of being recorded for future generations.' As the ulama filled the vacuum created by the demise of the caliphate, the biographical dictionaries proliferated. Prominent historians such as al-Khatib al-Baghdadi (d.1071), Ibn Asakir (d.1176), and Ibn Khallikan (d.1282) began explicitly to identify biography with history. Such historical writing regarded the history of the umma as the sum total of the lives of its notables, mostly ulama.

The biographical dictionaries contain a detailed picture of intellectual life and important material for social and economic history. They are also the richest source for the history of women. There are two distinct groups of women about whom there is a critical mass of information. First, the women of Mecca and Medina of the first Islamic century, and secondly the notable women of Egypt, Syria, and Arabia in the later Middle Ages (the fourteenth to fifteenth centuries). The total of about 3,000 entries represents the vast majority of all entries about women in the dictionaries, and divided nearly equally between the two groups. However, the nature of the information about the two groups is completely different.

In the beginning biographies of the Prophet's companions became necessary because their statements about his life and words depended for their authenticity on details of their own lives. Like the men, the early women entered the literature because of their proximity to the Prophet, as witnesses who related hadith. Beginning with Ibn Sad's (d.845) *Al-Tabaqat al-kubra* (The First Generations) in the third Islamic century, which contained 629 women (out of 4,250 persons), and culminating with Ibn Hajar's (d.1449) *Al-Isaba fi tamyiz al-sahaba* (The Accurate Measure of the Companions) in the ninth Islamic century (1,551 women out of 12,043 persons), all such biographical collections were historical in that they looked back at a distant past. Even the first book by Ibn Sad was separated by two centuries from the women he discussed. Later authors wrote mostly about the very same group of women, receiving their subjects from the earlier authors. The total possible number of these women of early Islam is probably the figure of 1,551 in Ibn Hajar's definitive *Al-Isaba*.

The biographies have a double significance: they not only tell us facts about their subjects, they do so in a way that fits them into certain 'ideal types' of personality to which Islamic culture attributed value. Here the seminal figures were the Prophet's first wife Khadija, his beloved young wife Aisha, and his daughter Fatima. Aisha was an extremely controversial figure through her own lifetime and beyond. As we shall see, she provides an important link across the centuries between the early and later groups of women.

It was Fatima who had the most illustrious posthumous history. Her fame grew as she became progressively exalted among the Shiis: thus the later the Shiite source, the more detailed her life becomes and the longer the list of her virtues. She became 'the Mistress of the Women of the Worlds', the 'Virgin', the 'Pure and Holy'. She was created from the light of God's greatness, or from the food of Paradise. She is the 'Mistress of Women on the Day of Judgment'. She will be the first to enter Paradise and she will intercede with God to save sinners provided they loved her family.

Fatima is not mentioned in the Quran – a privilege accorded to Mary, mother of Jesus – but Shii tradition gave her all the known attributes of Mary. In *Bihar al-anwar* (whose volume on Fatima is the most comprehensive in Shiism), al-Majlisi (1627-98) systematically claimed for Fatima the miracles of Mary. She was also called *Maryam al-kubra*, the Great Mary. In popular religion, the faithful rely on Fatima, who takes sides with the oppressed in the struggle against injustice which her father began, and which she and most famously her martyr son Husayn continued. Shiite women travel to shrines and commemorate her birth and death; they bring to her their everyday problems, sickness, pregnancy and childbirth, failed crops. She continues to be the constant protector, mother, and hope of her followers.

The second group consists of almost 1,300 women whose biographies were mostly written in their own lifetimes in the fourteenth and fifteenth centuries by their contemporaries Ibn Hajar and his student Sakhawi (d.1497) in two great centennial dictionaries. Ibn Hajar's *Al-Durar al-kamina* (Hidden Pearls) has 198 women out of 5,204 fourteenth-century notables (4 per cent), and Sakhawi's *Al-Daw al-lami* (Brilliant Light) on the fifteenth century, has 1,075 women out of 11,691 (9 per cent). Sakhawi's twelve-volume dictionary has the largest single group of women, with more detailed information about them, than any other source in Islamic history. It commemorates the notables of the ninth (fifteenth) century, mostly ulama but also the high-ranking officials of the Mamluk establishment, in the important cities of Egypt, Syria, and Arabia – Cairo, Mecca and Medina, Damascus, Jerusalem. He devoted the final volume to the women of the same families and classes, including certain concubines, and women who were merchants, poets, midwives, and entertainers.

The unique importance of Sakhawi's dictionary becomes clear when we recognize that, for reasons which we do not understand, women practically disappear from the centennial biographical dictionaries that followed him. Al-Ghazzi (d.1651), who wrote about the sixteenth century, included only twelve women among his 1,647 entries; al-Muhibbi (d.1699) included none in his dictionary of 1,289 biographies of his century; al-Muradi (d.1791) found a place for only one woman among 753 eighteenth-century notables; and the biographer of the nineteenth century, al-Baytar (d.1918), found room for two only women out of 777 persons.

The life of Umm Hani

(1376 – 1466)

Born, Cairo, Friday, mid-Shaban 778
Died, Cairo, Saturday 30 Safar 871

Umm Hani, also known as Maryam, the Cairene, the Shafiite, daughter of Nur al-Din Abu al-Hasan Ali the son of Judge Abd al-Rahman Ibn Abd al-Malik. On her mother's side she was the granddaughter of Judge Muhammad Ibn Muhammad al-Qayati.

She was born in Cairo on Friday night in the middle of the month of Shaban 778. Her maternal grandfather Judge al-Qayati took care of her upbringing. In 785 he took her to audit hadith in Mecca directly from four masters [names given]; and in Cairo she studied with her grandfather himself and many other masters [6 names given]. She obtained certificates of audition from a large number of important masters [13 names are given].

She married Muhammad Ibn Umar Ibn Qutlubugha al-Baktamuri and had the following children by him: Shuja al-Din Muhammad al-Shafii, Sayf al-Din Muhammad al-Hanafi, Fatima, Yunis al-Maliki, and Mansur al-Hanbali. Her sons studied and followed the schools of law by which they became known, the Hanafi in particular excelling. Her son Mansur the Hanbali was brilliant, but he died young, and it was said that his intelligence killed him.

After her first husband died she married Hasan Ibn Suwaid al-Maliki and had her children Ahmad and Aziza by him. When her grandfather Judge al-Qayati died her husband put his hand on her inheritance and used it freely, but then he died and she inherited all.

With the money she bought the great workshop, famous for its enormous size and many spinning wheels, known as Insha al Akram near Birkat al-Fil. One of the descendants of the original owner challenged the legality of the sale in court, but the Hanbali Judge Nasr Allah ruled that the sale was legal, and confirmed her ownership of the workshop.

She taught hadith for a long time, and many eminent scholars heard it from her; personally, everything I have learned from her teachers, I learned through her. Yet I believe that she knew much more than I was able to learn. Her grandfather had presumably taught her the rest of the Six Books [the canonical collections of hadith], and also Nashawiri's version of the *Sahih* of Bukhari.

She was a good woman who used to weep profusely when the names of God and the Prophet were mentioned; she was consistent in her fasting and night prayers, firm in her religion, and especially concerned with ritual purity. She wrote well, and was a natural poet, able to make up verse instantly. As a young woman she had memorized the Quran, Abu Shajja's *Mukhtasar* [abridgement] of jurisprudence, and *al-Mulha* [of al-Hariri, a treatise in verse] on word inflection, as well as other works. I heard her recite beautifully the Chapter of the *Saff* from the Quran [Chapter 61, 'The Battle Array', which begins: 'Whatever is in heaven and earth celebrates the praise of God'.].

She performed the pilgrimage 13 times, often staying for months to study and teach in Mecca and Medina.

As she grew older she lost her eyesight, but was patient, then she lost the use of her legs and became housebound. Her Hanafi son looked after her until she died on Saturday 30 Safar 871, while I was in Mecca. She was buried in the burial grounds of her grandfather Judge al-Qayati, near the Mausoleum of our Imam Shafii in the Qarrafa. May God have mercy on her, and on us.

Sakhawi basically followed the standard format of medieval biographical dictionaries. After the identification of the subject and a genealogical note, the date of birth, if known, is given. This is followed, in the case of someone who is a transmitter of hadith, by information about her education, certificates (*ijazat*), and details of her travels and pilgrimages. Supplementary information includes facts about wealth, social standing, and perhaps, through anecdote, personal character. Most entries give the date and place of death, and, quite often, its cause. Sakhawi departed from the standard in his determination to provide a complete record of the women's marriages. The length of the biographies varies, and most of the really short entries are incomplete. Sakhawi worked on the biographies for decades, and died without completing them all. Many of the women were still alive when he died, so their entries do not contain their dates of death or information that escaped him when he was alive.

Umm Hani's entry (no. 980, see box) is a representative complete biography. Only the long list of her teachers' names has been omitted. Note the precise dating of her birth and death; the record of an education carefully supervised from the age of seven by her maternal grandfather, a famous judge; her two marriages, and seven named children; her work in the transmission of Islamic learning as a teacher – she was one of Sakhawi's esteemed teachers of hadith; her involvement in the marketplace as owner of a textile workshop; and her close relationship to the son who took care of her in her long and difficult old age. The extreme mobility of the ulama comes across in her thirteen pilgrimages to Mecca and Medina.

In the fourteenth and fifteenth centuries women figured prominently among the teachers of the famous male scholars. Umm Hani was only one of sixty-eight women experts on whose authority Sakhawi recited hadith. Ibn Hajar named fifty-three women among his direct authorities, and al-Suyuti thirty-three. After the first Islamic century women hadith experts had become scarce until their remarkable efflorescence in the period of Ibn Hajar and Sakhawi. It is unlikely that this renaissance of women's religious learning is but a trick of the sources. It coincided with a new assertive promotion by the Syrian and Egyptian ulama of Aisha, wife of the Prophet and daughter of the first caliph Abu Bakr, as the foremost female source of hadith, and the unrivalled source of hadith concerning women. In particular, she was the acknowledged expert on ritual purity, a matter which, according to Sakhawi, especially interested Umm Hani and other women ulama.

Aisha was the most controversial woman in Islamic history. Unlike Fatima, she lived for fifty momentous years after the Prophet's death (she died in 678), and participated actively as a leader in the first civil war (*fitna*) which split the Muslim community. The events of her very public life were so familiar that later generations could hardly invent or suppress them. They could only interpret them. The twin sources of Aisha's blame as well as honour lay in her long life after the Prophet's death. Her involvement in active opposition to Ali, the fourth caliph and husband of Fatima, to the point of open warfare in the first civil war earned her an evil part in the foundation drama of the Shiites (originally the party of Ali) and their unrestrained condemnation. The Shiites highlighted the central problem of her life with the Prophet, the accusation of adultery, and the Sunni's countered by asserting her innocence, divinely guaranteed in the Quranic verses which the Shiites, in turn, refused to

Not only were there women famous for their learning, but there were also women famous for their skill at calligraphy. This picture from Isfahan of about 1600 shows a fashionable woman writing a letter. It is hard to believe that her handwriting and her thoughts were not as elegant as her pose and her dress.

accept as pertaining to her at all. When the Sunnis emphasized her primacy as the Prophet's preferred wife, the Shiites promoted another, Umm Salama, as the most favoured.

It was because of the horror of civil war that the medieval community rejected armed opposition to political authority, and this meant that Aisha's participation in the civil war was consistently condemned by the Sunnis themselves. Her political involvement made it difficult for the Sunnis to justify completely her behaviour. Attempts to reduce her culpability did not go beyond emphasizing her hesitancy to proceed to the Battle of the Camel in 656, which she lost, and blaming her associates' bad influence. The contrary evidence of her own headstrong will was considerable.

But in the formative years of Islam Aisha was the source of much of the oral information about the Prophet which developed into the hadith, and this was the abiding basis for Sunni faithfulness, for she was one of the six most prolific companions. When she finally came into her own in the later Middle Ages as the most honoured woman in the Sunni community, the indisputable basis of her primacy was her religious knowledge. Knowledge was the attribute that, without doubt or apology, made Aisha tower over all other women. Because the 'Mother of the Believers' was not a saint, but a scholar, she became the tangible model for women scholars, and the prestigious validation of their careers.

The biographical dictionaries have provided the information needed to understand the role late medieval women played in Muslim learning. Their evidence of women's direct involvement in economic life, property, and religious endowments is only the tip of an iceberg; for example, the surviving Ottoman charitable endowment (*waqf*) records show greater involvement than the biographies alone suggest. Women sometimes founded nearly 40 per cent of all endowments.

It is the personal information in Sakhawi's biographies which has hitherto proved unyielding. However, Sakhawi did complete the marriage records of 501 of his women. It is remarkable that 465 of these biographies provide full details of the number of marriages and the names of all the husbands (the remaining three dozen are of serial marriages where the name of one or more husbands is missing). The analysis of this sample yields important information about the incidence of marriage, divorce, remarriage, and polygamy, that is, the prevailing marriage pattern. Obviously, the analysis is meaningful because the women shared the same background, historical period, and social and political conditions.

Marriages	All Women	Ulama	Mamluk Establishment
Once	334	296	38
More than Once	167 (33.3 %)	138 (32 %)	29 (43 %)
Twice	86	72	14
Three Times	57	51	6
Over Three Times	24	15	9
Total	501	434	67

A third of all the women, 167 out of 501, married more than once, sometimes in close succession, and one woman, Faraj (no. 696), set a record with at least eight marriages. The decisive factor in this frequency of marriage was, of course, the frequency of divorce. Sometimes Sakhawi relates that a child grew up at home with both of her parents. Growing up with both of one's parents obviously could not be taken for granted: the author took the trouble to record it. The extreme physical mobility of the urban elite of ulama and merchants also undermined family life. A conditional divorce, which freed the wife from the bonds of matrimony if the husband did not return after a fixed time, was common, for example Sharifa (no. 409). Sakhawi's own niece brought family pressure to bear upon her husband until he eventually acceded to her demands for a divorce (no. 407). An economically self-supporting woman was able to obtain a divorce from a husband she disliked (no. 291), while another threw her husband out of the house impervious even to the pleas for his return made by the sharif of Mecca (no. 388). The high death rate of husbands, especially Mamluk husbands, also contributed to the termination of many marriages. So the question of a second or third marriage arose for many women in a society where universal marriage was the norm.

Divorce and polygamy were two features of the classical Muslim law of marriage, but in practice divorce was by far the commonest. In this record of 501 women there were only 9 clear cases (2 per cent) where the woman's husband took, or tried to take, another wife at the same time. All were highly problematic and carefully recorded by Sakhawi: the first wife either forced the husband to divorce the other woman, or she secured a divorce for herself, or, having failed to do either, she went mad!

Fatima's (no. 629) husband Ibn Hajji fell in love with her and divorced his other wife, who was a relative of his, for her sake. Similarly Umm al-Husayn's (no. 861) husband Ahmad had to divorce his erstwhile wife Kamaliyya for her sake. However, shortly thereafter Umm al-Husayn and their infant son died, crushed under a collapsing wall in their house. We get the other side of the story in the biography of Kamaliyya (no. 726), who refused to accept Ahmad's second marriage and who, even though they had several children, successfully insisted on a divorce for herself. But after Umm al-Husayn's sudden death, Kamaliyya remarried Ahmad – not happily ever after, for he soon died and she followed him two months and three days later.

Habibat Allah (no. 102) had long been married to her cousin Muhammad and they had had several children when he secretly married another woman. When she found out he was quick to divorce his new wife 'in fear of Habibat Allah's wrath'. Aziza (no. 505) entered into a delayed marriage contract with Ala Ibn Afif al-Din, who was already married. She travelled with her two brothers to join him, but he was forced to repudiate her because his other wife found out and 'he was not able to deal with her anger'. Later (possibly after his wife's death) Aziza was able to marry him and the marriage lasted until he died.

A husband and wife accuse each other before a qadi (judge). Note the scribe who is recording their complaints. Divorce would usually take place without reference to a qadi. A man could divorce a wife without giving a reason; a woman had much more limited rights to divorce. In practice, however, matters were never quite as simple as this, as Sakhawi's biographies show us. Whatever happened, the terms of the original marriage contract would have to be met.

Opposite The extent to which women might be permitted to leave the house varied from Muslim society to society, from time to time and from class to class. Strict Muslims in tenth-century Baghdad felt that women should never be seen on the street at all. An English visitor to eighteenth-century Aleppo, however, noted how women would picnic in the city gardens, singing and making merry. This charming miniature from sixteenth-century Iran shows women in the midst of preparing a picnic.

Muhammad was Umm Kulthum's (no. 923) third husband (and her first husband's brother). After the birth of their children he took another wife, Umm al-Hasan (no. 831), 'so Umm Kulthum went mad and never remarried until her dying day'. As for Umm al-Hasan, although her marriage to Muhammad produced several children it also ended in divorce. But she remarried and had more children. The rest of her life was quite sad: she divorced never to marry again, and she lived until she was eighty years old to die of a broken heart after all of her children had died before her. Umm al-Husayn (no. 866) was another wife who 'went mad because her husband married another woman'. Ultimately he divorced her, and she too never remarried.

The more common pattern among the notable women of the fifteenth century was that of serial monogamous marriages (strikingly similar to modern western patterns of marriage and divorce). Islamic law permitted equally polygamy and easy divorce. A man could, provided certain conditions were met, marry up to four women at the same time, and divorce was an uncomplicated procedure, at least for men. Sakhawi's lives of women show that the marriage pattern of Egyptian and Syrian urban society in the fifteenth century was greatly influenced by easy divorce, and practically untouched by polygamy. Earlier Egyptian documents from the eleventh to thirteenth centuries also showed a similar but more extreme pattern: in a sample of 273 women, 118 (45 per cent) married a second or third time. Edward Lane's careful observation of urban Egypt in the early nineteenth century suggests that the same regime of frequent divorce and rare polygamy still obtained in these last days of traditional society.

It was enormously important for a young wife to produce children, in particular sons. First, because they gave her a position – sons were required by the Quran to respect their mothers and by prophetic tradition to obey them – and second because it would reduce the incentive for her husband to take a second wife. Here we see the joyful celebrations at the court of the Mughal emperor Akbar on the birth of his eldest son, Salim. Despite numerous wives, Akbar had difficulty in producing an heir who survived. On this occasion he sought the help of the sufi Shaykh Salim Chishti and when one of his wives became pregnant sent her to the sufi's house to help insure a successful outcome. Hence the name of the prince who was later to become Jahangir.

The low incidence of polygamy and the sharp anguish and disruption that palpably comes across in the lives of those involved suggest that society did not really approve. The ideal of monogamous and permanent marriage of one man to one woman is conveyed sharply and clearly in certain biographies, for example when Amaim (no. 518) died, her husband mourned her deeply and refused to take another woman as wife or even concubine. Sakhawi says that 'all the women were envious of her'.

Umm Hani was not the only female child on whose education a caring grandfather, father, or mother lavished extraordinary effort. The value of children strikes us in the most heart-rending way in Sakhawi's inclusion of 'biographies', very short but all too final, of thirty-nine girls who died in infancy or early childhood. By any of the received definitions of the purposes of the biographical dictionary these notices are improbable. Two are for Sakhawi's own daughters (nos. 275 and 98): 'Zaynab, her parent's first-born, the daughter of the writer of these lines, Muhammad Ibn Abd al-Rahman al-Sakhawi. She died before completing her first month in Dhu al-Qida 849.' And twenty-eight years later, 'Juwayriyya, the daughter of the author of this book Muhammad Ibn Abd al-Rahman al-Sakhawi. She died a few months after her birth on 4 Dhu al-Hijja 877 and was buried next to her brothers and sisters. May God compensate them with Paradise.' In the biography of Sakhawi's wife and life-long companion, Umm al-Khayr (no. 895), we learn that they lost at least ten children in infancy.

FROM PAST TO PRESENT

> At this time we hear astonishing things about conditions in Cairo and Egypt as regards luxury and wealth in the customs of the inhabitants there. Indeed many of the poor in the Maghreb want to move to Egypt on account of that and because they hear that prosperity in Egypt is greater than anywhere else.
> *Ibn Khaldun*

When Ibn Khaldun (1332–1406) wrote the *Muqaddima* (Introduction) to his universal history (*Kitab al-ibar*) he was living near Oran in what is now Algeria. He had just fallen from favour with the Merinids in Fez and was enjoying a scholarly interlude before succumbing to Cairo's pull. He had his own explanation for Egypt's wealth: 'the reason is that the population of Egypt and Cairo is larger than that of any other city we can think of.' He called Cairo the 'metropolis of the universe, the garden of the world, the swarming core of the human species.' The word that Ibn Khaldun used for 'population' was *umran*. It derived from a root meaning 'to grow' or 'develop' and he used the same word for 'civilization'. In his view population growth was inseparable from the concept of civilized life. The more people, the more wealth, the more civilization.

In the late fourteenth century Cairo was not quite as 'astonishing' as Ibn Khaldun had heard. The Black Death (1348) had swept through Egypt and thereafter epidemics cut down every generation until the nineteenth century. Ibn Khaldun

Love between men and women was widely celebrated; the Arab love story of Layla and Majnun was arguably more widely known amongst Muslims than that of Romeo and Juliet in Europe. In this tender love scene from sixteenth-century Iran, a young man offers a girl a bowl of wine. 'Women are above men in many things', declared the ninth-century man of letters al-Jahiz, 'it is they who are wooed, wished for, loved, and desired, and it is they for whom sacrifices are made and who are protected.'

The rich farmland of the Nile delta was the source of Egypt's wealth. It supported both Cairo as a great city and the country's reputation for prosperity elsewhere in the Muslim world.

saw the plague as a worldwide phenomenon with worldwide consequences: 'In the middle of the eighth [fourteenth] century, civilization both in the East and West was visited by a destructive plague which devastated nations and caused populations to vanish…. Civilization decreased with the decrease of mankind. Cities and buildings were laid waste, roads and way signs were obliterated, settlements and mansions became empty, dynasties and tribes grew weak. The entire inhabited world changed.' The Black Death triggered in Ibn Khaldun the eerie sense of living at the end of a whole history and, not incidentally, a grand conception of the historian's vocation: 'When there is a general change of conditions, it is as if the entire creation has changed and the whole world been altered. Therefore there is need at this time that someone should systematically set down the situation of the world among all regions and races, as well as the customs and sectarian beliefs that have changed for their adherents. This should be a model for future historians to follow.' Ibn Khaldun's eulogy for a passing history was understandable but a little premature, for the world of the Middle Ages was to trudge on for another three centuries, during which the Muslim Ottoman, Safavid, and Mughal empires exhibited impressive energy.

After the plague came the West, and with it the 'general change of conditions' which Ibn Khaldun foresaw. Indeed this time the whole world was truly altered. At the end of the eighteenth century the profound changes which began to accelerate in northwestern Europe, the Industrial and French Revolutions (what Eric Hobsbawm has called the 'dual revolution') initiated 'the greatest transformation in human history since the remote times when men invented agriculture and metallurgy, writing, the city, and the state. This revolution has transformed, and continues to transform, the entire world.'

Western Europe, where the modern revolution first occurred, acquired massive social, economic, cultural, and military power over all the established civilizations, states, regions, and peoples of the world. In most places this took the form of a European conquest led by Britain. The Muslims, who had created a world in which they were sovereign for a thousand years, now found themselves in a world where the rules were being made – and more often than not blindly enforced – by others. In the nineteenth century the universal society of Islam, which before then was the closest thing to an international culture the world had known, was relegated to the margin and virtually destroyed. Fez and Cairo no longer looked to each other, but to Paris and London, which in any case did their best to cut the remaining links between them. The society of Ibn Battuta and Ibn Khaldun, of Ghazzali and Sakhawi and Umm Hani, no longer existed, but became something else, namely the common cultural and historical heritage of the Arabs, Iranians, Turks, and other modern Muslims.

There is, of course, much more to this. Islam and the West have always shared the common geography and humanity of the Mediterranean region; their relations were old and complex. The powerful domain of Islam was Europe's great cultural and human challenge in pre-modern times, and it was quite natural that Islam became Europe's dominant idea of the other. In any case, Europe did not have much of a choice: it was surrounded by Islam and water, and it conquered the oceans and what lay beyond them long before it subdued the Muslims. In the last two hundred years, even though conditions have been dramatically changed by the rise of the West, the fear and hatred of the earlier epochs have persisted. Even today it surfaces in the form of western cries about 'the return of Islam'.

The modern revolution spread from Europe but belonged to the whole world, in the same way that at the beginning the agricultural and urban revolutions, writing, and the wheel spread from the Middle East. In the Ottoman Empire in the first half of the nineteenth century, and especially in the precocious Egypt of Muhammad Ali from 1805, the process of adopting the modern techniques and ideas began. Nineteenth-century Muslim statesmen and thinkers in Istanbul and

Muhammad Ali (1769-1848), an Albanian officer in the forces which aimed to re-impose Ottoman authority on Egypt after the French invasion, was concerned not only to rule the country but to transform it. He gave Egypt new wealth from cotton production and reversed the country's demographic decline. His government, however, was ruthless and oppressive.

Cairo rightly understood this as necessary to survive and prosper in the modern world, two generations before anyone else outside Europe.

Egyptians call Cairo 'Misr', by which they also call Egypt. Today, more than ever, Cairo is Egypt, the home of over fifteen million people, a quarter of the entire Egyptian population. A glance at Egypt and Cairo might suggest that the great Ibn Khaldun had got it all terribly wrong about population. Far from creating wealth or sustaining civilization, today's over-population is seen as condemning Egyptians to chronic poverty, desperate over-crowding, and frantic migration.

Contemporary Cairo is not the Fatimid capital, or the walled metropolis of Saladin, but a modern creation. The modern transformation of Egypt began under Muhammad Ali (r.1805 – 48). Helped by his capable son Ibrahim and by his unusually long reign – forty-three years – he launched one of the earliest and most ambitious modernization programmes. It included reorganizing the entire government, creating an effective military machine, setting up colleges of technical and higher education, and establishing a policy for industrial development, all with the help of hired European consultants. But above all it was an agrarian revolution. Muhammad Ali appreciated that Egyptian prosperity and that of the government depended on the land. The system of land tenure was reformed, abolishing the Ottoman system and substituting a state monopoly of all agricultural land. Now the land tax alone supplied half the government's total revenue.

Likewise the extensive improvements in irrigation, communications, crop rotation, and seed. In the Delta perennial irrigation (permitting more than one crop a year) became the norm. This was essential for the success of the most celebrated and fateful innovation, the introduction of long-staple cotton. Egypt became one of the world's major cotton producers and cotton became one of the country's major sources of revenue. The cultivation of cotton was labour-intensive, which created a demand for more labour than was available until mid-century. Women and children filled this demand.

Muhammad Ali's rule was a classic example of a managed economy. It was also autocratic, authoritarian, repressive, and efficient. If anything it worked too well. The success of Muhammad Ali's forces occupying Syria in the 1830s provoked the hostility of the Ottoman government and its British ally; the success of cotton ultimately made the economy dangerously dependent on fluctuations in the world market; and the system of state monopolies and price fixing antagonized the influential European buyers and merchant houses.

In the 1840s an unholy alliance of the Ottoman Empire, the British, foreign business houses, and rural shaykhs forced Muhammad Ali to abandon his monopolies (after forcing him out of Syria). A new class of large landowners controlled the Egyptian countryside and the majority of peasants became either tenant farmers or labourers. The man who had done most to modernize Egypt was forced to legitimize the great agricultural estates, including those of the royal family, which frustrated land reform until the mid-twentieth century, and to open the door to direct manipulation of the rural economy by foreign business to comply with the Anglo-Turkish Convention of 1838. He was also forced to reduce his army, which had the fateful consequence of removing the incentive to industrialize.

After Muhammad Ali steps were taken to connect Cairo to the new world system of mechanized transportation. Roads were improved, and the first railway between Cairo and Alexandria was built (1852–54, long before, say, Sweden or Japan) to cut the time of travel between the capital and Egypt's seaport on the Mediterranean from four days to 4½ hours. But the most important event to fix Egypt's place in the imperial system was Khedive Said's (r.1854–63) decision of November 1854 to grant the Frenchman de Lesseps the concession to construct the Suez canal.

Said's successor in 1863, the Khedive Ismail, was committed to Cairo's development, and his reign (1863–79) was the decisive period for the birth of the modern city. In 1867 he went with a massive Egyptian delegation to the Exposition Universelle marking the climax of Baron Haussmann's replanning of Paris and was profoundly impressed by all he saw. In two years' time Ismail planned Egypt's own 'exposition' to open the Suez Canal. How better to declare Egypt 'a part of Europe' than by doing for Cairo what Haussmann had done for Paris? Whatever Ismail's other failings, he was no procrastinator; most of the city was planned and built in just two years. In Ali Mubarak (1824–92), his remarkable Minister of Public Works, he found the right man for the job. Luckily there was no need for whole-

Ali Mubarak, the Egyptian minister of public works who in the late 1860s oversaw the construction of the Khedive Ismail's vision of a modern Cairo. The Khedive was inspired by Haussmann's replanning of Paris.

Cairo's New Opera House where Verdi's *Rigoletto* was performed as the world visited the city in November 1869 to celebrate the opening of the Suez Canal.

sale demolition. In preceding centuries the bed of the Nile had been shifting slowly west. A tract of wasteland now intervened between the city and the river and it was here, facing west, that Mubarak laid out the grand façade of boulevards, parks, and *étoiles* that was to be Ismail's Cairo. Like Egypt itself, the new Cairo was 'the gift of the Nile'.

The Suez Canal was opened in November 1869. The crowned heads of Europe, the world's press, and the entrepreneurs came to Cairo looking for oriental mystery. They were confronted with Verdi's *Rigoletto* being performed at the New Opera House. The street lighting was on, the national Theatre was open, acres of wasteland were being transformed into wooded parkland, a new road conducted the visitors to the Pyramids and, for the first time, a bridge had been thrown across the Nile, thus inaugurating the city's expansion into the west bank. Ismail himself, resplendent with insignia, epaulettes, and drooping moustache, looked like a European. It is tempting to see Ismail's Cairo as a simple, even superficial, imitation of Haussmann's Paris. But then, new Cairo was equally, and perhaps more accurately, Ali Mubarak's Cairo. As such it acquires new meaning.

The harvest of Muhammad Ali's reforms was considerable, and Ali Mubarak was an outstanding example of that harvest. He was the youngest son of a poor family in the Delta who made it into the new state schools, and was sent by Muhammad Ali to specialize as a military engineer in France. He returned to become Egypt's most important civil servant from 1850 until 1882 – that is, until the British Occupation. He was often Minister of Education, of Public Works, and of Railroads. Mubarak, who wrote extensively, believed in science, progress, civilization, planning, machines, and in public service. In short, he was a utilitarian, a true son of the optimism and promise of the nineteenth century. According to him, science or knowledge is a universal and cumulative pursuit. It passed from the ancient Egyptians to the Greeks and then to the Arabs and then to the Europeans. Each in turn had borrowed from its predecessor and as the Muslims had once mastered and extended the discoveries of the Greeks, so now they must master those of Europe. Mubarak said these things in *Alam al-Din*, a four-volume book published in 1882. The date of publication is painfully symbolic, for this book and the attitudes it embodied became difficult after the British occupation of Egypt. It was one thing to admire the achievements of the West; it was another to have them mobilized against you. Arab and Muslim attitudes towards the West still reflect this ambivalence.

There was a mood of expansive optimism in Egypt as the country apparently leapt from the Middle Ages to the forefront of nineteenth-century progress. But without the alternative of a thriving industrial base, the foundations of modern Egypt remained weak. During the second half of the century the population doubled, as did the agricultural surplus; during the American Civil War the value of the cotton crop actually quadrupled. But the dispersal of land also continued and, by the time it reached the treasury, agrarian revenue was pitifully depleted. With each economic setback, with each heavily subsidized modernization, and with each royal extravagance, the state sank deeper into debt. Larger loans meant recourse to European bankers and the price of each loan became a concession to European interests. Soon new loans were required just to service the old. Egypt defaulted and the resultant Anglo-French receivership was threatened by the nationalist revolt of Urabi Pasha, to which the British responded in 1882 by occupying the country and imposing colonial rule.

The difference between Egypt and any of the other slabs of pink on the imperial map was that Egypt had already been through the traumas of modernization — a fundamental transformation in its land, economy, culture, and politics for seventy-five years. Under British rule the irrigation network was extended in the Delta and perennial irrigation to Upper Egypt, the first Aswan dams were built, cotton continued to flourish, and communications to be improved. But all this was a quantitative change, not qualitative. The point is well illustrated by Ismail's sensational transformation of Cairo. In India it was not until 1911 that the British decided to build a modern capital and a further twenty years before New Delhi was inaugurated. In Egypt 'new Cairo' was ready and waiting in 1882.

After the British Occupation of Egypt the rise of a man like Ali Mubarak was no longer possible because no Egyptian could hold a position of true responsibility. If a dam was built on the Nile it was an Englishman who made the decision. For

The terrace of Shepheard's Hotel, Cairo, a popular rendezvous for the British during their occupation of Egypt. It was a natural target for nationalist opposition and was burned down in January 1952 as the movement which was to bring the Free Officers to power began to gather way.

Huda Sharawi (1879–1947), who led demonstrations of women during the Egyptian revolt against the British in 1919 and who founded the Egyptian Feminist Union in 1923. Her feminism was politically nationalistic and westward looking; it meant overthrowing British rule and adopting western political institutions alongside a secular understanding of the state. She threw off the veil as part of her desire to liberate her society from western power; in the late twentieth century Egyptian women have begun to put on the veil, or Islamic dress, as a protest against western influence.

a few critical generations, Egyptians were forbidden to assume truly responsible roles in their own country, and this was the heavy, and hidden, price of imperialism. Some of the difficulties of the new nations of the third world relate directly to the gap which imperialism caused in the succession of responsibility for the affairs of their own societies.

The first steps on the road to women's rights, at least in the Arab world, are generally traced back to 1919 when there was a major Egyptian nationalist movement against the British. Huda Sharawi took part alongside her husband, an important figure in the movement, and she went on to lead women in demonstrations against the British, becoming widely respected and admired. One day, after returning from a women's conference in Rome in 1923, she took off the veil before a startled welcoming committee on the quay in Alexandria. From the 1920s until the 1970s the use of the veil declined, until only a minority of Muslim women outside the conservative societies of the Arabian peninsula still used it.

The veil or headscarf in the twentieth century has proved to be a symbol of progressive as much as retrogressive social trends, for both covering and uncovering have signified liberation of a sort. Many young Muslim women since the 1970s have returned to a traditional dress code, which covers the hair and neck, but leaves the face uncovered. They are often the daughters of mothers who were uncovered and the granddaughters of women like Huda Sharawi who threw off the covering in the 1920s as a sign of liberation. By taking on Muslim dress these granddaughters believe that they return to an indigenous culture, and symbolize their liberation from an imposed foreign culture. The point about the headscarf is that it has been subject to a variety of interpretations. The heated conflict over Muslim dress in France, which began in 1989 when the head teacher of a school in Creil refused to let three Muslim girls wear the headscarf to school, had reached a feverish stage at the beginning of the 1994 school year. The French education minister banished 'ostentatious' religious symbols in schools. For some reason crucifixes and Stars of David were not viewed as ostentatious.

When interviewed, many of the women – university students and graduates, doctors and lawyers – who have chosen to wear traditional Islamic dress give cultural and political explanations. Long before the French furore, this is how Safinaz Kazim, an Egyptian journalist and drama critic, put it:

> We became Muslims not to follow previous values, but to follow our own new values. And we are not forcing anybody to follow our values – we will not impose them on Christians, on western life…What I say is right, they will say is wrong. I say that this dress is to protect my dignity as a woman; Simone de Beauvoir will say that it is an attack against women and a violation of her dignity. I will not go and force Simone de Beauvoir to put on Muslim dress. And I refuse Simone de Beauvoir to tell Imam Khomeini with rudeness 'Don't apply this Muslim rule on Muslim women.' By God, this is very strange.

Women students wearing Islamic dress in a laboratory in Cairo University. Large numbers of Egyptian women now enter both higher education and the labour force. The adoption of Islamic dress enables them to carve out a legitimate area for themselves in public space and also to redefine that space itself. It signals the determination of women from the heart of Egyptian society to join modern life.

But cultural and political definitions are modified by the personal:

> I took up Muslim dress because this is part of Islam and I believe in it. It is not one of the basic things in Islam, but it is just a framework. I feel I am pleasing God in this way. I feel that I should be a complete Muslim – not only obeying some of its rules and rejecting other rules.

These are the words of a young Egyptian medical student. Neither her status as a medical student nor her choice to cover are unusual, which illustrates the dilemma: is a young Egyptian woman attending medical school 'traditional' or 'modern'? How does her free choice to wear Islamic dress qualify one's response to this question?

The early Egyptian feminists led by Huda Sharawi went on to lobby for women's rights to education, the right to vote, and equal rights in other fields. But for later feminists, like the Egyptian Dr Nawal Sadawi, the early feminists did not go nearly far enough. The problem is, as ever in both the Muslim world and the rest of the world, what to do with the family. And how does one change it? Feminist reformers, like most Muslim reformers, argue that Islamic law itself must adapt to modern times, assuming that laws regarding women would thus become more liberal or progressive. But the reinterpretation of Islamic law to suit modern conditions is not without unexpected ironies.

All the Islamic schools of law from the tenth to the nineteenth century gave contraception their serious consideration. They dealt principally with *coitus interruptus*, the most common method, and unanimously agreed that it was licit provided the free wife gave her permission, because she had rights to children and to sexual fulfilment which withdrawal was believed to diminish. From the writings

The head of the delegation from Kuwait to the 1994 Cairo Conference on population and development is interviewed. The conference saw similar views on birth control and abortion expressed by Islamists and Roman Catholic Christians. The concerns of the Islamists are new. Traditionally, Muslim physicians have always paid attention to methods of birth control in their writings, and its practice had support in Islamic law.

of the jurists it emerges that other methods of birth control – mostly intravaginal tampons – were also used by premodern women and the commonest view was that these should only be employed if the husband also agreed.

Given the dates and the fact that both Christian and Jewish tradition outlawed contraception, the Muslims had a remarkably pragmatic attitude towards birth control and a sophisticated knowledge of possible methods. Medieval doctors like Ibn Sina (Avicenna) regarded birth control as a normal part of medicine, and devoted chapters to contraception and abortion in their textbooks. According to medieval Muslims, birth control was employed to avoid a large number of dependants; to safeguard property; to guarantee the education of a child; to protect a woman from the risks of childbirth, especially if she was young or sickly; or simply to preserve her health and beauty.

The Muslim condemnations of birth control which accompanied the Cairo Population Conference in the summer of 1994 were therefore not the repetition of age-old attitudes, but something else altogether. When birth control was reintroduced as a question in twentieth-century Islam it produced a normal response: the modern jurist consulted the old books and repeated the classical permission. But the old Islamic law had never envisioned birth control as a concern of the state. The religious permission applied to individual couples, who alone had the right to limit their families according to their own perceived economic, medical, or personal interests. After the Second World War 'over-population', particularly in the third world, has engaged national governments, international agencies, and also western governments and institutions. Responding both to government involvement in their personal lives, and to the jealous advocacy of family planning by some western circles, many Muslims have seen the whole effort as yet another foreign intervention in Muslim societies. The official family planning programmes in place by the 1970s engendered enough fear and resentment to persuade some religious leaders forthrightly to reject the classical permission. Both this attitude and the official population policies are equally distant from the spirit of classical Islamic law and its view of birth control as strictly a matter of personal choice.

Knowledge, its Transmission, and the Making of Muslim Societies

One day, goes a story concerning al-Shafii (d.820), the founder of one of the four Sunni schools of law, his pupils brought him a slave girl. Frustrated, after waiting in vain for the eminent jurist throughout the night, she complained to the slave dealer that he had sold her to a 'crazy man'. Hearing this al-Shafii declared 'crazy is he who knows the value of knowledge, and who then squanders it, or hesitates so that it passes him by.' This story and many like it emphasize the centrality of the search for knowledge in good Muslim lives.

At the heart of this search was the Muslim concern to command all that could be known of the Quran, the life of the Prophet, and the skills to make the guidance that they represented socially useful. This was knowledge needed to gain salvation. Nevertheless, the high value placed on learning also came to include knowledge which might give power in the world, such as the rational sciences, medicine, technology, always provided that it did not run counter to Islamic purposes.

Thus, learning for Muslims was an act of worship. It was, moreover, a supremely important one. 'An hour of learning', went the saying, 'is worth more than a year of prayer.' This emphasis had two outcomes of major significance in Islamic history. First, wherever Muslims went in the world there was a central core of knowledge in which all could share, although they might interpret it differently, and a central core of religious duties, which all should perform, although there might be minor differences. Second, Muslims themselves, whether the state was concerned to play a role or not, took responsibility for preserving knowledge in their generation and transmitting it to the next.

THE FORMATION OF ISLAMIC KNOWLEDGE

The core of Islamic knowledge was shaped in the first five Muslim centuries. In the era that followed, this core was to be further elaborated, but not significantly changed. To this day traditional Muslim scholars use many of the texts written by the great scholars of the Islamic middle ages, and often in ways that do not differ greatly from those of their medieval forebears. The elements that went to make this most influential body of knowledge came together as a consequence of the Arab conquests of the seventh century. Just as the material wealth of the early Islamic world derived from the Arab achievement in uniting the great economic regions of the Mediterranean basin and Asia, so its wealth in knowledge derived from the opportunities it created for the mingling of a new complex of Semitic, Hellenistic, Iranian, and Indian strands of culture.

Revelation, tradition, and the law

At the heart of Islamic knowledge lay the Quran, which Muslims believed to be the word of God revealed to men and women through the Prophet Muhammad. From its opening chapter, which the faithful use as Christians might the Lord's Prayer, the Quran reminded Muslims of the central reality of God in human life:

> In the name of Allah, Most Gracious, Most Merciful.
>
> Praise be to Allah
>
> The Cherisher and Sustainer of the Worlds:
>
> Most Gracious, Most Merciful;
>
> Master of the Day of Judgment.
>
> Thee do we worship,
>
> And Thine aid we seek.
>
> Show us the straight way,
>
> The way of those on whom
>
> Thou has bestowed Thy Grace,
>
> Those whose [portion]
>
> Is not wrath.
>
> And who go not astray.

Humans had a fundamental choice. They could submit to God and follow the commandments, or they could turn away from him, follow human desire, and

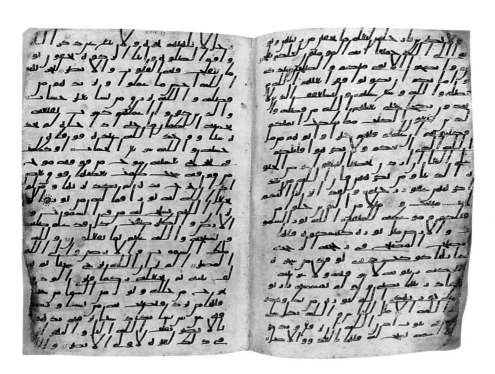

The earliest datable fragments of the Quran go back to the first quarter of the eighth century. They are written in kufic, the most widely used script for liturgical purposes in the early Muslim world, and usually on vellum. This page from an eighth-century Quran is in the slanting form of kufic, known as *mail*; this page was written before diacritical marks and vowel signs were added to texts to prevent misreadings of the sacred word.

take the consequences. Men and women are left in no doubt as to the awesome nature of the Last Day, the pleasures of paradise, and the horrors of hell. Much guidance is given about what they should believe in religion and how they should behave in worship, about what rules they should follow with regard to their fellows and the gratitude to God which should infuse their daily lives.

Muslims refer to the Quran as the 'noble' or the 'glorious'; its Arabic is regarded as being without compare. Copying the Quran has been an act of piety performed by rich and poor alike. Learning the Quran has been the normal starting point of Muslim education, whether or not the young children concerned could understand its Arabic. Although the revealed word was first written down in full under the third caliph, Uthman, and copies were sent to the major cities, the classical way of transmission was oral. Early Arabic script left possibilities for variant readings; in time seven traditions of recitation, distinguished by only minor differences, came to be regarded as canonical. As the written text of the Quran became

The primacy of God's word for Muslims is reflected in its almost universal use to decorate surfaces dedicated to a religious purpose: minarets, the interior and exterior of mosques, mosque furniture, tombs, and of course the *kiswah* (cloth), renewed each year, which covers the Kaaba at Mecca. Here, the south arch of the Taj Mahal, India, displays in magnificent calligraphy verses 1–21 of Sura 36 of the Quran, 'Ya Sin'. The remaining sixty-two verses are presented on the other three arches. The calligraphy in marble inlay was the work of Amanat Khan, a distinguished scholar from Shiraz.

available so the work of interpretation and exegesis began. Inevitably, the resulting commentaries were subject to the sectarian controversies of the time. The first
attempt to make an overarching critical study was produced in thirty volumes by
the historian and theologian al-Tabari (d.923). Over three centuries later the task
was done again by al-Baydawi (d.1286). To the present day his work has remained
the standard for Muslim and non-Muslim alike.

The second source of knowledge was the record of the sayings and doings of
the Prophet. Given that the Prophet was the model of the perfect Muslim life, it
was only natural that believers should wish to know all he said and did. The collective memory of these sayings and doings came to be known as the *sunna*, the
'beaten path' or 'custom' of the Prophet. Individual statements of the sunna were
known as *hadith*, which might go thus: 'Ibn Umar reported that the Messenger of
Allah said: Whoever imitates a people, he belongs to them.' As time went on the
hadiths multiplied till they numbered hundreds of thousands; they came to be
invented to support legal, political, and theological positions of the day. In the
ninth and tenth centuries, therefore, men travelled throughout the Muslim world
to collect hadiths. After analysing them to see whether their chain of narration
from the time of the Prophet was sound and whether their content was in harmony with the Quran, already authenticated hadiths, and reason, they were classified as either sound (*sahih*), acceptable (*hasan*), or weak (*daif*). Six collections
of hadiths came to have canonical status, of which those of Bukhari (d.870) and
of Muslim (d.875) were the most esteemed. Bukhari winnowed the multiplicity of
hadiths down to 2,762. Subsequently, different movements built different collections of hadiths. The Shias, for instance, accepted only those traditions transmitted through Ali and his followers.

Western scholars and some Muslim modernists have tended to cast doubt on
the authenticity of some long-accepted traditions. Nevertheless, the traditions
have played a major role in forming the character of Muslim communities and in
developing like behaviour through much of the Sunni world. When Muslim communities have felt particularly under threat, moreover, it is to the traditions that
they have often turned for renewed direction.

The guidance of the Quran and hadiths was encapsulated in practical form for
Muslims in the law. This is usually referred to as the *sharia*, which meant originally in Arabic 'the path leading to the water', that is the path to the source of life.
The sharia grew from the attempts of early Muslims, as they confronted immediate social and political problems, to derive systematic codes of behaviour from the
word of God and the example of the Prophet. Four main schools of legal interpretation developed: the Hanafi, which grew up in the Abbasid capital of Baghdad
and was founded by Abu Hanifa (d.769); the Maliki, which grew out of the practice of the Medinan judge Malik bin Anas (d.795); the Shafii, which developed
under the leadership of al-Shafii, a disciple of Malik; and the Hanbali, founded by
Ahmad ibn Hanbal (d.855) in Baghdad. The first three schools all had formal

differences of emphasis and technique; Hanafis, for instance, allowed more room for *ijtihad*, personal reasoning, than the others, while the Shafiis were concerned to distinguish their use of the hadiths from the more limited practice of the Malikis. All agreed, however, on important matters; all recognized each other's systems as equally orthodox. The Hanbali school, on the other hand, developed as a traditionalist reaction against what it regarded as the speculative innovations of the earlier established schools. But, until the later middle ages its influence tended to be limited to Iraq and Syria. The Hanafis were strong throughout mainland Asia, the Shafiis in lower Egypt, the Hijaz, Southeast Asia, and east Africa, and the Malikis in the rest of Muslim Africa.

Ulama, that is scholars, those with *ilm* (knowledge), developed these systems roughly thus. They treated the Quran as containing the general principles by which all matters should be regulated, and when the Quran was unclear they sought clarification in the hadiths. The foundations of the sharia, then, were the unambiguous commands and prohibitions to be found in these sources. When points of law arose, on which the Quran and the hadiths offered no firm guidance, most ulama turned to *qiyas*, which meant arguing by analogy and applying to the problem the principles underlying a decision which had already been reached on a comparable issue. As the years passed, ulama increasingly came to agree on points of law, and the principle of *ijma*, or consensus of the community, came into play. 'My community', went a very important hadith, 'will never agree upon an error.' So, if the community as embodied in its legal experts came to agree on a point, that agreement gained the authority of revelation itself and the development of new ideas on the subject was forbidden. Steadily, more and more of the law was underpinned by ijma, and the area in which personal reasoning might be deployed was increasingly diminished. By the mid-tenth century most scholars had declared the 'gate of ijtihad' shut. Henceforth, if the meaning of a text was re-interpreted in such a way as to challenge the understanding supported by ijma, *bida* was committed, an act of innovation, which was as near as Islam came to the Christian concept of heresy.

The sharia was comprehensive. It embraced all human activities, defining the relations of men and women with God and with their fellows. In the first role it prescribed what they should believe and how by ritual acts they should express their beliefs; in the second it covered those areas which in European codes might come under the heading of civil, commercial, penal, personal law, and so on. No formal legal code was created at this time, or subsequently, the sharia being more a discussion of how Muslims ought to behave. In the process, human actions were classified on a five-point scale: obligatory, meritorious, indifferent, reprehensible, forbidden. The sharia told men and women all they needed to know about how to live righteously in this world and how to be prepared for the next.

The sharia defined the constitution of the Muslim community. This said, it was never to be applied in full. For one thing, it was impossible to enforce a system

A qadi, or judge, administering the law. From Abbasid times such judges might sit by themselves with just a secretary to record decisions. In general, only oral testimony from reputable witnesses was acceptable; written evidence was only accepted if supported by reputable witnesses. In making his rulings the qadi could draw on a *fatwa* (legal opinion) from a mufti. Moreover, in applying the law he had a degree of flexibility. For instance, in order to improve the chances of preserving social harmony, he might choose to act as a conciliator between two parties rather than applying the letter of the law. Here, a qadi settles an argument between two litigants.

which included moral obligations as well as hard-and-fast rules. For another, it would always be subject to the realities of political power. Rulers could not afford to permit the interpreters of the law a completely free hand in the legal arena. They were unlikely to think it wise, even if they had the power, to impose the sharia over local customary law. Nevertheless, the sharia was to be a potent ideal. Those who accepted Islam accepted in principle the idea that the knowledge it represented should be spread as widely as possible so that it might fashion the lives of all.

Greek and other knowledge

A second strand was the great heritage of the ancient world in science, technology, the humanities, and the arts of government, which was drawn into the new Islamic civilization. One element was from the former Sasanian lands and found in large part in the Pahlawi language. There was the store of Iranian expertise contained in the *adab* literature – guides on government, office-holding, and etiquette before princes. There was the technical literature in fields ranging from arms and horsemanship to agriculture and irrigation. There was scientific literature, notably in the fields of medicine, astronomy, and mathematics; not least amongst the last was the Indian system of numerical notation which in Arab hands began its transformation to those in widespread use today. Of course, there were works of Iranian literature such as the moralistic fables of animal life, the *Kalila wa Dimna* and stories which were to be included in the Arabian Nights. The impact of this heritage was such that under the Abbasids the Shuubiyya tried to assert the

Aristotle teaching. Hellenistic culture had an immense impact on the growth of Islamic civilization. The greatest source of influence was in philosophy, which embraced a wide range of rational investigations including logic, natural science, and physics. Such was the respect for Aristotle and his influence that in madrasas down to the twentieth century he was known as the 'first teacher'.

superiority of Iranian culture over Arab, and Iranian ideas of kingship over Islamic ideas of caliphate. By the end of the ninth century the specific religious threats had been met by theologians and the more general challenges of Iranian culture had been countered by writers such as al-Jahiz (d.869) and Ibn Qutayba (d.889) who developed a literature of Iranian themes and forms expressed within a framework of Arab and Islamic values.

More important was the impact of Greek culture which came to the Islamic world not in its classical form but as it had come to be elaborated in the late antique world. The Hellenistic traditions of Athens were sustained by Nestorian Christians working under Sasanian patronage at their educational centre of Jundishapur in southern Iran. The Hellenistic traditions of Alexandria were sustained successively in Antioch in Syria, Marv in Khurasan and Harran in Mesopotamia. Theological debate in the eighth and ninth centuries led to curiosity about Greek thought and both traditions were transferred to Baghdad. A great programme of translation of works from Greek, and also from Syriac into which many Greek works had been translated, was established under Hunayn Ibn Ishaq (d.873) and high standards were maintained in publishing accurate and reliable editions. By the eleventh century at least eighty Greek authors had been translated, many major figures such as Aristotle, Plato, Galen, and Euclid being represented by several works. Among the subjects covered were philosophy, medicine, mathematics, physics, optics, astronomy, geography, and the occult sciences of astrology, alchemy, and magic. Like the later Hellenes, the Muslims were not interested in Greek literature and history.

The most important aspect of knowledge transferred from the Hellenistic tradition was philosophy, with its emphasis on reason, logic, and the laws of nature. This knowledge was used for theological purposes by the Mutazilites, 'those who keep themselves apart'. Confronted by pagan, Manichean dualistic and Christian Trinitarian, conceptions of God, they were determined to assert His absolute unity and transcendence. They focused on the following questions: were the attributes of God stated in the Quran part of Him or merely metaphorical? Was the Quran part of the essence of God or created? Were the lives of humans predetermined or were humans morally responsible for their own actions? Many Muslims, believing in the literal truth of the Quran, took the former positions; the Mutazilites, deploying the insights of philosophy, the latter. Thus, in the eighth and ninth centuries two theological positions developed: one in which God was understood through revelation and one in which He was understood through reason.

An all-important bridge was built between these conflicting positions by al-Ashari (d.935). A pupil of the leading Mutazilite theologian of Basra, al-Ashari was converted to the opposing position by dreams he had during the fast of Ramadan. He now asserted the literal truth of the Quran but, in his bridge-building mode, justified his position with reason. Reason, however, could operate only up to a certain point, beyond which faith had to take over. So God was One: He had eternal attributes, but these were not Him, nor were they apart from Him. So the Quran was 'uncreated' but might become created when transmitted to humankind. So God willed all things, good and evil, but men and women acquired responsibility as the instrument of these actions. Through history al-Ashari's synthesis of reason and revelation remained the classic Sunni theological position.

Al-Ashari's achievement set limits to the rationalist enterprise in the mainstream of Islamic thought, but it in no wise put an end to philosophical speculation. Indeed, Islamic civilization, as it responded to Greek thought in the early centuries, produced a majestic series of philosophers: al-Kindi (d.870), who was known as the 'philosopher of the Arabs'; al-Farabi (d.950), who came from Turkistan; Ibn Sina (Avicenna, d.1037), who worked as both physician and official; Ibn Tufayl (d.1185), who worked as physician and vizier at the Almohad court; and Ibn Rushd (Avarroes, d.1198), who succeeded Ibn Tufayl. Amongst the ideas asserted were that philosophical truth was universally valid, that religious symbolism was an inferior way of conveying truth, that reason was the surest path to truth, and that God was the first cause in which essence and existence were one. Such ideas were bound to be unacceptable to the vast majority of the faithful. Philosophical knowledge was doomed to subsist on the margins of Muslim civilization and to have a greater influence on medieval Europe than on the Muslim world which conveyed it there.

Mystic knowledge

The third strand of knowledge was mysticism or sufism, as it is generally called. Whereas the sharia dictated the formal relations of Muslims towards God and their fellows, sufism taught Muslims how to know God in their hearts. Sufis lived their lives and ordered their thoughts in ways designed to make possible a direct and personal experience of God.

Sufism grew as a distinct strand of Muslim devotion, which was inspired by the Quran, the religious practices of the Prophet and the early Muslim community. It did so in part as the Arab Muslims came into contact with the Christian and other mystic traditions of the lands they conquered, and in part in reaction to the moral laxity and worldliness of the Umayyad court at Damascus. The term 'sufi' is probably derived from the Arabic *suf*, wool, which referred to the simple woollen clothes worn by mystics in contrast to the rich apparel of the worldly.

In the beginning the basis of sufi feeling was fear of God and of judgment. 'The believer wakens grieving and goes to bed grieving', declared the famous early

A sufi with a cat. There is considerable love for cats amongst Arab Muslims at least, which originated in Egypt where cats had long been holy animals. Cats were loved by the Prophet, who regarded them as clean animals, and were mentioned in many biographies of sufis. Such holy men have been known to say that they learned how to meditate quietly and intensely by imitating the cat that waits in tense concentration in front of a mousehole.

mystic Hasan al-Basri (d.725), 'and this is all that encompasses him, because he is between two fearful things: the sin which has passed, and he does not know what God will do with him, and the allotted term which remains, and he does not know what disasters will befall him.' But, by the second Islamic century, the doctrine of love had become prominent. 'I love Thee with two loves,' the woman saint Rabia (d.801) declared to God, 'love of my happiness, and perfect love, to love Thee as is Thy due.' Sufis, however, did not remain satisfied with this intense gospel of love. By the third Islamic century they had begun to develop the doctrine of the 'inner way' or the spiritual journey towards God. There were different stages of the way corresponding to the different levels of sufi experience. The mystic, who was usually a man, was first seeker, then a traveller, and then an initiate. He progressed along the way through processes of self-abnegation and enhanced awareness of God. The nearer he came to God, the more God spoke with his lips, controlled his limbs, and moved the desires of his heart until he reached the final stage when self was annihilated and totally absorbed in God.

By this time two attitudes had developed, one ecstatic, the other sober. Both resigned themselves to God's will by embracing poverty. The ecstatic ignored the Quran and the Law in moving to the final stages when the self was annihilated and totally absorbed in God. Typical of this attitude was al-Hallaj (d.922) who carried his sufi message through northern India and Central Asia. In manifesting his union with God he declared 'I am the Truth' and was brutally executed in Baghdad for his pains. The sober attitude was typified by al-Junayd (d.911) who was known as the 'peacock of the poor'. He insisted that mere self-annihilation was not enough. The self still had to persevere in the real world and that could only be done by living in conformity with the Quran and the Law.

Side by side with these varying ways of approaching the Divine there were attempts to develop a metaphysical understanding of God and His relationship to humankind. Sufis proposed a transcendent God whose spiritual radiance was reflected in humanity. To discover the divine essence that lay within them human beings had to overcome their worldly nature. After the translation of Hellenistic learning into Arabic, sufis also proposed a way profoundly influenced by Neoplatonic mysticism. The universe emanated from God in stages of spiritual and then material manifestation. Human beings were able by developing inner knowledge to ascend through the stages of material and then spiritual manifestation to the ultimate vision of God.

By the tenth and eleventh centuries social and political rivalries mingled with different strands of knowledge in Islam to express a series of tensions. The decline of the Abbasid caliphate had led to the rise of Shia regimes throughout the Middle East. While the Twelver Shias were largely unconcerned with proselytizing, the Ismailis were great missionaries: the Ismaili Fatimid rulers of Egypt sponsored missions from north Africa through to Central Asia and Afghanistan. Shia power,

moreover, was not just a challenge to Sunni dominion and understandings of authority in Islam; it also created circumstances in which Hellenistic knowledge could flourish. The defence of Sunni Islam was taken up most vigorously in Baghdad and by followers of the Hanbali school of law, who permitted no place for the rational sciences in developing their understandings of Islam. The Hanbalis were at the heart of the second tension; they were no less concerned about the influence of rational schools of theology, such as the Ashari, amongst the Sunni community. For them Hellenistic learning was unnecessary as a support to revelation and the example of the Prophet. This tension, however, grew greater as the Asharite theologians in their struggle to check the influence of philosophy increasingly came to use philosophical methods in displaying their theology. Then, the claims of some sufis, in particular those of the ecstatic variety, to achieve knowledge of God through direct personal experience were a further source of tension; they challenged the upholders of the sharia, lawyers and theologians alike. Such claims devalued the role of law in Muslim society. They were, moreover, justified by a Hellenistic theosophical metaphysics; they were often associated with a belief in the miraculous prowess of saints as instruments of God's will or both; they had growing support amongst the Muslim population at large.

That these tensions did not open up an unbridgeable gulf between those immersed in the different strands of knowledge has much to do with the achievement of one man, the greatest figure in medieval Islam, indeed, the most influential figure after Muhammad, Abu Hamid al-Ghazzali (d.1111). As a relatively young man al-Ghazzali had been appointed to the senior professorship at the

The arms and legs of al-Hallaj (d.922) being cut off. 'When morning came', goes the official testimony of the Baghdad Clerk of the Court, Zanji, 'the commissioner had Hallaj led out on the very esplanade of the police headquarters on the western end of the bridge of boats, and ordered the executioner to scourge him. A large crowd formed whose numbers were considerable, countless. Once the thousand lashes had been administered, they cut off one of his hands, then a foot; then the other hand, followed by the other foot. [He was then hoisted in full view on a post.] His head was cut off and the trunk was burned. I was there, that very moment, motionless, on the back of my mule; the trunk twisted on the embers and the flames blazed forth.'

Nizamiyya College in Baghdad. He was brilliant, but, as he tells us in his moving autobiography, the *Deliverer from Error*, 'my teaching was concerned with branches of knowledge which were unimportant and worthless,...my motive in teaching...was not sincere desire to serve God but that I wanted an influential position and widespread recognition.' He had a physical and mental breakdown, left his post and lived the life of a sufi. During his scholarly life al-Ghazzali examined the main strands in the thought of his time and produced a synthesis that has lain at the centre of Sunni Islam to this day. He explored the arguments of the Ismaili Shias and refuted them one by one. He explored the potential contribution of the rational sciences to religious understanding, particularly in his attack on Ibn Sina, *The Incoherence of the Philosophers*, and demonstrated that while they were of great value in mathematics and logic, they could never enable Muslims to know a transcendent God. Thus, al-Ghazzali reaffirmed the rational theology of al-Ashari in which reason was firmly subject to revelation. Finally, and very much as a result of his own personal crisis, he explored the possibilities of building a bridge between sufism and sharia Islam. In building that bridge he demonstrated that God was not to be discovered by intellect alone, but by personal experience. The Muslim must expect to know not just that knowledge which God had revealed to him but also to know God in his heart. Al-Ghazzali's religious vision was published in his most important work, *Revival of the Religious Sciences*. He was given the title 'Renewer of Islam'.

By al-Ghazzali's death at the beginning of the twelfth century the basic shape of normative Islamic knowledge had been fashioned from the interaction between the knowledge revealed to man by God and the actions of His Prophet and the great heritage of knowledge in the Middle East derived from pre-Islamic sources. At the apex of Islamic knowledge stood the Quran and hadiths, whose guidance was embodied in the sharia. These were serviced by the twin strands of rational and mystical knowledge, whose insights helped to make the sharia of value both to individuals and to society, but were not permitted to trespass beyond the bounds set by revelation. This is what the American Islamicist Ira Lapidus has termed the 'Sunni-Sharia-Sufi' consensus. Around this consensus, however, which was it itself a very broad 'church', he points to other Islamic possibilities. There was the gnostic vision, present in sufism, Ismaili Shiism, and philosophy, which saw the purpose of life not in fulfilling God's word on earth but in purification of the soul and detachment from earthly things. There was popular Islam, which was most frequently represented in the worship of saints whom it was believed could intercede for humankind with God and whose cults often mingled with pre-Islamic beliefs and customs. There were the Shias, whose practices differed from those of the Sunnis in few respects, but for whom the vital issue was loyalty to the family of Ali. These various traditions of Islamic knowledge and understanding represent, in the words of Lapidus, 'a repertoire of cultural and religious ideas which remain operative in Islamic lands to the present day.'

THE TRANSMISSION OF KNOWLEDGE TO 1800

Islamic knowledge was made available to society and transmitted to the generations to come by ulama and sufis. It is important for those from a non-Muslim
background to realize that these transmitters were not priests and performed no
sacerdotal functions; in theory, at least, normative Islam tolerated no intermediaries between man and God. In most Muslim societies ulama existed less because
a state willed their existence than because society valued the functions they performed. We now consider ulama and sufis as transmitters of the knowledge which
shaped both the outward form and the inner nature of Muslim societies down to
the European irruption in the nineteenth and twentieth centuries.

The Ulama: transmitters of formal knowledge

The ulama were to be found in almost every corner of the Islamic world. They
bore different titles in different regions: Mulla in the Persian-speaking lands of
Iran, Central Asia, and northern India; Shaykh in the Arabic-speaking central
Islamic lands; Kiyayi on the Indonesian islands; and Mallam or Karamoko in west
Africa. They performed a wide range of functions. They might administer
mosques, schools, hospitals, and orphanages; they might also be courtiers, diplomats, or leading bureaucrats. Their first task, however, remained the preservation
and transmission of the sharia. As scholars they defended their understandings of
it, as qadis they administered it on behalf of the state, as muftis they expounded it
on behalf of the community for whom they issued *fatwas* (legal decisions) free of
charge. They reminded Muslims of their obligations under it in their sermons and
instructed their children in it in their schools.

Ulama might have a range of sources of support. Some lived off land grants or
salaries from the state, but the majority were supported by the community – by
the endowments of the pious, by the donations of the grateful, or by the proceeds
of the crafts or trades in which they were engaged. In some areas where the state
had periods of notable strength, as in the Ottoman empire, numbers of ulama
might come under state control, forming a kind of bureaucracy. In other areas,
where the state was often weak, as in Indonesia or west Africa, they existed largely
free from state control. Of course, during this long period there could be great
shifts in the relationship between the ulama and a particular state. Nowhere was
this more obvious than in Safawid Iran, to which Shia ulama were transplanted
in order to bolster Safawid rule only to achieve such power in Iranian society that
they came to challenge the authority of the state. This said, the ulama embraced
a wide range of distinction and function, from those of the patrician families
of Cairo, Damascus, and Baghdad, or those of the great clerical families of
west Africa, such as the Jakhanke of Senegambia who can be traced back to the
thirteenth century, or the Saghananughu who can be traced back to the fourteenth century, to the leader of prayers in a small-town mosque or to the village
school teacher.

The qadi was the particular victim of those who wished to draw attention to the hypocrisy of the ulama. For instance, anonymous versifiers praised the Mamluk chief justice, Ibn al-Naqib thus:

A qadi who, when two parties
   part in peace,
Rekindles their dispute with
   binding words.
Indifferent to this world and its
   luxuries, he seems,
But in secret, he wouldn't say no
   to a camel's dung.

Oh, people pause and hark
To the charming qualities of our
   qadi,
A homosexual, drunkard, forni-
   cator, and takes bribes,
A tell-tale liar whose judge-
   ments follow his whim.

A similar theme was taken up in a story in the *Gulistan* of Shaykh Saadi of Shiraz. In this illustration to a fine copy of the *Gulistan* commissioned by the Mughal emperor Shah Jahan, a qadi who was famed for his modesty and honour is discovered by the king with a boy, both exhausted after a night of drinking and love-making. In spite of the grim future for the qadi suggested by this painting, the tale ends happily with the judge winning the king's pardon as a result of a clever and witty defence.

Such men, who were both important and often prominent in their communities, were inevitably a focus of criticism. In fourteenth-century Cairo their pretensions were satirized by street players wearing outsize turbans and sleeves. Under the Ottomans, Khoja Chelebi, Sulayman the Magnificent's great Shaykh al-Islam, was accused of having 'an excess of complaisance and softness towards men of government'. The corrupt qadi was a theme in poetry and painting. That such comments should take place at all indicates the esteem in which ulama were generally held. 'Verily,' declared the Prophet, 'the men of knowledge are the inheritors of the prophets.'

Ulama taught in the reception rooms of their houses, in the courtyards of mosques and shrines, and also in madrasas, or specially constructed colleges. Indeed, through much of the medieval Muslim world the madrasa, a term directly derived from the verb meaning 'to study', was the focus of education. The madrasa seems first to have developed as a specific institution in Khurasan. During the eleventh and twelfth centuries it became established in Iraq and Syria as part of an assertion of Sunni tradition in a region long threatened by Shia power. At the end of the twelfth century there were at least thirty madrasas in Damascus and a similar number in Cairo.

By this time the madrasa had become a major Islamic institution. Some foundations from this medieval period exist to the present day, such as al-Azhar in Cairo, established in 972, or the Bu Inaniyya in Fez, established in the mid-fourteenth century. So too, in its arrangement of students' and teachers' rooms around a courtyard, the madrasa had come to represent a classic form of Islamic architecture to set alongside the mosque and shrine. Magnificent relics of this form can be seen in the monumental madrasas which fill three sides of the Registan Square in Samarqand, or in the four fine madrasas which form part of the Sulaymaniye complex in Istanbul. Nevertheless, the number, and sometimes the magnificence, of madrasas in many parts of the Muslim world should not lead one to believe that teaching and learning were highly formal or institutionalized processes. There were no examinations at entrance, no degrees on leaving. Moreover, salaries for teachers and stipends for students, as research on medieval Cairo has revealed, were often low priorities for those making endowments. The madrasas were primarily a location in which teaching took place. The arrangements were normally informal; they were a person-to-person affair.

At the heart of the person-to-person nature of teaching was the fact that it was essentially oral. This was the way in which the Prophet had first transmitted the messages he received from God to his followers. Learning the Quran by heart and then reciting it out loud was the first task of Muslim boys and girls. The methods of learning and of transmitting the Quran laid their impress on the transmission of all other knowledge. 'The Quran', declared the great fourteenth-century historian Ibn Khaldun, in a fine chapter on the art of teaching in his *Muqadimmah*, 'has become the basis of instruction, the foundation of all habits that might be

Knowledge has traditionally been highly prized by Muslims. 'Nothing is more powerful than knowledge', goes one tradition, 'kings are the rulers of the people, but scholars are the rulers of kings.' By the same token the transmission of knowledge was a major act of piety. It was a person-to-person activity. The pupils depicted here would probably have deliberately sought this teacher as an expert in a particular text. He would dictate the text to them and discourse upon it. They would memorize the text and repeat it back to him. Once they had repeated the full text back to the teacher to his satisfaction, the teacher would issue an *ijaza* (licence) to transmit the text. On that licence would be listed the names of those who had transmitted the text, going back to the original author. Here, we see teaching taking place in a well-stocked library.

acquired later on.' Thus, when a teacher taught a text in the madrasa curriculum, he would dictate it to his pupils (usually boys), who might write it down, and frequently commit it to memory – many pedagogical texts were written in rhyme to assist this process. Subsequently, there might be an explanation of the text depending on its nature. The study of the book was completed by the pupil reading back the text with the explanation. If this was done to the teacher's satisfaction, the pupil would be given an *ijaza* (meaning 'to make lawful'), which was a licence to teach that text. The personal and oral nature of the process of transmission is captured in the words of a tenth-century ijaza from the author of a text: 'I entrust my book to you with my writing from my hand to yours. I give you authorization for the poem and you may transmit it from me. It has been produced after being heard and read.' The pupil would also see in his ijaza a list of all the names of those who had transmitted the text going back to the original author. He would know that he was but the most recent link in a continuing chain of oral transmission.

It might reasonably be asked why a culture which placed a high value on the book – which saw great libraries amassed, in which students were urged to buy

books, and many opportunities for silent reading existed –
should place such emphasis on oral transmission. The reason was that Muslims were fundamentally sceptical of the
written word, and particularly the written word studied
without supervision, as a reliable means of communication. 'When a student has to rely on the study of books and
written material and must understand scientific problems
from the forms of written letters in books', declares Ibn
Khaldun, 'he is confronted by...[a] veil...that separates
handwriting and the form of the letter found in writing
from the spoken words found in the imagination.' To
approach the true meaning of the text, which the author
intended when he first published the text by reading it out
loud, the student had to read it out loud. To have authority
over the transmission of the text the student had to read it
out loud to the satisfaction of a teacher who himself had
authority over the text.

Two enduring features of Islamic culture illuminate the
importance of person-to-person transmission. One is the
literary form of the *tazkirah*, collective biography. This
might cover the scholars of a particular time, place, or family. It would record, after family details, who a scholar's
teachers were, what the scholar had learned, and whom the
scholar had taught. Contributions to knowledge would be
listed along with anecdotal evidence bearing on the

A page from Mir Sayyid Sharif
Jurjani's notes on Qutb al-din
Mahmud al-Razi al-Tahtani's
*Tahrir al-Qawaid al-
Mantiqiyya fi sharh al-risala
al-shamsiyya*, which was
Tahtani's commentary on *Al-
Risala al-Shamsiyya* 'The
Logic of the Arabs' by Najm
al-Din Abul Hasan Ali bin
Umar (d.1276), a leading
Shafii scholar and logician.
Al-Tahtani's commentary and
the notes of his pupil Jurjani
were used in madrasas in the
Ottoman empire, through Iran
to India. Much Muslim schol-
arship was carried on in the
form of commentaries and
glosses such as these.

scholar's reliability as a transmitter of knowledge. Such biographies, which record
the person-to-person transmission of the central messages of Islam, have been
kept to the present day. The second feature is the enormous respect given to the
teacher in the Islamic tradition. 'Know that...one does not acquire learning nor
profit from it', declared a thirteenth-century educational manual, 'unless one
holds in esteem knowledge and those who possess it. One [must also] glorify and
venerate the teacher.' The situation was little different at the beginning of the
twentieth century. 'The pupil should walk several paces behind his teacher',
declared a leading north Indian scholar, 'he should strive to be the first to do his
teacher's bidding...and should they differ his teacher's word is final.'

When learning began in a madrasa, the student would already know some Arabic, and, if fortunate, would have memorized the Quran. Now the student would
study books of Arabic grammar and syntax, the hadiths, Quran commentary,
rhetoric, the law, and jurisprudence. Occasionally there was a little arithmetic,
which ulama needed if they were to give a fatwa on inheritance; there might also
be some works on medicine or sufism. Theology, and its supporting subjects of
logic and philosophy, was not acceptable to all. Madrasas in the Hanbali, Maliki,

Previous page
Scholars, the ulama (those with *ilm,* knowledge), were to be found in almost every corner of the Muslim world. They performed a wide range of functions, administering mosques, schools, hospitals, and orphanages and acting as courtiers, diplomats, and bureaucrats. Their most important function, however, was the preservation and transmission of the holy law, and to make it available to the society of their time. Although there was a strong tradition that scholars should avoid the powerful – 'the worst of scholars is he who visits princes', went an oft-quoted hadith, 'and the best of princes is he who visits scholars' – nevertheless there was a strong predisposition amongst the ulama to support princes so long as they upheld the law. In this charming picture of about 1640, full of circumstantial detail, the Mughal emperor Shah Jahan entertains ulama to a banquet. There appears to be little doubt about the respect which these scholars offer their worldly ruler.

and Shafii traditions either banned it altogether or offered it a fitful toleration; only madrasas in the Hanafi and Shia legal traditions found it generally acceptable.

By 1500 great classical texts had become established in most of the fields of madrasa knowledge. There was, for instance, the *Hidaya,* the basic work of Hanafi law written by Shaykh Burhan al-Din al-Marghinani (d.1196). There was also the widely accepted commentary on the Quran by al-Baydawi. As time went on classical works such as these gained in authority; few new books were introduced. Ulama tended to confine themselves to writing commentaries and supercommentaries on the classical version until the point where it was all but overwhelmed by layers of annotation. Sometimes, as in the case of the commentaries of the two great rivals at the court of Timur, Saad al-Din Taftazani (d.1389) and Mir Sayyid Sharif Jurjani (d.1413), such works helped to make classical texts highly accessible to madrasa students. Indeed, they remained in use right down to the twentieth century.

The tendency of this educational system was conservative. It was understandable. Ulama knew that they had received the most precious favour from God in the Quran and the life of Muhammad; they also knew that up to the day of judgment there would be no further guidance for humankind. It was their foremost duty to strive to pass on this gift in as pure a form as possible alongside the skills to interpret it for the benefit of the community. The further they got from the time of the Prophet, the greater was the chance that part of God's precious favour would be corrupted or lost. There was no likelihood of Muslims discovering more of the truth, only a danger that they might preserve less of it. Rote learning played an important part in the process of preservation and transmission, although at the higher levels scholars were concerned to emphasize the importance of understanding. Knowledge tended to be normative: Muslims learned how things ought to be.

This educational system was often elitist. There seems to have been an enduring fear amongst the ulama of late medieval Cairo, for instance, that a democratization of education might lead to a lowering of standards. They inveighed against those colleagues who made much of their fine clothes and huge turbans for fear that emphasis on finery rather than learning might enable the ignorant to parade themselves as scholars. They inveighed against those who were so unprofessional as to repeat themselves, fall asleep in class, or be just plain wrong; such poor performance made it difficult to distinguish between the merely lazy and the fundamentally unqualified. Nevertheless, there were also ulama who believed that all Muslims should have access to madrasa learning. 'To lock the door of a madrasa', declared Ibn al-Hajj (d.1336–37) 'is to shut out the masses and prevent them from hearing the [recitation of] knowledge...and being blessed by it and its people [i.e. the ulama].' If the ulama kept knowledge from the common people, they would not benefit from it themselves.

It is evident, despite the fear of some ulama for their elite professional stand-ing, that knowledge and the special privilege of transmitting it did seep into the wider community. Sixteenth-century Timbuktu, for instance, was not only a great centre of learning but also one in which there is reason to believe there may have been universal male literacy; well over 150 Quran schools served a population of roughly 70,000. In fourteenth- and fifteenth-century Cairo the many madrasas were well integrated into the local community. Madrasa functionaries – for instance, Quran readers, muezzins, and porters – took lessons as well as students, and so did the common townspeople. At no point, however, were the people so involved in the transmission of knowledge as in the public recitations of hadiths. On these occasions, which were manifestations of piety as well as of learning, ordinary Muslims were able to acquire ijazas and become transmitters of precious knowledge which reached back through the Prophet's companions to Muhammad himself. Here women were able to play their part. Al-Sakhawi (d.1497) offers 1,075 biographies of women amongst some 11,000 in his collective biography of the notables of his time. Of these 400 had some form of religious education. Amongst the various fields of knowledge, women were most prominent in hadith, where they were able to rival men. Remarkable in the field was Aisha of Damas-cus. Such was her learning that the noted scholar of Hadith Ibn Hajr al-Asqalani

The Sankore mosque, first built in the fourteenth and fif-teenth centuries, and one of the two oldest mosques in Timbuktu. In the sixteenth century, under the patronage of the Aqit family, this mosque was the leading cen-tre of learning in the city and renowned for the exposition of the *Kitab al-Shifa* which took place in its madrasa. This book by al-Qadi Iyad (d.1149) was popular throughout north Africa and the Sudan on account of its arguments concerning the mission of the Prophet and their implications for the hadiths and sharia.

Science

Islamic science was built on earlier achievements, especially those of the Greeks, Iranians, and Indians. Forged with speed in the first hundred years of the Islamic era, the Islamic world system enabled scientists to interact across the world from Central Asia and India to Spain and north Africa. Science began to develop a significant international dimension. For six centuries or more Arabic was the world's leading language of science, a fact which has left its mark on European languages in terms such as algebra and algorithm.

Muslim contributions to the sciences were great and wideranging, and their full extent is still unknown. Mathematics was one such area of achievement. In number theory and computation, for instance, the Central Asian al-Biruni (d.1046) wrote many studies of series. The contemporary historian of Islamic science Sayyed Hossein Nasr describes al-Biruni's famous chessboard problem thus:

> asked to be given the amount of grain which would correspond to the number of grains on a chessboard arranged in such a way that there would be one grain in the first square, two in the second, four in the third, and so on up to the 64 squares. The ruler first accepted but soon realized that there was not that much grain in his whole kingdom.

Al-Biruni found the answer to be 18, 446, 744, 073, 709, 551, 615, which in modern form would be $\sum^{64} 2^{n-1} = 2^{64} - 1$. By 950 al-Uqlidisi had already discovered the decimal fraction, the approximate method for calculating problems which have no exact solution. This discovery was taken into the mainstream of the subject by the fifteenth-century Iranian mathematician Jamshid al-Kashani, who amongst other things may have been the first to invent a calculating machine. In geometry Muslims followed the paths laid out by the Greek mathematicians, solving many previously unsolved problems. Notable were Omar Khayyam (1048–1131) of *Rubaiyyat* fame and the great Shia scientist Nasiruddin Tusi (d.1274), who re-examined the very foundations of Euclidean geometry. Trigonometry as studied to this day was developed to its full extent by Muslim mathematicians; the word 'sine' is a direct translation of the Ara-

Nasr al-Din Tusi's version, based on earlier Arab translations, of Euclid's proof of Pythagoras' theorem.

bic *jayb* (curve). So, equally, Muslims were the founders of algebra (from the Arabic *al-jabr*, meaning 'restoration'). The subject was first established by Muhammad ibn Musa al-Khwarazmi (d.c.846), whose name gives us 'algorithm', and was brought to its peak by Omar Khayyam, great poet but greater mathematician. The influence of mathematics in Islamic civilization is manifest throughout its architecture and decorative arts.

A second area of major achievement was astronomy. Muslim astronomers drew on Greek, Iranian, and Indian sources. From the ninth century, as the works of Ptolemy and other Greek astronomers came to be translated, their studies began to take major steps forward. Many improvements were made to astronomical tables and there were remarkable feats such as the measurement of the meridian near Mosul. In the eleventh century these and many others were drawn together by al-Biruni whose compendium of Islamic astronomy, *al-Qanun al-Masudi*, is the equal for this subject of Ibn Sina's *Qanun* for medicine. In the same century Ibn al-Haytham (the Latin Alhazen, d.1039), also well known for his work on optics, measured the thickness of the atmosphere and its effect on astronomical observations. In the eleventh and twelfth centuries scientists in Spain and the Maghrib became increasingly critical of Ptolemaic astronomy. In the thirteenth century Nasiruddin Tusi and his circle, working in the famous observatory which Tusi established at Maraghah in northwest Iran, developed a powerful critique of the Ptolemaic understanding of interplanetary motion. The work was translated by the Byzantines into Greek and ultimately reached Copernicus and other European astronomers who used it to develop their heliocentric theory.

Medicine was a third area of both achievement and influence. Many scholars applied themselves to its practice because it brought the living which enabled them to sustain other researches. The early Islamic physicians drew on Graeco-Alexandrian, Near Eastern, Iranian, and Indian traditions. The first great figure was Muhammad ibn Zakariyya al-Razi (Rhazes, d.925). Al-Biruni catalogued 184 of his works, of which 50 are extant. His most important work was a vast encyclopaedia of medicine, *al-Hawi*, found in the Latin West under the title *Continens*. For each disease he gave the views of Greek, Syrian, Indian, Iranian, and Arab writers, added notes from his daily clinical observations, and then gave his own opinion. The greatest writer on medical matters, however, was Ibn Sina. His *al-Qanun fil-tibb* is arguably the most influential work in the history of medicine. Translated into Latin in the twelfth century, it dominated the teaching of medicine in Europe until at least the sixteenth century. Among other figures of note were the Andalusians Ibn Zuhr (Avenzoar, d.1161) for his work on diet and Ibn Rushd (Averroes, 1121-1198) for his work on general principles, and the Syrian Ibn al-Nafis (d.1288) for his discovery of the minor circulation of the blood. In the nineteenth and twentieth centuries, in much of the Muslim world Islamic systems of medicine gave way to those of the West. However, they remain vigorous in India, Pakistan, and Bangladesh.

So brightly did the star of Muslim science shine, so far did its light travel, that the questions must be asked: why

Medicine for Muslims, like its Hippocratic and Galenic predecessors, was based on understanding the harmony of the four humours, that is blood, phlegm, yellow bile, and black bile. This harmony differed from individual to individual; diagnosis sought to discover how this harmony had been upset; treatment was concerned to restore harmony. Treatment was essentially non-invasive; Muslim physicians disapproved of surgery. However, it was recognized that there were some occasions when it could not be avoided, as is demonstrated by this caesarean operation illustrating a work of al-Biruni.

did its advances peter out? Why, as in the case of interplanetary motion, were studies not taken to their logical conclusion? The reasons are several; amongst them is the problem that Muslim scientists were subject to a world view in which knowledge was to be judged by whether it conformed to Islam or not. This said, the Chinese and Indian civilizations were no more successful in carrying forward their scientific and mathematical discoveries than the Muslim. Ultimately, the question needs to be asked why Europe made such spectacular advances rather than why others failed to do so.

Ottoman astronomers working in the observatory established by Taqi al-Din at Istanbul in 1575: note the wide range of instruments displayed and the hive of activity the place seems to be.

A page from the work of Ibn al-Shatir, a fourteenth-century astronomer from Damascus, who suggested non-Ptolemaic models for the motion of the sun, moon, and planets. He continued the work of Nasr al-Din Tusi in questioning the geocentric theory of interplanetary motion.

(1372–1449) listed her amongst his teachers with pride. Such was Aisha of Damascus' reputation that a seventeenth-century historian rated her the most reliable transmitter of her time.

The ulama were not only an elite within their own society. Many formed part of an international elite, because learning was a truly international affair shared across the Islamic lands. As one might expect, many books tended to be shared within regions dominated by a particular school of law. So, for instance, the Maliki ulama of Timbuktu used many of the same books as those of Morocco and Egypt. So, too, did the Hanafi ulama of the Ottoman Empire, Central and South Asia, where the helpful texts of Taftazani and Jurjani were especially popular. Moreover, because of the greater openness to the rational sciences of the Hanafis and the Shias, there was a considerable commonality of texts in this field between the Shia ulama of the Safawid empire and the Sunni ulama of the Mughal empire. Then there were works used throughout the Sunni world regardless of law school. This was naturally the case with the six canonical collections of hadiths, but also with great works of synthesis such as al-Ghazzali's *Revival of the Religious Sciences*, which was used from Spain to Southeast Asia, or al-Suyuti's Quran commentary *Jalalain*, as popular in west Africa as in north India.

A shared world of books meant a shared world of debate and reference. When in 1637 ulama in the Sumatran sultanate of Atjeh fell out over the appropriate attitude to adopt to the works of Ibn al-Arabi (d.1240), echoes of the dispute reached Medina where one of the leading scholars of the day, Ibrahim al-Kurani (1615–90), wrote a magisterial work to resolve the points at issue. Notable in the seventeenth and eighteenth centuries was the export of knowledge and understanding in the rational sciences from Iran into India, and then the subsequent export of outstanding Indian scholarship in the field to Egypt and west Asia, where it helped to revive studies in the field.

Ulama had wideranging connections throughout this world of shared knowledge. There were family connections within a region – the descendants of Ghulam Allah, who from at least the fifteenth century spread throughout the Upper Nile valley, or the Farangi Mahal family of Lucknow, who from the late seventeenth century spread throughout India. There were family connections across regions – those of the Majlisi family, which from the seventeenth century spread from the cities of Iraq and Iran through to Murshidabad and Bengal, or those of the Aydarus family, which expanded from south Arabia in the sixteenth century to the point in the eighteenth century when it had important branches throughout the Indian Ocean rim from the islands of Southeast Asia through India to east Africa. No less important were the travels of the ulama and the connections of teachers and pupils which resulted. Indeed, ulama took very seriously the exhortation in the hadiths that they should travel in pursuit of knowledge. Al-Ghazzali, for instance, studied in his native Tus in Khurasan, then in Jurjan and Nishapur, and travelled as a scholar to Baghdad, Mecca, Damascus, Egypt, and back to Tus.

Ulama travelled from Timbuktu to the great centres of learning in Egypt and west Asia, but equally, a noted scholar such as al-Maghili of Tlemcen thought it worth his while to travel to west Sudan. Great schools, such as Ibrahim al-Kurani's school of hadiths at Medina, attracted pupils from all over Asia, from the Hijaz, the Fertile Crescent, Anatolia, India, and the Indonesian islands. No recorded life reveals more dramatically how much was shared through the Islamic world than that of the great traveller Ibn Battuta (1304–69), who between 1325 and 1354 journeyed its length and breadth – the equivalent of well over forty modern countries – worked as a qadi from time to time, lived well, and dangerously, and survived to dictate a humane and engaging account of his adventures.

The sufis: transmitters of spiritual knowledge

Sufis, or the 'friends of God' as they were known, were more ubiquitous than the ulama. The latter tended to flourish in cities and areas where there was state power willing to support the law. Sufis, on the other hand, reached all levels of society and all parts of the world where Muslims lived. Their style and methods, moreover, were particularly well adapted to those areas, often on the frontiers of Islam, where kin and tribal organization were paramount.

From the tenth century groups of disciples had begun to gather round particular sufi shaykhs in order to learn how to follow his (or occasionally her) particular *tariqa*, way of travelling, towards direct experiential knowledge of God. Sometimes they came together in *khanqa*s (sufi hospices), in which they might live an ordered devotional life and which were often dedicated to charitable and missionary work. Whether part of a khanqa community or not, all disciples performed the central ritual of their tariqa, which was their shaykh's *dhikr* – special way of remembering God. This might involve repeating the name of Allah to focus the mind away from earthly things, or using breathing techniques to intensify concentration. Often there was a collective ritual in which adepts sought ecstatic religious experience by means of chant, music, or dance. Once a disciple had placed himself in the hands of a shaykh he had to obey him at all costs, even if it meant going against the sharia; he was to be, as the saying went, 'like a corpse in the hands of the washer of the dead.'

Central to the transmission of mystical knowledge across time and space were the connections of shaykhs and disciples. Particularly important were the shaykh's *khalifa*s, successors, gifted disciples, who were designated to pass on the shaykh's teaching and to make disciples of their own. They became part of their shaykh's *silsila*, chain of transmission, which went back through him and his predecessors to the saint who had founded their mystical way. Often khalifas became saints themselves.

On being initiated into a mystical way the disciple would swear an oath of allegiance to his shaykh, receive from him a *khirqa*, cloak, and be told the special protective prayer, *hizb al-bahr*, of the founder of the way. The disciple would also

Each sufi shaykh (master) would carefully supervise the spiritual development of his disciples and pass on to them his particular dhikr or way of remembering God. In this mid-seventeenth-century Mughal painting, disciples perform a dhikr of dancing before six shaykhs. Some dancers have already collapsed in ecstatic trance. The inscription above the door declares in Persian: 'What a session in which they bestow a treasure of magnificence, they bestow a thousand royal crowns on a beggar'.

receive a certificate showing the chain of transmission of spiritual knowledge, starting with the Prophet, moving down through a companion, usually Ali, and then through one or two of the great mystics of the early Abbasid period, down to the saint who founded his way, and then down to his shaykh. The newly initiated mystic would know, in the same way as a pupil who received an ijaza to transmit hadiths, that he had become a repository of precious knowledge that went back to the foundation of the Muslim community.

The focal point for the followers of a particular sufi way was the shrine of the founding saint. This was often managed by the saint's physical descendants whose functions might well have become more ceremonial than spiritual. They administered the fabric of the shrine, its sufi community, its endowments, and its charitable works. The shrine of the founder of a major sufi order, say that of Abd al-Qadir al-Jilani (d.1166) in Baghdad, whose chains of succession spread throughout much of the Islamic world, was a focus of international pilgrimage. Lesser shrines were the focus of regional and local cults. As in the case of the madrasa, the rectangular shrine, often surmounted by a dome and surrounded by a compound with a khanqa and cells in which disciples might stay, became a feature of Islamic architecture. Visiting the shrines of saints, moreover, became a custom in Islamic devotional life. Some Muslims did so because they felt that the resting places of those who were close to God were propitious for prayer, others because they wished to beg the saint to intercede for them with God. Each year the shrine would hold a major rite, known as the *urs*, wedding; it celebrated the moment when the saint's soul became united with God. A major part of the rituals on this day would often be the recollection of the stages, in some traditions in devotional songs, by which spiritual knowledge passed down from the Prophet to the saint.

The Muslim world is covered with saints' shrines, places where the pious Muslim can be close to those who are close to God. In the pre-modern period most Muslims would have called upon a saint to intercede for them with God. Here we see the shrine of the eighteenth-century Siraiki poet, Sachal Sarmast, at Daraza near Khayrpur in Sindh. The shrines of this Indus valley province are famed for their magnificent tilework. Today Sachal Sarmast is second only to Shah Abd al-Latif of Bhit as a symbol of Sindhi identity.

From the thirteenth century sufis began to organize in orders, which came to number in hundreds. The differences between them stemmed partly from variations in their rituals and ways of remembering God and partly from the extent to which they followed the sharia or permitted deviations from it. Overall they represented relatively loose affiliations, indeed, loose enough for Naqshbandi sufis in one part of the world to follow practices deeply disapproved of by Naqshbandis in another. Nevertheless, these connections of spiritual brotherhood through Muslim lands were key channels along which Islamic knowledge travelled and by means of which it might, when the need arose, be reshaped and revitalized.

Some orders achieved influence across the Islamic world. The Suhrawardiyya, for instance, who were notably careful in observing the sharia and who looked back to the Baghdadi sufis Abu Najib al-Suhrawardi (d.1168) and his nephew Shihab al-Din (d.1234), spread their influence from west Asia to the east Indian province of Bengal. The Shadhiliyya, who found the roots of their tradition in the Spanish sufi Abu Madyan Shuayb (d.1197), not only broadcast their message from Morocco through north Africa to west Asia but also inspired several modern revivalist movements, as well as becoming the favoured home of European and American recruits to sufism. The Naqshbandiyya, who derive their name, although not their specific way, from Shaykh Baha al-Din Naqshband (d.1389) whose mausoleum lies outside Bukhara, expanded throughout Asia; from the eighteenth century they were both the inspiration and channel for the most vigorous movements of Islamic assertion. The Qadiriyya, however, descended from the Baghdadi saint Abd al-Qadir al-Jilani, became the most widespread order. In west Africa in recent centuries they too have been associated with movements of Islamic assertion.

A sufi hospice in the village of Blagaj 6 miles south of Mostar in Bosnia-Herzegovina. Note the dhikr invocation 'hu' in Arabic script on the wall. The sufi brotherhoods of the Balkans acknowledged historical links to Central Asia. Among those present in the region were: the Bektashiyya, Qadiriyya, Mawlawiyya, Khalwatiyya, Naqshbandiyya, and Malamiyya. The Bektashiyya had particularly strong roots in Albania.

Many orders, while still of great importance, have been restricted to a particular region. In India the most influential order was the Chishtiyya, who made a point of eschewing those with political power. India, however, was also host to many irregular orders, such as the Malamatis and the Qalandaris, who followed many indigenous customs and were not bound by the sharia. In west Asia the Rifaiyya were remarkable for their dhikr, which made a loud and harsh sound – hence their sobriquet the 'Howling Dervishes', and their strange practices such as fire eating and biting the heads off live snakes. In Anatolia and the Ottoman empire there were the Bektashiyya, the favoured order of the Janissaries, who made confessions to their shaykhs, observed a Christian-like ritual involving bread, wine and cheese, and believed in a quasi-Trinity of God, Muhammad, and Ali. There were also the Mawlawiyya, who were inspired by the great mystical poet Jalal al-Din Rumi (d.1273) and who, on account of their dhikr of a constantly turning dance, have come to be known in the West as the 'Whirling Dervishes'.

Alongside the consolidation of the sufi orders there also grew a mystical understanding of enormous importance to the development of Islam. Its author was Ibn al-Arabi, a Spanish sufi educated in Seville. On a pilgrimage to Mecca he had a vision of the divine throne in which he was told that he stood foremost amongst the saints. This inspired his masterwork *The Meccan Revelations*, in which he developed his doctrine of the unity of being. God was transcendent. Yet because all creation was a manifestation of God, it was identical with Him in essence. It followed that God was necessary for men and women to exist but equally they were necessary for God to be manifest. In expounding his doctrine Ibn al-Arabi turned frequently to the famous tradition which conveys a message from God but is not included in the Quran: 'I was a hidden treasure and wanted to be known, thus I created the world that I might be known.' Moreover, in expressing this vision he both generated a rich symbolic vocabulary and produced a masterly synthesis of sufi, philosophic, and neo-Platonic thought.

For centuries Ibn al-Arabi has been accused of pantheism by scholars, Muslim and Christian alike, and banned in parts of the Islamic world. Nevertheless, western scholars have come to accept that he always maintained God's transcendence and that his vision rested firmly on the Quran. What concerns us, however, is his impact on the later development of sufism and Muslim religious understanding.

Such was Ibn al-Arabi's achievement and authority that he set the agenda for sufi discourse, which from then on focused on his concept of the unity of being

Women approach the shrine of Ayyub (Job) Ansari at Eyup (Ayyub in Turkish) on the Golden Horn just outside the walls of Istanbul. Ayyub Ansari was the friend and standard-bearer of the Prophet and is said to have been killed in the first Arab siege of the city in the years 674–78. Eyup is one of the holiest places of pilgrimage in the Islamic world. After his conquest of Constantinople in 1453 Sultan Mehmet Fatih raised a complex of buildings around the tomb of Ayyub Ansari. Subsequent Ottoman sultans, on acceding to the throne, came to Eyup to be girded with the sword of Uthman (Osman).

and on the problems of reconciling his vision of God's relationship to the material world with that of the Quran. Not least among the vehicles of his ideas was poetry. And this was as much the case for poetry in Arabic or the African languages as for poetry in the high Persian tradition – that of Jalal al-Din Rumi, whose *Mathnawi* is talked of as the Persian *Quran*, Hafiz (1325/6– 89/90) of Shiraz, whose *Diwan* contains some of the world's most sublime poetry, or Jami (1414–92) of Herat, whom many regard as the last of the great mystical poets – and in the languages of Asia – that of Yunus Emre (d.1321) in Anatolia, Bullhe Shah (d.1754) in the Indian Punjab, and Shah Abd al-Latif (d.1752) in Indian Sind. The outcome of such widespread absorption of the idea of the unity of being was to lessen the importance of observing the sharia. If everything was God, it made it less important to strive to put into practice on earth His revelation. Ecstatic union with Him would be enough. But, if some might regard this as the down side of Ibn al-Arabi's impact on Islamic history, they could not fail to see that it also had an up side. The greater tolerance and flexibility which Ibn al-Arabi's vision brought to Muslim approaches to non-Muslim traditions, whether he intended the outcome or not, helped sufis throughout the world build bridges between Islam and a myriad of local religious traditions.

Sufis had a key role in transmitting the message of Islam into regions and societies where ulama were unlikely to move with confidence or ease. Indeed, in the wider Islamic world they were often the first bearers of the faith. We know relatively little of their role in the central Islamic lands but rather more of their achievement in north Africa, Anatolia, the Balkans, and Central and South Asia. Here they filtered into lands freshly conquered by Muslim armies or worked their way along international trade routes and prepared the ground for the consolidation of Islam. It is not possible to consider the firm establishment of Islam in Central Asia or in the Sind and Bengal regions of India without considering the role of sufis. Further afield sufis were also crucial. In some parts of sub-Sarahan Africa the founding myths of Islam go back to the arrival of wandering holy men. In Java they refer to the work of nine saints; in Sumatra to the arrival of a sufi on a ship sent by the 'king of Mecca'.

In transmitting their messages to non-Muslim societies, sufis, bolstered by the apparently latitudinarian thought of Ibn al-Arabi, tended not to insist on a strict application of the sharia. For one thing they did not have the power to do so; for another they usually tried to minimize conflict with local religious traditions. Their policies, in fact, were normally to seek points of contact and social roles in the host community. They shared their knowledge of religious experiences with those of other spiritual traditions. They operated as intermediaries and buffers between people and all the uncertainties of life beyond their control. By accommodating themselves to local needs and customs they gradually built a position from which they might draw their clients into an Islamic milieu and educate them in Islamic behaviour. They insinuated their ideas into daily human life, as indicated by these verses created by a sufi for women in India's Deccan to sing as they ground corn:

> The *chakki*'s [grindstone] handle resembles *alif*,*
>> which means Allah,
> And the axle is Muhammad, and is fixed there.
> In this way the truth-seeker sees the relationship
>> Ya *bism Allah*, hu hu Allah.
> We put grain in the *chakki*
> To which our hands are witnesses.
> The *chakki* of the body is in order
> When you follow the *shari'at*.
>> Ya *bism Allah*, hu hu Allah.

Sufis headed the transmission of Islamic knowledge, both to the masses in long-conquered societies and to largely non-Muslim societies as a whole. On the front-line the shrines of the saints were the fortresses and outposts. Here sufis tendered religious services to the people in the process fostering manifold expressions of what has come to be known as 'popular Islam'. Worship of trees, fish, or crocodiles might become associated with particular shrines, and pre-Islamic cults relating to St George or Khwaja Khidr (the spirit of life and renewal worshipped from Mesopotamia through to Bengal) might be incorporated into local Muslim beliefs; shrines and also mosques were often built on former Christian or Hindu holy places. A range of ritual practices might be tolerated: lighting candles, sweeping the tomb, or tying a piece of cloth to the shrine to remind the saint of a request. Relics there were a-plenty. Most shrines had the relics of a saint – cloak, rosary, or turban. One or two places, not necessarily saint's shrines, might have relics of the Prophet, hairs from his beard or casts of his footprint. At such points the practice of Islam tended to reflect more the beliefs and customs of the societies it embraced than the behaviour and attitude laid down in the sharia.

That sufis through much of the Islamic world should permit such practices could be a major source of tension with the ulama. The latter were bound to feel ill-at-ease when they witnessed the flouting of the sharia. Some ulama of the Hanbali school refused to have anything to do with sufis. Most notable amongst them was Ahmad ibn Taymiyya of Damascus (d.1328). When Ibn Battuta, who accepted most sufi practices, heard him preach in 1326, he thought he had 'a kink in his brain'. Soon afterwards, moreover, the Mamluk government seemed to agree and placed him in prison where he died of a broken heart. Nevertheless, from the seventeenth century onwards there was increasing sympathy for his uncompromising attitude to sufism. Today he is regarded as embodying the spirit of the Muslim revival and his books are much reprinted. This said, the tension between the bearers of the two great shaping forces of Islam should not be over-

*vertical letter, the first of the Arabic alphabet

Through the work of sufis many pre-Islamic cults came to be incorporated into Muslim beliefs in localities. One of the most widespread was that of Khwaja Khidr, here seen in a Bengali incarnation of the late eighteenth century. This figure first appeared in the Mesopotamian *Epic of Gilgamesh* and its subsequent Babylonian developments. From Turkey through to Bengal he is associated with springtime renewal, fertility, happiness, and often the colour green. He helps those in distress, in particular those in danger of drowning at sea or being lost in the desert. In Delhi, washermen used to celebrate his anniversary by launching grass boats on the Jumna; in Murshidabad (Bengal) it was done by launching paper rafts with peacock-shaped prows on the Ganges.

estimated. Many ulama were sufis, many sufis were deeply learned in the sharia. It was widely felt that the best learned and holy men were those who had achieved a judicious balance of the two forms of knowledge.

No less a tension was that between the transmitters of the two great Islamic traditions of knowledge and the wielders of political power. Different groups of sufis and ulama had conflicting attitudes towards princes. 'My room has two doors', declared the great Chishti saint Nizam al-Din Awliya, whose order laid especial emphasis on avoiding princes; 'if the sultan comes through one door, I will leave by the other.' Yet other sufi orders, like the Suhrawardiyya and the Naqshbandiyya, had a particular interest, for some of their history at least, in political power. Moreover, ulama have always tended to support political order, however much they may have disapproved of individual princes, because such order was necessary to administer the sharia.

On occasion there was an actual breakdown of relationships between the transmitters and princes. It was such a breakdown which led the Mughal emperor Jahangir to throw a Naqshbandi shaykh, Ahmad Sirhindi (1564–1624), into prison after he had crowed over the death of the emperor's father, Akbar, in whose reign, Sirhindi declared, 'the sun of guidance was hidden behind the veil of error'. In such a breakdown, too, the leading scholar of late seventeenth-century Iran, Muhammad Baqir al-Majlisi (1627–98), had tens of thousands of wine bottles in the Shah's cellars publicly smashed. But ultimately the two sides had a considerable degree of interdependence; Muslim princes often needed the legitimation of sufi and ulama support no less than the transmitters needed the support of state power for their knowledge.

ULAMA AND SUFIS REVITALIZE ISLAM

When in the eighteenth century Muslim power began to decline, tensions between the transmitters of knowledge and the wielders of political power were exacerbated. Scholars and mystics responded by reassessing the knowledge appropriate to their societies. There was a return to first principles, the Quran and the hadiths, and increasing scepticism of the value of the rational sciences, which by the nineteenth century extended to much of the scholastic inheritance from the past. Criticism of activities at sufi shrines also grew, particularly saint worship and anything that suggested that saints or the Prophet might intercede for men and women with God. Alongside this, as might be expected, Ibn al-Arabi's sufi vision was increasingly to be questioned, although his vocabulary retained a powerful hold over all discourse. The arguments of Ahmad Sirhindi, who had countered Ibn al-Arabi's doctrine of the 'unity of being' with one of 'unity of witness', replacing the concept that 'all was God' with one that 'all was from God', became more widely accepted. Associated with the process were scholars who restricted their sources of authority to the Quran and the hadiths, not least the adherents of the Hanbali school of law, who had always resisted both sufism and the rational sciences. Among those taking up this new position, influenced by the works of Ibn Taymiyya, was its extreme exemplar, Muhammad ibn Abd al-Wahhab (1703–87), the Arabian reformer whose name became a metaphor for puritanism. These new emphases in the repertoire of Islamic knowledge were of great importance. They meant a shift from an Islam which was inclusive to one which was increasingly exclusive, and from an Islam which was otherworldly to one which was concerned to put God's guidance into practice on earth.

The new emphasis in knowledge and on action was conveyed through much of the Islamic world by sufis. This might seem odd as the new position attacked many sufi practices and in its extreme manifestation sufism itself. Sufis, however, responded creatively to the reforming challenge; they absorbed the emphasis on the Quran and hadiths as authorities within their sufi framework, reduced the significance of ecstatic practices, and reviewed the metaphysical tendencies in their beliefs. A notable feature of this reformed sufism was a new attention to the life of the Prophet, shown in growing numbers of ceremonies celebrating his birthday and of biographies of his life. To stress how they followed the path of the Prophet some gave themselves the title *Tariqa Muhammadiyya* (Muhammad's Way). Not all sufis were swept into these new forms of thought and behaviour. Nevertheless, from the eighteenth-century the overall outcome was a sufi revival in which old orders were revitalized and new ones founded.

Medina in the nineteenth century, the two domed buildings by the minarets being the tomb and the mosque of the Prophet. From the eighth century Medina was an important intellectual centre. In the seventeenth and eighteenth centuries it was the seat of a famed school of hadith scholarship to which learned men travelled from all over the Muslim world.

This new sufi spirit was carried through much of Asia by the Naqshbandiyya who inspired notable movements in Indonesia, China, Central Asia, and the Caucasus. Networks of Naqshbandi scholars, moreover, played important roles in much of India and the Middle East. The new sufism was spread through Africa by orders flowing directly or indirectly from the Khalwatiyya, who were influential in Egypt, in particular amongst the ulama of Cairo's al-Azhar. There were, for instance, the Tijaniyya, whose influence spread to the Maghrib and Nilotic and central Sudan, the Sammaniyya, whose influence also spread to the Nilotic Sudan, Eritrea, and Ethiopia; the Sanusiyya, who spread from their headquarters in the Libyan desert through much of the Sahara, and the Sahiliyya, who became the dominant force in Somalia. Not infrequently these and other sufi movements raised calls for jihad. On occasion such jihads led to the successful founding of Islamic states as in the case of the Sultanate of Sokoto, which was established early in the nineteenth century by Uthman dan Fodio in northern Nigeria, or as in the

Mahdist state established in the late nineteenth century by Muhammad Ahmad in Nilotic Sudan.

Many of the connections between ulama and sufis which helped to underpin this Islam-wide revival and reform have recently been revealed: for instance, those of leading scholars of hadiths in Medina such as Ibrahim al-Kurani, Shaykh Abu Muhammad al-Kurdi, Taj al-Din al-Hanafi and Muhammad Hayya al-Sindhi. Among their pupils were many figures influential in the eighteenth-century revival: Abd al-Rauf al-Sinkili (1617–90) of Sumatra, Shah Wali Allah of Delhi, Mustafa al-Bakri (d.1749) of Cairo, Muhammad ibn Abd al-Wahhab, Shaykh Muhammad Samman (1717–95), and at one remove Uthman dan Fodio. The pupil-teacher connections of the Mizjaji family of the Yemen overlapped with those of the Medinan teachers of hadiths, including several of the figures above as well as Muhammad Murtada al-Zabidi (d.1791), an Indian pupil of Shah Wali Allah who became a great figure in late eighteenth-century Cairo. Many revivalist scholars were also members of the Naqshbandi order. Ma Ming Hsin (d.1781), who spread the 'New Sect' teaching amongst the Chinese Naqshbandiyya from 1781, studied under a member of the Mizjaji family; Mawlana Khalid Baghdadi (1776–1827), who stimulated Naqshbandi activity throughout Syria, Iraq, Kurdistan, Anatolia, and the Balkans, some of which has continued down to the present, studied under the successors of Ahmad Sirhindi in Delhi. Probably at no previous time in Islamic history were the connections between ulama and sufis across the world as many and as vigorous as they were in the eighteenth century. Nevertheless, their interactions were complex. We are well advised to be cautious when ascribing meaning to these connections and to be aware of the importance of local circumstances in stimulating developments. This said, the movement of ideas and also of mood along the connections of ulama and sufis does illustrate the very real way in which these links were the arteries and veins of the Islamic world along which the lifeblood of knowledge and fresh vitality flowed.

RESPONSES TO THE CHALLENGE OF THE WEST AND WESTERN LEARNING SINCE 1800

The success of the West and the expansion of its sway over much of the Muslim world in the modern era transformed the context in which Islamic knowledge existed. The questioning and subversive presence of western knowledge year by year became more accessible and began to compete for a place in Muslim minds. European scientific achievement and the secular philosophies of the Enlightenment came to challenge belief in God and the idea that He created the world, that He revealed Himself to humankind, and that through following His revelation men and women might gain salvation. Such knowledge also came to challenge much of the vast store of learning which Muslims had cherished down the centuries for the support of revelation and for the service of the community.

The Nizami curriculum

This curriculum was developed by Mulla Nizam al-Din (d.1748) of the Farangi Mahal family of Lucknow, north India, in the early eighteenth century. Nizam al-Din drew substantially on the achievements of Iranian and north Indian scholars in the rational sciences over the previous 150 years. The curriculum shares a similar structure to and a good number of books with courses taught in the Ottoman and Safawid empires. It was popular in part because it laid emphasis on comprehension as much as rote learning so that able students were able to finish more quickly than before; and in part because it came to be recognized as an excellent training for government service. Curriculums such as this lost favour as Muslims responded to western knowledge and the supremacy of the west.

Nizam al-Din divided the curriculum thus:

Revealed Sciences	No. of Books	Rational Sciences	No. of books
Grammar and Syntax	1	Logic	11
Rhetoric	2	Philosophy	3
Jurisprudence	2	Theology	3
Principles of		Mathematics and	
Jurisprudence	3	Astronomy	5
Traditions	1		
Quranic Exegesis	2		

A glance at a couple of major texts in the curriculum indicates how it was rooted in the scholarship of the Islamic middle ages. In jurisprudence pupils studied *Sharh-i Wiqaya*, a commentary by Ubayd Allah ibn Masud (d.1346-47) on *Wiqaya* by his grandfather Taj al-Sharia Mahmud. In logic they studied the *Sharh-i Shamsiyya* of Najm al-Din Umar (d.1099), with the help of commentaries by Qutb al-Din Razi (d.1364-65) and Saad al-Din Taftazani (d.1389). In the rational sciences there was the more recent scholarship of Iran and India, to which Indians added significant contributions in the eighteenth century.

This mufti, a scholar entitled to give a fatwa (opinion) in Islamic law, painted in Lucknow around 1775, probably followed the Nizami syllabus and may even have been a member of the Farangi Mahal family who performed this role for the Sunni community of the city for more than 200 years. Reasoning power was a particular quality expected in a mufti.

However, not only did western knowledge become steadily more widely available in the Muslim world, it also drew the support of the state: Islamic knowledge came to be uncoupled from power. To a great extent this was a consequence of colonial rule. The British, the French, the Dutch, the Russians developed the structures of the modern state in their empires and made them the means both to provide western systems of education and to replace much of the sharia with western law codes. To a lesser extent the growth of state support for western knowledge was also a consequence of resistance to the possibility of colonial rule. Thus, the *tanzimat* reformers of the Ottoman empire in the nineteenth century or the Pahlawis of Iran in the twentieth strove to make their states strong enough to keep the foreigner out. The independence of Muslim states from the mid-twentieth century, moreover, made little difference. The process of entrenching western knowledge in Muslim societies continued, their states usually adopting an ethnic or secular identity rather than an Islamic one. Admittedly, some token state support might be available for Islamic learning, but if it existed in any force it did so because society wished it.

To this challenging environment for Islamic knowledge should be added economic, social, and technological changes sparked off by the west. The penetration of western trade and capital into Muslim societies stimulated large commodity trades, and, as Muslims learned to buy western finished goods, the destruction of local industries. Associated social changes saw the emergence of new elites to manage the new economic and political structures – technocrats, bureaucrats, bankers, intellectuals, industrial workers, all people who belonged to an existence outside the old urban communitarian world of the artisan workshop, the bazar trader, the caravansarai, and the quarter, which had long supported the work of ulama and sufis. Associated technological changes introduced steam and electrical power, the telegraph, telephone, wireless, and television communications.

In this rapidly changing context Muslims found that they had to review the body of Islamic knowledge inherited from the past and see how they might make it relevant to the present. They discovered that the application of technology to the transmission of Islamic knowledge transformed access to it. They came to note, moreover, the increasing marginalization of ulama and sufis from the activities of Muslim societies as a whole. In each society responses to the new context differed according both to the nature of western imperialism and to the particular balance of social, economic, and political forces within it.

Responses to Western knowledge
There were three broad strands of response: reformism, which re-evaluated but did not change in essence Islamic knowledge inherited from the past; modernism, which aimed to reconstruct that knowledge in the light of western knowledge and the new economic and political realities; and Islamism, which was no less respectful of the new economic and political realities but wished to make them, and western knowledge, subordinate to their utopian understanding of revelation. With-in and beyond these broad strands there were many competing voices.

Sayyid Ahmad Khan, the leader of Muslim modernism in nineteenth-century India. Note the Turkish fez which he and his followers adopted as a symbol of his identity with the modernist reforming movement in the Ottoman empire. Sayyid Ahmad came from an aristocratic family long associated with the Mughal court. In the second half of the nineteenth century he led the modernist movement in education, religious thought, and Urdu prose. The Muhammadan Anglo-Oriental College founded at Aligarh, some 80 miles southeast of Delhi, was the focus of his achievement. The College, which became a university in 1920, was to produce many leading Muslims, including several key figures in the movement for Pakistan.

Reformism carried the spirit and principles of the eighteenth-century movement of revival into the period of European domination. In the process it developed a form of 'Protestant' Islam. Without worldly power to create an Islamic society, responsibility for doing so was transferred to the individual Muslim conscience. Reformists knew, and it was often a heavy burden of knowledge, that they must will God's purpose on earth. The dissemination of knowledge of God's word and of the life of His messenger were at the heart of the reformist effort. Typical vehicles were the Deoband movement founded in north India in 1867, which by its centenary claimed to have established 8,934 schools; or the Muhammadiyya of Indonesia founded in 1912, which by 1938 had founded 1,700 schools; or the Nurcular, who learned their message of personal discipline and moral responsibility from the writings of the Turkish Naqshbandi shaykh Said Bediuzzaman Nursi (1873–1960). Reformists attacked the presence of logic and philosophy in the madrasa curriculum; the historic victories of al-Ashari and al-Ghazzali were no longer seen to be enough. Only amongst the Shias, and particularly in Iran, did the flame of Islamized Hellenic learning continue to burn brightly.

In their concern to shape the human conscience, reformists continued the assault on Ibn al-Arabi's doctrine of the unity of being, on sufi practices which suggested intercession for men and women with God, and on the host of local customs which mingled with Islamic practice. To compensate for the loss of the emotional and spiritual dimensions of the faith which went with successful attacks on sufism, yet more attention was paid to the life of the Prophet. His biography became a prolific genre of devotional literature in the twentieth century. Thus the reformists allowed only a sanitized proportion of the inheritance of Islamic knowledge from the past to continue into the present. At the same time, they paid varying attention to what the new learning from Europe had to offer; the Deobandis continued to emphasize traditional learning, while the Muhammadiyya found a place for modern science. Reformism was typically the response of the ulama, more often than not supported by traditional mercantile elites.

Modernism was concerned to face up to the reality of western knowledge and western dominance. At the least modernists wanted Muslims to command western science and technology, which they perceived to be the source of western strength. At the most they wished to review Islamic knowledge as a whole, including its founding pillars, the Quran and the hadiths, in the light of western learning. Leading figures amongst the modernists were Sayyid Ahmad Khan of India, Namik Kemal of Turkey (1840–88), Shaykh Muhammad Abduh of Egypt, and Jamal al-Din al-Afghani. Not all these men had the same approach to western and Islamic knowledge, but they knew that the way of the ulama was insufficient to meet the challenges of the times. In the nineteenth and early twentieth centuries many modernists were attracted to pan-Islamic responses to the west but, after the First World War brought the final onset of western domination, they began to focus

Dr Ali Shariati. A striking development of the second half of the twentieth century has been the establishment of a new type of transmitter of Islamic knowledge, trained outside the madrasas of the ulama and often involved in the Islamist movement. One important figure was Shariati, who was educated in Mashhad and Paris; in the latter he was particularly influenced by Sartre, Fanon, and Massignon. In the 1960s and 1970s his teaching and writing had great influence over Iranian youth. He formulated a coherent Islamic world view with an ideology of social, political, and economic change, which contributed much to the Iranian revolution.

their attention on the nation-state. For the Indian modernist Muhammad Iqbal, this was a nation-state to be built
on Islamic principles, a Pakistan, but for the great majority
modernism became secularism and the future was envisaged in secular states -the Turkey of Ataturk or the Iran of
Riza Shah – in which religion was a private affair. Modernists, therefore, had little place for the medieval inheritance of Islamic knowledge. In the schools they
established, and even more in the educational systems fostered by secular Muslim states, western languages and
some of the western humanities came to be studied alongside western science and technology. Modernism was typi-

cally the response of Muslim ruling elites. For many, these elites in seeking
western material strength ran the grave risk of throwing out the Islamic baby with
the bathwater.

It is not surprising that reformism and modernism attracted criticism. 'You
have been throttled at the outset by schoolmen', complained Iqbal of the madrasa-
educated and their obsession with matters irrelevant to contemporary life,
'whence shall come the cry "There is no God but Allah".' 'Give up your literature',
announced the Indian satirical poet Akbar Allahabadi (1846–1921), to the products of secular education, 'forget your history, break all your ties with shaykh and
mosque – it could not matter less. Life's short. Best not worry overmuch. Eat English bread, and push your pen, and swell with happiness.'

It was in part because neither reformism nor modernism produced satisfactory
answers to the problem of what was appropriate knowledge for a Muslim society
that Islamist answers came to be proposed. Islamists started from the principle
that all human life, and therefore all knowledge, must be subordinated to the
guidance sent by God to human beings. As one Islamist said of the essence of that
guidance, the sharia offers a complete scheme of life 'where nothing is superflu-
ous and nothing wanting'. Notable leaders of Islamism have been Sayyid Abul Ala
Mawdudi of Pakistan, Hasan al-Banna and Sayyid Qutb (1906–66) of Egypt, Ali
Shariati and Ayatollah Khomeini of Iran; notable organizations are the Jamaati-e-
Islami of South Asia and the Muslim Brotherhood of the Arab World. Islamists
have little difficulty with most of western knowledge, although Darwinian evolution which contradicts the Quranic story of the creation, literally understood, has
been a sticking point. They are alarmed, however, by the failure of the reformists
to face up to the meaning of western knowledge and are horrified by the way in
which the modernists and the secular nationalists seem to have capitulated to it in
its entirety. The dominance of the views of the latter, whom they characterize as
suffering from 'Westoxification' or 'Occidentosis', over the educational systems of
most Muslim states is the great object of their attention. They have striven to
Islamize the scholarly disciplines of the West; thus has been born, for instance,

Sayyid Qutb, left, here seen
on trial in 1966, was the dominant figure in the second
phase of the development of
the Muslim Brotherhood from
the 1950s. Educated at the
University of Cairo, he first
made his name as a modernist
literary critic in the 1930s
and 1940s. A trip to the USA
in 1948–50, followed by an
introduction to the ideas of
the Indian Islamist Mawdudi,
converted him to Islamism.
Jailed by Nasser's regime from
1955 to 1964 he produced his
masterwork, *Signposts on the
Road*, in which he urged that
an all-out offensive, a jihad,
be waged against secular society in which 'numerous man-
made idols – from agnosti-
cism to capitalism – hold
sway'. His struggle to bring
about an Islamic system on
earth has been taken up by
splinter groups from the
Muslim Brotherhood and
other organizations through
much of the Muslim world.
On 29 August 1966 he was
hanged by the Egyptian government for plotting against
the regime.

Islamic economics and Islamic sociology, indeed a whole Islamic system or <u>nizam</u>, as an equivalent to capitalism or socialism. Islamists represent, by and large, new elites who are competing for power. They have little desire to bring back into service the Islamic learning of the past but rather aim to place western learning in an Islamic mould and direct it to Islamic ends.

Over the past 200 years the proper relationship of revealed knowledge to all the knowledge available in Muslim societies has been hotly disputed. If the trend for much of the period has been for western learning to command centre stage, recent years have seen this position challenged by new champions of Islam. But there has been one clear loser in this age of revolution: it is the mystical understanding of the faith. Reformists have subjected much of sufism to withering fire. Modernists and secularists have fostered the wintry climate of post-Enlightenment knowledge. For Islamists sufis are an irrelevance. The new Muslim understandings of the past two centuries, and the new Muslim mastery of self and the environment, have rendered the world a less 'enchanted' place; the realm in which the spiritual knowledge of Islam could flourish has shrivelled.

KNOWLEDGE IS DEMOCRATIZED

Side by side with the uncoupling of Islamic knowledge from power in many societies, there has been a revolution in its transmission. This change began with the adoption of print during the nineteenth century. In some societies, for instance Egypt, the process was tentative; leading scholars saw printing as a danger to religion and social order. In others, particularly where, as in India, Muslims were acutely aware of the threat to their faith from colonial rule, it was more positive. Reformist ulama seized upon print technology as a key means to spread their understanding of Islamic knowledge widely through society so that it might be defended both against the corruptions of local cults and the seductions of western learning. By the end of the nineteenth century in north India over 700 newspapers and magazines in Urdu, the main Muslim language, had been started; 400 to 500 books were being published every year, many of them on religious matters.

The adoption of print was just the first stage in the democratization of Islamic knowledge. Further stages came with the translation of the Quran, the hadiths, and other major Islamic texts into many of the languages of the Muslim peoples of the world. For the first time many Muslims have been able to read these texts in languages they understand. This development has been accompanied by the adoption of other forms of media technology and mass communication–radio, television, film, tape cassettes; it is now well known that the telephone and the tape cassette were crucial in bringing the voice of Ayatollah Khomeini to the Iranian people in the months before the Iranian revolution in 1979. These new technologies of communication have opened up new forums of interaction and new forms of contact among Muslims: they are the arenas in which the great disputes over knowledge take place; they are the vehicles through which new Islamic understandings, and especially those of the ulama, have been taken to the margins of the Islamic world; they are the means through which official versions of Islam are broadcast to the peoples of those states where Islam is once more aligned with power.

The rapid spread of print culture brought about a decline in the oral transmission of Islamic texts and a weakening of that person-to-person transmission of the central messages of the faith which reached back to the time of the Prophet. The process of change was already far advanced in Mecca in the 1880s. 'All students now bring to lecture printed copies of the text which is being treated', observed the Dutch orientalist Snouck Hurgronje on his visit in 1884–85, 'which circumstance has entirely changed the mode of instruction.' Arguably, changes of religious understanding accompanied the penetration of the printed

text into the believer's world; processes barely perceptible in the era of manuscripts were greatly intensified. Other aspects of the modern transformation of Muslim societies were also influential but the new technology encouraged new forms of awareness: Muslims came less to see their faith as one in constant decline since the time of the Prophet and more one which might achieve greater stages of perfection on earth; they came to understand Islam as a system of beliefs and practices to which a commitment might or might not be made rather than part of the natural warp and weft of life; they tended to see the Quran less as ritual object and more as the subject of contemplative study; and they began to transform their image of the Prophet from Perfect Man to perfect person on which different groups of Muslims might impose their ideal vision. This said, oral transmission of religious guidance continues to have greater meaning for the Muslim than it does for the Christian. In all Muslim societies the memorization and recitation of the Quran remains a highly prized feat.

It is unlikely that print will ever have quite the impact it has had on the West; already the electronic media, which help to sustain some forms of oral transmission, make rapid headway. The Tablighi Jamaat (Preaching Society), which was founded in India in the 1920s, is the most widely followed organization in the Muslim world: it insists that its missionaries learn texts by heart and communicate them person to person.

The coming of print, and the spread of translations, brought much greater freedom of access to religious knowledge. Muslims now could study with relative ease the great religious texts outside the madrasa framework and the ulama's authoritative interpretations. Moreover, they increasingly did so from a basic education in western learning. Not surprisingly, this new freedom of access led to the new freedom of interpretation represented by the modernist and Islamist strands, as well

Over the past 200 years the adoption of print in Muslim societies has transformed access to Islamic knowledge. Not only has it helped to break the monopoly of the ulama over religious learning but it has been employed by most movements, reformist, modernist, and Islamist, to spread their messages. The Turkish reformer Bediuzzaman Said Nursi sent his followers through the villages of Anatolia carrying sacks of books. Pamphlets such as these, most of which are Islamist texts, can be found on bookstalls in much of the Muslim world.

The emergence of modern knowledge transmitted through the secular systems of the modern state led in many societies to the marginalizing of the ulama. Increasingly, the ulama and their claims were seen as less relevant to society, and they became the objects of mockery on the part of their opponents, as in this cartoon, published in the satirical weekly, *Mulla Nasruddin*, of Tiflis in the Caucasus, on 7 October 1907.

as a host of sectarian positions. But, if print and translation helped to liberate Muslims from the monopoly of the ulama, it also helped to dissipate religious authority. Now, there were many new voices claiming to speak for Islam that drew force from their acceptance of the realities of western strengths in knowledge and power. The authority embedded in interpretations of texts handed down over hundreds of years became much reduced.

Inevitably, the changing position and nature of Islamic knowledge in Muslim societies have led to changes for classical transmitters of learning. The status of sufis declined with that of sufism. Some sufis continue to give comfort to the pious, but others are now seen to be less the cherishers of the glories of spiritual understanding at the heart of the Islamic tradition than as tricksters fleecing the ignorant and deluding the gullible. Their devotional practices have come to be performed less for the service of God – the whirling dance of the Mawlawiyya of Turkey or the mystical songs (*qawwali*) of the sufis of South Asia – than for that of the television programme or the tourist office. Only where sufis were able to provide some substantial function for modern Muslim societies have they remained at the centre of affairs. This is the case of the Muridiyya, who have maintained a leading position in Senegal through their dominance of the peanut business, or of the Naqshbandiyya and the Qadiriyya in the Caucasus, who kept the flame of Islam alight under Soviet rule.

Ulama, too, were pushed towards the margins of society as their functions of teacher and lawyer were supplanted by the secular systems of the modern state. For many Muslims in the twentieth century the ulama have remained symbols of a Muslim backwardness from which they wished to escape. Their decline, however, does not equal that of the sufis: they still command residual respect in many societies. They may be treated as state employees, as in Turkey, or given places of honour on state occasions – the rector of al-Azhar was sitting with Egypt's president, Anwar Sadat, at the official parade where he was shot in 1981. Nevertheless, for much of the twentieth century the ulama have been moving steadily down the paths of marginalization trodden by the Christian clergy of the western world since the Enlightenment. But, as for sufis, there have been specific circumstances where the ulama have been able to remain at the centre – notably in the Lebanon, Iraq, and Iran, where the Shia ulama have led movements of resistance against state oppression and in Iran have come to control the state themselves.

As ulama have been pushed to one side, their role as transmitters and interpreters of Islam to their societies has been challenged, if not supplanted, by scholars from outside the madrasa world. There are many such Muslim thinkers whose writings are prime sources of Islamic understanding for their societies: Iqbal and Mawdudi of Pakistan and al-Banna and Sayyid Qutb of Egypt, Khurshid Ahmad, an economist from Pakistan, Hasan al-Turabi, a lawyer from the Sudan, Rashid Ghannoushi, a teacher from Tunisia, and Mehdi Bazargan, an engineer from Iran. The people who carry forward the missionary and educational pro-grammes of the more notable Islamic organizations of the latter part of the twen-tieth century – for instance, the worldwide Tablighi Jamaat, the populist Muslim Brotherhood, the elitist Jamaat-e-Islami, the Islamic Tendency movement of Tunisia, or the Islamic Salvation Front of Algeria – are almost entirely lay edu-cated. They have, moreover, in common with many other Islamic groups born in recent years, strong support amongst students.

Since 1800 western learning has confronted the Islamic world with very much the same problem that Hellenistic learning presented it from the ninth to the eleventh centuries. There is, however, one substantial difference. Al-Ashari and al-Ghazzali met the Hellenistic rational and philosophical challenges from a posi-tion of Muslim dominance; modern Muslims have confronted the challenges of western science from a position of weakness. In spite of this they have shown con-siderable creativity in their responses. They have striven to move Islamic civiliza-tion forward in the world while keeping it rooted in revelation. As the ulama and sufis have seemed to fail to meet the challenge, new types of scholar have emerged from the community to provide answers. All these scholars, whether old or new, have interacted with each other across the Islamic world – so Muhammad Abduh was influenced by Jamal al-Din al-Afghani and Sayyid Qutb by Mawdudi. As yet, however, there has been no widely accepted consensus which would enable Mus-lims once more to regard the pursuit of learning as an act of worship. The issue of the proper relationship of revealed and earthly knowledge remains acute. What is important is that it remains the subject of vigorous debate.

CHAPTER 8

Stephen Vernoit

Artistic Expressions of Muslim Societies

Since the emergence of Islam there have been remarkable achievements in all aspects of art – literature, music, and the visual arts – encouraged by Muslim patrons. The sheer breadth and scope of this output is all the more remarkable when we consider that the arts throughout the Islamic lands often have a very distinct character. Islamic culture has been, and continues to be, multi-faceted and, fortunately, eludes simple analysis.

THE PURPOSE OF ART IN ISLAM

It is useful to distinguish between Islamic, that is religious, definitions of art and the arts of the Muslim world as they have emerged as manifestations of Muslim culture. Religious attitudes towards art are based primarily on two sources, the Quran and the *hadith*. The Quran, which is believed by Muslims to be the word of God, has ultimate authority, but the hadith, or the traditions reporting the words and actions of the Prophet Muhammad, also have a great validity. The hadith are believed, in content at least, to proceed from divine inspiration. Collected after Muhammad's death, they shed light on matters about which the Quran is silent. The Quran, for example, contains some outspoken references to poetry, but seldom refers to music and the visual arts. This emphasis reflects the fact that in Arabian society at the time of Muhammad the issue of artistic creativity in music and the visual arts was not as significant as it was for poetry.

Poetry

In pre-Islamic Arabian society poetry played a leading role in political life. Poets were the propagandists of their tribes and it was thought that they were inspired by jinns. The Prophet knew, therefore, that he had to harness the power of poetry to the cause of Islam. In Arabic poetry the *qasida* (ode) was the most highly valued poetic form. This was a relatively lengthy poem, written in one of a number of accepted metres with a single rhyme, and consisted of three parts: a prologue, in which the poet expressed sadness at leaving the camp of his beloved's tribe and recalled the time he passed with her; an account of a journey in the desert; and a eulogy or condemnation of the tribe, family, or person that was the object of the journey. As qasidas were intended to be recited in public, either by the poet or a reciter, there was probably scope for improvisation, and there might not have been a single version of a poem.

With the Islamic conquests the Arabic language was spread over a wide area. It became both a spoken language, in various local dialects influenced by the previous vernacular languages, and a written language, sanctified as the language

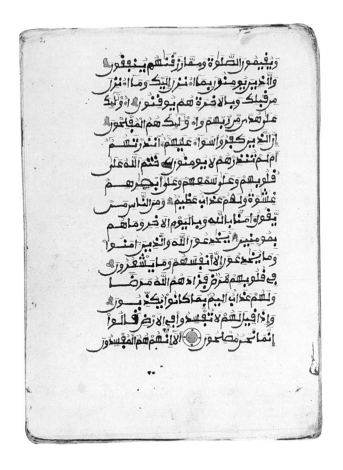

uttered by God in the Quran. This gave Arabic a new and unequalled power and significance. At the same time, pre-Islamic poetry was preserved and admired for its literary excellence, despite the frequent conflict of its ideals with the tenets of Islam. Such themes in pre-Islamic poetry as self-glorification and indulgence in love and wine conflicted with the new faith, but were accepted by later generations, in much the same way that ancient Greek and Roman attitudes were accommodated in Christian civilization.

The esteem among Arabs for their language and its expressive potential gave cohesion to the early Islamic community; later Persian, Turkish, and Urdu became vehicles for profound mystical expression. Apart from texts directly concerned with the faith, such as commentaries on the Quran, and prayers, however, the written word also served a didactic role through such literary forms as the 'instructions for princes', and by extension the manuals for courtiers that became popular in the Abbasid era.

Music

Early in the Islamic era music accompanied such events as pilgrimages, weddings, and wars. The nature of such music is difficult to reconstruct because it was not

Islamic art from west Africa has only recently begun to attract detailed study. The two folios from this nineteenth-century Quran contain the first chapter, *al-fatiha* (The Opening Chapter) and verses 1–11 of the second chapter, *al-Baqara* (The Heifer). The text is written in *Sudani* script with the vowel points marked in red. Each verse is indicated by clusters of three yellow circles and each tenth verse by a large yellow circle. The rectangular panel indicates the end of a chapter. Such Qurans were often carried in leather satchels or cases.

written down. But the emphasis was on vocal music; indeed it seems likely that in pre-Islamic times poetry was chanted or sung to a musical accompaniment. Among the musical instruments in use in the seventh century were the lute, pandore, psaltery, harp, flute, reed-pipe, horn, tambourine, castanets, and drums; while the Quran indicates that trumpets will sound on the last day (suras 6.73: 74.8). The idea of instrumental music independent from song may not have arisen before the Abbasid period.

In the wake of the Islamic conquests, Arabic music spread rapidly across Islamic lands, although ethnic and regional styles continued. Fortunately, much information about music and musicians of the early centuries of Islam has been preserved in the *Kitab al-aghani* (The Book of Songs) compiled by Abul-Faraj al-Isfahani (897–967). Musical theory also developed, usually in relation to the *ud* (short-necked lute), which was one of the most popular instruments.

Music in the Muslim world is melodic and uses a greater and more subtle range of intervals than is normal in the West. Harmony in the western understanding of the term is unknown. In the days of the *Kitab al-aghani* there were eight musical modes, but, drawing on Iranian culture, this number was increased to eighteen or more. Music served various religious purposes. The chanting of the Quran emphasized the pattern of God's words, and thereby communicated them to the faithful. During the Abbasid period in various centres of culture the Quran was apparently sung to a variety of secular tunes as well. The call to prayer was also chanted or sung, and from the tenth century military bands took part in it, employing such instruments as the drum and large kettle-drum. Major religious events such as pilgrimage, the month of fasting, and the celebration of the Prophet's birthday were accompanied with songs.

In the medieval Islamic world, as elsewhere, music was understood in the broader context of correspondences. In the work of the ninth-century Arab philosopher al-Kindi (c.790–c.874), the four strings of the lute allowed associations to be made with the elements, humours, seasons, and points of the compass. Instruments were also ordered according to the number of their strings, each with particular associations. Al-Farabi (d. 950) and Ibn Sina (Avicenna, 980–1037), however, examined music more as a science in our understanding of the word, ignoring cosmology and numerology.

As an aspect of sufism, music, singing, chanting, and measured recitation were employed to encourage religious emotion and ecstasy. Early sufi music tended to avoid secular tunes, and use only reed-pipes, flutes, and drums, but it later became more elaborate. Indeed, in Turkey music gained acceptance in the mosques through the influence of such sufi orders as the Mawlawi. Among Shiites music accompanied the *taziya* (passion plays) about the life and death of Husayn and his followers during the month of Muharram.

Secular music was patronized at numerous courts, and the prince in the company of musicians was an important motif in royal iconography through the ages.

Although the status of musicians put them on the outer fringes of society, some became close companions to the caliphs and other rulers.

Architecture and the visual arts

The central theological message of the Quran, that of the total power and uniqueness of God, means that God alone creates. Idolatry, since it was an abnegation of God, was, of course, considered particularly reprehensible. However, it is reported in the hadith that when Muhammad destroyed the idolatrous images in the Kaaba he put out his hand to protect a picture of the Virgin and Child, an indication that representation as such was not a threat to his understanding of faith. It is interesting to note that Caliph Umar (r.634–44) was reported to have used a censer with figures on it, which he had obtained in Syria, to perfume the mosque at Medina. This censer was presented to the mosque by Umar, but in 783 a governor of Medina had its figures erased. Representations of animate beings have been absent from mosques throughout Islamic history.

Some valuable insights concerning the relationship between architecture and the state can be found in the work of the Maghribi historian Ibn Khaldun (1332–1406), who emphasized that cities and other monuments reflected the dynasties that created them. From extant buildings we can also deduce that mathematics and geometry were often considered part of the medieval architectural aesthetic. As Islamic society developed, different types of buildings emerged, to express particular needs. In a sense, these different types of buildings were in existence from the outset in the mosque, which not only functioned as a place of worship, but could also offer shelter, food, facilities for teaching, administration, and burial. The emergence of caravansarais, madrasas, mausolea, and other buildings with specific functions was, however, connected with specific groups of interested parties at different times in history and, in consequence, their fortunes were tied to the fate of those parties. One other important role of architecture was to enhance the authority of the ruler. In the early Abbasid period, for example, when the caliphs adopted the ceremonies of the ancient Iranian courts, they created domed throne-rooms for private audiences, preceded by an *iwan* (large vaulted hall) or four radiating iwans for public audience. Axial planning was a marked feature of Abbasid palaces.

The duty to propagate the word of God led to the primacy accorded to writing, which quickly gained the most exalted position in Islamic art. The profession of the calligrapher was dignified because he was engaged in copying the Quran. At the time of Muhammad's death, some parts of the Quran were already written down. Verses were written on palm leaves, flat stones and other materials. Tradition associates the collection of this material, together with what the faithful had memorized, with the first caliph Abu Bakr (r.632–34), or his successor Umar, who died before the work was completed. An authorized text and arrangement of the Quran was probably produced during the reign of Uthman (r.644–56).

The motif of a prince or ruler listening to music is recurrent in Islamic art. The scene on this carved pyxis, however, which was probably made in Cordoba, is unusual for its informality, with two young men in similar poses occupying the throne, and a lutenist standing in the centre. The figure to the left holds a goblet or bottle and a flower on a stalk, while the one on the right holds a fan. The two lions beneath the throne symbolize royal power. The inscription states that the pyxis was presented in 968 to al-Mughira, the younger son of Abd al-Rahman III (r.912–61).

The earliest Arabic inscriptions, written in Aramaic script, can be dated to the fourth century. Arabic script evolved in the following centuries. Historical sources mention an angular script known as *maqili*, which was invented, according to legend, by the prophet Idris. From this script Ali (r.656–61) is credited with developing the so-called kufic script, in which five sixths of the lines were straight and one sixth curved. Different forms of Kufic script developed in various centres but the town of Kufa, with which Ali was associated, was probably one of the most important. The script in which the Quran was originally written contained no diacritical marks and signs for vowels; these were added in coloured ink during the reign of the Umayyad caliph Abd al-Malik (r.685–705) in order to avoid misreadings.

Epigraphy became an integral part of the decoration of architecture and artefacts, and it is probable that the high status of the arts of illumination and bookbinding in the Muslim world was a consequence of their role in the perpetuation of the word of God. For a long time calligraphy was also the only art in which the practitioners were remembered by their names. Unlike the calligrapher, the painter did not have religious sanction, and consequently had a lower status in society.

A further characteristic of Islamic art was that objects of daily use were often transformed into art and endowed with an aesthetic significance. Apart from calligraphy, certain qualities evolved in Islamic designs that enabled them to be easily transferable: arabesque patterns, for example, with their potential for infinite repetition, were applied to objects in a range of media.

When historical enquiry into Islamic architecture and art developed in the nineteenth century it was primarily a western preoccupation. Among the misconceptions that were introduced at that time about the visual arts, the western view of human change as an evolutionary process in history encouraged scholars to assume that the European 'fine' arts of painting and sculpture were among the highest spiritual attainments. Inevitably, Islamic art could not fit into this view, which, though challenged in the twentieth century, still exerts a powerful influence. Thus, Islamic painting has attracted far more attention than calligraphy, while so-called ethnographic items are still regarded as ahistoric and representative of a static culture. The artistic significance of the use of precious materials is also often obscured by the modern belief that an idea or feeling should be embodied in a work of art. Furthermore, the study of Islamic art and architecture is still understood largely as a medievalist discipline, with historical surveys terminating in the seventeenth century. Vast areas of sub-Saharan Africa and Southeast Asia, regions in which Islam has a strong presence, tend to be excluded from the subject.

A common thread is apparent in much Islamic art, but the attempt to define cultures in the modern world (whether by 'Islamic' or 'national' boundaries), has led various scholars to seek some vague essence from the past to support their assertions. Art in the Muslim world, however, can best be described as the art produced for or by Muslim patrons and peoples.

THE ART OF TRIUMPH: SEVENTH TO TENTH CENTURIES

As the Islamic empire expanded, Muslims took control of wealthy Byzantine provinces, with their legacy of Graeco-Roman art and culture, while to the east they encountered the artistic traditions of the Sasanian empire. In 661 Muawiya, the governor of Syria, defeated Ali and founded the Umayyad dynasty, which ruled a huge empire from Damascus. With the rise of the Abbasid dynasty in 750, however, there was a shift of power from Syria to Iraq, yet closer to the Sasanian heartland. In 762 the Abbasid caliph al-Mansur (r.754–75) founded the round city of Baghdad as his new capital, at the centre of which was the royal palace and mosque. Baghdad remained the Abbasid capital until the demise of the dynasty, except for the period 836 to 883 when a new capital was built at Samarra, some sixty miles along the Tigris to the north of Baghdad. Samarra became a huge sprawling city extending over thirty miles. It was at the capitals of Damascus, Baghdad, and Samarra, therefore, that Islamic civilization flourished in the initial years of triumph, and its achievements were reflected in a host of other cities and towns throughout Asia, north Africa and Spain.

The first Islamic poetry and prose

Arabic was carried across the vast empire by the Quran, whose remarkable language entranced those who heard it, providing a basis for written Arabic and a continual inspiration for literature. Bedouin poetry continued to flourish, and the feuds and political controversies of the Umayyad era are captured in the works of the most famous poets, al-Farazdaq (d.728), Jarir (d.728), and al-Akhtal (d.c.710), all active in Damascus. Al-Farazdaq was both a satirist and panegyrist, and many of his qasidas are reduced to laudatory elements alone to praise the caliph. Jarir wrote laudatory poems and some elegies, but satire predominates. Although al-Akhtal was a Christian, he nevertheless became a close companion of Yazid I (r.680–83), whom he praised in his panegyrics. He also continued the pre-Islamic tradition of poetry that celebrated a life of wine and love, as did the Umayyad caliph al-Walid II (r.743–44) in his poems. Increasingly, however, this theme turned from reflecting bedouin to urban life.

In Mecca and Medina, meanwhile, a lighter form of poetry arose, probably from the prologue of the qasida. Umar ibn Abi Rabia (d.712/19) was a master of this genre, later imitated in Basra, Kufa, and Baghdad. In other regions of the Islamic empire, Arabic poems were often simple works, which expressed pride in the victories of Islam and the homesickness of those on campaign in distant lands.

Under the Abbasids, new genres were developed from the qasida. The blind poet Bashshar ibn Burd (d.784/85) produced both panegyrics in the classical style and innovatory amorous pieces, excelling in epigram and parody. The erotic and bacchic pieces, with their frankness and irony, of Abu Nuwas (d.813/15) made him the most famous poet of the early Abbasid period in Baghdad:

> When she left me, stopped writing notes,
> My desire hurt. The thought of her
> So upset me I nearly died.
> I got Satan into a corner
> And, blubbing like a child, told him,
> 'She's hooked me: tears and lack of sleep
> Cause my eyes to look like ulcers.
> Unless you make that girl love me,
> And you can, I won't write poetry,
> I won't listen to songs, and I won't
> Pickle my bones with drink. Day and night
> I'll fast, pray, and read the Quran.
> I'll follow the path He commands.'
> Shamefaced she was back in a flash.

At the Hamdanid court in Aleppo the great virtuoso poet al-Mutanabbi (915–65), who excelled in classical panegyrics, found patronage for nine years of his wandering life. At the same court was a group of minor poets who interspersed their panegyrics with descriptions of nature, a form that was widely imitated. The cultural life that flourished at this court indicates how patronage was now developing at centres other than Baghdad. The *muwashshah,* a strophic poem that did not respect classical metres and combined Romance elements, arose under Umayyad rule in Spain (756–1031), and then spread eastwards. Literary prose under the Abbasids can be largely credited to government scribes and those who translated foreign texts into Arabic: the Iranian Ibn al-Muqaffa (d.c.756), for example, translated the renowned book of animal fables known as the *Kalila wa Dimna,* which was later frequently illustrated. Skill in Arabic literature was highly prized in the new courtly society, and al-Jahiz (d.868/69), who was active in Baghdad and Samarra, raised to a new artistic level a mannered, anecdotal, and didactic form. As prose writings became more numerous, authors tended to embellish their work with poetic devices, such as rhymes and tropes.

Music in the early Islamic world

In the first century of Islam influences from Iran and the former Byzantine provinces were incorporated into Arabian music, especially at Mecca and Medina. A new type of musician, effeminate and professional, emerged during the reign of Uthman, one of the first being the famous singer Tuways ('Little Peacock',

632–711), who was inspired by Iranian melodies and accompanied himself on the square tambourine. Under the Umayyads the centre of music shifted to their capital at Damascus. Yazid I, who had a passion for music and was himself a poet, introduced singers and musicians to the court, and during the reign of al-Walid I, the chief musicians of Mecca and Medina were summoned. Under Al-Walid II an early collection of Arab songs, the *Kitab al-nagham* ('The Book of Melodies'), was compiled by Yunus al-Katib (d.c.765).

Music also flourished under Abbasid patronage. Unrivalled as a singer, instrumentalist, and composer was Ibrahim al-Mawsili (742–804), who was a companion of Harun al-Rashid (r.786–809) and became extremely rich. He was succeeded by his son Ishaq al-Mawsili (767–850). A new type of lute was introduced by Zalzal (d.791), replacing the earlier Iranian lute, and the addition of a fifth string to the lute was made by Ziryab (d.c.850), who left Baghdad for the Umayyad court in Spain, where he arrived in 821. Ziryab became chief court musician and companion to Abd al-Rahman II (r.822–52) in Cordoba, where his school of music survived until the extinction of the Spanish caliphate.

The acquisition from Byzantium of treatises on the Greek theory of music and their translation into Arabic was of great importance to musical culture, encouraged by the caliphs al-Mamun (r.813–33) and al-Mutasim (r.833–42). The philosopher al-Kindi wrote several short treatises that served as textbooks for musicians for several centuries. Al-Kindi was the first of the Greek-inspired theorists, and his treatises encompass material of a descriptive, scientific nature, as well as cosmological affiliations and numerology.

In the following century al-Farabi explored music theory in the *Kitab al-musiqi al-kabir* ('The Great Book of Music'), and in the early eleventh century Ibn Sina tackled the subject in the *Kitab al-Shifa* ('The Book of the Cure'). These works marked a peak in music theory, especially in such areas as the physics of sound and the analysis of intervals and scales. Cosmology and numerology were treated in the tenth century *risala* (epistle) on music by the Ikhwan al-Safa (The Brethren of Purity), a work that relates the rhythms and strings of the lute to associations, including the seasons, colours, and scents. Behind these associations was the conception of a cosmic harmony governed by numerical relationships, which also informed discussion of the medical effects of music. Throughout the period, songs continued to be collected and biographies of famous musicians were compiled, the most notable being the *Kitab al-aghani*.

Early Islamic architecture

The formation of mosques for communal worship was the central architectural achievement of the early centuries of Islam. As the earlier pagan structures of Arabia appear to have been simple buildings of a different type, such as the Kaaba in Mecca, it seems that the earliest mosques were based on another source, probably the house of the Prophet in Medina, which was used for prayer during

Muhammad's lifetime. It consisted of a square courtyard built of sundried bricks, with a number of small rooms on the east wall and short colonnades of palm trunks supporting palm branches on the south and north sides. The south wall became the *qibla,* the direction of prayer towards the Kaaba, and Muhammad delivered sermons from a simple *minbar* (pulpit). This plan probably inspired the design of the early Iraqi mosques at Basra (635, rebuilt 665), Kufa (637, rebuilt 670) and Wasit (702), whose courts included a small structure serving as the treasury of the Muslim community. The governor's palace was built flanking the mosque, usually on the south side. In Syria, Iran, and possibly Egypt, churches or other cultic buildings were sometimes converted into mosques. The minaret probably originated in Syria or Egypt, deriving perhaps from the square Syrian towers used for hermits' cells. The earliest surviving Islamic monument is the Dome of the Rock (691) in Jerusalem, situated on Mount Moriah, traditionally the site of the Jewish Temple. The Dome of the Rock was intended to emphasize the victory of Islam and to compete with the Christian sanctuaries of Palestine. This was attempted through its architectural form, scale, construction techniques, decoration, and use of Quranic inscriptions, which included Christological passages.

The newly acquired power of Islam was also expressed in the congregational mosque of al-Walid I at Damascus (706–714/15). The Great Mosque is built on the site of a Roman sanctuary, and made use of salvaged architectural elements. The prayer hall consists of three aisles that are parallel to the qibla wall, probably imitating Christian basilical churches, and the novel addition of a nave perpendicular to the qibla wall and carrying a dome. These latter features were also to be found in the mosques at Medina (706–10) and Jerusalem (709–15). As at the Dome of the Rock, the main decorative material was mosaics. Although the compositions at Damascus are aniconic, they contain architectural images that perhaps symbolize the Umayyad conquests.

The Umayyad royal palace flanking the Great Mosque of Damascus no longer remains, but there exist numerous Umayyad country or desert residences, including Jabal Says, Rusafa, Khirbat al-Minya, Qasr al-Hayr East, Qasr al-Hayr West, and Mshatta. Their construction of stone follows the Syrian tradition, with some Mesopotamian features, and the bath is a common feature, using Roman heating systems. One significant innovation found at Qusayr Amra and Khirbat al-Mafjar is the enlargement of an entrance room, perhaps as a reception area for Umayyad princes. Figurative mosaics, paintings, stucco sculpture, and carved stonework in the Hellenistic tradition decorated many of the palaces. At Qusayr Amra the figurative paintings, now in a poor condition, show a rich iconography of court life, with images of musicians, drinkers, acrobats, regal giftbearers, hunting, wrestling, and bathing, as well as a domed ceiling with the constellations.

The surviving architecture of the early Abbasid period tells a somewhat different story. Although nothing remains of al-Mansur's round city of Baghdad, there are ruins of other cities, as well as a large isolated palace at Ukhaydir (c.778),

Opposite At Damascus, the capital of the Umayyad empire, an imperial mosque was constructed from 706 to 714/15 under al-Walid I that was a tour de force of early Islamic architecture. No expense was spared. The mosque consists of a court surrounded on three sides by a portico, while on the fourth (south) side the sanctuary is formed by three arcades set parallel to the south or qibla wall, intersected in the middle by a transept perpendicular to the qibla wall. The mosque was lavishly decorated with marble panelling and mosaics, and most of the columns were taken from older buildings. Although this view of the sanctuary gives a sense of the interior space, much of it was rebuilt following a fire in 1893.

Little now survives of Abbasid painting, although it is known that palaces were decorated with murals and that illustrated manuscripts were produced. German excavations conducted in Samarra in the years immediately before the First World War revealed fragments of wall paintings that adorned part of the harem of the Jawsaq al-Khaqani palace, built by Caliph al-Mutasim (r.833–41). The two women dancers pouring wine in this reconstruction of a wall painting are painted in a style similar to that found on Sasanian vessels.

which show the persistence of Sasanian methods and materials of construction. At Samarra are the remains of large palace complexes. These included mosques and baths, as well as reception and residential areas, surrounded by extensive gardens. The foremost decoration of the palaces and houses of Samarra is stucco work, which has been divided into three styles, ranging from the most naturalistic, with a characteristic vine leaf, to the most abstract, in which the designs are in deep relief and bevelled. This latter style, with its potential for infinite repetition, had new and far-reaching implications for Islamic design. Mural paintings of court life, found in the Jawsaq al-Khaqani (palace of al-Mutasim), have stylistic parallels with Sasanian art.

Two remarkable ruined mosques at Samarra were both built under the caliph al-Mutawakkil (r.847–61). The Great Mosque of Samarra is the largest of all medieval mosques (261 by 170 yards), with a hypostyle (many-columned) prayer hall, a courtyard, and porticoes. On an axis with the mihrab but outside the walls is a large spiral minaret, the source of which remains uncertain. The second mosque, known as the Abu Dulaf, has a similar minaret. It is slightly smaller (233 by 147 yards) than the Great Mosque and introduces the 'T-plan', or wider axial nave and qibla aisle, into the prayer hall.

Outside Iraq the governor of Egypt, Ibn Tulun, who spent many years in Samarra, built a mosque in Cairo (879) that clearly looked to the mosques of Samarra in its plan, spiral minaret, brick construction, and stucco decoration. The mosque is remarkable for its fine proportions. In Tunisia the Great Mosque of Qayrawan (c.670, 836, 862, and 875) is built of stone with plentiful columns and capitals from local Graeco-Roman ruins. The mihrab area is well preserved, with lustre tiles and carved marble panels.

The Great Mosque of Cordoba in Spain had a series of extensions (784–86, 833–52, 961–76 and 987), and includes the major innovation of the ceiling being supported by two tiers of arches, with tall impost blocks of brick over the columns. The mihrab area is also distinguished with a variety of finely wrought domes and arches, a separate room for the mihrab, and splendid mosaics that were executed by Byzantine craftsmen. The secular architecture of Umayyad Spain is known principally through the partially excavated city of Abd al-Rahman III, Madinat al-Zahra, near Cordoba.

From Spain to Central Asia in the formative Abbasid era other building types emerged, from the so-called nine-domed mosque (a small mosque open on three or four sides and whose precise function is unclear), and the *ribat* (fortified monastery) to mausolea. During this period Graeco-Roman and Sasanian traditions were absorbed into characteristically Islamic forms and functions, and exported to the extremes of the Muslim world.

The spectacular ruins of the Great Mosque of Samarra (848–52) are surrounded by an outer enclosure that contains to the north of the mosque, on the axis of the mihrab, a huge conical minaret, mounted by a spiral ramp. Built of fired brick, the mosque consisted of a large court with a covered sanctuary to the south. The roof of the sanctuary was supported on twenty-four rows of columns. The outer walls of the mosque may have been decorated with mosaics, but none survive in situ.

Umayyad and Abbasid calligraphy and arts

The most distinctive art form of the emerging Islamic world was calligraphy. The earliest known fragments of the Quran probably date to the beginning of the eighth century. Early Quran manuscripts were written in Kufic script on parchment or vellum and tend to have a horizontal or almost square format. The most spectacular form of embellishment was the frontispiece and finispiece, on single or double pages.

Gradually the angular kufic scripts were supplanted by rounded hands. By the late ninth century more than twenty of these scripts were in use. It was the achievement of Ibn Muqla (885/86–940), calligrapher and vizier to the Abbasid caliphs, to introduce rules by which cursive script could be written, though no works in his hand appear to have survived.

Apart from the introduction of calligraphy, the nature of material culture in the Middle East remained relatively constant. On the whole it is difficult to distinguish Umayyad from pre-Islamic metalwork, and Sasanian forms and decoration persist, as in bronze incense burners in the shape of a bird. Precious metals were widely used in the Abbasid palaces at Baghdad and Samarra, but they have not survived and we must look instead to gold and silver objects associated with such provincial dynasties as the Buyids (r.932–1062) to get a fuller impression of metalwork in this period.

The ninth-century historian al-Yaqubi reports that potters were brought from Basra and Kufa to Samarra, where the earliest examples of the metallic lustre technique on pottery have been found. A major inspiration to Islamic pottery was Chinese ware, which began to arrive in the Middle East in the mid-eighth century. Abbasid production includes green, yellow, and brown 'splashed' wares imitating Tang pottery; *scraffiato*, a technique where the designs were scratched through the surface clay to reveal the underlying reddish earthenware body; and most importantly, wares imitating Chinese white porcelains. These Abbasid white wares were created by adding tin to the lead-glazed earthenware, with innovative additions of designs and inscriptions in cobalt blue.

Provincial centres in Iran and elsewhere rapidly succeeded those of the Abbasids: Samarqand and Nishapur, in particular, became major locations of ceramic manufacture. Among the wares that owed nothing to Abbasid models was a type decorated with bold Kufic inscriptions, or Kufic characters transformed into zoological shapes.

One of the few extant (and the oldest) examples of Umayyad and Abbasid carved wooden objects is the minbar (c.862) of the Great Mosque of Qayrawan. Many of its motifs echo the designs of stucco and stone carving in architecture. In a group of ivory boxes from tenth- and eleventh-century Umayyad Spain, some

The technique of decorating ceramic wares with designs painted in metallic lustre was developed by Abbasid potters with outstanding results. The decorative repertoire included highly stylized forms, as seen in this example from Samarra, in which a bird is combined with a palmette, while hatchings, spirals, and dots fill the spaces between the main elements of the design.

are identified by inscriptions as being made for royal or court personages, and include both abstract and figurative decoration, capturing in their exquisite carving the refinement of the period's patronage.

THE ART OF THE COURTS AND THE PEOPLE: ELEVENTH TO FIFTEENTH CENTURIES

The dissolution of the Abbasid empire from the tenth century onwards and the rise of provincial dynasties signalled changes in art production and patronage. Regional centres arose around the courts of these rulers, some of which were of nomadic origin, while others propagated heterodox and puritanical doctrines. Scholasticism and sufism became the guiding movements, and the emergence of an urban bourgeois milieu imitating court patronage might well explain why this period was one of the richest and most productive in Islamic history.

Arabic, Persian and Turkish poetry and prose

In time, only the educated elite could understand the classical Arabic poetic tradition, and poets began to use dialect verse forms. In Arabic prose, a new genre known as the *maqama* (session) was created by Badi al-Zaman al-Hamadhani (968–1008). The maqama is a fictional work that features two characters, a hero and a narrator who recounts the adventures of the former in rhyming prose. Such narratives were used to display the wealth of the Arabic vocabulary and the verbal acrobatics of the author. It was in this genre that the poet and philologist al-Hariri (1054–1122) produced his *Maqamat* early in the twelfth century, whose great popularity is attested by many illustrated copies.

The tales known as *The Thousand and One Nights* – so attractive to the westerner – which originated in India, Persia, and the Arabic world, were being circulated at this time by storytellers, though they were never regarded by Arabs as classical literature.

In Spain the local (*taifa*) princes wrote poetry and encouraged poets, the most important of whom was Ibn Zaydun (1003–70). Under the Almoravids (r.1056–1147) the colloquial language of Andalusia asserted itself in the poems of Ibn Quzman (d.1160). By the time Ibn Sahl (d.1251) wrote his muwashshahs, they were a dying form. The advance of the Reconquista was lamented by the poet Abul-Baqa ibn Sharif (d.1285), and the Nasirid vizier Ibn al-Khatib (1313–74) marked the end of the muwashshah with his anthology *Jaysh al-tawshih*. Both the poems of Ibn al-Khatib and his successor as vizier, Ibn Zamrak (d.1393), were inscribed on the walls of the Alhambra palace in Granada.

As the vitality of the Arabic literary tradition began to wane, Persian literature was growing in strength. It had emerged among the autonomous states in north-eastern Iran, especially at the court of the Samanids (r.819–1005) at Bukhara. The Ghaznawids (r.977–1186) inherited this legacy and their capital at Ghazna became a centre of intellectual and literary life, graced by Firdawsi (d.1020), whose epic masterpiece, the *Shahnama* (The Book of Kings), relates the history of the mythical sovereigns of ancient Iran and the successive dynasties.

A verse form known as the *rubai* became popular and was adopted by Omar Khayyam (1048–1131) and other poets. But until the Mongol invasions, the qasida remained the dominant form for lyrical poetry, inspiring such poets of the Seljuq court as Muizzi (1048–1124) and Anwari (d.c.1190), as well as the work of Khaqani (d.1199) in Azarbayjan. The Mongols brought to an end the predominance of the north-eastern provinces in Persian literature. Among the new centres were Konya, the capital of the Seljuqs of Rum, and Shiraz in southern Iran. From the thirteenth century the *ghazal* emerged as the principal form for lyrical poetry. For both romantic and didactic poetry the *mathnawi*, using rhyming couplets, was employed. The magnificent romantic poems composed by Nizami (d.1209) relate such stories as *Layla wa Majnun* and *Khusraw wa Shirin*, while Farid al-Din Attar's *Mantiq al-tayr* (The Conference of the Birds, 1177) is a mystical mathnawi.

After the foundation of the Sultanate of Delhi in 1206, Persian literature was also cultivated in the Indian subcontinent by such poets as Amir Khusraw (1253–1325). Mystical poetry flourished, its foremost representative being Jalal al-Din Rumi (d.1273). Shiraz was the home of Saadi (d.1292) and Hafiz (c.1319/20–1389/90). The former's fine didactic mathnawi *Bustan* (The Garden) and his prose and verse poem, *Gulistan* (The Rose Garden) were much admired and frequently illustrated in later years. Hafiz in a series of sublime ghazals presented a vision of the world that combined sensual imagery with mystical thought:

> The rose has flushed red, the bud has burst,
> And drunk with joy is the nightingale -
> Hail, Sufis! lovers of wine, all hail!
> For wine is proclaimed to a world athirst.

This vibrant period of Persian literature came to a close with the mystical poetry of Jami (1414–92) in Harat.

Literary works in Turkish appeared in Anatolia from the thirteenth century onwards, and by the fifteenth century, when the Ottoman court was encouraging scholars and poets, fine poems in Turkish were being composed. In Harat, Mir Ali Shir Nawai (d.1501), minister to the Timurid ruler Husayn Bayqara (r.1469–1506), wrote in Chaghatay Turkish as well as Persian, and Turkish was also promoted in Egypt under the Circassian Mamluks (r.1382–1517). By the late fifteenth century Turkish was established as a vehicle for literary endeavour.

Music theory and practice

In the same way that the use of sensual imagery became a means of expressing religious experiences in poetry, so it was argued by the theologian Abu Hamid al-Ghazzali (1056–1111) that the sensual art of music could reflect the spiritual domain. The towering figure in musical theory was Safi al-Din (d.1294), who was in the service of the last Abbasid caliph al-Mustasim (r.1242–58) and the Mongol Hulagu (r.1256–65). His treatises *Kitab al-adwar* (The Book of Modes) and the *Risala al-sharafiyya fi al-nisab al-talifiyya* (The Sharafian Treatise on Intervallic Relations) supplied the theoretical framework that was used by nearly all major writers on music in the following two centuries. Safi al-Din's most influential successor was the composer and performer Abd al-Qadir al-Maraghi (d.1435), who was active in Baghdad and Samarqand.

By the mid-thirteenth century the fusion of Arab and Iranian music brought a common idiom to most of the eastern Islamic world. In north Africa and Spain music had continued to develop an Andalusian style, while in Turkey the Mawlawis began to cultivate music in their ritual at least from the time of Rumi's son, Sultan Walad (1226–1312). In India, Islamic and regional music began to intermingle fruitfully. Various Muslim rulers in India also became keen patrons – Sultan Muhammad ibn Tughluq (r.1325–51) had 1200 musicians in his service and a further 1000 slave musicians.

New building types in the Muslim empires
The movement of Turkic tribes into Iran from the tenth century brought innovations in building typology, plan and construction. The foremost congregational

After the Great Mosque of Isfahan was destroyed by fire in 1121/22 it was rebuilt with an iwan in the centre of each of the four facades. The iwan on the south side appears to have been built first, followed by those on the east and west, and finally the north iwan. Since the twelfth century, however, the court has been restored several times. This view across the court shows the west iwan, which was substantially restored in the late Safawid period, as indicated by the tilework and inscriptions.

This remarkable tower mausoleum, the Gunbad-i Qabus, was built by the Ziyarid prince Qabus ibn Vashmgir in 1006–07 near Gurgan, southeast of the Caspian Sea. Circular in plan, with ten triangular flanges on the exterior, it is positioned on an artificial platform and dominates the landscape. As no tomb was found inside the tower, the coffin may have been suspended, as related by a medieval chronicler. Two small bands of inscriptions break up the expanse of brick. The family of Qabus had converted to Islam from Zoroastrianism, and the use of a solar as well as a lunar calendar on the monument is further evidence of the survival of pre-Islamic traditions.

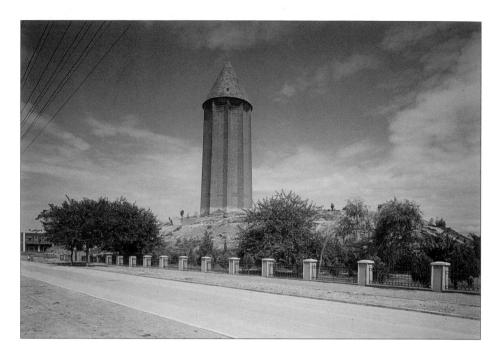

Opposite The Mamluk sultan Qaytbay (r.1468–96) was a prolific patron, and the architectural masterpiece of his reign was his own funerary complex in the Northern Cemetery of Cairo. The tall portal in the foreground is flanked on the left by a water dispensary, with a Quran school on the first floor; to the rear is the madrasa and mausoleum. The exterior of the building is decorated with horizontal masonry stripes, while the dome and minaret display fine Mamluk carved stonework.

mosque of the Seljuqs, the Great Mosque at their capital Isfahan, received two major alterations. The first was the addition of two domed units, one before the mihrab and another to the north of the mosque, in 1072–75 and 1088 respectively. Their function is unclear but the latter may have served as a royal oratory or anteroom. The second alteration took place after 1121/22, when Ismaili Shiites set fire to the Great Mosque, which was a centre of Sunnism. It consisted of the addition of an iwan in the centre of each courtyard façade. This four-iwan plan created a new cross-axial sense of space and was to characterize Seljuq and later mosques in Iran, as well as other building types that appeared at that time, such as madrasas and hospitals. It has been suggested that the interest in both the single domed units and the four-iwan plan are revivals of pre-Islamic Iranian architecture.

While the Seljuq interest in vaults and domes, constructed in the finest fired brick technology, can be appreciated in the two domes of the Great Mosque at Isfahan, the Seljuq interest in structural innovation and decorative brickwork can be seen in the numerous mausolea constructed from the tenth century onwards. The 'canopy tomb', consisting of a domed cube, is exemplified by the mausoleum of Ismail the Samanid at Bukhara (early tenth century), while the tomb tower is seen most spectacularly in the Gunbad-i Qabus (1006/07) near Gurgan, southeast of the Caspian Sea. The latter, a flanged tower surmounted by a conical roof, is 165 feet high. In the Iranian world, there are also a number of isolated eleventh- and twelfth-century minarets or towers, usually tall and conico-cylindrical. Some of them might have functioned as monuments to the victory of Islam, or as 'lighthouses' for desert caravans.

In Anatolia the Seljuqs adopted stone as their principal building material, the plasticity of whose carving is extraordinary. A characteristic Anatolian innovation is the use of triangular pendentives instead of squinches in the zone of transition of domes. Because of the severe climate, later Seljuq mosques had a small courtyard, some covered with a dome, this centralized plan presaging the single-domed mosques of the Ottoman period. Numerous mausolea, hospitals, caravansarais and madrasas also survive from Seljuq Anatolia.

After the Mongol capital was established at Tabriz in northwest Iran, the ilkhan Ghazan (r.1295–1304) and his grand vizier Rashid al-Din constructed entire new

Ibn al-Bawwab

The calligrapher and illuminator Ibn al-Bawwab (Abul-Hasan Ali ibn Hilal, d.1022) followed the calligraphic school established by Ibn Muqla (d.940), studying penmanship with the latter's daughter. His great achievement was to refine and lend elegance to Ibn Muqla's six 'proportioned scripts'. Ibn al-Bawwab was fluent in all six scripts, but especially favoured naskh and muhaqqaq. He was active in Baghdad and also served as librarian to the Buyid ruler Baha al-Dawla

(r.998–1012) at Shiraz, where he copied a *juz* (one-thirtieth of the Quran) that was missing from a Quran written by Ibn Muqla. Ibn al-Bawwab's work was so similar to the original that the two hands were indistinguishable. During his lifetime Ibn al-Bawwab is said to have copied sixty-four manuscripts of the Quran, as well as an epistle and poem on calligraphy. A devout man, well-versed in theology and law, and notable for his long beard, Ibn al-Bawwab achieved fame during his lifetime. After his death the school of calligraphy he had established was continued in Baghdad by his numerous pupils, among whom was a woman, Zaynab Shuhda al-Katiba (d.1178). Through her the chain of transmission of Ibn al-Bawwab's school led to the last of the great medieval calligraphers, Yaqut al-Mustasimi (d.1298).

Only one Quran by the hand of Ibn al-Bawwab appears to have survived. Copied at Baghdad in 1000–01, this Quran contains 286 folios measuring 6³/₄ by 5¹/₄ inches, with fifteen lines of naskh script on each page of text. The letters, which are of uniform thickness, were written with a straight-cut reed pen. The graceful script with long swinging curves and the illumination in sepia, blue, and gold make this Quran a masterpiece. It is the earliest known Quran written in cursive script on paper, older examples having been lost.

The text of this Quran by Ibn al-Bawwab is written in naskh script with headings in thuluth script. The page illustrated here (folio 9 verso) begins with *al-Fatiha* (The Opening Chapter) and the roundel in the margin to the right, marking the drop shape in the text, indicates the start of the fifth verse. The second heading indicates the beginning of the second chapter, *al-Baqar* (The Heifer).

quarters to the city, of which the only major Mongol monument surviving today is the immense vaulted hall of the ruined mosque of Ali Shah (c.1310–20). A new Mongol capital was built at Sultaniyya by Uljaytu (r.1304–17), and this too has vanished except for his enormous mausoleum (1307–17). Its double-shell dome is carried on an octagonal base, covered with blue tiles, and was surrounded by eight minarets, all features developed by the Timurid dynasty.

The distinctive domed mausolea of the Timurid period can be seen best at Timur's capital at Samarqand, at the Gur-i Amir (1404), where Timur was himself buried in 1405, and the extramural cemetery of the Shah-i Zinda. At the Gur-i Amir and at the tomb of Gawhar Shad, wife of Shah Rukh (r.1405–47), at Harat, the outer dome is bulbous and the surface ribbed, and in all the examples the dome is sheathed in brilliant glazed ceramics, usually turquoise. Both in these mausolea and the Timurid mosque complexes at Samarqand, Harat, Mashhad, and Tabriz, the structures are covered with beautiful multi-coloured tiles, unique in the history of colour in architecture.

In Egypt an equally distinctive architecture developed under the Fatimid caliphate (r.909–1171), whose Shiite doctrine and royal ceremonial is reflected in the plan and decoration of their mosques. Two large congregational mosques have survived in their capital Cairo, al-Azhar (970) and al Hakim (990 1013). A num ber of mausolea date to the early Fatimid period, perhaps attributable to the Fatimid claims to the caliphate and their veneration of tombs of the descendants of Ali. From the mid-eleventh century the Fatimids built smaller mosques in Cairo, with elaborate stone-carved façades. The most spectacular remains of their secular architecture are the three stone gates in the city walls of Cairo, which reveal an affinity with military architecture in Syria and northern Mesopotamia.

Under the Mamluks (r.1250–1517) the architectural forms and decoration of earlier dynasties attained a high level of achievement. The majority of Mamluk constructions were funerary complexes, usually consisting of mosques, madrasas, and hospitals grouped around the mausoleum of the patron. The most impressive is the complex of Sultan Hasan (1354–62) in Cairo, for its size and the strength of its stone-carved decoration. Fifteenth-century examples are generally smaller but have the distinctive Mamluk carved stone domes and polygonal minarets, as, for instance, at the complex of Qaytbay in Cairo (1472–75). Although characteristic of Mamluk Egypt, many features such as the funerary complex plan, the form of the dome and the monumental portals, as well as the stone decoration, can be related to architecture in contemporary Iran and Anatolia.

As with literature and music, the Maghrib and al-Andalus early acquired their own styles. The emerging cities of the Almoravid and Almohad empires all received new congregational mosques, or had existing mosques rebuilt, as in Almoravid Algiers (1096), Tlemcen (1136), and the Qarawiyyin mosque at Fez (mostly 1135) or the Almohad congregational mosques of Marrakesh (1146–96), Seville (1171) and Rabat (1196/97). These mosques followed the pattern set at

Opposite This miniature painting by Bihzad, showing the caliph Mamun at a Turkish bath, was executed in Harat in 1494–5. Bihzad demonstrates his skill in creating a formal structure for the painting, with internal rhythms and carefully arranged colours. The scene also shows his genius for characterization.

Below The wounded Rustam shoots Shaghad, from an illustrated copy of Firdawsi's great epic poem, the *Shahnama* (The Book of Kings), which relates the history of the Iranian kings and heroes. Here, the dying hero Rustam, whose horse Rahksh is impaled in a pit, is shooting his treacherous half-brother Shaghad through a tree-trunk.

Qayrawan and Cordoba, with immense hypostyle prayer halls with the T-plan, and the typical square-plan minaret. From the Nasirid period (r.1232–1492) the best-known monument is the Alhambra palace in Granada, a uniquely well preserved Islamic palace that has been a source of fascination for centuries because of the wealth and delicacy of its decoration. A series of intimate courts, mostly dating to the mid-fourteenth century, are decorated with glazed tile mosaic, and carved and painted wood and stucco, elements first developed under the Almoravids and Almohads. The most elaborate forms are the stucco domes of *muqarnas* or stalactite, a feature first expressed in the brick structures of Seljuq Iran, here playing a purely decorative role.

Visual arts

Naskh, *thuluth*, *muhaqqaq*, *rayhan*, *tawqi* and *riqa* scripts were canonized in the tenth and early eleventh centuries. Naskh was used for copying manuscripts and small Qurans, thuluth often for chapter headings in Qurans and architectural inscriptions; muhaqqaq and rayhan for large Qurans, and the more fluid tawqi and riqa for chancellery documents and colophons in manuscripts. Ibn Muqla's system for giving proportion to calligraphic scripts was refined by Ibn al-Bawwab (d.1022) and later improved by Yaqut al-Mustasimi (d.1298). From the fourteenth century, calligraphers increasingly signed their works, and their names are preserved in other written sources. In Egypt and Syria the styles of writing established by Yaqut and his pupils flourished under Mamluk patronage. Some of the finest copies of the Quran are those copied in muhaqqaq for the Mamluk Sultan Shaban II (r.1363–76) and his mother.

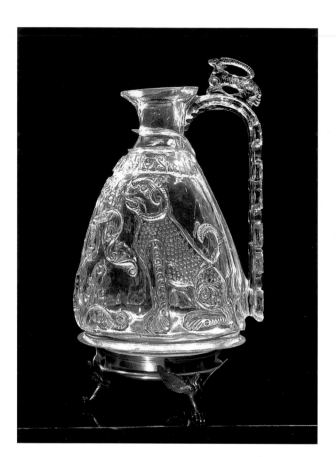

Rock crystal was a highly esteemed medium in the Fatimid period. This ewer, which is decorated with the carved figure of a lion, carries an inscription that refers to the Fatimid caliph al-Aziz (r.975–96).

This sheet brass ewer of c.1180–1200 (*above right*), with a twelve-sided body and tall spout, is decorated with benedictory inscriptions, astrological iconography, and scrollwork in repoussé and silver inlay, with copper for the eyes of the embossed birds. It was probably made in Harat, a major centre for the manufacture of inlaid metalwork in the Seljuq period.

From the late twelfth century there was a growth of figurative imagery in Muslim lands in various media, including illustrated manuscripts, and by the thirteenth and fourteenth centuries various styles of painting had emerged. That current under the Seljuqs was mannered and decorative, while the style practised in Mesopotamia and Syria for Arab patrons exhibited a keen sense of realism. Some Syrian manuscript paintings show elements of the local Hellenistic tradition. Persian painting began to flourish from the fourteenth century; several styles, including Chinese influences, gradually fused to create this new idiom. The paintings from a great Mongol *Shahnama*, probably painted in the second quarter of the fourteenth century in Tabriz, portray an atmosphere of intense emotion and fierce action. By the late fourteenth century under the Jalayrid and Muzzafarid dynasties, however, a new delicate style of painting with complex spatial compositions had appeared, heralding the Timurid style of the fifteenth century. Timurid painting was produced for various royal patrons, thriving particularly in Harat under prince Baysunghur (d.1433). The final flowering of this extremely refined art in Harat came at the end of the century, when the famous painter Bihzad was active.

A large range of media attracted Muslim artisans in this period. Some carved rock crystals survive from Fatimid rule in Cairo, inscribed with the names of

In addition to a wide range of vessels and tiles, the potters of Kashan produced fine mihrabs. Their decorative repertoire was sober, based on inscriptions and non-figural motifs. This underglaze- and lustre-painted ceramic mihrab, which was made in Kashan in 1226, consists of a series of niches surrounded by inscriptions in naskh and kufic scripts.

caliphs or high officials. Examples of Fatimid cut glass also survive, while under the Mamluks the technique of enamelled and gilt glass reached its apogee in mosque lamps decorated with calligraphy and heraldic emblems. Fine jade carvings were produced during the Timurid era. Knotted rugs exist from Seljuq Anatolia, a technique probably brought to western Asia by Turkish tribes; Spain, meanwhile, became a leading manufacturer of silks. The metalwork of the Islamic world was unrivalled, primarily bronze and brass objects (such as ewers, basins, trays, candlesticks, and incense burners) inlaid with gold and silver, in designs at once abstract, calligraphic, and figurative. This tradition first appeared in Seljuq Khurasan, was developed in thirteenth-century Iraq, and flourished again at the Mamluk court in Cairo. Along with the rise of architectural tilework in Iran and Anatolia, a variety of ceramic techniques were also generated from the twelfth century. The most common is polychrome underglaze painted pottery, but, later, overglaze painted pottery appeared as well. The most spectacular technique was metallic lustre, seen first under the Abbasids in Iraq and the Fatimids in Egypt, and then established at Kashan in Iran, where lustre tiles and vessels were manufactured in quantity. The iconography on such vessels, which include scenes of enthronement, drinking, hunting, and sport, is that of courtly life, established under the Umayyads and Abbasids, but now decorating wares made increasingly for bourgeois consumption.

THE ART OF THE GUNPOWDER EMPIRES: SIXTEENTH TO EIGHTEENTH CENTURIES

The three major empires of the Muslim world in the sixteenth century – the Ottomans, Safawids, and Mughals – each evolved distinctive forms of artistic expression that eventually led them on divergent cultural paths. At the same time there was much shared culture and interaction between them; for example, as patronage declined at the Safawid court many artists from Iran travelled to India to seek their fortune under the Mughals. By the eighteenth century there was also political disruption in each region, caused either by internal strife or the growing intervention of European states.

Ottoman, Safawid, and Mughal poetry and prose

Under the Ottomans the qasida and ghazal were adapted to Ottoman Turkish. Fuzuli (d.1556), a brilliant linguist, wrote in Turkish, Persian, and Arabic, although he never travelled beyond his native Iraq. In Istanbul, however, the sultans and their dignitaries were eager to provide patronage. Sulayman the Magnificent (r.1520–66) recognized the talent of the poet Baqi (1526–1600), and the grand vizier Ibrahim Pasha was the patron of Khayali (d.1556). Turkish mystical poetry also developed, under the influence of Rumi. The most prominent poet of the so-called Tulip Age was Nedim (d.1730):

Get your mother's leave, say it's for holy prayers this Friday:
Out of time's tormenting clutches let us both steal a day,
And slinking through the secret roads and alleys down to the quay,
Let's go to the pleasure gardens, come, my sauntering cypress.
Just you and I, and a singer with exquisite airs – and yet
Another: with your kind permission, Nedim, the mad poet;
Let's forget our boon companions today, my joyful coquette –
Let's go to the pleasure gardens, come, my sauntering cypress.

After Nedim, Ottoman poetry tended to move further away from the Persian poetic tradition, and attempts were made to simplify the language.

The style of Turkish prose favoured in the sixteenth century was characterized by artificial language with complicated images. Works on history came to the fore, especially chronicles extolling the successes and virtues of the sultans. Geographical works, travels, and biographical dictionaries based on Arabic models were also popular. In the following century Katib Chelebi (Hajji Khalifa, d.1657) devoted some twenty years to the compilation of his *Kashf al-zunun* (The Removal of Doubts), a vast encyclopaedia and bibliography, while the *Siyahatname* of Ewliya Chelebi (1611–c.1684) became important for its commentary on all aspects of social life.

In Safawid Iran the efforts of many writers were channelled into works of religious propaganda and manuals of religious conduct. Religious poetry also became prominent, with themes taken from stories of Shia imams and martyrs. Sufism, which had stimulated poetry in previous centuries, was now less visible, and traditional court patronage likewise declined, while the day-to-day language of the Safawid court was Turkish and not Persian.

Many Iranian poets in the second half of the sixteenth century were attracted to India, where the Mughal emperors were generous patrons. Urfi (1555/56–90), who was a native of Shiraz, sought patronage under the Mughals, and at the court of Akbar (r.1556–1605) there were fifty-one poets from Iran. The migration of talent also stimulated a new style of poetry in both India and Iran. Known as the Indian style, *sabk-i hindi*, it was characterized by a preference for the ghazal and the use of rich imagery and original metaphors. The most talented of the Iranian poets working in the Indian style was Saib of Tabriz (1601/02–76/77), who received much acclaim in India.

Iranian poets continued to migrate to India during the reigns of Jahangir (r.1605–27) and Shah Jahan (r.1627–58). Preeminent among Jahangir's poets was Talib Amuli (d.1626/27), while those active under Shah Jahan included Kalim (d.1651) and Saib. Under Awrangzeb (r.1658–1707), however, the official patronage of poetry came to an end, although it was continued to an extent by some members of his court. The best-known poet of this period was Bedil (1644/45–1720), in whose verse the Indian style of Persian poetry reached its culmination. From the eighteenth century Urdu steadily gained importance and began to replace Persian as the medium of literary expression.

Mughal prose, which had an ornate tendency, is notable for historical and biographical writings, such as Babur's record of his life in Chaghatay Turkish, the *Baburnama* (The Book of Babur). This genre also includes Jahangir's *Tuzuk-i Jahangiri* (The Memoirs of Jahangir), which reveals in an unadorned style the emperor's interest in the arts and natural history.

Music under the Ottomans and Mughals

Several sufi orders created an Ottoman liturgical music, with an independent style and repertoire. The compositions were performed during the canonical prayer service, Islamic festivals, and especially during the sufi *dhikr*, which involves a breathing technique that allows the rhythmic utterances of God's name and his attributes. In the seventeenth and eighteenth centuries some of these genres were accepted into the public mosque service. Among the sufi orders, the Mawlawi ceremony *ayin-i serif*, in which the whirling dance is performed, uses singers and a large ensemble including flutes, kettledrums, framedrums, fiddles, and long-necked lutes.

Music was played in various Ottoman hospitals, for instance at the Bayazid II complex at Edirne, for its therapeutic value. It was also played by the Ottoman military band (*mehter*) which arose in the fourteenth century and made use of the base drum and shawm. By the seventeenth century at the latest other instruments had been added – trumpets, pairs of small kettledrums, cymbals, and Turkish crescents. The latter, known in the West as the jingling Johnny, was a percussion stick in the form of an ornamental standard.

Since Muslim music was transmitted almost entirely by oral tradition it is difficult to judge whether it was ever influenced by European music. When Ewliya Chelebi visited Vienna, however, he noted that music there was quite different from Turkish music. Early in the eighteenth century a treatise on Turkish musical theory was written by the Romanian prince Dimitrie Cantemir (d.1723), who lived for some time in Istanbul and composed in the Turkish manner. Cantemir analysed the structure of Ottoman music, left a record in notation of the instrumental repertoire, and described the vocal and instrumental forms in vogue.

From Abul Fadl's *Ain-i Akbari* (1597) we learn that all the vocal musicians at Akbar's court were probably Indian, while many of the instrumentalists were foreigners, some of whom came from Harat, Mashhad, and Tabriz. Under Awrangzeb in the late seventeenth century, music suffered a setback, but it revived under Bahadur Shah (r.1707–12) and Muhammad Shah (r.1719–48). From the mid-eighteenth century musical culture was increasingly maintained at the provincial courts, but on a less lavish scale, when many Mughal musicians dispersed to courts in Rajasthan, and a large number gathered at Lucknow in the service of the nawabs of Oudh (Awadh).

Sinan

Sinan (d.1588) entered the Janissaries in 1521 and had a successful army career before being appointed court architect in 1538. His Sehzade Mosque in Istanbul (1544–48), which he described as the work of his apprenticeship, was built in commemoration of Sulayman the Magnificent's son, Mehmed, who died of smallpox in 1543, aged twenty-two. To create a large domed prayer-hall for this mosque, Sinan employed four half-domes around a central dome, which gave the resulting building a centralized plan. His next major project was the Sulaymaniye Mosque in Istanbul (1550–57). For this he returned to the design of earlier Ottoman mosques in which two half-domes supported the central dome, and he made the height of the dome (174 feet) twice the diameter (87 feet). The structure of the mosque is expressed in its outer profile, which dominates the Istanbul skyline. Thin 'pencil' minarets rise at the four corners. The mihrab area was decorated with Iznik tiles and calligraphic roundels designed by Ahmad Karahisari (1469–1566). Sulayman's tomb is in a cemetery to the south of the mosque, and that of Sinan himself was eventually added to the complex.

The building that Sinan regarded as his masterpiece, completed when he was nearly eighty, is the Selimiye Mosque at Edirne (1569–75). The plan of this mosque consists of a circle on an octagon in a square. The dome, the largest in Ottoman architecture (102 feet in diameter), is carried on eight massive piers, which made the large half-domes of earlier mosques unnecessary. The mihrab is flanked by a tiled dado and the minbar is carved in openwork in Marmara marble. A tribune in the centre of the mosque was used for chanting; below it is a small fountain. Outside, four soaring minarets surround the dome.

Sinan was also engaged on many other projects in Istanbul, Edirne, and on the route between the two cities. In Istanbul he worked on the mosque of Rustem Pasha (d.1561), the Mihrimah Sultan complex (1562–65), the Sokollu Mehmed Pasha Mosque (1571), the mausoleum of Selim II (1577), the Kilic Ali Pasha complex (1580), and the Zal Mahmud Pasha complex (1580). He was also responsible for various engineering works. A total of 477 buildings have been attributed to him, of which 196 are still standing. This immense activity, forming the urban topography of Istanbul, ensured his great fame, during his lifetime and after.

The beauty of the Selimiye Mosque is expressed in the clarity of its structure. The great dome, which equals in width the dome of Hagia Sophia in Istanbul, is supported by 8 piers, the tops of which are expressed on the exterior by 8 external buttresses, while 4 small semi-domes placed below the dome mark the transition from an octagon to a square. The whole ensemble is anchored by 4 great fluted minarets that reach a height of 230 feet.

Religious and court architecture

Mosque architecture under the Ottomans was characterized by a progressive experimentation with the use of domes to cover a large floor space. The process began at the Fatih Mosque complex in Istanbul (1463–70, 1766), where a large dome and a single half-dome over the southern mihrab area, flanked by domed bays, were the central elements in a square plan. At the mosque complex of Bayazid II in Istanbul (1501–06), a second half-dome was added on the north or courtyard side, while the central dome, which collapsed in 1766, rested on four great piers. This design was clearly inspired by the Byzantine church of Hagia Sophia, which Mehmed II had converted into a mosque. Further experimentation with the domed form was carried out in the sixteenth century by the architect Sinan (d.1588), in whose work this mosque type reached its zenith. After him, a reversion to the four semi-dome plan was made by Mehmed Agha for the mosque of Ahmad I (the Blue Mosque) in Istanbul (1609–17). From the time of Ahmad III (r.1703–30), a new architectural style was developed, known as Ottoman Baroque. Although initially inspired by European architecture, it acquired a character of its own, typified by drooping eaves and mouldings, as seen, for example, in the fountain of Ahmad III in Istanbul (1738). The Nuruosmaniye Mosque in Istanbul (1755) is notable for its rounded courtyard, curved buttresses, and portals in this style.

The residence of the Ottoman sultans and the seat of government from the sixteenth to the nineteenth century was the Topkapi Palace, begun under Mehmed II, with further buildings and renovations proceeding through the centuries. The palace consists of a sequence of courts, surrounded by cloisters and pavilions, each courtyard separated by imposing gates. There is an area known as the *haremlik*, a system of small courts that contained the private quarters of the sultan and his harem. A variety of styles was used for the different pavilions, including a Timurid plan and decoration for the Cinili ('Tiled') Kiosk (1465–72). A great range of building types were also undertaken by the Ottomans all over their empire – mosques, dams, bridges, baths, and fountains.

Safawid architecture reached its apogee during the reign of Shah Abbas I (r.1588–1629), who rebuilt the capital Isfahan after 1598 on lavish scale. He began with the Chahar Bagh, a long garden avenue with a water channel running along its centre and pavilions constructed on either side. To the east of the Chahar Bagh a monumental open area, the Maydan-i Shah (560 by 174 yards), was constructed, one of the largest public squares of its time. The Maydan formed the heart of the new city and was the site of markets, troop reviews, polo games, and executions. It was enclosed by a two-storey wall with shops on the lower level. On the short sides of the Maydan was a portal leading to the bazar, and opposite, the entrance to the Shah's Mosque (1612/13–30). On one of the long sides of the Maydan was the mosque of Shaykh Lutfullah (1602/03–18/19), and, on the other, the palace-pavilion known as the Ali Qapu. The latter, which served as a gate to

Opposite The Masjid-i Shah (Shah Mosque; now renamed Masjid-i Imam), begun during the reign of Shah Abbas I (r.1588–1629), is situated on the south side of the Maydan in Isfahan. While the entrance to the mosque is aligned with the Maydan, the mosque itself is oriented towards Mecca. The mosque has a four-iwan plan around a court. This view shows the sanctuary iwan with paired minarets, behind which floats the large sanctuary dome. The latter has a double shell to allow different inner and outer profiles. The mosque was decorated throughout with polychrome glazed tiles, although the original tilework was largely replaced in the twentieth century.

Persian court carpets of the sixteenth century are among the most magnificent ever produced. This is the so-called Ardabil carpet, which may in fact have come from the shrine of Imam Riza in Mashhad. A cartouche bears the words: 'Except for thy heaven there is no refuge for me in this world; other than here there is no place for my head'.

the royal gardens, was also a place where the Shah could watch events in the May-dan and receive ambassadors. Both mosques were fitted with impressive domes and portals flanked with minarets, the whole adorned with tiles. Subsequent Safawid shahs continued building works in Isfahan. After the fall of the Safawids the unrest in Iran prevented further building, except at the court of Karim Khan Zand (r.1750–79) in Shiraz.

The first Mughal emperor Babur (r.1526–30) is best remembered for the construction of gardens. The most celebrated building associated with his successor Humayun is the latter's mausoleum surrounded by a garden at Delhi. In the 1560s Akbar renovated the Red Fort at Agra and in 1571 founded his palace–city at Fathepur Sikri. He also began work on a mausoleum for himself at Sikandra, near Agra: completed by Jahangir, it too is situated in a garden. Elements of the Sikandra mausoleum were brought together on a smaller scale, but with exquisite effect, for the mausoleum built by Nur Jahan at Agra for her father Itimad al-Daulah (d.1622); she also built a mausoleum for Jahangir at Lahore. The most famous of the Mughal mausolea, however, is the sublime Taj Mahal (1632–47), which became the resting place of Shah Jahan. The Taj Mahal combines perfect harmony of proportions with luxurious surface decoration comprised of carved and inlaid marble. Shah Jahan's passion for architecture is also displayed in work at the palace forts at Agra and Lahore, while the Shalamar Garden at Lahore (1641–42) is among the finest laid out by the Mughals. The new palace–city at Delhi, Shahjahanabad (1639–48), includes the Red Fort, which became the centre of the Mughal empire. Afterwards, in the eighteenth century provincial styles began to develop at the local courts, principally at Lucknow.

Visual arts in three empires

Ottoman calligraphy in the early sixteenth century was dominated by Shaykh Hamd Allah (1436–1520), who was greatly admired by Sultan Bayazid II and was also something of an athlete: it is reported that he swam the Bosphorus carrying his writing implements between his teeth. Hamd Allah adapted the six scripts canonized by Yaqut al-Mustasimi and refined the *divani* script used for documents in Ottoman chancelleries. He trained many followers, including Ahmad Karahisari (1469–1566).

In Iran, an elegant cursive script known as *nastaliq*, an ideal vehicle for poetic texts, was elaborated by such calligraphers as Sultan Ali of Mashhad (c.1442–1519), Mir Ali (d.1556), Mahmud Nishapuri (d.c.1564) and Mir Imad (d.1615). Shah Abbas I's favourite calligrapher, Ali Riza of Tabriz (d.c.1627), excelled in thuluth script, and wrote many of the inscriptions on buildings in Isfahan. Nastaliq script also flourished in India, carried by calligraphers who migrated from Iran towards the end of the reign of Shah Tahmasp (r.1524–76). Other calligraphers went to Turkey, where this style became popular and was later refined under the Ottomans.

Turkish painters became noted for depicting contemporary historical events in a style quite separate from Iranian work, especially the tendency towards a more prosaic observation of the world. The Safawids, on the other hand, were direct heirs of the Timurid traditions of Harat and of the Turkman style in western Iran. The foremost patron was Shah Tahmasp, for whom was made perhaps the finest of all illustrated Shahnamas (now dispersed) in the 1520s. By the reign of Shah Abbas I painting focused on single figures or couples, on loose folios. The most prominent artist in this style was Riza, and it was continued by his follower Muin Musawwir. Thereafter Persian painting increasingly incorporated stylistic conventions of European art.

In India, the Mughal school of painting developed from 1549 when Humayun, then ruling in Kabul, was joined by the painters Mir Sayyid Ali and Abd al-Samad, both of whom had worked for Shah Tahmasp. The major project of Akbar's workshop in the 1560s and 1570s was the *Hamzanama* (The Book of Hamza), which contained some 1400 illustrations. Akbar also commissioned illustrated copies of such works as the *Baburnama* and *Akbarnama*. About a hundred painters, many of them Hindus, worked in Akbar's workshop. Jahangir employed fewer painters but took a great interest in the art, encouraging a more static style of painting and commissioning allegorical works. As in Iran, single paintings were executed and collected in albums with calligraphic specimens. Jahangir's interest in natural history also led to fine studies of plants and animals. With the breakup of the Mughal empire in the eighteenth century, painting became established at various provincial courts, where the Mughal style merged with local traditions.

A great range of court art in various mediums also survives from this period, including inlaid furniture and textiles, especially silks and brocades made for court consumption. Under the Safawids, carpets of breathtaking beauty were manufactured, and were highly prized in Europe. Ottoman metalwork was practised in two styles, so that highly decorated bejewelled wares were made at the

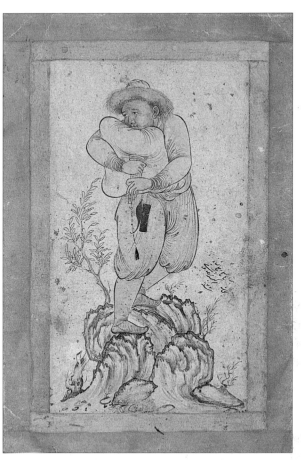

This tinted drawing of a man playing a bagpipe is signed Riza-i Abbasi, who was the leading artist at the Safawid court in the early seventeenth century. It is one of a number of single-figure studies by Riza in which his virtuosity is combined with a satirical observation of life. According to his contemporaries, Riza developed a reputation for indulging in low company and he enjoyed watching wrestling. This bagpipe player was apparently not among the musicians of the court.

The fine ceramic mosque lamp, underglaze-painted in black cobalt and turquoise, is an example of the so-called Damascus group of Iznik ware. On the base is a fragmentary inscription which gives the date 1549 and a dedication to the shrine of Esrefzade (Abdallah-i Rumi) at Iznik. In the nineteenth century the lamp was in the Dome of the Rock in Jerusalem.

same time as unadorned wares that relied on their outline and proportions for effect. Mughal carved jade and rock crystals inlaid with gems survive from the seventeenth century onwards, as do ivory powder-horns with grotesque combinations of animal forms. Ceramics of the sixteenth and seventeenth centuries are dominated by the great Ottoman production at the potteries of Iznik. The affinity of the designs on ceramics, textiles, and other Ottoman arts suggests that there was a centralized design atelier at the Turkish court of this period.

ART IN THE MODERN AGE: 1800 TO THE PRESENT

Two trends have characterized the arts of the modern era in the Muslim world. First, there has been a rediscovery and renewal of Muslim traditions, and, second, an assimilation of western culture as a means of encouraging development in Muslim lands. Underlying both of these trends has been a new consciousness of history, while the emergence of an educated class of Muslims formed by secular institutions has been important for their growth. Both trends have also played a part in the nationalist and religious movements that grew up over this period. In all areas of art a need has been felt to protect traditional practices, whether in music, where the survival of the oral tradition depends on an adequate musical education in each subsequent generation, or in architecture, where numerous urban renewal schemes have destroyed traditional buildings and the crafts that maintained them.

Literature revitalized

In Muslim lands from the nineteenth century various attempts have been made to reform and revitalize literature from within. In the Arab world, in particular, a sustained movement revived classical Arabic and its literary genres. The maqamat, for example, inspired the Lebanese writer Nasif al-Yaziji (1800–71). In Iran, Persian poetry received patronage at the Qajar court. Under Fath Ali Shah (r.1797–1834), a circle of poets gathered who emulated classical Persian poetry, the most important among them being Saba of Kashan (d.1822/23). This cultivation of classicism reached a height in the work of Qaani (d.1854). At the same time the task of reforming Persian prose began with Qaim Maqam Farahani (1779–1835), and continued during the nineteenth century. In India, meanwhile, the Persian language as a medium of literary expression continued to lose ground to Urdu. Ghalib (1797–1869), the last great poet of the Mughal era, composed in both languages.

Increasingly writers in the Muslim world laboured to adapt their language to express new ideas, which they encountered in the recent translations of scientific and literary works from European languages. A central figure in Turkey was Namik Kemal (1840–88) who wanted to revive Ottoman culture. He and his pupil Abd al-Haqq Hamid exercised a profound influence through their poetry and the former's novels, dramas, and other writings. Poets and writers such as Muallim Naji, Tewfiq Fikret, and Khalid Ziya also attempted to introduce modern conventions into their work. Early in the twentieth century literature became preoccupied with national issues. When the Arabic alphabet was replaced by the Latin alphabet in 1928 the break with previous Ottoman literature seemed complete, even though some texts were reprinted in the new alphabet.

New ideas also began to permeate Arabic poetry, although such poets as Khalil Gibran (1883–1931), who discarded classicism at an early date, were exceptions; he lived in the West and was more exposed to its poetry. In the Arab world Ahmad Shawqi (1868–1932) used high language to commemorate public events and praise rulers, and he was also a spokesman for Egyptian nationalism. Attempts to modernize Arabic poetry were made by Khalil Matran (1871–1949) and later by Ahmad Zaki Abu Shadi (1892–1955). Meanwhile, the novel, itself a western genre, was passing through several stages –historical, romantic, realist, and symbolic – in search of a modern form. A new way of looking at Egyptian life was expressed in Husayn Haykal's *Zaynab* (1914). During the 1920s there was a growing output of realistic short stories dealing with contemporary life. The writer who best expressed the aspirations of his generation was Taha Husayn, whose autobiographical *Al-Ayyam* (The Days, 1926) is a prose masterpiece.

In Iran political changes had put an end to court patronage and writers became more involved with politics and the society in which they lived. The historical novel achieved popularity in the early twentieth century, often carrying nationalist sentiments. Many writers preferred the short story; Muhammad Ali Jamalzada's satirical stories *Yaki bud yaki nabud* (Once Upon a Time, 1921) were particularly influential. Although Jamalzada lived in Europe most of his life, he never lost his interest in colloquial Persian. Sadiq Hidayat, who translated Franz Kafka into Persian and incorporated elements of western Surrealism in his own work, received international acclaim for his novel *Buf-i kur* (The Blind Owl, 1937).

In India, the ghazal and mathnawi forms were adapted in Urdu to express new social and ideological concerns, beginning in the work of the poet Altaf Husayn Hali (1837–1914) and continuing in the poetry of Muhammad Iqbal (1877–1938). In the poetry of Iqbal, which he wrote in Persian, to speak to a wider Muslim audience, as well as Urdu, a memory of the past achievements of Islam is combined with a plea for reform. He is considered the greatest Urdu poet of the twentieth century.

After the Second World War a poetic revolution in the Arab world, led by poets from the Lebanon, Syria, Palestine, and Iraq, aimed to replace the subjectivism of

Um Kulthum first sang as a child under the supervision of her father, who was the village shaykh in the Egyptian Delta. She developed her repertoire of religious music in Cairo in the early 1920s, guided by Shaykh Abu al-Ila, one of the leading exponents of the classical tradition of Islamic singing, and she also performed some secular songs. Her fame grew, especially after she appeared in popular films, and from the 1940s until her death in 1975 she was a legendary figure. Um Kulthum's great following in the Arab world is indicated in this image by the halo-like lighting surrounding her head.

earlier poets with a new realism and commitment. A leading poet in this movement was the Syrian Ahmad Said (b.1929), known as Adonis. The petty bourgeoisie of Cairo were depicted in a series of novels by Najib Mahfuz (b.1911). Women writers became more prominent, while poetic drama in classical language, which had flourished in the work of Tawfiq al-Hakim (1899–1987), was overtaken by new dramatic forms using more accessible language.

Music in the modern era

After Mahmud II (r.1808–39) destroyed the power of the Janissaries in 1826, their military bands of reed pipes, trumpets, cymbals, and kettle–drums were replaced by western-style bands as part of the reforms of the army. In 1828 Guiseppe Donizetti (1788–1856), brother of the opera composer Gaetano Donizetti, was invited to Istanbul to command the imperial band, and he was also responsible for introducing European notation to Turkish music. Prior to this, a system of notation had been introduced by the Armenian musician Hamparsum Limonicyan (1768–1839), which enabled much Turkish classical music, mainly of the religious repertory, to be written down. From the late nineteenth century, however, Turkish classical music has played a decreasing role in musical life. With the closure in 1925 of Turkish monasteries the music of the sufi orders also declined.

Musical performances and education became more focused on western forms. Caught between two equally valid traditions, some twentieth-century composers, such as Ulvi Cemal Erkin (1906–73) and Adnan Saygun (b.1907), sought a synthesis between Turkish and western music.

The encroachment of western musical culture was vividly symbolized by the construction of an opera house in Cairo in 1869. In the presence of westernization, the popularity of Arab classical music began to diminish, and in the twentieth century an attempt was made at the Cairo Congress on Arab Music (1932) to define aspects of Arab music to ensure its survival. New, popular styles of Arab music introduced by such composers as Sayyid Darwish (1892–1923), Muhammad Abd al-Wahhab (b. 1910) and Farid al-Atrash (d.1974), were successful because they were both rooted in tradition and borrowed features from western music. The outstanding performer was Um Kulthum (1908–75), whose voice gained her an international reputation. After the Second World War a new Egyptian art music used western forms and techniques of composition. The principal composers of the first generation were Yusef Greiss (1899–1961) and Abu Bakr Khayrat (1910–63), followed by Abd al-Rahim (b.1924) and others.

Iranian classical music had followed a somewhat independent path in the preceding centuries and during the nineteenth century a concept known as the *dastgah-ha* was developed, in which musical modes were used in groups, each group making up one dastgah. By the second half of the nineteenth century, however, European music was beginning to reach Iran, especially when French musicians were employed to create an imperial military band and organize musical education. With increasing European influence, Iranian musicians were attracted by the idea of ensemble music, which led to the use of fixed melodic and rhythmic forms. The growing interest in 'display' pieces in the twentieth century, as opposed to the more improvisatory nature of earlier music, was also a result of westernization. During the century some European instruments, especially the violin, found wide application in Persian music, while the *ud* (lute), the *qanun* (psaltery), and Persian vocal techniques were employed less. The instruments that continue to be widely used in Persian classical music are the *sitar* (long-necked lute), *tar* (another long-necked lute), *santur* (dulcimer), *kamancha* (spike fiddle), *nay* (flute), and *tumbak* (goblet drum).

In India from the late eighteenth century Lucknow became the main musical centre until the Indian uprising in 1857, after which other princely courts offered

Conceived by the Iraqi artist Ismail Fattah (b. 1934) and built in 1981-83 by the Mitsubishi Corporation to the specifications of Ove Arup and Partners, the Martyr's Monument in Baghdad commemorates the dead from the Iraq–Iran war (1980–88). A giant turquoise dome, split into two halves, has been built on a circular platform, situated in the middle of an artificial lake. Ismail Fattah won international recognition with his powerful design.

The Great Mosque of Hassan II (completed 1993), built by Michel Pinseau and the Royal Architectural Workshop, is situated on the coast at Casablanca in Morocco. It has a prayer hall designed to accommodate 25,000 worshippers, and a soaring minaret. Adorned with marble, mosaics, and stucco decoration, the roof of the mosque can be opened to allow light to enter. The mosque is part of a complex that includes public baths, a madrasa, library, and amphitheatre.

patronage. As Indian music was generally ignored by the British, court patronage continued as a lifeline for musical traditions until Indian independence. However, the emergence of new forms of technology, including the radio and India's flourishing film industry, had a marked effect on musical development. Most films produced are musicals and their songs have a wide audience in the Muslim world.

Revivalism and modernism in architecture

The growth of historical revivalism in Muslim architecture and art, and the desire to produce works of art considered acceptable as 'fine' art in the western sense, are two processes that reflect the issue of how Muslim culture should be represented in the modern world. Both also filled the vacuum that was created by the breakdown of previous forms of patronage.

European architectural ideas were introduced in various parts of the Muslim world during the nineteenth century. In Istanbul they were propagated in buildings designed for the Ottoman sultans by the Armenian Balyan family of architects, and by the early twentieth century there was an eclectic style of architecture in which Ottoman features were grafted on to European forms, especially in the architecture of Vedat (1873–1942) and Kemalattin (1870–1927). From the late 1920s, under the Republican government, European modernist styles were promoted, although during the 1930s there was a shift in emphasis as architects began to express in their work a new awareness of indigenous Turkish culture, although without totally rejecting modernism. Sedad Hakki Eldem emerged as an influential voice in this defence of indigenous styles over international ones.

In Egypt the nineteenth-century rebuilding of Cairo entailed the demolition of medieval buildings, in whose place European-style boulevards and plazas were created. By the early twentieth century, a revivalist style of architecture became fashionable in which 'Islamic', usually Mamluk, features were applied on the surface of buildings. Mahmud Fahmi (1856–1925) designed the Ministry of Waqf building (1915) in an Islamic revivalist style, while for the mausoleum of Saad Zaghlul (1928–31) his son Mustafa (1886–1972) adopted a 'neo-Pharaonic' style recalling ancient Egyptian civilization. Both of these revivalist styles made claims on nationalist sentiments. By the mid-twentieth century, Egyptian architects – Hasan Fathi (1900–89) and others – began to derive inspiration and learn lessons from the indigenous tradition of mud-brick village architecture.

Architecture in Iran was influenced by European ideas during the reign of Nasir al-Din (r.1848–96), when the capital Teheran was enlarged and rebuilt. Under Pahlawi rule (r.1925–79) new priorities came to the fore and various old buildings were replaced by modern structures. An awareness of the dislocation of traditional values led such architects as Nader Ardalan and Kamran Diba to confront these issues in their work in the 1960s and 1970s.

In the contemporary Muslim world traditional architectural forms have been used in a variety of ways. The Martyr's Monument in Baghdad (1981–83), for example, which was conceived by the Iraqi artist Ismail Fattah (b.1934), takes advantage of the familiar form of a dome, but here split into two halves, with a poignant result. The Great Mosque of Hassan II in Casablanca (completed 1993), one of the largest in the world, retains a traditional design and form, but rendered on a massive scale, for which modern technology was required.

Innovation and tradition in the visual arts

The art of calligraphy has continued to be vibrant and has also inspired painters in the late twentieth century. In the nineteenth century Ottoman calligraphy flourished in the work of Mustafa Izzet (1801–76) and his followers. Calligraphy in Turkey, however, was an immediate casualty of the introduction of the Latin alphabet in 1928. Despite this, various masters of the art managed to pass on their knowledge to younger enthusiasts, and the Turkish tradition was also kept alive by calligraphers in Egypt and Iraq. Among twentieth-century Arab calligraphers one of the greatest has been Hashim Muhammad al-Baghdadi (1917–73) in Iraq. Calligraphy has also thrived in Iran and among Iranians abroad, as seen in the work of Shams Anwari Alhuseyni (b.1937) and others.

In the nineteenth century, the military colleges in Istanbul included painting in the curriculum as a means of training officers to produce topographic and technical drawings for military purposes, and European values in painting were thus assimilated. Turkish and Egyptian students were sent to Europe to complete their education, some of whom studied painting, including the Turkish military painters, Ahmed Ali (1841–1907) and Suleyman Seyyid (1842–1913), both of whom attended the Ecole des Beaux Arts in Paris. Their work consists largely of oil paintings of landscapes and still-life subjects. The opening of the Academy of Fine Arts in Istanbul in 1883, directed by Osman Hamdi (1842–1910), who had himself studied painting in Paris, marked a turning point in the promotion of western-style painting in Turkey. In his own work Osman Hamdi introduced western-style figurative compositions, adopting a detailed realistic manner for which he employed photographs to attain accuracy. By the early twentieth century a Turkish school of orientalist painting had developed. In Egypt a school of fine arts opened in Cairo in 1908. The first students, who included the painters Muhammad Nagi (1888–1956), Mahmud Said (l897–1964), and Raghib Ayyad (1892–1980) and the sculptor Mahmud Mukhtar (1891–1934), laid the foundations of Egypt's modern art movement. By the mid-twentieth century artists in Turkey and Egypt were deriving inspiration from popular, folk images and Surrealism. An important art movement also developed in Iraq, where at the Institute of Fine Arts in Baghdad painting and sculpture were taught from the 1940s. The most significant figure to emerge in this milieu was the painter and sculptor Jawad Salim (1920–61).

At the Qajar court in Iran artists had been employed in the early nineteenth century to glorify the reign of Fath Ali Shah with numerous portraits of the sovereign, including full-size oil paintings and murals. The foremost court painters were Mirza Baba (fl.c.1785–1830), Mihr Ali (fl.c.1795–1830), and Abd Allah Khan (fl.c.1810–50), while other artists worked in painted enamel or lacquer. In

Abul-Hasan Ghaffari

Abul-Hasan Ghaffari (c.1814-66) was an Iranian court painter active in Teheran. Born into a family of painters from Kashan, he was by 1829 a pupil of the painter Mihr Ali. In 1842 Muhammad Shah (r.1834-48) appointed him court painter, and from 1846 to 1850 he studied in Italy where he became acquainted with European painting. On his return to Iran, he was appointed *naqqash-bashi* (painter laureate), and supervised the illustration of a six-volume Persian translation of the *Thousand and One Nights*. For this monumental task, which was completed by 1855, he led a team of thirty-four painters, and executed some of the finest miniatures himself. Pages of text and pages of miniature paintings alternate in this manuscript, which numbers a total of 1134 pages of paintings, each containing from two to six miniatures. In 1856 he led his team on another project, a set of seven large oil panels for the Nizamiyya Palace in

Teheran of Nasir al-Din enthroned in state and surrounded by his sons, courtiers, and foreign ambassadors. Each figure is a life-like portrait; Abul-Hasan concentrated most of his attention on the faces. In 1861 he received the title Sani al-Mulk ('The Painter of the Kingdom'). His major achievement was the development of a psychological realism in Iranian portraiture. His nephew, Muhammad Ghaffari (1848-1940), known as Kamal al-Mulk ('The Perfection of the Kingdom'), was the central figure in Iranian painting in the late nineteenth and early twentieth century.

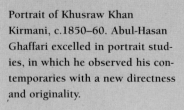

Portrait of Khusraw Khan Kirmani, c.1850–60. Abul-Hasan Ghaffari excelled in portrait studies, in which he observed his contemporaries with a new directness and originality.

The Algerian artist Rachid Koraïchi (b.1947) is an influential figure in the mod-ern calligraphic school of Islamic painting and graphics, exploring the potential of abstract calligraphic composi-tions to great effect, often with a minimal use of colour. Since 1970 he has exhibited his work in Europe, Japan, South America, and the United States as well as in Islamic lands.

the mid-nineteenth century Abul-Hasan Ghaffari (c.1814–66), who had studied in Europe, introduced a new style of psychological realism. From the 1850s paint-ing was taught at the Dar al-Funun college in Teheran. Late nineteenth-century Qajar painting is represented by the work of Mahmud Khan (1813–93), who was the Qajar poet laureate, and Muhammad Ghaffari (1848–1940), who was appointed court painter. Towards the end of the century he studied in Paris, where he perfected the use of perspective and light and shade. In 1911 he opened his own art school in Teheran, which he directed until 1928. This promoted west-ern-style academic painting in Iran, and when the College of Fine Arts opened at Teheran University in 1938 several of Muhammad Ghaffari's pupils occupied key positions. His own mature style was completely Europeanized. After the Second World War a greater number of Iranian painters studied in the West, and by the 1950s a modernist movement had developed, an important advocate being the painter Jalil Ziapur (b.1928).

Throughout the nineteenth and twentieth centuries craft skills in the Muslim lands have been challenged by imports of machine-made western goods. In many instances craft skills have declined, as they had in the West with industrialization, or they have been channelled into revivalist work, often for the European market. In Cairo and Damascus, for example, inlaid metalwork and other items in the style of the Mamluks were produced in the late nineteenth and early twentieth century, while in Iran lacquerwork and ceramics were manufactured that referred to the Safawid period or earlier. A revivalist trend also emerged in Iranian painting associated with the artist Husayn Bihzad (1894–1968). Such work, whatever the outlook of the artist who produced it, tended to reinforce in the political sphere the idea that there were regional schools in Islamic art that approximated to modern national boundaries. In a similar fashion such art movements as the Saqqakhana school in Iran during the 1960s, in which artists combined motifs from Shiite iconography and folklore with western techniques, have been susceptible to this interpretation. In the late twentieth century, however, this outlook began to be countered by such trends as the rise of calligraphic painting, expressive of the pan-Islamic heritage. The dialogue between regional schools and a distinct language for Islamic art as a whole seems set to continue.

Conclusion

The history of Islamic civilization is one of notable human endeavour; we have been concerned to illustrate the achievement. Within a century of Muhammad's death Muslims held sway over the most widespread empire the world had yet seen. At its heart in West Asia they drew on a Hellenic, Iranian, and Semitic heritage to create the rich and sophisticated world of the Arab caliphate. The high culture of this civilization was carried to Spain, north and west Africa, to Central, South, and Southeast Asia; mingling with indigenous traditions it resulted in distinctive regional forms. In the sixteenth and seventeenth centuries three of these forms reached remarkable peaks in the Ottoman, Safawid, and Mughal empires. Over a millennium, ideas, people, commodities, and skills were distributed widely through the Muslim world, from the Atlantic to the Pacific, as traders sought goods and markets; scholars, knowledge and jobs; and those with skills, opportunity and patronage. But equally, Muslims interacted with the world beyond the borders of their civilization. They made use of key inventions such as paper and gunpowder from China, in turn transmitting to the West much philosophical and scientific knowledge.

It is important to understand the duration and extent of Muslim success in world affairs to be able to appreciate Muslims' sense of loss, as European power enveloped almost all their lands between 1800 and 1920, and as they came to reflect on the glory that was past. Their worldly success had served to bear out the Quranic statement that they were the best community raised up for humankind. Their failure meant blows to faith and confidence which hampered their response to the western challenge. The withdrawal of formal European power, moreover, brought little respite. In some places – in Egypt or Iran – it was replaced by the influence of the USA and the USSR, as these great powers sought to build their Cold War alliances. But, more important, the worldwide processes, which had disrupted urban and rural life as they had existed through much of Islamic history, continued apace. The growth of the international economy eroded old forms of production in town and countryside and the societies which rested upon them; the growth of the modern state brought a much more intense relationship between government and people, in which little place could be found for the autonomy of urban communities and nomadic tribes; the internationalization of culture and communication meant not only that public space was threatened more and more by western influences but also what came to be seen as that holy of holies, the private world of the home. During the second half of the twentieth century the threat to Muslim civilization from outside began to seem more intense and more dire than ever before.

Islamic history, however, is not simply about material progress, or lack of it, it is also about one of the main routes down which humankind has travelled in seeking answers to the challenges of being human. Through the guidance of the Quran and the life of the Prophet, mediated by a host of learned and holy persons, Muslims have sought to live moral lives, urging what is right and forbidding what is wrong. Through such guidance they have built human communities in which men and women have striven to live together well and to sustain a workable balance between the public good and the individual ego. Through such guidance, too, they have sought to understand the signs of God, to know Him better, realizing all the while that they would never ultimately comprehend Him; 'if one could comprehend God', as the mystic Rumi said, 'then that would not be God.' Many of the illustrations in this book are tributes to this search, from the sacred space of the mosque in which Muslims come together to submit to God, to the saint's shrine where they come to approach God, to the works of art created in the name of God. Given the achievement of Islam in bringing meaning to human lives, and that of Muslims in shaping human history, there are several issues in the contemporary Muslim condition that demand consideration.

RELIGIOUS REVIVAL

A powerful movement of religious renewal has animated all parts of the Muslim world since the eighteenth century. It has been expressed differently in different social and political contexts, from the holy wars of west Africa, Arabia, and Central Asia to the educational movements of north Africa, India, and Indonesia. Usually it has involved attacks on local Islamic cults, a host of superstitious customs, and all ideas that give saints undue power to intercede for humankind with God; it has required that Muslims follow the precise guidance of the sharia as known in the Quran and the hadiths. This movement has been carried forward by learned and holy leaders who sought to reach out to Muslims at large by preaching, by fostering literacy, by adopting print, and by translating the Quran and other forms of guidance into languages the people could understand. Millions of Muslims, as Richard Bulliet points out, have been caught up in movements referred to variously as *islah* (reform), *tajdid* (renewal), *dawa* (call), or *jihad* (struggle). We have already noted that one such movement, the Tablighi Jamaat of South Asia, is thought to be the most widely followed in the Muslim world today..

The impact of this drive to know the requirements of Islam better and to realize them more fully contributed to the formation of states, as with the Mahdiyya in the Sudan, the Sanusiyya in Libya, or the Wahhabi movement in Saudi Arabia; it also helped Muslims develop strategies for coping with colonial rule, as in the Deoband movement of India or the Muhammadiyya of Indonesia. Moreover, by leading Muslims away from local cults and local identities towards a shared set of Islamic principles, it played a part in fashioning a Muslim identity. In many cases, Islamic renewal enabled Muslims to contribute to modern mass political formations – nationalist movements, nation-states, and Islamist opposition parties and groups. Equally, by making the creation of an Islamic society more a matter of personal effort and individual responsibility than the observance of popular customs and communal rites, it helped to prepare Muslims for the egalitarian nature and disciplined requirements of modern industrial and urban society.

The desire to effect Islamic renewal has not been limited to the missionary campaigns waged by ulama and their associates against local cults: it has also been expressed by those who have interacted powerfully with the West and been much formed by it. The Muslim modernists, such as Muhammad Abduh, Sayyid Ahmad Khan, and Muhammad Iqbal, aimed to build bridges between Islam and western knowledge, and eventually between Islam and the modern nation-state. The modernists have had limited success in capturing Muslim imaginations. Their political successors, as leaders of Muslim nation-states, have tended to reduce the role of Islam in public life, sometimes confining it to no more than a symbolic position. Such policies, moreover, have been combined with economic and social programmes that have in a good number of cases failed to meet the material aspirations of their peoples. Given the low levels of education in many Muslim societies, modernism was never likely to have broad popular appeal, but the problems experienced by secular leaders in meeting material aspirations have diminished its attractions as a way forward for Muslims.

Since the 1970s the desire to effect renewal has been more powerfully expressed in the Islamist movements. Often led by western-educated professionals and run by university students, these movements have aimed to fill the

Shaykh Abbassi Madani, the leader of Algeria's Islamist party, the Islamic Salvation Front (F.I.S.), voting in municipal elections in June 1990. In these elections F.I.S. won 55 per cent of the vote and gained control of 800 local government offices. When in the 1991 general elections. F.I.S. won 188 of the 228 seats contested, the army declared a state of emergency and stopped the second round of voting in order to prevent F.I.S. taking power.

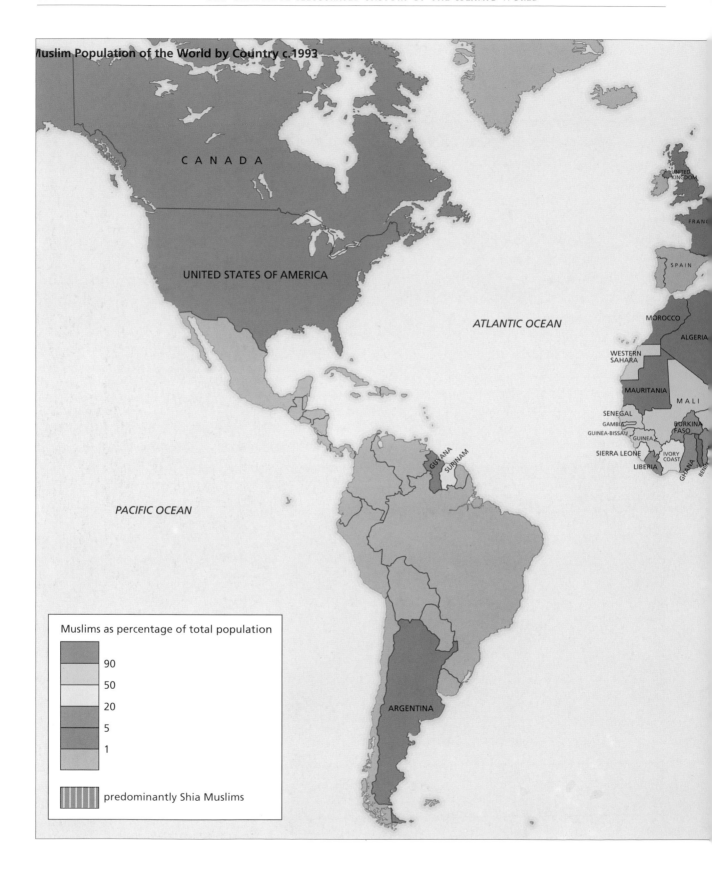

Muslim Population of the World by Country c.1993

CANADA

UNITED STATES OF AMERICA

ATLANTIC OCEAN

PACIFIC OCEAN

UNITED KINGDOM

FRANCE

SPAIN

MOROCCO

ALGERIA

WESTERN SAHARA

MAURITANIA

MALI

SENEGAL

GAMBIA

GUINEA-BISSAU

GUINEA

BURKINA FASO

SIERRA LEONE

IVORY COAST

LIBERIA

GHANA

BENIN

GUYANA

SURINAM

ARGENTINA

Muslims as percentage of total population

90

50

20

5

1

predominantly Shia Muslims

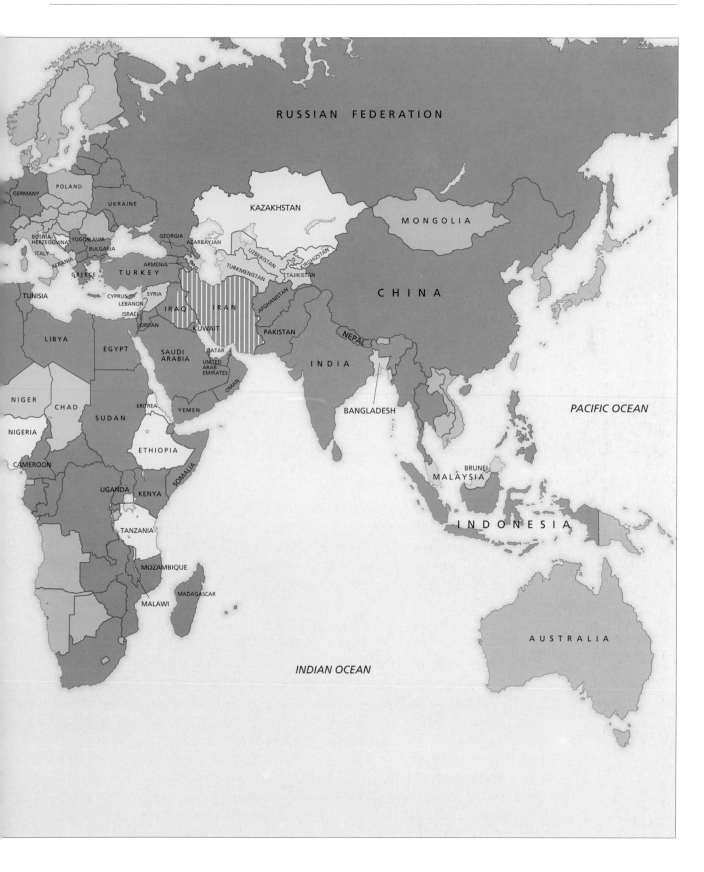

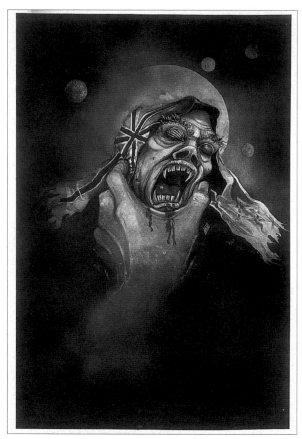

This poster issued by the Iranian Ministry of Islamic Guidance in 1985 illustrates Iran's enemies and their fate. The demonic head of imperialism, draped in the flags of Britain and Israel and seeing with the eyes of the USA and the USSR, is being crushed by the strong hand of Islam.

vacuum created by the failures of the state at the local level in cities and towns through much of the Muslim world. By providing schools, clinics, welfare, and psychological support, they have served the needs of urban communities disrupted by the penetration of the modern state and the international economy. They have also attracted the millions who have flocked to the cities in recent decades from the countryside. The rhetoric of these movements is profoundly opposed to western culture and western power. Their programmes, which start from the premise that the Quran and the holy law are sufficient for all human circumstances, aim to establish an Islamic system to match those of capitalism or socialism. They are to be implemented by seizing power in the modern nation-state. This understanding of Islam as a system, an ideology, is new in Islamic history. So too, although it was part of the classical ideal, is the complete merger between religion and political power.

Islamist movements have transformed the politics of Muslim societies. Everywhere they have brought Islam closer to the centre of the political identity of Muslim peoples. In some places, such as Iran or the Sudan, they have taken power. In others, such as Algeria, Egypt, or Turkey, they are poised in the mid-1990s to make a serious bid for power. In yet others, such as Malaysia or the former Yugoslavia, their very presence may disturb a delicate ethnic balance. Each political struggle has its own cast of players, its particular pattern, but a common theme of many is that Islamism offers a language, as well as organizational structures, through which relatively disadvantaged urban groups can negotiate their place in the modern economy and state.

Amidst the various expressions of Islamic renewal of recent centuries two distinct processes of long-term religious change are evident. One is a move away from other-worldly religion towards this-worldly religion. Reformists, modernists, and Islamists all attack aspects of sufism. In particular they have attacked ideas of intercession for humankind with God, emphasizing instead the need for Muslims to act on earth, here and now, to ensure the establishment of an Islamic society. In consequence the past 200 years have seen a decline in spiritual piety focused on the sufi shaykhs and the saints' shrines and the growth in its place of an ethical Islam centred on study groups, voluntary associations, sports clubs, business organizations, paramilitary groups, and political parties.

The second and associated process is a change in the way in which Muslim society is understood. Traditionally it has been seen to be composed of separate individuals who have fashioned their personalities through lives of submission to

God and service to His word. This understanding of society as made up of faithful individuals was exemplified in the classical Muslim view of history as collective biography – the record of individuals who sustained in their time and transmitted to future generations the skills and knowledge that made Muslim societies. The Islamists, however, tend to view society as a system, or indeed a machine. Thus for the Islamist thinker Mawdudi, God was the great engineer in his workshop:

> It is His explicit Will that the universe – this grand workshop with its multi-farious activities – should go on functioning smoothly and graciously so that man – the prize of creation – should make the best and most productive use of all his powers and resources, of everything that has been harnessed for him in the earth and in the high heavens ... The shariah is meant to guide the steps of man in this respect.

It is important to ask to what extent the great religious movements of the past two centuries, and the elements of religious change which they embrace, point to processes of secularization. Clearly, the move away from sufi ideas of intercession for humankind with God represents a 'disenchantment' of the world, a decline in belief in magic, and increasing confidence both in scientific explanations of human circumstances and in human capacity to control them. It is arguable, too, that the emphasis amongst reformists in particular, but amongst the other movements as well, on personal responsibility for making an Islamic society represents a Muslim form of Protestant ethic. Furthermore, modernism as it came to support secular national identities – Turkish or Arab nationalism with little or no space for an Islamic identity – led to the privatization of religion. Belief became a purely personal matter; many educated Muslims became Muslims only by culture. At first sight it would seem that Islamism might be tending in the opposite direction. However, by absorbing the whole political world within the religious sphere, the Islamists may provoke a stricter confinement of religion to the private sphere than before and a more firmly established secular public arena. If Islamism were to fail politically, as did Communism in eastern Europe, it might well lead to the discrediting of Islamist ideas.

ISLAM AND THE WEST

The Islamic resurgence in the politics of Muslim states has given rise to fears about the threat which it is supposed to represent to the security of the West and the safety of western peoples. Such fears, at first glance, are not unreasonable. Many have been shocked by the rhetoric of the Iranian revolution, the casting of the USA as the 'Great Satan', and the apparently mass popular hostility to the West. Few westerners can have gained comfort from the ideology of the Muslim Brotherhood as developed in the hands of Sayyid Qutb: all those who do not form part of a culture based on the fundamentals of the Islamic world view are castigated as part of a *jahili* (ignorant) culture against which it is the duty of righteous Muslims to struggle 'until all religion belongs to God'. Confidence has not been increased by the savagery of the assaults on those in Muslim societies whose world view inclined towards the West, the gunning down of Egypt's President Sadat in 1981 or the slitting of the throats of Algerian newspaper editors, government servants, and young women since 1991 (notwithstanding the no less vicious oppression of the Algerian military regime). Real fears are raised by the fatwa seeking the death of the English author Salman Rushdie, and the attempted day of devastation which was allegedly planned for New York in 1993 by the blind Egyptian Shaykh Umar Abd al-Rahman and his followers in Islamic Jihad. Nor are the fears laid to rest when westerners hear of the nuclear ambitions of states such as Iran and Pakistan. We are bound to ask if the relationship between Islam and the West, which on both sides in the past has had its periods of holy war, might not be moving towards a new phase of militant hostility. Indeed, an eminent US political scientist, Samuel Huntington, suggested in a notorious article in *Foreign Affairs* (1993) that the era of nation-states has come to an end and is to be replaced by a clash of civilizations: in such a clash the Confucian and the Islamic worlds are the competitors with the West, but the latter is the only remaining ideological competitor.

Such fears are greatly exaggerated. The Islamists are striving to win power in their own states; for all their rhetoric their battle is more with their fellow citizens than with the outsider. Their enemies are the rulers of their states – the westernized elites and international business classes of Cairo and Istanbul, the royal family of Saudi Arabia, the emirs of the Gulf and their supporters. At the international level their enemy is the state of Israel, which has for so long obstructed the attempts of a Palestinian state to struggle into existence and which, as a stake of western provenance driven into the Islamic heartland, seems to symbolize the problems of Muslims worldwide. If the Islamists attack the West, which includes the Soviet Union and its Russian successor, it is because western political and economic power is seen to be the source of the crisis of Islam. It is the West which usually supports the regimes they wish to overthrow, and it is the West, the USA in particular, which is seen to be the prime reason for the existence and what is felt as the intransigence of Israel. Of course, in an era of increasingly interconnected communities, it is possible that the struggle for power in Muslim societies will affect the West, as that in Europe for much of the nineteenth and twentieth centuries spilled over into the Muslim world. The key struggle, however, is internal, not between Islam and the West. In this light, a western fear of Muslim states acquiring nuclear weapons should rest less on the fact that they are Muslim than on the more general fact of the spread of nuclear danger. Iran and Pakistan in this respect are no different from North Korea and India.

The essentially state-based quality of the Islamist movement is emphasized by the nature of its supra-state organizations and by a tendency to put the needs of the local political context before ideology in decision-making. With the exception of the Muslim Brotherhood, as Olivier Roy states, all attempts at international

Islamist union (the World Muslim League of Jidda, the Bureau of Islamic propaganda of Qum, and the Arab-Islamic People's Conference of Khartoum) have derived from the policies of individual states aimed at rivals in the Muslim world. Different branches of the Muslim Brotherhood have had to respect the constraints of local political conditions, entering the political process in Jordan and Kuwait, opposing peacefully in Egypt but with arms in Syria and Libya. The responses of different branches of the Brotherhood to alliances between the conservative states of the Gulf, Saudi Arabia, and Egypt with the West against Saddam Husayn's Iraq in the Gulf War only emphasize this point. The Islamists in Sudan, Tunisia, and Jordan all supported Iraq; the Brotherhood in Egypt and the Islamic Salvation Front in Algeria tried to sit on the fence until popular demand forced them into the Iraqi camp; Hamas, paid for by Saudi Arabia and opposed to the Palestine Liberation Organization, supported the Allies, as did the Muslim Brotherhood organizations in states throughout the Gulf. The extent of the non-ideological approach which both Islamists and the West adopted is demonstrated by the USA's support for Islamist groups throughout the 1980s as it strove to contain both Soviet expansion in Afghanistan and Iran's attempts to export its revolution.

In struggling for power within their nation-states, Islamist groups have been forced to respect the disciplines of politics, and are still so constrained once they gain power. These constraints, moreover, operate not just in internal but also in international affairs. The experience of Iran since the revolution of 1979 illuminates the point. The rival interests of its neighbouring states of Iraq and Saudi Arabia limited the possibilities of revolutionary expansion to the west as did the Cold War struggle for influence in Afghanistan to the east. The revolutionary regime also remained a member of almost all the diplomatic, social, and economic organizations (OPEC, UNCTAD, and so on) which the Shah's regime had previously

This cartoon for the London-based Iranian satirical magazine, *Asghar Agha*, December 1990, mocks the conservative Arab states of the Gulf and Saudi Arabia for looking to the USA for help in their time of need rather than God.

Although conservative Arab governments sided with the West in the Gulf War, Saddam Husayn had much popular support in the Arab world. Here in October 1990 Algerians demonstrate in support of the Iraqi dictator. Demonstrations such as these forced the Islamic Salvation Front to come out in support of a regime which was strongly opposed to their interests.

joined. In the economy, after a decade of revolutionary policies of nationalization and expanded social welfare, the country embarked on policies of liberalization from state control – handing back business and industry to the private sector, raising the limit on foreign capital invested in Iranian enterprises from 35 per cent (set by the Shah's regime) to 49 per cent, and revitalizing the Teheran stock market. Apart from the removal of the USA from the scene, the overall patterns of Iran's foreign trade have not significantly changed; 40 per cent of all trade in the 1980s, for instance, continued to be with the European Community. In politics the need to pass essential legislation led to Ayatollah Khomeini revising his interpretation of Islamic government. In a letter to President Khamenei of 6 January 1988, which represents a major turning point in the history of the Islamic republic, he insisted on a new interpretation which resulted in the will of Parliament in legislation prevailing over that of the Islamic jurist. Power had shifted in the direction of the elected representatives of the people.

That Islamist regimes when they come to power are subject to the disciplines of politics and economics does not mean that they will not be a source of irritation to other societies; the tensions of their internal political struggles may well be reflected by movements of refugees or campaigns directed against particular foreign powers or people. This said, there is notable irony in the success they have had and may have in future. They claim to be restoring an ideal Islam of the past, but in fact their utopian vision has little precedent in Islamic history. They speak with profoundly anti-western tongues yet their ideas are no less profoundly influenced by the West; Sartre, Fanon, and Massignon influenced the Iranian revolutionary thinker Ali Shariati; we could equally point to the influence of the French

Fascist thinker Alexis Carrel on Sayyid Qutb, or even the lingering influence of Plato, studied in madrasas for over 1,000 years, on Khomeini's theory of Islamic government, in which the Islamic jurist is but a philosopher king by another name. Islamists seek to restore the glory of Islam but they reject much of the achievement of its civilization as set out in this book, whether it be in music, philosophy, poetry, the visual arts, or spiritual insight.

WOMEN AND THE SOCIAL TRANSFORMATION OF MUSLIM SOCIETIES

Over the past two centuries of Islamic renewal and western power, the issue of the proper place and conduct of Muslim women, one tenth of humankind, has been hard-fought territory. Classically the denizens of the very private world of home and family, women found themselves in the front line of the struggle to control the social transformation of Muslim societies, in which Muslims, their public world invaded by western power and culture, have endeavoured to preserve a private Islamic space; in which Muslim elites, eager to build up state power, have striven to increase the influence of government in society and to reduce loyalties to local kin, tribe, and community; and in which Islamists, keen to seize state power from secular elites, have carried forward their campaigns against the corrupting presence of western values and culture. The attitudes adopted on the issue of women, for instance, whether they should be encouraged to go uncovered or uncovered in public, have tended to depend on the social position of the espousers no less than the outcome of the debate has been subject to the play of power. If the elites of Ataturk's Turkey mocked women veiled in black as 'beetles', the Islamist opposition of the Shah's Iran mocked the unveiled as 'painted dolls'. Amidst this cross-fire of insult women themselves have become increasingly significant social actors in the public sphere.

From the nineteenth century the influence of reformism mingled with the context of western power to bring about a transformation in the position of urban women. Before then, the household, as compared with the public realm where the sharia ruled, had been regarded as the place of the weak, of slaves, of boys, and of women. Here local dialects as opposed to 'Islamic' languages might still be spoken. Here many pagan customs might be followed and magical beliefs upheld. Here most of all lay the sexual attractions which might challenge a man's devotion to God. Urban women in the reformist world, however, came to be seen less as erotic distractions from the good Muslim life than the sustainers of that life itself. Thus, in one of the classics of reformist literature in India, the *Bihishti Zewar* (Jewels of Paradise) of Mawlana Ashraf Ali Thanawi (1864–1943), women were expected to have all the Islamic knowledge that would enable them to uphold an Islamic rule for themselves and their households. Thus Thanawi made women equally responsible with their men for sustaining Islamic society. The Islamist Mawdudi was to go further and make them bear the greater part of the responsibility. 'The *harem*', he wrote in the 1930s, 'is the strongest fortress of the Islamic civilization, which was built for the reason that, if it ever suffered a reverse, it may then take refuge in it.'

For Muslim modernists and secular elites concerned to build Muslim nation-states, the unveiling of women in the public sphere has been a symbol both of progress and of the state's capacity to impose its national ideology over religious forces within. In Turkey, for instance, the Young Turk revolution of 1908 saw the establishment of what one woman visitor described as a 'Turkish Feminist Government'. The ideology of Turkism spoke of a pan-Islamic golden age for women, while the impact of war from 1912 onwards brought women into the workforce in unprecedented numbers. Ataturk continued where the Young Turks left off, attacking the veil in the 1920s and enfranchising women in 1934. In 1937 eighteen women were elected to the National Assembly making up 4.5 per cent of the total. Ataturk's nation-building project required women to have full citizenship of the modern state while Islam was relegated to the private sphere. For similar reasons, on 8 January 1936 Riza Shah of Iran ordered women to abandon their veils and join the state bureaucracy. In the 1960s and 1970s his son made substantial attempts to win women's loyalty to the state, or rather his person, by giving them the vote, by permitting them to stand for high offices of state, and by passing much legislation in their favour. Needless to say, the project of modernization and the building of state power have always been more important than women's issues themselves.

The extent to which the position of women is subject to the play of political forces is well illustrated by recent events in Pakistan and India. In the former, where Islam is integral to nationhood, General Zia ul-Haq, keen to entrench his power, announced the introduction of an Islamic system from 1979. He made women the focal point of his Islamization programme; they were subject to a series of discriminatory laws. Women were to pay the price of his bid to bring new ideological strength to the Pakistani state. That the country has had a woman prime minister in Benazir Bhutto since then has made little difference; the political pressures which led to the legislation remain strong. In India, whose community of over 100 million Muslims form about one-eighth of the population, their ability to live under Muslim personal law rather than a common Indian Civil Code has become a symbol of their ability to sustain their identity. In the mid-1980s the issue came to a head when Shah Bano, a divorced Muslim women, tried to escape destitution, which was her position under Muslim personal law, by pressing for her maintenance rights under the Indian Criminal Procedure Code. The issue brought Muslim women to the forefront of the debate over the future of the Muslim community, indeed of India itself. Muslim religious leaders moved to protect the integrity of Muslim personal law; leaders of the Hindu right wing used the issue to attack the secular basis of the Indian state, which allowed minorities special privileges but not the majority Hindus. There followed an

In the early 1990s over 300 million Muslims were ruled by women – Khaleda Zia of Bangladesh, Benazir Bhutto of Pakistan, and Tansu Ciller of Turkey. Here Bhutto and Ciller present themselves to the crowd outside the Bosnian Presidency building in February 1994. They had braved the dangers of visiting Sarajevo, which was at that time being shelled by besieging Serb forces, in order to draw attention to Bosnia's plight.

intensification of India's communal politics. In this process, which has seen the Hindu right wing achieve power as never before, Muslim women have been made to bear the burden of being key markers of Muslim identity both for Muslim men and for the Hindus.

The rise of Islamism has brought extra pressures to bear on women. If, in the mid-twentieth century, at the height of the era of secular nation-building, it was the veiled woman who seemed marginal in most Muslim cities, now it is the woman without a veil. This change, like Islamism itself, has been interpreted as a return to tradition as well as a protest against the West. Recent study of Egyptian women who have adopted the veil – which, as Musallam has pointed out, may not necessarily be a veil itself but a form of dress which meets Islamic standards of propriety – reveals that something more is taking place than an affirmation of cultural authenticity. The dress being adopted is different from traditional dress. Those who don it are usually children of first-generation immigrants to the city. They are characterized by educational achievement. They are upwardly mobile and aim to take their place in the vanguard of their society. Islamic dress enables these women to move in public with reasonable ease and to interact with men without being dubbed immoral because it establishes their Islamic credent-ials. The dress enables them to act legitimately in public space. Analysis of the views of these women suggests that they are by no means conservative; most want education, jobs, and political rights, and divide only on the issue of equality in marriage. The reappearance of large numbers of veiled women in the streets of Muslim cities represents less a return to tradition, or an affirmation of cultural authenticity, than, as Leila Ahmed has put it, 'a uniform of arrival, signalling entrance into, and determination to move forward in, modernity.'

Opposite The rapid development of electronic means of contact and the globalization of media systems suggest that Muslims interact much more intensely with non-Muslim cultural influences than before. The satellite discs decorating the skyline of an Indonesian town, with the roofs of its mosque and temple, illustrate the process.

A woman student at Gadjah Mada university, Jakarta, Indonesia, parks her moped. The wearing of Islamic dress, such as the student wears, may represent an element of liberation. It enables this woman to move freely in the university environment.

Unfortunately, not all male Islamists share this view. As it turns out, veiled women in negotiating their own paths forward may well be supporting movements which are determined that these paths go nowhere. The Iranian revolution led immediately to the annulment of un-Islamic legislation, the banning of women from the judiciary, their segregation from men in public and enforced veiling on penalty of seventy-four lashes. The Islamic Salvation Front in Algeria, operating in a context of massive unemployment, opposes women's right to work, aims to limit their right to vote, and makes them unwelcome at the Front's political demonstrations. It proposes to close off the avenues opened up by Islamism elsewhere. In the long run, however, as we have argued above, Islamist regimes have to respect the disciplines of politics and economics. In Iran this happened quickly. The war with Iraq, and the huge loss of men involved, offered many roles for women in military support activities as well as in government offices. Dress codes remain vigorously enforced but now they are more to enable the participation of women in public life. Similarly, Islamist regimes, as they fight for economic progress, will find that they too cannot ignore the economic energy represented by half their population. The upshot will be that Muslim societies will not be able to avoid the most profound social revolution of recent centuries – the re-ordering of male-female relations. Arguably, it is the greatest challenge they face today.

GLOBALIZATION AND THE MUSLIM WORLD

The contemporary Muslim world, from the shape of its map to the shape of its ideas, is to a large extent the outcome of its painful interaction with the West. Western power left it a world of nation-states; western influence helped to fashion the elites which rule these states. Moreover, few in these societies from traditional scholars in the towns to peasants in the fields remain untouched by one aspect or another of western civilization. This world is one of many voices: different national voices, different voices within nations, different voices within movements. Muslims are no more likely than westerners to speak and act as one. This said, there are expressions of feeling widely shared. The large-scale celebrations of great religious rites each year, for instance the fasting in Ramadan or the pilgrimage to Mecca, remain at the religious level remarkable affirmations of Muslim unity. There subsists, moreover, a lingering resentment at what are regarded as the double standards of the West. It is prepared to intervene on the side of 'justice' when its interests are challenged in the Gulf but either has done so only in a limited and tardy fashion or not at all when those interests are not seen to be involved, as in the Muslim causes of Palestine, Bosnia, Chechnya, or Kashmir. There is a widespread feeling that Muslims are not given the respect they deserve.

In future the Muslim world is likely to be even more powerfully engaged with outside forces and more fully shaped by its interaction with them. The contemporary Muslim community forms a world community whose diaspora is in constant contact with its heartland. New electronic means of contact, telephones, fax machines, satellite television, the internet, make possible the exchange of ideas and culture with unprecedented speed and intensity. This exchange, moreover, is unlikely to be halted for long by the rising influence of Islamist movements; that is checked by the sharia, as Musallam has shown, at the threshhold to the Muslim home. Islamists can drive alien influences out of public space, but their ability to prevent them from affecting domestic space is limited.

History demonstrates the capacity of Muslims to contribute to many cultures in creating a remarkable human achievement. In doing so they have stored up riches not just for themselves but for all humankind. A constant source of inspiration, as this volume has endeavoured to show, has been the Quran, the life of the Prophet, and the moral vision which they offer human beings and their communities. In this vision and in their achievement lie our hopes for the Muslim future.

'Verily we belong to God, and to him do we return.'
(Calligraphy from the Shifaiye Madrasa, Sivas, Turkey, 1278.)

Reference guide to The Cambridge Illustrated History of the *Islamic World*

Rulers of the Islamic World

Glossary

Bibliography

Rulers of the Islamic World

THE CALIPHS

The Orthodox or Rightly guided Caliphs
632   Abu Bakr
634   Umar ibn al-Khattab
644   Uthman ibn Affan
656   Ali ibn Abi Talib

Umayyad Caliphs
661   Muawiya I ibn Abi Sufyan
680   Yazid I
683   Muawiya II
684   Marwan I ibn al-Hakam
685   Abd al-Malik
705   al-Walid I
715   Sulayman
717   Umar ibn Abd al-Aziz
720   Yazid II
724   Hisham
743   al-Walid II
744   Yazid III
744   Ibrahim
750   Marwan II al-Himar

Abbasid Caliphs (in Iraq and Baghdad)
749   al-Saffah
754   al-Mansur
775   al-Mahdi
785   al-Hadi
786   Harun al-Rashid
809   al-Amin
813   al-Mamun
817–19 Ibrahim ibn al-Mahdi, in Baghdad
833   al-Mutasim
842   al-Wathiq
847   al-Mutawakkil
861   al-Muntasir
862   al-Mustain
866   al-Mutazz
869   al-Muhtadi
870   al-Mutamid
892   al-Mutadid
902   al-Muktafi
908   al-Muqtadir
932   al-Qahir
934   al-Radi
940   al-Mutaqqi
944   al-Mustakfi
946   al-Muti
974   al-Tai
991   al-Qadir
1031   al-Qaim
1075   al-Muqtadi
1094   al-Mustazhir
1118   al-Mustarshid
1135   al-Rashid
1136   al-Muqtafi

1160   al-Mustanjid
1170   al-Mustadi
1180   al-Nasir
1225   al-Zahir
1226   al-Mustansir
1242-58   al-Mustasim

Abbasid Caliphs (in Cairo)
1261–1517

SPAIN AND NORTH AFRICA
Spanish Umayyads
756–976

Almoravids (North Africa and Spain)
Early 11th century–1147

Almohads (North Africa and Spain)
Muhammad ibn Tumart (d.1130)–1269

Saadians (Morocco)
1511–1659

Filalis (Morocco)
1631–1927
1927   Muhammad V (first reign)
1953   Muhammad
1955   Muhammad V (second reign)
1962   al-Hasan II

WEST AFRICA
Sokoto Caliphate (Nigeria)
1754–1938 (succession of last caliph)

EGYPT, SYRIA AND IRAQ
Tulunids (Egypt and Syria)
868–905

Ikhshidids (Egypt and Syria)
935–69

Fatimids (North Africa, and then Egypt and Syria)
909–1171

Ayyubids (Egypt)
1169–1252

Mamluks (Egypt and Syria)
1. Bahri line
1250–1389

2. Burji line
1382–1516

Muhammad Ali's Line (Egypt)
1805   Muhammad Ali Pasha
1848   Ibrahim Pasha
1848   Abbas I Pasha
1854   Said Pasha
1863   Ismail (Khedive from 1867)
1879   Tawfiq
1892   Abbas II Hilmi
1914   Husayn Kamil (Sultan)
1917   Ahmad Fuad I (King from 1922)
1936   Faruq
1952–53 Fuad II

Presidents (Egypt)
1953–54 Neguib
1956   Nasser
1970   Sadat
1981   Mubarak

Seljuqs
1. Great Seljuqs (Iraq and Persia)
1038–1194

2. Seljuqs of Syria
1078–1117

3. Seljuqs of Kirman
1041–1186

ANATOLIA AND THE TURKS
Seljuqs of Rum (Anatolia)
1077–1307
Danishmendids (Central and eastern Anatolia)
1. Sivas branch
c.1071–1174

2. Malatya branch
c.1142–1178

Qaramanids (Central Anatolia)
c.1256–1483

Ottomans (Anatolia, the Balkans, the Arab lands)
1281   Uthman (Osman) I ibn Ertoghril
c.1324 Orkhan
1360   Murad I
1389   Bayazid (Bayezit) I Yildirim ('the Lightening-flash')
1402   Timurid invasion
1403   Muhammad (Mehmet) I Chelebi (first in Anatolia only, after 1413 in Rumelia also)
1403   Sulayman I (in Rumelia only till 1410)
1421   Murad II (first reign)
1444   Muhammad II Fatih ('the Conqueror', first reign)
1446   Murad II (second reign)

1451 Muhammad II Fatih (second reign)
1481 Bayazid II
1512 Selim Yavuz ('the Grim')
1520 Sulayman II Qanuni ('the Law-giver', also called in western usage 'the Magnificent')
1566 Selim II
1574 Murad III
1595 Muhammad III
1603 Ahmad I
1617 Mustafa I (first reign)
1618 Uthman II
1622 Mustafa I (second reign)
1623 Murad IV
1640 Ibrahim
1648 Muhammad IV
1687 Sulayman III
1691 Ahmad II
1695 Mustafa II
1703 Ahmad III
1730 Mahmud I
1754 Uthman III
1757 Mustafa III
1774 Abd al-Hamid I
1789 Selim III
1807 Mustafa IV
1808 Mahmud II
1839 Abd al-Majid I
1861 Abd al-Aziz
1876 Murad V
1876 Abd al-Hamid II
1909 Muhammad V Rashad
1918 Muhammd VI Wahid-al-Din
1922–24 Abd al-Majid II (as Caliph only)

Turkey
1923 Mustafa Kemal (Ataturk)
1938 Ismet Inonu
1950 Celal Beyar
1961 General Gursel
1966 Senator Cevdet Sunay
1973 Senator Fahri Koroturk
1980 General Kenan Evren
1989 Turgut Ozal
1993 Suleyman Demirel

MODERN WEST ASIA
Lebanon
1920 French mandate
1926 republic

Presidents
1926 Charles Dabbas
1934 Habib Saad
1936 Emile Edde
1941 independent
1941 Alfred Naccache
1943 al-Khuri
1952 Camille Chamoun
1958 Faud Chehab
1964 Charles Helou
1970 Sulayman Franjiya

1976 Elias Sarkis
1982 Bachir Gemayel
1982–88 Amin Gemayel
1989 Rene Moawwad
1989 Elias Hrawi

Syria
1918 Faysal (son of Amir Husayn, heads autonomous government in Damascus)
1920 French mandate
1941 independent
1943 republic

Presidents
1943 Shukri al-Quwatli
1949 Hashim al-Atassi
1951 General Fawzi Selo
1953–54 General Shishakli
1955 Shukri al-Quwatli
1958 Nasser (United Arab Republic)
1961 Nazim Qudsi
1963 Major General Amin al-Hafiz
1966 Nur al-Din Atasi
1970 Ahmad Khatib
1971 General Assad

Hijaz
Hashimites
1908 Amir Husayn (Sharif of Mecca, takes the title of King from 1916)
1924 Ali
1925 Hijaz conquered by Saudis

Transjordan
1920 British mandate

Hashimites
1921 Amir Abd Allah (takes the title of King from 1946, of Jordan from 1949)
1951 Talal
1952 Husayn

Iraq
1920 British mandate

Hashimites
1921 Faysal I ibn Husayn
1933 Ghazi
1939 Faysal II
1958 republic

Presidents
1958 Major General Najib al-Rubai
1963 Field Marshal Abd al-Salam Muhammad Arif
1966 Lt.-General Abd al-Rahman Muhammad Arif
1968 Major General Ahmad Hassan Bakr
1979 Saddam Husayn al-Takriti

ARABIAN PENINSULA
Yemen
Zaydi Imams
1. Rassid line
9th century–c.1281

2. Qasimid line
c.1592–1962
1962 Republic.

Presidents
1962 Colonel Abd All Sallal
1968 Abd al-Rahman al-Iriani
1974 constitution suspended
1977 Lt-Col Ahmad ibn Husayn
1978 Lt. Col Ali Abd Allah Saleh (of both North Yemen and republic of Yemen from 1990).

Oman and Zanzibar
1. United Sultanate
1741–1856 (Sultanate divided)

2. Zanzibar
1856–1964 (Revolution and incorporation in the Republic of Tanzania)

3. Oman
1856–1932
1932 Said ibn Taymur
1970 Qabus ibn Said

Saudis
1764 Muhammad ibn Saud
1765 Abd al-Aziz
1803 Saud ibn Abd al-Aziz
1814 Abd Allah I ibn Saud
1818–22 Ottoman occupation
1823 Turki
1834 Faysal I (first reign)
1837 Khalid ibn Saud
1841 Abd Allah II (as a vassal of Muhammad Ali of Egypt)
1843 Faysal I (second reign)
1865 Abd Allah III ibn Faysal (first reign)
1871 Saud ibn Faysal
1874 Abd Allah III (second reign)
1887 conquest by Rashidis of Hail, Abd Allah remains as governor of Riyad till 1889
1889 Abd al-Rahman ibn Faysal
1891 Muhammad ibn Faysal (vassal governor)
1902 Abd al-Aziz
1953 Saud
1964 Faysal II
1975 Khalid
1982 Fahd

Iranian World
Buyids
Lines in: Fars and Khuzistan 934–1062
       Kirman 936–1048
       Jibal 932–77
       Iraq 945–1055

Samanids (Khurasan and Transoxania)
819–1005

Saffarids (Sistan)
867–1480

Timurids (Transoxania and Persia)
1. Supreme rulers in Samarqand
1370   Timur (Temür)
1405   Khalil (till 1409)
1405   Shah Rukh (at first in Khurasan only)
1447   Ulugh Beg
1449   Abd al-Latif
1450   Abd Allah Mirza
1451   Abu-Said
1469   Ahmad
1494–1500 Mahmud ibn Abi-Said

2. Rulers in Khurasan after Ulugh Beg's death
1449–1506

3. Rulers in western Iran and Iraq after Timur's death
1404–15

Qara Qoyunlu (Azarbayjan and Iraq)
1380–1468

Aq Qoyunlu (Diyarbakr, eastern Anatolia, Azarbayjan)
1378–1508

IRAN
Safawids
1501   Ismail I
1524   Tahmasp I
1576   Ismail II
1578   Muhammad Khudabanda
1588   Abbas I
1629   Safi I
1642   Abbas II
1666   Sulayman I (Safi II)
1694   Husayn I
1722   Tahmasp II
1732   Abbas III (nominal ruler in certain parts of Persia only)
1749   Sulayman II (nominal ruler in certain parts of Persia only)
1750   Ismail III (nominal ruler in certain parts of Persia only)
1753   Husayn II (nominal ruler in certain parts of Persia only)
1786   Muhammad (nominal ruler in certain parts of Persia only)

Afsharids
1736–95

Zands
1750–94

Qajars
1721–1924

Pahlawis
1925   Riza Shah
1941   Muhammad Riza Shah
1979   Islamic Republic

Presidents
1980   Abol Hassan Bani-Sadr
1981   Hojjatolislam Sayad Ali Khamenei (Leader of the Islamic Revolution from 1989)
1989   Ali Akbar Hoshemi Rafsanjani

Presidents of Azarbayjan
1991   Ayaz Mutalibov
1992   Abulfaz Elchibey
1993   Gaydar Aliev

AFGHANISTAN AND INDIA
Ghaznawids (Khurasan, Afghanistan and northern India)
977–1186

Ghurids
1. Principal line in Ghur and then Ghazna
c. end 10th century–1215

2. Line in Bamiyan and Tukharistan
1145–1215

Delhi Sultans
1. Muizzi or Slave Kings
1206–90

2. Khaljis
1290–1320

3. Tughluqids
1320–1414

4. Sayyads
1414–51

5. Lodis
1451–26

6. Suris
1540–55

Mughal Emperors
1526   Zahir al-Din Babur
1530   Nasir al-Din Humayun (first reign)
1540–55 Suri sultans of Delhi
1555   Nasir al-Din Humayun (second reign)
1556   Jalal al-Din Akbar I
1605   Nur al-Din Jahangir
1627   Dawar Baksh
1628   Shihab al-Din Shah Jahan I
1657   Murad Bakhsh (in Gujarat)
1657   Shah Shuja (in Bengal till 1660)

1658   Muhi al-Din Awrangzeb Alamgir I
1707   (line continues to 1858)
1858   under British crown
1947   dominion

Governors-general
1947   Earl Mountbatten of Burma
1948   Chakravarti Rajagopalachari
1950   republic

Presidents
1950   Rajendra Prasad
1962   Sarvepalli Radhakrishnan
1967   Zakir Husayn
1969   Varanagri Venkata Giri
1974   Fakhruddin Ali Ahmed
1977   Neelam Sanjiva Reddy
1982   Giani Zail Singh
1987   Venkataraman
1992   Shankar Dayal Sharma

Pakistan
Governors-general
1947   Muhammad Ali Jinnah
1948   Khwaja Nazimuddin
1951   Ghulam Muhammad
1955   Major General Iskander Mirza
1956   Islamic republic

Presidents
1956   Major General Iskander Mirza
1958   Field Marshal Ayub Khan
1969   Major General Yahya Khan
1971   Zulfiqar Ali Bhutto
1973   Fazl Elahi Chaudhry
1978   General Zia ul-Haq
1988   Ghulam Ishaq Khan

Bangladesh
1971   republic

Presidents
1971   Shaykh Mujibur Rahman
1972   Abu Sayeed Chowdhury
1973   Mohammadullah
1975   Shaykh Mujibur Rahman
1975   Mushtaq Ahmad
1975   Abusadat Muhammad Sayem
1977   Major General Ziaur Rahman
1981   Abdus Sattar
1982   Abul Chowdhury
1983   General Muhammad Hossain Ershad
1990   Shahabuddin Ahmad (Acting President)
1991   Abdur Rahman Biswas

Afghanistan
Durranis
1747–1842
Barakzais
1819–1973

Presidents
1973 Sardar Muhammad Daud
1978 Nur Muhammad Taraqqi
1979 Hafiz Allah Amin
1979 Babrak Karmal
1986 Muhammad Chamkari (Acting President of Revolutionary Council)
1987 Sayyid Muhammad Najibullah
1992 Burhanuddin Rabbani

CENTRAL ASIA
Mongol Great Khans (Mongolia and northern China)
1206 Chingiz Khan
1227–1370

Chaghatayids (Transoxania, Semirechye and eastern Turkey)
1227–1363

Ilkhanids (Persia)
1256–1353

Shaybanids (Samarqand)
1500–99

Janids (Bukhara)
1599–1785

Mangits
1785–1868

President of Uzbekistan
1991 Islam Karimov

President of Turkmenistan
1991 Sapermurad Niyazov

Presidents of Tajikistan
1991 Rakhman Nabiev

1992 Imamali Rakhmanov

President of Kirghistan
1991 Asker Akaev

President of Kazakhstan
1991 Nursultan Nazarbaev

Indonesia
Sultanates
Mataram 1575–1748 (accession of last sultan)
Surakarta 1788–1944 (accession of last sultan)
Jojakarta 1755–1939 (accession of last sultan)
Atjeh 1496–1874 (accession of last sultan)

Presidents
1950 Muhammad Ahmad Sukarno
1966 Presidium
1968 General Suharto

Glossary

amin trustworthy; title for the holder of an official position such as the head of a guild.

amir title of a military commander or prince, commonly transliterated 'emir'.

caliph see **khalifa**.

dhikr recollection of God, a spiritual exercise to render God's presence throughout one's being.

emir see **amir**.

fatwa opinion on a point of Islamic law given by a **mufti**.

ghazi a frontier warrior for the faith.

hadith a report of the sayings or doings of the Prophet transmitted by his companions.

hajj the annual pilgrimage to Mecca which every Muslim should make at least once in a lifetime.

Hanafi one of the four **Sunni** schools of law founded by Abu Hanafi (d.767).

Hanbali one of the four **Sunni** schools of law founded by Ahmad ibn Hanbal (d.855).

hijra the flight of the Prophet and his followers from Mecca to Medina and the point from which the Islamic calendar begins.

hisba the primary duty of every Muslim to 'promote what is right and to prevent what is wrong'.

ijaza a certificate given by a teacher to a pupil granting permission to transmit a text.

imam the supreme leader of the Muslim community; the successor to the Prophet, used commonly by the **Shia** for Ali and his descendants.

ilmiye the **ulama**, those learned in Islam under the Ottoman empire.

Ismailis a branch of the **Shia** who look to the leadership of Ismail, a son of Imam Jafar and his descendants; this branch includes the Fatimids; it later divided again; a significant surviving branch is the Nizariyya, the followers of the Aga Khan.

jami mosque for Friday prayers.

jihad struggle, which might be directed both at inner weakness and outwardly as holy war against infidels.

Kaaba the cube-shaped building in the centre of the sanctuary of the great mosque at Mecca where Muslims believe that Abraham built the first house for the worship of the one God; the focus of Islam to which all Muslims turn when praying.

khalifa successor of the Prophet and hence head of the Muslim community, hence caliph; for **sufis** the successor of a **shaykh**.

khan a Turkish title, originally the ruler of a state; also a hostel for travelling merchants.

khanqa a sufi hospice, where the **shaykh** may live and instruct his disciples.

madrasa a college whose primary purpose was to be an environment for transmitting Islamic knowledge.

Maliki one of the four **Sunni** schools of law founded Malik Ibn Anas (d.796).

mamluk a slave or freedman in military service.

mihrab niche in the place of prayer indicating the direction of Mecca.

mufti learned exponent of the **sharia** who issues **fatwa**s when consulted.

muhtasib official who supervises market practices and public morals.

qadi judge, the caliph's designated representative to adjudicate disputes on the basis of **sharia**.

qasbah a fortified building; residence of government officials; chief town.

sayyid prince, lord, chief; descendant of Husayn the son of Ali.

Shafii one of the four **Sunni** schools of law founded by Imam al-Shafii (d.820).

sharia the path to be followed; Muslim law; the totality of the Islamic way of life.

shaykh literally 'old man'; the chief of a tribe; any religious leader; in particular an independent **sufi** 'master' in a position to guide disciples in his **sufi** way.

Shaykh al-Islam the **mufti** of Istanbul and supreme religious authority in the Ottoman state.

Shia group or 'party' of Muslims who, against the orthodox **Sunni** view, insist on the recognition of Ali as the legitimate successor of Muhammad.

sufi a Muslim mystic.

sultan 'power', authority, the title of a Muslim ruler.

Sunna 'the beaten path', custom, the practice of the Prophet and the early community, which is for all Muslims an authoritative example of the correct way to live a Muslim life.

Sunnis those who accept the **Sunna** and the historic succession of the caliphs, as opposed to the **Shia**; the majority of the Muslim community.

sura chapter of the Quran.

Tanzimat Reorganization; the name for the Ottoman reforms of the nineteenth century.

ulama the collective term for the learned men of Islam.

umma people or community; the Islamic community as a whole.

Bibliography

This bibliography aims to help the reader go further into the subject. More detailed bibliographical references can be found in most of the works listed below. J. D. Pearson, *Index Islamicus*, Cambridge, 1958 to the present, covers the periodical literature from 1906 and books from 1976. *The Encyclopaedia of Islam*, ed. H. A. R. Gibb *et al*, 2nd edn, Leiden, 1960 to the present, is the outstanding reference work in all areas of the subject. Useful atlases are: R. Roolvink, *Historical Atlas of the Muslim Peoples*, Amsterdam 1957; F. Robinson, *Atlas of the Islamic World since 1500*, Oxford, 1982; and J. L. Bacharach, *A Middle East Studies Handbook*, Seattle, 1984.

Introduction

There are two outstanding overviews of Islamic history: M. G. S. Hodgson, *The Venture of Islam*, 3 vols., Chicago, 1974, and I. M. Lapidus, *A History of Islamic Societies*, Cambridge, 1988. Both should be read alongside Hodgson's essays in which he places Islamic civilization in a global historical framework, *Rethinking World History: Essays on Europe, Islam and World History*, ed. Edmund Burke III, Cambridge, 1993. Pioneering work on western attitudes to Islam has been done by N. Daniel, *Islam and the West: the Making of an Image*, Edinburgh, 1960, and *Islam, Europe and Empire*, Edinburgh, 1966. This should be supplemented by R. W. Southern, *Western Views of Islam in the Middle Ages*, Cambridge, Mass,. 1962, M. Rodinson, *Europe and the Mystique of Islam*, Seattle, 1987, A. Hourani, *Islam in European Thought*, Chicago, 1991, and the powerful critique of western study of the East, E. Said, *Orientalism*, London, 1978. The best introduction to Muslim attitudes to the West before 1800 is B. Lewis, *The Muslim Discovery of Europe*, London, 1982. There is a number of delightful Muslim records of journeys to the West in the nineteenth century, of which *Disorienting Encounters: Travels of a Moroccan Scholar in France in 1845-46*, S. C. Miller, trans. and ed., Berkeley, 1992, is an excellent example. Aspects of Muslim antipathy and anger towards the West can be found in M. Iqbal, *Javid-nama*, trans. A. J. Arberry, London, 1966, S. A. A. Maududi, *Purdah and the Status of Women in Islam*, trans. and ed. al-Ashari, Delhi, 1974, and J. Al-i Ahmed, *Occidentosis: A Plague from the West*, trans. R. Campbell, Berkeley, 1984. For the European debt to Islam see W. M. Watt, *The Influence of Islam on Medieval Europe*, Edinburgh, 1972, and G. Makdisi's two important books *The Rise of Colleges: Institutions of Learning in Islam and the West*, Edinburgh, 1981, and *The Rise of Humanism in Classical Islam and the Christian West*, Edinburgh, 1990. For issues surrounding interdependence see Akbar Ahmed, *Postmodernism and Islam: Predicament and Promise*, London, 1992. The speech by Ataturk is quoted in B. Lewis, *The Emergence of Modern Turkey*, 2nd edn, Oxford, 1968, and the statement by Mawdudi is in *Purdah and the Status of Women in Islam*, cited above.

Chapter 1

There is a highly readable (and beautifully illustrated) introduction to the pre-Islamic Middle East in P .Brown, *The World of Late Antiquity*, London, 1971, and reprints, though on Arabia the reader is better served by I. Shahid's chapter in the *Cambridge History of Islam*, vol. 1, Cambridge, 1970, and I. Goldziher's classic *Muslim Studies*, trans. S. M. Stern, vol. 1, London, 1967 (first published 1889).

The controversy over the origins of Islam has barely reached the level of introductory works, though the reader will find something about it in M. A. Cook's little book *Muhammad*, Oxford, 1983 and reprints, which is highly commendable in other respects too. The reader will probably appreciate its merits better by first reading some more conventional biographies, such as W. M. Watt, *Muhammad, Prophet and Statesman*, Oxford, 1961, and reprints, or F.

Gabrieli, *Muhammed and the Conquests of Islam*, London, 1968, which is an easy introduction to the conquests too. My own views are most accessibly set out in the last two chapters of P. Crone, *Meccan Trade and the Rise of Islam*, Princeton, 1987.

The most recent works on the conquests are F. M. Donner, *The Early Islamic Conquests*, Princeton, 1981, and W. E. Kaegi, *Byzantium and the Early Islamic Conquests*, Cambridge, 1992, both of which concentrate on the Fertile Crescent. On the emergence of Islamic civilization there is a brilliant sketch by M. A. Cook in *The Origins and Diversity of Axial Age Civilizations*, ed. S. N. Eistenstadt, Albany, N.Y., 1986.

For the political and social history of the Umayyad period, the reader is well served by G. R. Hawting, *The First Dynasty of Islam*, London, 1986, which is short and lucid. For the development of the sects and early religious thought, there is a comprehensive survey in W. M. Watt, *The Formative Period of Islamic Thought*, Edinburgh, 1973. M. Momen, *An Introduction to Shi'i Islam*, New Haven and London, 1985, is also helpful, though it covers only Imami Shiism. The first chapters of J. Schacht, *An Introduction to Islamic Law*, Oxford, 1964, introduce the reader to both law and traditionism. The briefest introduction to the controversy over the dating of hadith is in P. Crone, *Roman, Provincial and Islamic Law*, Cambridge, 1987, ch. 2. For the Abbasid revolution the reader may start by consulting the first chapter of E. L. Daniel, *The Political and Social History of Khurasan under Abbasid rule, 747-820*, Minneapolis and Chicago, 1979.

For the political history of the Abbasids up to al-Mamun there is an accessible account in H. Kennedy, *The Early Abbasid Caliphate*, London, 1986. The best introduction to the Shuubiyya is Goldziher's Muslim Studies, vol. 1 (see above), though the best interpretation is to be found in H. A. R. Gibb, *Studies in the Civilization of Islam*, London, 1961. On the mamluk institution, the reader will find D. Pipes, *Slave Soldiers and Islam*, New Haven and London, 1981, easier to read than P. Crone, *Slaves on Horses, the Evolution of the Islamic Polity*, Cambridge, 1980, on which I have drawn for my account of the Umayyads and Abbasids here.

F. Daftary, *The Isma'ilis*, Cambridge, 1992, offers a helpful survey of Ismaili history and doctrine from the beginning until today. The clearest account of the political history of the tenth and eleventh centuries is H. Kennedy, *The Prophet and the Age of the Caliphates*, London and New York, 1986, which covers the entire period from the sixth to the eleventh century. For all aspects of Iranian history from the conquests to the Turkish invasion, the reader may start by consulting *The Cambridge History of Iran*, vol. 4, Cambridge, 1975, which is mostly excellent. For the society and culture of the tenth and eleventh centuries, A. Mez, *The Renaissance of Islam*, Patna, 1937 (German original, 1922) is still unsurpassed.

Chapter 2

P. M. Holt, *The Age of the Crusades: The Near East from the eleventh century to 1517*, London, 1986, covers the political history of the Arab lands, plus the Sudan and Anatolia. For the history of lands to the east of Iraq, see D. Morgan, *Medieval Persia 1040-1517*, London, 1988. R. S. Humphreys's *Islamic History: A Framework for Inquiry*, rev. edn, London, 1991, provides a thoughtful, bibliographically orientated guide to some of the key historical issues in this period. C. E. Bosworth, *The Ghaznavids: Their Empire in Afghanistan and Eastern Iran 994–1040*, Edinburgh, 1963, and *The Later Ghaznavids*, Edinburgh, 1977, cover a wider range of topics than their titles may suggest and they are particularly useful for the history of the early Seljuqs and for the study of medieval Islamic military organization. On the latter topic, one should also consult the essays by Bosworth and others in *War, Technology and*

Society in the Middle East, ed. V. J. Parry and M. E. Yapp, London, 1975. S. D. Goitein's monumental, stylish and learned *A Mediterranean Society: The Jewish Communities of the Arab World as Portrayed in the Cairo Geniza*, 5 vols., Berkeley and Los Angeles, 1967–88, is an acknowledged masterpiece of historical writing. Although it is based almost entirely on Jewish source material, it is nevertheless fundamental for the understanding of the Muslim economy and society in the eleventh and twelfth centuries.

The history of the Crusades is covered at length (though patchily) in *A History of the Crusades*, ed. K. M. Setton *et al*, 6 vols., rev. edn Madison, 1969–89, and the articles on Islamic topics by B. Lewis, H. A. R. Gibb, and C. Cahen are particularly useful. Those wishing to know more about the Muslim counter-crusade should consult *Arab Historians of the Crusades*, ed. and trans. F. Gabrieli, London, 1969, and M. C. Lyons and D. E. P. Jackson, *Saladin, the Politics of Holy War, Cambridge*, 1982. Those interested in the other important area where Muslims and Christians were in conflict will find R. Fletcher's *Moorish Spain*, London, 1992, to be exceptionally stimulating reading. More specialized aspects of Spanish Muslim history are dealt with in the same author's *The Quest for El Cid*, London, 1989, and in *The Legacy of Muslim Spain*, ed. S. K. Jayyusi, Leiden, 1992, a massive volume. E. W. Bovill's *The Golden Trade of the Moors*, rev. edn, Oxford, 1968, not only covers the Almoravids and the Almohads, but also discusses Muslim penetration of sub-Saharan Africa.

M. Dols's *The Black Death in the Middle East*, Princeton, 1977, highlights one of the most important causes of growing economic and political difficulties in the later Middle Ages. On the Mamluk dynasty in Egypt and Syria, see the numerous important studies by D. Ayalon collected under the titles *Studies on the Mamluks of Egypt (1250–1517)*, London, 1977, and *The Mamluk Military Society*, London, 1979, as well as R. Irwin's *The Middle East in the Middle Ages: The Early Mamluk Sultanate 1250–1382*, Beckenham, 1986. Cultural and social aspects of Mamluk rule are covered in E. Atil, *The Renaissance of Islam: Art of the Mamluks*, Washington, DC, 1981, and in *Muqarnas*, ed.O. Grabar, vol. 2 of *The Art of the Mamluks*, New Haven and London, 1984. Also R. Irwin's *The Arabian Nights: A Companion*, Harmondsworth, 1994, covers such topics as medieval Arab literature, popular culture, sex, occultism and crime.

D. Morgan, *The Mongols*, Oxford, 1986, offers an extremely readable account of the history of the Mamluks' chief adversaries and assesses the effects of their occupation of Iran and Iraq. The best guide to Iran in the post-Mongol period and to the rise of the Timurids is provided in the chapters contributed by H. R. Roemer to *The Cambridge History of Iran*, ed. P. Jackson and L. Lockhart, vol. 6, Cambridge, 1986. The history of Anatolia prior to the rise of the Ottoman empire is not well served, though C. Cahen, *Pre-Ottoman Turkey*, London, 1971, provides most of the materials from which a history might be constructed. H. Inalcik's *The Ottoman Empire: The Classical Age 1300–1600*, London, 1973, is lucid and more than just a political history. The value of F. Babinger's *Mehmed the Conqueror and his Time*, Princeton, 1978, has been greatly increased by the updating and corrections in the footnotes provided by the American editor R. Mannheim. K. N. Chaudhuri's *Trade and Civilization in the Indian Ocean: An Economic History from the Rise of Islam to 1750*, Cambridge, 1985, and *Asia before Europe: Economy and Civilization of the Indian Ocean from the Rise of Islam to 1750*, Cambridge, 1990, take a Braudelian approach to their subject matter and make exciting if taxing reading.

Perhaps the best way of capturing the flavour of the period is to read some primary sources. Usamah ibn Munqidh, *An Arab-Syrian Gentleman and Warrior in the Period of the Crusades*, New York, 1929, is a remarkably lively autobiography. *The Travels of Ibn Jubayr*, trans. and ed. R. J. C. Broadhurst, London, 1952, by a Spanish Muslim pilgrim, describes his journey from Granada to Mecca and on to the lands of Saladin and the Abbasid caliph. Ibn Battuta travelled even more widely through Africa and Asia. Although only three volumes of his *Travels* have so far been translated into English by H. A.

R. Gibb (Hakluyt Series, Cambridge, 1958–71), R. E. Dunn's *The Adventures of Ibn Battuta: A Muslim Traveller of the Fourteenth Century*, Beckenham, 1986, uses the man's travels as a peg on which to hang an excellent synoptic account of how the medieval Muslim world worked.

Chapter 3

The period from 1500 to 1800 is well documented in comparison with earlier centuries of Islamic history. This is particularly true of the four major Turco-Mongol states. The foremost source of documents, histories, literary texts, and religious treatises is the Ottoman archives, which contain materials relevant to Iran and eastern Europe as well as the Ottomans' Arabic-speaking provinces. No similar collections of sources are extant for the Safawid, Uzbek, and Mughul states, or for the emerging Islamic states of Africa and Southeast Asia. Yet traditional narrative histories, collections of religious biographies, memoirs, and European travellers' accounts still offer a remarkable range of information about these states and regions. Data on socio-economic history is scarce for all regions, although Ottoman records contain a relative wealth of this material, but coins and wakf deeds still offer considerable information about economic trends, prices, and wages. Those who wish to read further about the Islamic lands in this period should begin by consulting F. Robinson's, *Atlas of the Islamic World since 1500*, Oxford, 1982, which covers the same material as in this chapter but in much greater depth. A second general study with an exemplary annotated bibliography is I. M. Lapidus, *A History of the Islamic Societies*, Cambridge, 1988.

The Turco-Mongol States: our knowledge of Ottoman provincial and imperial history is constantly being supplemented by a stream of articles and monographs. H. Inalcik, *The Ottoman Empire: The Classical Age, 1300–1600*, London, 1973, remains the obvious starting point. For a survey of the empire see S. Shaw, *History of the Ottoman Empire and Modern Turkey*, Cambridge, 1976. B. Lewis surveys the history of the Ottoman capital in *Istanbul and the Civilization of the Ottoman Empire*, Norman, Okla., 1963. C. Fleischer offers important insights into sixteenth-century cultural and intellectual history in, *Mustafa Ali: Ottoman Bureaucrat and Intellectual*, Princeton, 1986. For Ottoman religious classes see H. A. R. Gibb and H. Bowen, *Islamic Society and the West*, Oxford, 1950–57, and J. Birge, *The Bektashi Order of Dervishes*, London, 1937. M. Cook and S. Faroqhi are two important socio-economic historians. See their respective works, *Population Pressure in Rural Anatolia, 1450-1600*, London, 1972, and *Towns and Townsmen in Ottoman Anatolia, Trade, Craft and Food Production in an Urban Setting*, Cambridge, 1984.

In comparison to Ottoman history that of the Safawid empire is relatively poorly documented. The best introduction to the empire's Timurid antecedents and the Safawids themselves is *The Cambridge History of Iran*, ed. J.A. Boyle, vol. 5, Cambridge, 1968. For the artistic aspect of the Timurid legacy in Iran see T. W. Lentz and G. D. Lowrey, *Timur and the Princely Vision*, Los Angeles, 1979. An excellent German survey of Iranian political and religious history is H. R. Roemer, *Persien Auf dem Weg in die Neuzeit: Iranische Geschichte von 1350–1750*, Beirut, 1968. Two important works on economic history are M. Keyvani, *Artisans and Guild Life in the Later Safavid Period*, Berlin, 1982, and J. Quiring-Zoche's *Isfahan im funfzehnten und sechzehnten Jahrhundert*, Freiburg, 1980. The topic of state and religion in Iran has been largely discussed in journal articles, for which see Lapidus' citations. See also F. Rahman, *The Philosophy of Mulla Sadra (Sadr al-Din al-Shirazi)*, Albany, N.Y., 1976. For the collapse of the empire see the two volumes by L. Lockhart, *The Fall of the Safavi Dynasty and the Afghan Occupation of Persia*, Cambridge, 1958, and *Nadir Shah: A Critical Study*, London, 1938.

For an introduction to the Mughal empire see J. F. Richards, *The Mughal Empire*, Cambridge, 1992. As was the case in Iran the Mughal archives were largely destroyed in the eighteenth century, but Mughal historians are fortunate to have a number of memoirs, contemporary histories, and administrative studies – especially for the sixteenth and seventeenth centuries. Foremost among these is the remarkably frank, idiosyncratic autobiographical memoir of the founder of the dynasty, *The Babur-nama*, trans. A. S. Beveridge, London, 1969. One of Babur's daughters left her reminiscences, especially of womens' court life, in the *Humayun-nama*, trans. A. S. Beveridge, Delhi, 1972. Babur's grandson Akbar, was largely responsible for consolidating the empire, and while he was illiterate his friend and official, Abul Fazl left both a detailed history of the reign, *The Akbar Nama*, Delhi, 1987, and an invaluable gazetteer of the empire in the late sixteenth century, the Ain-i Akbari, Delhi, 1988. His son Jahangir also left a memoir of his reign, which is especially rich in comments on court life and the arts, *Tuzuk-i-Jahangiri*, trans. A. Rodgers, Delhi, 1978. The socio-economic history of Mughal India has long been the focus of the 'Aligarh school', led by I. Habib: see his *The Agrarian System of Mughul India, 1556–1707*, Bombay, 1963. For a sophisticated introduction to Indo-Muslim intellectual and religious life see A. Ahmad, *Islamic Culture in the Indian Environment*, Oxford, 1969. M. Alam analyses Mughal decline in, *The Crises of Empire in Mughal North India, Oudh and the Punjab, 1707–1746*, Delhi, 1986.

It is difficult to reconstruct the history of the Uzbek Turan, but for background see the volumes on Timurid history cited under Safawid history. Russian scholars have done much of the most important work on the region, but the single best introduction to this entire period is R. D. McChesney's, *Waqf in Central Asia*, Princeton, 1973.

Africa and Southeast Asia: the study of Islam in the vast, culturally diverse regions of Africa and Southeast Asia is a daunting problem. Apart from Lapidus' citations, the best starting point for Africa are the bibliographies of P. E. Ofori, *Islam in Africa South of the Sahara: A Select Bibliographic Guide*, Mendelin, 1977, and S. M. Zoghby, *Islam in Subsaharan Africa: A Partially Annotated Guide*, Washington, D.C., 1978, and the relevant vols. in the *Cambridge History of Africa*, Cambridge, 1975 to the present. A comparable bibliographic guide to Islam in Indonesia is that of B. J. Boland and I. Farjon, *Islam in Indonesia, A Bibliographic Survey*, Dordrecht, The Netherlands, 1983. For a general survey of the region in the tradition of F. Braudel, which includes much information on Islam, see A. Reid, *Southeast Asia in the Age of Commerce, 1450–1680*, New Haven, 1988 to the present. Apart from the works cited by Lapidus see M. Majul, *Muslims in the Philippines*, Quezon City, the Philippines, 1973.

Chapter 4

One of the most satisfying doorways through which to enter this period of Muslim history is that offered by M. G. S. Hodgson, *The Venture of Islam: Conscience and History in a World Civilization*, 3 vols., Chicago, 1974, in particular vol. 3, *The Gunpowder Empires and Modern Times*, which in its second half offers a masterful analysis of the Islamic world system and the development of Islamic ideas from the end of the eighteenth century. This study has been complemented more recently by F. Robinson, *Atlas of the Islamic Islamic Societies World since 1500*, Oxford, 1982; J. O. Voll, *Islam, Continuity and Change in the Modern World*, Boulder, Colorado, 1982; I. M. Lapidus, *A History of Islamic Societies*, Cambridge, 1988. A. Hourani, *A History of the Arab Peoples*, Cambridge, Mass., 1991, provides a similar treatment for one, albeit a very significant, part of the Muslim world.

Turning to the upsurge in reform and revival which has taken place so widely since the turn of the nineteenth century, *The Cambridge History of Islam*, 2 vols, Cambridge, 1970, provides a good starting point from which to approach studies such as G. Rentz, 'Wahhabism and Saudi Arabia' in *The Arabian Peninsula*, ed. D. Hopwood, London, 1972; P. Hardy, *The Muslims of British India*, Cambridge, 1972; M. Ahmed, *Saiyid Ahmad Shahid*, Lucknow, 1965; Q. Ahmad, *A History of the Fara'idi Movement in Bengal, 1818-1906*, Karachi, 1965; R. Israeli, *Muslims in China: A Study of Cultural Confrontation*, London, 1980; B. G. Martin, *Muslim Brotherhoods in Nineteenth Century Africa*, Cambridge, 1976; J. Abun Nasr, *The Tijaniyya: a Sufi Order in the Modern World*, Oxford, 1960; M. Hiskett, *The Sword of Truth: The Life and Times of Shehu Usuman dan Fodio*, New York, 1973; E. E. Evans-Pritchard, *The Sanusi of Cyrenaica*, Oxford, 1949; and *Charisma and Brotherhood in*

African Islam, ed. D. B. Cruise O'Brien and C. Coulon, Oxford, 1988.

For the rise of Europe and the variety of Muslim reactions which this invoked, to the introductory works mentioned above may be added studies which have taken as their subject the challenge to Islam of new frameworks of power, namely the modern state and western knowledge. F. Rahman, *Islam and Modernity: Transformation of an Intellectual Tradition*, Chicago, 1974; H. Enayat, *Modern Islamic Political Thought*, Austin, Texas, 1982; and J. P. Piscatori, *Islam in a World of Nation States*, Cambridge, 1986, represent just a small selection of these. For the responses of particular Muslim thinkers see, for example, N. R. Keddie, *An Islamic Response to Imperialism: Political and Religious Writings of Sayyid Jamal ad-Din "al-Afghani"*, Berkeley, 1968; M. Abduh, *The Theology of Unity*, London, 1966; C. Troll, *Sayyid Ahmad Khan: A Reinterpretation of Muslim Theology*, New Delhi, 1978, and M. Iqbal, *The Reconstruction of Religious Thought in Islam*, Oxford, 1934.

Likewise, for the responses that occurred in various parts of the Muslim world, see B. Lewis, *The Emergence of Modern Turkey*, 2nd edn, London, 1968; Lord Kinross, *Attaturk: The Rebirth of a Nation*, London, 1964; P. J. Vatikotis, *The History of Egypt*, 2nd edn, London, 1980; T. Mitchell, *Colonising Egypt*, Cambridge, 1988; V. A. Martin, *Islam and Modernism*, London, 1989; H. E. Chehebi, *Iranian Politics and Religious Modernism*, London, 1990; H. Carrere d'Encausse, *Reforme et revolution chez les Musulmans de l'empire Russe, Bukhara 1867–1924*, Paris, 1964; A. Ahmed, *Islamic Modernism in India and Pakistan 1857–1964*, London, 1967; F. Robinson, *Separatism among Indian Muslims: The Politics of the United Provinces' Muslims 1860-1923*, Cambridge, 1974; B. Metcalf, *Islamic Revival in British India: Deoband, 1860–1900*, Princeton, 1982; A. Jalal, *The Sole Spokesman: Jinnah, the Muslim League and the Demand for Pakistan*, Cambridge, 1990; J. L. Peacock, *Purifying the Faith: The Muhammadiyah Movement in Indonesian Islam*, Menlo Park, California, 1978; M. K. Hassan, *Muslim Intellectual Responses to New Order Modernization in Indonesia*, Kuala Lumpur, 1980; M. Nakamura, *The Crescent Arises over the Banyan Tree*, Yogyakarta, 1983; A. Benningsen and S. Enders Wimbish, *Mystics and Commissars: Sufism in the Soviet Union*, Berkeley, 1985; P. B. Clarke, *West Africa and Islam*, London, 1982; and D. B. Cruise O'Brien, *The Mourids of Senegal: The Political and Economic Organisation of an Islamic Brotherhood*, Oxford, 1971.

An introduction to Islamism is provided in *Islamic Fundamentalism*, ed. R. M. Burrell, London, 1989. R. P. Mitchell, *The Society of Muslim Brothers*, London, 1969; G. Kepel, *The Prophet and Pharaoh: Muslim Extremism in Egypt*, London, 1985; A. Weiss, *Islamic Reassertion in Pakistan: The Application of Islamic Laws in a Modern State*, New York, 1986, and *Religion and Politics in Iran: Shi'ism from Quietism to Revolution*, ed. N. Keddie, New Haven, 1983, all examine the rise and consequences of 'fundamentalist' Islam. Abul A'la Maududi, *Towards Understanding Islam*, Karachi, 1960; C. Wendell, *Five Tracts from Hasan al-Banna (1906-1949): A Selection from the Majmu'at Rasa'il al-Imam al-Shahid Hasan al-Banna*, Berkeley, 1978; and H. Algar, *Islam and Revolution: Writings and Declarations of Imam Khomeini*, Berkeley, 1981, provide insights into the thinking of leading 'Islamist' thinkers, whose combined political impact, as J. L. Esposito, in *The Islamic Threat: Myth or Reality*, New York, 1992, explores, has come to be seen as the major contemporary challenge to Western political hegemony.

The quotation about Nasser is from M. E. Yapp, *The Near East since the First World War*, Harlow, 1991.

Chapter 5

There is no single adequate and modern treatment of the economic and social history of Islam from its rise in 622 AD, to the present age. The following titles are all valuable and should be studied by anyone seriously interested in learning about Islamic people, their economy, and social history. It is not possible to guide the reader through the selected list without appearing opinionated and prejudiced.

F. Aalund, 'The wakalat bazar'a: the rehabilitation of a commercial structure in the old city' in *Islamic Cairo: Architectural Conservation and Urban Development of the Historic Centre*, Art and Archaeology Research Papers, ed. M. Meinecke, London, 1978. Al-Abbas, and Al-Malik al-Afdal ibn Ali, *Bughyat al-Fallahin*, trans. R. B. Serjeant, 'The cultivation of cereals in medieval Yemen', *Arabian Studies*, vol.1, 1974. R. McC. Adams, *Heartland of Cities: Surveys of Ancient Settlements and Land Use on Central Floodplains of the Euphrates*, Chicago and London, 1981, *The Evolution of Urban Society*, London, 1966, and *Land beyond Baghdad: A History of Settlement on the Diyala Plains*, Chicago and London, 1965. W. E. D. Allen, *Problems of Turkish Power in the Sixteenth Century*, London, 1963. *Arid Lands: A Geographical Appraisal*, ed. E. S. Hills, London, 1966. D. Ayalon, *Gunpowder and Firearms in the Mamluk Kingdom: A Challenge to a Medieval Society*, London, 1955. Khatib al-Baghdadi, *The Topography of Baghdad*, trans. J. Lassner, Detroit, 1970. Al-Baladhuri, *The Origins of the Islamic State*, trans. P. H. Hitti, London, 1916. Ziya al-Din Barani, Ta'rikh-i Firuz Shahi in *The History of India as Told by its Own Historians*, ed. and trans. H. M. Elliott and J. Dowson, 8 vols., vol. 3, London, 1866–77. K. Barbir, *Ottoman Rule in Damascus, 1708–1758*, Princeton, 1980. R. Brunschvig, *La Berberie orientale sous les Hafsides: Des Origines à la fin du XV siècle*, 2 vols., Paris, 1940–47. K. N. Chaudhuri, *Trade and Civilisation in the Indian Ocean from the Rise of Islam to 1750*, Cambridge, 1985, and *Asia before Europe: The Economy and Civilization of the Indian Ocean from the Rise of Islam to 1750*, Cambridge, 1990. K. A. C. Creswell, *Early Muslim Architecture*, 2 vols., Oxford, 1969. *The Desert and the Sown: Nomads in the Wider Society*, ed. C .Nelson, Berkeley and Los Angeles, 1973; esp. T. Asad and F. Barth. S. Digby, *War-horse and Elephant in the Delhi Sultanate: A Study of Military Supplies*, Oxford, 1971. P. W. English, *City and Village in Iran: Settlement and Economy in the Kirman Basin*, Madison, 1966. H. Gaube, *Iranian Cities*, New York, 1979. R. Gazzard, 'The Arab house: its form and spatial distribution' *The Arab House*, ed. A. D. C. Hyland and A. al-Shahi, Newcastle, 1986. S. D. Goitein, *Studies in Islamic History and Institutions*, Leiden, 1966. L. Golvin and M.-C. Fromont, *Thula: Architecture et urbanisme d'une cité de haute montagne en république arabe du Yemen*, Paris, 1984. J. Goody, *Technology, Tradition, and the State in Africa*, London, 1971. N. Hanna, *Construction Work in Ottoman Cairo 1517-1798*, Supplément aux Annales Islamologiques, Cahier 4, Cairo, 1984. H. Helbaek, 'Ecological effects of irrigation in ancient Mesopotamia', *Iraq*, vol. 22, 1960. D. Hill, *A History of Engineering in Classical and Medieval Times*, London, 1984. *A History of Land Use in Arid Regions*, ed. L. D. Stamp, Paris, 1961. *The Islamic City: A Colloquium*, ed. A. H. Hourani and S. M. Stern, Oxford, 1970. G. F. Hourani, *Arab Seafaring in the Indian Ocean in Ancient and Early Medieval Times*, New York, 1975. al-Idrisi, *La Géographie d'Idrisi*, Fr. trans. P.-A. Jaubert, Paris, 1836-40. H. Inalcik, *Studies in Ottoman Social and Economic History*, London, 1985. *The Islamic Middle East, 700–1900: Studies in Economic and Social History*, ed. A. L. Udovitch, Princeton, 1981; esp. A. K. S. Lambton and I. M. Lapidus. C. Issawi, *An Economic History of the Middle East and North Africa*, London, 1982. M. Keyvani, *Artisans and Guild Life in the Later Safavid Period: Contributions to the Socio-Economic History of Persia*, Berlin, 1982. A. M. Khazanov, *Nomads and the Outside World*, trans. J. Crookenden, Cambridge, 1984. A. K. S. Lambton, *State and Government in Medieval Islam*, London, 1981; 'Kanat' in *The Encyclopedia of Islam*, ed. H. A. R. Gibb et al, 2nd edn, Leiden, 1960 to the present. C. J. Lamm, *Cotton in Medieval Textiles of the Near East*, Paris, 1937. H. S. I. Lammens, *Le Berceau de l'Islam: L'Arabie occidentale à la veille de l'Hégire*, vol. 1, *Le Climat - Les Bedouins*, Rome, 1914. *Land Tenure and Social Transformation in the Middle East*, ed. T. Khalidi, Beirut, 1984. I. M. Lapidus, *Muslim Cities in the Later Middle Ages*, new edn, Cambridge, 1984. J. Lassner, *The Topography of Baghdad in the Early Middle Ages: Texts and Studies*, Detroit, 1970. G. Le Strange, *The Lands of the Eastern Caliphate*, London, 1966. Ma Huan, *Ying-yai Sheng- lan [The Overall Survey of the Ocean's Shores]*, ed. J. V. G. Mills, Cambridge, 1970. Al-Maqrizi, *Les Marches du Caire: Traduction annotée du texte de Maqrizi*, trans. A. Raymond, Cairo, 1979, and *A History of the Ayyubid Sultans of Egypt*, trans. R. J. C. Broadhurst, Boston, 1980. M. Meyerhof, *Studies in Medieval Arabic Medicine*,

ed. P. Johnstone, London, 1984. Ibn Miskawaihi, *The Eclipse of the Abbasid Caliphate*, trans. and ed. H. F. Amedroz and D. S. Margoliouth, Oxford, 1921. M. G. Morony, *Iraq after the Muslim Conquest*, Princeton, 1984. Al-Muqaddasi, *Ahsanu- t-Taqasim fi Ma'rifati-l-aqalim*, ed. and trans. by G. S. A. Ranking and R. F. Azoo, Calcutta, 1901. A. Musil, *Arabia Deserta: A Topographical Itinerary*, New York, 1927; *The Manners and Customs of the Rwala Bedouins*, New York, 1928; and *The Middle Euphrates: A Topographical Itinerary*, New York, 1927. C. Niebuhr, *Travels through Arabia and Other Countries in the East*, trans. R. Heron, 2 vols., Edinburgh, 1792. R. Owen, *The Middle East in the World Economy 1800-1914*, London, 1981. *Pastoral Production and Society: Proceedings of the International Meeting on Nomadic Pastoralism*, Paris, 1–3 December 1976, Cambridge, 1979. C. Pellat, *Etudes sur l'histoire socio-culturelle de l'Islam (VIIe-XVe s.)*, London, 1976. *Perspectives on Nomadism*, ed. W. Irons and N. Dyson- Hudosn, Leiden, 1972. A. Raymond, *Artisans et commercants au Caire au XVIIIeme siècle*, 2 vols., Damascus, 1974. A. ibn Ridwan, *Medieval Islamic Medicine: Ibn Ridwan's Treatise, 'On the Prevention of Bodily Ills in Egypt'*, trans. with intro. by M. W. Dols, Arabic text ed. A. S. Gamal, Berkeley, Los Angeles and London, 1984. M. Rodinson, *Islam and Capitalism*, London, 1980. F. Rosenthal, *A History of Muslim Historiography*, Leiden, 1952. *Sa'na: An Arabian Islamic City*, ed. R. B. Serjant and R. Lewcock, London, 1983. R. B. Serjeant, *Islamic Textiles*, Beirut, 1972, and *Material for a History of Islamic Textiles*, London, 1942. A. Sousa, *Irrigation and Civilization in the Land of the Twin Rivers*, Baghdad, 1969 [English and Arabic text]. Ibn Taghri Birdi, *History of Egypt 1382–1469*, trans. W. Popper, vols. 3 and 4, Berkeley and Los Angeles, 1957–8. A. M. Watson, 'A Medieval Green Revolution', in Udovitch, ed. *The Islamic Middle East, 700-1900*, ed. A. L. Udovitch (see above), and *Agricultural Innovation in the Early Islamic World*, Cambridge, 1983. G. Wiet, *Cairo: City of Art and Commerce*, trans. S. Feiler, Oklahoma, 1964. J. C. Wilkinson, *Water and Tribal Settlement in South-East Arabia: A Study of the Aflaj of Oman*, Oxford, 1977.

Chapter 6

For medieval Muslim cities in general see: I. M. Lapidus, *Muslim Cities in the Later Middle Ages*, Cambridge, Mass., 1967, and *The Islamic City*, ed. A. H. Hourani and S. M. Stern, Oxford, 1970. For Fez in particular see: R. Le Tourneau, *Fez in the Age of the Marinids*, Norman, Oklahoma, 1991, and T. Burckhardt, *Fez, City of Islam*, trans. W. Stoddart, Cambridge, 1992. For other cities see: J. Abu Lughod, *Cairo: 1001 years of the City Victorious*, Princeton, 1971; *Alep*, Paris, 1941; M. Burgoyne and D. S. Richards, *Mamluk Jerusalem: An Architectural Study*, London, 1987; *San'a, an Arabian Islamic City*, ed. R. B. Serjeant and R. Lewcock, London, 1983; S. Blake, *Shahjahanabad*, New Delhi, 1993; B. Lewis, *Istanbul and the Civilization of the Ottoman Empire*, Norman, Oklahoma, 1963; and S. Faroqhi, *Towns and Townsmen of Ottoman Anatolia*, Cambridge, 1984. For aspects of urban life see: B. Shoshan, *Popular Culture in Medieval Cairo*, Cambridge 1983; S. D. Goitein, *A Mediterranean Society*, 5 vols., Berkeley, 1967–88; G. Wiet and A. Raymond, *Les Marches du Caire*, Cairo, 1979; A. L. Udovitch, *Partnership and Profit in Medieval Islam*; and for the voices of the inhabitants of Muslim cities see *Ibn Khaldun: the Muqaddimah*, trans. F. Rosenthal, 3 vols., London, 1958; for Ibn Battuta's travels see H. A. R. Gibb, *The Travels of Ibn Battuta*, 3 vols., Cambridge, 1958–71; and Leo Africanus, *The History and Description of Africa*, trans. J. Pory, London, 1986 For al-Ghazzali's life see W. M. Watt, *Muslim Intellectual*, Edinburgh, 1963, and for his masterwork G. H. Bousquet, *Ihya ouloum ed-din ou vivifaction des sciences de la foi: analyse et index*, Paris, 1951, and M. Fazul-ul-Karim, *Imam Gazzali's Ihya Ulum-id-din*, Lahore, n.d. The chapter's view of the relationships between the individual, society, and the state is much influenced by a number of writings, principally G. E. von Grunebaum, *Islam: Essays in the Nature and Growth of a Cultural Tradition* (The American Anthropologist, vol. 57, no. 2, part 2, memoir no. 81, April 1955), especially chapters 7 and 8; I. M. Lapidus, 'The Separation of State and Religion in the Development of Early Islamic Society', *International journal of Middle Eastern Studies*, vol. 6, 1975, pp. 363–85; J. A. Nawas, 'A

Reexamination of Three Current Explantions for Al-Ma'Mun's Introduction of the Mihna', *International Journal of Middle Eastern Studies*, vol. 26 (1994), pp. 615–29; and M. Hinds' article 'Mihna' in the *Encyclopedia of Islam* (new edition). See also A. K. S. Lambton, *State and Government in Medieval Islam*, Oxford, 1981; T. Khalidi, *Arabic Historical Thought in the Classical Period*, Cambridge, 1994; R. P. Mottahedeh, *Loyalty and Leadership in an Early Islamic Society*, Princeton, 1980; and articles by A. K. S. Lambton and C. Hillenbrand,in *Iran*, vol. 26, 1988 On the *hisba* see the article in the *Encycopledia of Islam* (new edition), and on the *muhtasib* as market inspector see Ibn al-Ukhuwwa, *Ma'alim Al-Qurba Fi Ahkam Al-Hisba*, ed. R. Levy, (E. J. W. Gibb Memorial Series, new series, xii), Cambridge, 1938, with an abstract of contents in English.

For introductions to issues relating to women see: Leila Ahmed, *Women and Gender in Islam*, New Haven, 1992; W. Walther, *Women in Islam*, trans. C. S. V. Salt, London, 1981, and *Women in Middle Eastern History: Shifting Boundaries in Sex and Gender*, ed. N. R. Keddie and B. Baron, New Haven, 1991. For early Muslim women see: N. Abbott, *Aishah, the Beloved of Muhammad*, Chicago, 1942, *Two Queens of Baghdad: Mother and Wife of Harun al-Rashid*, Chicago, 1946, and M. Smith, *Rabi'a the Mystic and her Fellow-Saints in Islam*, Cambridge, 1928. For women in the Muslim middle ages see: A. Abd al-Raziq, *La Femme au temps des Mamlouks en Egypte*, 2 vols., Cairo, 1973.; and for their biographies see R. Roded, *Women in Islamic Biographical Dictionaries: from Ibn Sa'd to Who's Who*, Boulder, Colorado, 1994. For the view of an Englishwoman who experienced a Turkish harem in the early eighteenth century *The Complete Letters of Lady Mary Wortley Montagu*, ed. R. Halsband, 2 vols., Oxford, 1965; and for women in Cairo at the beginning of the modern transformation see: E. W. Lane, *The Manners and Customs of the Modern Egyptians*, London, 1836, repr. london, 1978, and J. Tucker, *Women in Nineteenth-Century Egypt*, Cambridge, 1985.

On the modern history of the Middle East the best introduction is A. H. Hourani, *A History of the Arab Peoples*, London, 1991. For the modernization of Egypt see: A. Lutfi al-Sayyid Marsot, *Egypt in the Reign of Muhammad Ali*, Cambridge, 1984; E. R. Toledano, *State and Society in mid-Nineteenth-Century Egypt*, Cambridge, 1990; D. Landes, *Bankers and Pashas*, London, 1958; R. Hunter, *Egypt under the Khedives*, Pittsburgh, 1984; and T. Mitchell, *Colonising Egypt*, Cambridge, 1988. For a study of the reshaping of a Muslim city apart from Cairo see Z. Celik, *The Remaking of Istanbul: Portrait of an Ottoman City in the Nineteenth Century*, Seattle, 1986. Issues relating to women are well covered in Ahmed (above), while classical Muslim attitudes to birth control are examined in B. Musallam, *Sex and Society in Islam*, Cambridge, 1983.

Chapter 7

There are many useful introductions to Islam of which the following are particularly recommended: H. A. R. Gibb, *Islam*, Oxford, 1975; F. Rahman, *Islam*, 2nd edn, Chicago, 1979; J. L. Esposito, *Islam: The Straight Path*, New York, 1988, and A. Schimmel, *Islam: An Introduction*, Albany, N.Y., 1992. Many feel that the best representation of the Quran in English is A. J. Arberry, *The Koran Interpreted*, London 1980, but a more precise translation is the official Saudi Arabian version, *The Holy Quran: English Translation of the Meanings and Commentar*, Al-Madinah Al-Munawarah, 1410/1989/90. A popular anthology of hadiths drawn from the six compilations is *Al-Hadis: an English Translation and Commentary of Mishkat-ul-Masabih*, trans. F. Karim, 4 vols., Lahore, 1938. N. J. Coulson, *A History of Islamic Law*, Edinburgh, 1964, offers an excellent introduction as does W. M. Watt, *Islamic Philosophy and Theology*, Edinburgh, 1962. For Islamic science see Seyyed Hossein Nasr, *Islamic Science: An Illustrated Study*, London, 1976. For early sufism see M. G. S. Hodgson, *The Venture of Islam*, vol. 1, Chicago, 1974, and the masterwork of L. Massignon, *The Passion of al-Hallaj*, trans. H. Mason, 4 vols., Princeton, 1982. Al-Ghazzali is made readily accessible in W. M. Watt, *Muslim Intellectual: A Study of al-Ghazali*, Edinburgh, 1963.

The ulama and the transmission of formal knowledge: for the social organi-

sation of the ulama see R. P. Mottahedeh, *Loyalty and Leadership in an Early Islamic Society*, Princeton, 1980, and R. W. Bulliet, *The Patricians of Nishapur*, Cambridge, Mass., 1972. For the work of teaching see J. Berkey, *The Transmission of Knowledge in Medieval Cairo: A Social History of Islamic Education*, Princeton, 1992, Burhan al-Din al-Zarnuji, *Instruction of the Student: Method of Learning*, trans. G. E. von Grunebaum, New York, 1947; Ibn Khaldun, *The Muqaddimah: An Introduction to History*, trans. F. Rosenthal and N. J. Dawood, New York, 1967, ch. 6. For the work of the ulama further afield see E. N. Saad, *Social History of Timbuktu*, Cambridge, 1983, J. R. I. Cole, *Roots of North Indian Shi'ism in Iran and Iraq*, Berkeley, 1988; and F. Robinson, 'Problems in the History of the Firangi Mahall Family of Learned and Holy Men' in *Oxford University Papers on India*, ed. N. J. Allen *et al*, vol. 1, part 2, New Delhi, 1987. For the life and world of a distinguished Ottoman scholar of the sixteenth century see C. H. Fleischer, *Bureaucrat and Intellectual in the Ottoman Empire: The Historian Mustafa Ali (1541–1600)*, Princeton, 1986.

Sufis and the transmission of mystical knowledge: the best introductions to sufism and its development are A. Schimmel, *The Mystical Dimensions of Islam*, Chapel Hill, N.C., 1975, and J. S. Trimingham, *The Sufi Orders in Islam*, Oxford, 1971. For the working of sufi institutions and their impact see L. Fernandes, *The Evolution of a Sufi Institution in Mamluk Egypt: The Khanqah*, Berlin, 1988, and two important books by R. M. Eaton, *Sufis of Bijapur 1300–1700: Social Roles of Sufis in Medieval India*, Princeton, 1978, and *The Rise of Islam and the Bengal Frontier 1204-1760*, Berkeley, 1993. Ibn Arabi can be approached through H. Corbin, *Creative Imagination in the Sufism of Ibn 'Arabi*, trans. R. Mannheim, Princeton, 1969, and C. Addas, *Quest for the Red Sulphur: The Life of Ibn 'Arabi*, trans. P. Kingsley, Cambridge, 1993. An approach to Islam instinct with sufi understanding is A. Schimmel, *Deciphering the Signs of God: A Phenomenological Approach to Islam*, Edinburgh, 1994. Ulama, sufis, their Islam-wide connections and revival: for an introduction to the movement see F. Robinson *Atlas of the Islamic World since 1500*, Oxford, 1982, ch. 4, and see also *Eighteenth-Century Revival and Reform in Islam*, ed. N. Levtzion and J. O. Voll, New York, 1987, and B. G. Martin, *Muslim Brotherhoods in Nineteenth-Century Africa*, Cambridge, 1976.

Responses to the challenges of the West and western learning since 1800: for overviews of the challenges and Muslim responses see I. M. Lapidus, *A History of Islamic Societies*, part 3, Cambridge, 1988, and J. O. Voll, *Islam: Continuity and Change in the Modern World*, Boulder, Colorado, 1983. For important attempts to portray the nature and meaning of the changes and how Muslims have seen them see R. P. Mottahedeh, *The Mantle of the Prophet: Religion and Politics in Iran*, London, 1986; T. Mitchell, *Colonising Egypt*, Cambridge, 1988; and S. Mardin, *Religion and Social Change in Modern Turkey: The Case of Bediuzzaman Said Nursi*, Albany, N.Y., 1989. B. D. Metcalf, *Islamic Revival in British India: Deoband, 1860–1900*, Princeton, 1982, reveals the variety and creativity of Muslim responses to colonialism, R. P. Mitchell, *The Society of Muslim Brothers*, London, 1969 and S. V. R. Nasr, *The Vanguard of the Islamic Revolution: The Jama'at-i Islami of Pakistan*, Berkeley, 1994, offer the most thorough studies of Islamist responses to western civilization. F. Rahman, *Islam and Modernity: Transformation of an Intellectual Tradition*, Chicago, 1982, focuses specifically on the challenge of modernity in the field of knowledge. For the impact of new technologies on the transmission of knowledge see F. Robinson, 'Islam and the impact of print in South Asia' in *The Transmission of Knowledge in South Asia: Essays on the Social Agenda*, ed. N. Crook, New Delhi, 1995; B. Messick, *The Calligraphic State: Textual Domination and History in a Muslim Society*, Berkeley, 1993; D. F. Eickelmann, *Knowledge and Power in Morocco: The Education of a Twentieth-Century Notable*, Princeton, 1985; and M. M. J. Fischer and M. Abedi, *Debating Muslims: Cultural Dialogues in Postmodernity and Tradition*, Madison, 1990. The charming story about al-Shafii is quoted by J. Berkey (see above) Sura Fatiha is from the official Saudi Arabian translation of the Quran (see above), the translation of the ijaza is by J. Pedersen, *The Arabic Book*, trans. G. French, ed. R. Hillenbrand, Princeton, 1984; and the sufi song of the

Deccani women has been translated by R. Eaton.

Chapter 8

Literature: a number of useful anthologies of Muslim poetry and prose are available, such as R. A. Nicholson's *Translations of Eastern Poetry and Prose*, London, 1987, which ends in the fifteenth century, and *Anthology of Islamic Literature: From the Rise of Islam to Modern Times*, ed. J. Kritzeck, Harmondsworth, 1964. For Persian poetry see *Persian Poems: An Anthology of Verse Translations*, ed. A. J. Arberry, London, 1954. A good anthology of Turkish poetry is *The Penguin Book of Turkish Verse*, ed. F. Iz, London, 1978. A fine introductory survey of Arabic literature is R. A. Nicholson's *A Literary History of the Arabs*, rev. edn, Cambridge, 1953. Early Arabic poetry is discussed in A. F. L. Beeston *et al*, *Arabic Literature to the End of the Umayyad Period*, Cambridge, 1983, and medieval literature in A. Hamori, *On the Art of Medieval Arabic Literature*, Princeton, 1974. A concise inrtoduction to modern Arabic literature is M. M. Badawi's *A Short History of Modern Arabic Literature*, Oxford, 1993; other writings by Badawi on modern Arabic poetry and drama should also be consulted. A detailed account of twentieth-century Arabic poetry is S. K. Jayyusi's *Trends and Movements in Modern Arabic Poetry*, 2 vols., Leiden, 1977, while modern Egyptian literature and literary criticism are discussed in J. Brugman, *An Introduction to teh History of Modern Arabic Literature in Egypt*, Leiden, 1984. Persian literature is surveyed in J. Rykpa *et al, History of Iranian Literature*, Dordrecht, The Netherlands, 1968; shorter accounts include R. Levy, *An Introduction to Persian Literature*, New York and London, 1969,and G. Morrison, J.Baldick, and S. Kadkani, *History of Persian Literature from the Beginning of the Islamic Period to the Peșent Day*, Leiden, 1981. An excellent introduction to Urdu literature is A. Schimmel's *Classical Urdu Literature from the Beginning to Iqbal*, Wiesbaden, 1975. Schimmel has explored Islamic mystical poetry in *As Through a Veil: Mystical Poetry in Islam*, London, 1978. Ottoman poetry is surveyed in E. J. W. Gibb's *A History of Ottoman Poetry*, 6 vols., London, 1958, although his approach is somewhat dated; a more recent discussion of the subject is W. G. Andrews, *Poetry's Voice,Society's Song*, Seattle and London, 1985. For modern Turkish literature see *Contemporary Turkish Literature*, ed. T. S. Halman, Toronto and Rutherford, 1982.

Music: the student of Arab music will still find the works of H. G. Farmer indispensable, especially his *History of Arabian Music to the XIIIth Century*, London, 1973; *Historical Facts for the Arabian Musical Influence*, London, 1970; and *The Sources of Artabian Music*, 2nd edn, Leiden, 1965. A recent study of eary Abassid music is G. D. Sawa's *Music Performance Practice in the Early Abbasi Era*, Toronto, 1989. The theory and practice of Persian music is introduced in E. Zonis, *Classical Persian Music*, Cambridge, Mass., 1973. For Turish music see K. Reinhard and U. Reinhard, *Musik der Turkei*, 2 vols., Wilhelmshaven, 1984; for a summary of K. Reinhard's views in English see his article 'Turkey' in the *New Grove Dictionary of Music and Musicians*, ed. S. Sadie, London, 1980. A detailed study of Turkish folk instruments is in L. Picken, *Folk Instruments of Turkey*, London, 1975. The theories of Safi al-Din are discussed in O. Wright, *The Modal System of Arab and Persian Music A.D. 1250–1300*, Oxford, 1978.

Architecture and visual arts: a well-illustrated introduction to this subject is R. Ettinghausen and O. Grabar's *The Art and Architecture of Islam, 650–1250*, Harmondsworth, 1987, which has been continued by S. S. Blair and J. M. Bloom in *The Art and Architecture of Islam, 1250–1800*, New Haven and London, 1994. A useful shorter introduction is B. Brend's *Islamic Art*, London, 1991. A highly readable and stimulating survey of Muslim architecture to the seventeenth century is R. Hillenbrand's *Islamic Architecture*, Edinburgh, 1994. Many of the issues concerning the nature of early Muslim architecture and art are tackled by O.Grabar in *The Formation of Islamic Art*, New Haven and London, 1973. The most comprehensive survey of early Muslim architecture is K. A. C. Creswell's *Early Muslim Architecture*, Oxford, vol. 1, 1969, vol. 2, 1940. Creswell also wrote a detailed survey of Egyptian architecture to the Mamluk period in *Muslim Architecture of Egypt*, 2 vols.,

Oxford, 1952–9. Other regions of the Muslim world have not been so well investigated. A. U. Pope and P. Ackerman edited the *Survey of Persian Art*, 6 vols., London and New York,1938–39, 2nd edn, Tokyo, 1964–65,which is dated but useful for its plates. The reader will probably derive more from shorter studies, such as D. N. Wilber's *Persian Gardens and Garden Pavilions*, Rutland, Vermont, 1962. The Ottoman tradition is surveyed in G.Goodwin's *A History of Ottoman Architecture*, London, 1971. Calligraphy is introduced in Y. H. Safadi's *Islamic Calligraphy*, London, 1978, and A. Schimmel's *Calligraphy and Islamic Culture*, New York, 1984. The issue of the lawfulness of figural painting in Islam is explored by T. W. Arnold in *Painting in Islam*, London, 1965. Illustrated accounts of Muslim painting include R. Ettinghausen's *Arab Painting*, Geneva, 1962; B. Gray's *Persian Painting*, London, 1977; and G. Renda *et al*, *A History of Turkish Painting*, London and Seattle, 1988. Carpets are discussed by K. Erdmann in *Oriental Carpets: an Account of their History*, trans. C. G. Ellis, London, 1960. For metalwork see J. W. Allan, *Islamic Metalwork: The Nuhad Es-Said Collection*, London, 1982, and A. S. Melikian-Chirvani, *Metalwork from the Iranian World, 8th–18th Centuries*, London, 1982, the latter concerned with items in the Victoria and Albert Museum, London. The ceramic arts are surveyed in A. Lane's *Early Islamic Pottery*, London, 1947, and *Later Islamic Pottery*, 2nd edn, London, 1971. Studies of pottery production in specific regions include O. Watson's *Persian Lustre Ware*, London, 1985, and N. Atasoy and J. Raby's lavishly illustrated I*znik: the Pottery of Ottoman Turkey*, London, 1989.

The poem by Abu Nuwas and the extract from a poem by Nedim are from *The Elek Book of Oriental Verse*, ed. K. Bosley, 1979. The extract from a poem by Hafiz is from G. Bell, *Teachings of Hafiz*, London, 1979.

Conclusion

The magisterial conclusion to I. M. Lapidus, *A History of Islamic Societies*, Cambridge, 1988, remains the best overview of the current condition of the Muslim world; further useful insights can be gained from M. G. S. Hodgson, *Rethinking World History: Essays on Europe, Islam and World History*, ed. E. Burke III, Cambridge, 1993, and R. W. Bulliet, *Islam: The View from the Edge*, New York, 1994. The movement of renewal is surveyed in J. O. Voll, *Islam: Continuity and Change in the Modern World*, Boulder, Colorado, 1982. More detailed studies of renewal in its reformist and modernist manifestations can be found in B. D. Metcalf *Islamic Revival in British India: Deoband 1860–1900*, Princeton, 1982, and A. Hourani, *Arabic Thought in the Liberal Age, 1789–1939*, with new preface, Cambridge, 1983. Local studies of the emergence of Islamism can be found in G. Kepel, *The Prophet and Pharaoh: Muslim Extremism in Egypt*, London, 1985, and S. V. R. Nasr, *The Vanguard of the Islamic Revolution: The Jamaat-i Islami of Pakistan*, Berkeley, 1994; S. Zubaida, *Islam, the People and the State: Political Ideas and Movements in the Middle East*, London, 1989, is an excellent introduction to the sociological context of the phenomenon. The aims and limitations of Islamism are explored in the following: H. Dabashi, *Theology of Discontent: The Ideological Foundation of the Islamic Revolution in Iran*, New York, 1993; J. L. Esposito, *The Islamic Threat: Myth or Reality?*, New York, 1992; O. Roy, *The Failure of Political Islam*, London, 1994; A. al-Azmeh, *Islams and Modernities*, London, 1993; and A. Ehteshami After Khomeini: *The Iranian Second Republic,* London, 1995. L. Ahmed, *Women and Gender in Islam*, New Haven, 1992, and *Women, Islam and the State*, ed. D. Kandiyoti, Basingstoke, 1991, offer excellent overviews of the issues at stake for Muslim women. *Forging Identities: Gender, Communities and the State*, ed. Z. Hasan, examines specific problems in India, *In the Eye of the Storm: Women in Post-Revolutionary Iran*, ed. M. Afkhami and E. Friedl, London, 1994, does the same for Iran. The real lives of some contemporary women can be savoured in G. Brooks, *Nine Parts of Desire; the Hidden World of Islamic Women*, London, 1995, and V. L. Barnes and J. Boddy *Aman: the Story of a Somali Girl*, London, 1994. *Islam, Globalization and Modernity*, ed. A. Ahmed and H. Donnan, London, 1994, offers an introduction to the meaning of globalization for Muslim societies.

Picture Acknowledgements

The following abbreviations have been used:
APP: Associated Press Photo, London
BM: The Trustees of the British Museum, London
BN: Bibliothèque Nationale, Paris
Bodleian: Bodleian Library, University of Oxford
BL: By permission of The British Library, London
Chester Beatty: Chester Beatty Library, Dublin
Coll: Collection
Harding: Robert Harding Picture Library, London
Hulton: Hulton Deutsch, London
Mary Evans: Mary Evans Picture Library, London

Half title page Mohamid Amin/Harding. **Title page** Musée d'Art et d'Histoire, Geneva. **Foreword** Gemeentmuseum, The Hague. **xi** Escorial Monastery, Madrid/Oronoz. **xiv** Mathaf Gallery Ltd, London. **xv** Francis Robinson. **xviii** from Allen Douglas and Fedwa Malti-Douglas: *Arab Comic Strips* (1994). **xx** Coll Prince Sadruddin Aga Khan. **xxii** APP. **xxiii** Stuart Franklin/Magnum. **xxiv/1** F. Jackson/Harding. **3** University Museum, University of Pennsylvania. **4** Harding. **6** Middle East Archives, London. **9** Harding. **11** Museo Arqueologico, Madrid. **12** Francis Robinson. **13** American Numismatic Society, New York. **15** Harding (external view); Magnum (internal view). **18** Israel Antiquities Authority, Jerusalem. **19** Israel Antiquities Authority, Jerusalem. **22** Israel Antiquities Authority, Jerusalem. **23** Ashmolean Museum, Oxford. **24** Ashmolean Museum, Oxford. **25** Hutchison Library, London. **26** Benedikt Taschen Verlag, Cologne. **27** *above and below* Benedikt Taschen Verlag, Cologne. **30** Harding. **32** Edinburgh University Library. **35** James H. Morris Picture Library, London. **38** Patrimonio Nacional, Madrid. **40** The Nasser D. Khalili Coll of Islamic Art, London. **44** Dr Hugh Kennedy. **46** Jean Dieuzaide. **49** Bodleian, MS Pococke 400 fol 48r. **50** Ross Greetham/Harding. **51** Topkapi Seray Museum, Istanbul. **52** Tunney-Lee/Aga Khan Visual Archives, MIT. **54** *above* Novosti **54** *below* BM, 1961 2 B.1. **55** Sonia Halliday. **57** above and below Harding. **58** Wellcome Institute, London, MS Per 474 fols 70v-70r. **59** Réunion des Musées Nationaux, Paris. **62** Sonia Halliday. **64** Francis Robinson. **67** Sonia Halliday. **68** BM, 1520-66. **69** Coll Prince Sadruddin Aga Khan. **70** Al-Sabah Collection, Ministry of Information, Kuwait; MS 75 fol 82a. **72** *above* Harding. **72** *below* Hasham Khosorovani Coll, Geneva. **73** Momem's Coll. **74** courtesy of S. N. Lambden. **75** Christine Osborne Pictures, London. **77** BL, Add Or 1039. **78** BM, 1921-10-11-03. **79** Harding. **80** Christina Gascoigne. **82** Harding. **83** Hulton. **84** BL, C7392 (1) OPP. Pa 28. **88** Harding. **93** Réunion des Musées Nationaux, Paris. **94** University of Leiden. **95** Hulton. **96** Hulton. **99** *above* from Allen Douglas and Fedwa Malti-Douglas: *Arab Comic Strips* (1994); **99** *below* from Khalid Kishtainy: *Arab Political Humour* (1985). **100** BL, 14797 d 21, pl. 19. **101** Hulton. **104** Hulton. **105** APP. **107** APP. **108** Popperfoto. **109** APP. **110** APP. **112** Rassol/GAMMA, Frank Spooner Pictures. **113** Makram Karim/Al Akbar/GAMMA, Frank Spooner Pictures. **116** C. Hires/Frank Spooner Pictures. **120** Popperfoto. **122/3** Ellen Barnett Moinard/Aramco. **125** Bodleian, MS Pococke 375. **127** Al-Sabah Collection, Kuwait. **129** Desmond Harney/Harding. **131** BN, Arabe 5847 fol 119v. **132** Hasham Khosrovani Coll, Geneva. **133** left Ashmolean Museum, Oxford. **133** centre Victoria and Albert Museum, London. **133** below right BM, OA + 6291. **134** T'oung Paa Archives. **135** Mary Evans. **136.** BL, Add Or 484. **138** Landesbildstelle Rheinland, Düsseldorf. **140** BN, Arabe 5847 fol 94v. **143** James H. Morris Picture Library, London. **145** Circa Photo Library, Manchester. **146** Jane Taylor/Sonia Halliday Photographers. **148** Mary Evans. **149** Inge Morath/Magnum. **150** BN, Arabe 2964 fol 22. **153** John Hatt/Hutchison Library. **154** Peter Fraenkel. **156** Hulton. **157** Hulton. **158** Mary Evans. **162** Harding. **167** Dr G. Gerster/Comstock. **168**

Dr G. Gerster/Comstock. **169** Bruno Barbey/Magnum. **170** Bruno Barbey/Magnum. **171** Roland and Sabrina Michaud/John Hillelson Agency. **172** H. Gruyaert/Magnum. **175** BN, Arabe 5847 fol 138r. **177** Chester Beatty, MS 419 fol 310r. **179** Bodleian, MS Ouseley Add 24 fol 55v. **180** BN, Arabe 5847 fol 19. **183** BN, Arabe 5847 fol 29v. **187** Chester Beatty, MS 419 fol 40v. **191** BL, J-13-4. **194** BN, Arabe 5847 fol 21. **195** Bodleian, MS Elliott 189 fol 192. **196** Chester Beatty, MS 3 fol 143r. **197** Museum of Fine Arts, Boston. **198** Photographers Library, London. **200** Hulton. **201** *above* from *L'Illustration*, 14th October 1882. **201** *below* Hulton. **203** Mary Evans. **204** Saudi Research and Marketing (UK) Ltd, London. **205** A. Abbas/Magnum. **206** Stuart Franklin/Magnum. **209** BL, MS Or 2165 fol 67b. **210** Harding. **213** BN, Arabe 6094 fol 24r. **214** BL, Or 2784 fol 96r. **216** Freer Gallery of Art, Washington. **217** Edinburgh University Library, ORMS 161 fol 94r. **220** Hashem Khosrovani Coll, Geneva. **222** BN, Arabe 5847, fol 5v. **223** Royal Asiatic Society, MSS 35. **224** Freer Gallery, Washington. **225** Freer Gallery, Washington. **227** A. Abbas/Magnum. **228** BL, Add 23387 fol 28r. **229** above right Edinburgh University Library, ORMS 161 fol 16r. **229** *below left* Topkapi Seray Museum, Istanbul. **229** *below right* Bodleian. **232** BL, J-7-3. **233** Sarah Ansari. **234** Francis Robinson. **235** Roland and Sabrina Michaud/John Hillelson Agency. **238** BL, J-55-3. **240** Mary Evans. **242** BL, J-1-20. **243** BL, 306 22 D 23. **245** Saudi Research and Marketing (UK) Ltd, London. **251** Chester Beatty, MS 1599 fols 1v-2r. **254** Réunion des Musées Nationaux, Paris. **259** Roland and Sabrina Michaud/John Hillelson Agency. **260** Ernst Herzfeld. **261.** Aerofilms. **262** Staatliche Museen zu Berlin/Preussischer Kulturbesitz Museum für Islamische Kunst. **265** Vivienne Sharpe. **266** Josephine Powell. **267** A. F. Kersting. **268** Chester Beatty, MS K16 fol 9v. **270** BM, no. 1948 12-11 025. **271** BM, Or 6810 fol 27v. **272** *above left* S Marco Treasury, Venice. **272** *above right* BM, 1848 0805.2. **273** Staatliche Museen zu Berlin/Preussischer Kulturbesitz Museum für Islamische Kunst. **277** Roland and Sabrina Michaud/John Hillelson Agency. **278** Vivienne Sharpe. **280** By courtesy of the Board of Trustees of the Victoria & Albert Museum, London. **281** The Syndics of the Fitzwilliam Museum, Cambridge. **282** BM. **284** from Sarah Graham-Brown: *The Portrayal of Women in Photography in the Middle East, 1860-1950* (1988). **285** Steve McCurry/Magnum. **286** Stephen Vernoit. **288** BM, Or 4938 no 12. **289** Courtesy of the artist. **293** APP. **296** from *The Graphic Art of the Islamic Revolution*, The Publication Division of the Art Bureau of the Islamic Propagation Organization, n.d.. **300** Nacerdine Zebar/GAMMA, Frank Spooner Pictures. **303** APP. **304** Ron Giling/Panos Pictures. **305** Chris Stowers/Panos Pictures.

Maps: 7 The Pre-Islamic Middle East, source, I. M. Lapidus, *A History of Islamic Societies*, Cambridge, 1988, p. 12. 21 The Islamic Middle East, source: I. M. Lapidus, *A History of Islamic Societies*, Cambridge, 1988, p. 40. 33 Egypt and Southwest Asia on the Eve of the Mongol Invasions, source: J. Bacharach, *A Middle East Studies Handbook*, rev. edn, Cambridge, 1984, p. 63. 47 Expansion of the Islamic World to 1500, source: F. Robinson, *Atlas of the Islamic World since 1500*, Oxford, 1982, pp. 24–5. 91 Islamic Revival in the Eighteenth and Nineteenth Centuries, source F. Robinson, *Atlas of the Islamic World since 1500*, Oxford, 1982, pp. 118–19. 103 European Imperialism in the Muslim World c. 1920, source: F. Robinson: *Atlas of the Islamic World since 1500*, Oxford, 1982, pp. 134–35. 114-15 The Achievement of Independence in the Muslim World, source: F. Robinson, *Atlas of the Islamic World since 1500*, Oxford, 1982, pp. 158-59. 126 Trade Routes and Centres 600–1500, source: F. Robinson, *Atlas of the Islamic World since 1500*, Oxford, 1982, p. 88. 166-67 The Travels of Ibn Battuta between 1325 and 1354, source: R. Dunn, *The Adventures of Ibn Battuta*, Berkeley, 1986, pp. 28, 42, 82, 107, 138, 175, 184, 256, 267, 277.

Index